# The Gun Digest Book Of PISTOLSMITHING

By Jack Mitchell

Edited By Jack Lewis

DBI BOOKS INC., NORTHFIELD, ILLINOIS

**Art Director**
SONYA KAISER

**Art Assistant**
JOHN VITALE

**Production Coordinator**
BETTY BURRIS

**Copy Editor**
DORINE IMBACH

**Contributing Editors**
DEAN A. GRENNELL
CLAY MERRILL
WAYNE NOVAK
ARMAND SWENSON
PAT VOIGHT

**Associate Publisher**
SHELDON FACTOR

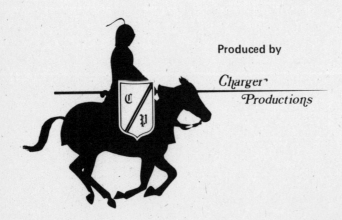

Produced by

*Charger Productions*

ISBN 0-910676-18-6                                      Library of Congress Catalog Card Number 80-66470

# Contents

# INTRODUCTION

Just as the medical profession has its particular fields of endeavor, the gunsmithing trade is the same. A truly custom pistolsmith is a specialist in his own right. To be a good pistolsmith requires certain traits: Almost without exception, he must be a shooter; he must have a thorough knowledge of ballistics; he must be mechanically inclined and be as stubborn as a Missouri mule.

A great part of knowing when a pistol is right is by the feel. If the pistolsmith can't shoot a tight group with the fruits of his labors, the probability is that his customer won't either.

Pistols have a lot of parts confined within a small frame; each can be the cause of problems. Being a good pistolsmith requires the tenacity to solve each problem, returning to the customer a firearm that is as durable as the mechanical design will permit, as reliable as though a life might depend upon it and as accurate as the particular model is able to perform.

I began this book with some misgivings, but with a lot of help from practicing gunsmiths, as well as the knowledge I gained in the Colorado School of Trades' gunsmithing course. I feel that the pistol enthusiast can profit by studying and practicing the basic pistolsmithing techniques outlined in this book; there also are some novel approaches that the professional might find useful.

I'll be the first to admit that much of this volume results from picking the brains of the best and most respected craftsmen in this unique trade. Without the generous assistance from many fellow gunsmiths willing to share their knowledge and methods, as well as the cooperation of numerous manufacturers, this book would not be done yet. In fact, it might never be done.

My wife, Cyndi, deserves special recognition for her moral support. Wayne Novak, good friend and an excellent gunsmith, assisted in many of the technical aspects of pistolsmithing. Frank Brownell's help always was just a phone call away and he never failed me.

Without the excellent instruction and warm friendship of Sid Cross, my instructor at the Colorado School of Trades, I doubt that I would have been graduated. Finally, I have to thank my Mom, who always said someday I'd write a book; and my Dad, who gave me my first gun and taught me firearms safety, responsibility and the unique kinship of my comrades in arms.

Jack Mitchell,
Vista, California

# You Can Do It All With A File, But There Are Better Ways To Go!

# TOOLS FOR THE PISTOLSMITH

### Chapter 1

*For top competition performance, a smooth functioning action is a virtual requirement. Much of this can be done in your own shop, if you know the proper techniques of pistolsmithing and are equipped with the right tools.*

**O**NE OF THE most prolific gunsmiths in the country is Ralph Walker, who operates out of Selma, Alabama. He has some pretty definite ideas as to what an amateur pistolsmith should have at his command in the way of tools, if he is to do the job right.

So we asked Walker to put his thoughts on paper in his own inimitable style and below is what he reports:

## BASICS AND HAND TOOLS

The tools used in pistolsmithing, at first glance, seem almost endless and far above the financial capabilities of the average person. Not so, provided you do a little bit of inventorying and decide what phase or category you will be working in with handguns.

If you already have some tools on hand, many of those used on rifles and shotguns also will serve for handgun work. If this is the case, conduct an inventory, listing all dual-purpose tools. Utilizing this list, you can slowly add the necessary special handgun tools, jigs, and fixtures on an as-needed basis — when you cannot do a specific job or the tools you are using are not correct for a quality job. The only rule to follow is always to buy the best quality tool, jig, or fixture you can afford. There is no such thing as a good cheap tool.

For those who have only their bare hands and the desire, tool selection should be planned carefully and purchases made on a needed basis with the same attention to the quality. Let's assume you are in this category, starting from square one.

Before you rush out on a tool-buying spree, first decide which phase of handgun work you will perform. While there are no strict and rigid lines, and some phases overlap, there are four basic phases, and I emphasize the word *basic*.

The first phase is general repair. This primarily involves malfunctioning handguns or replacement of broken, worn, or missing parts or components. In the average gunsmithing shop this accounts for fifty percent or more of the handgun work performed. If you include correcting someone else's mistakes, the percentage is even higher. This type of pistolsmithing is the best place for the beginner to start working on handguns.

The goal is to correct the malfunction through parts and component replacement, or modifications and adjustments. In short, the operating cycle of the handgun is placed in its correct sequence. Any effort toward modification, customizing, et cetera, is useless and due to fail until the original correct operating cycle is thoroughly understood by the workman. Needless to say, the workman must be fully capable of restoring a malfunctioning handgun to this status. To use an old phrase, "You must learn to crawl before you can walk, and walk before you can run."

The second phase goes by many names such as slick up, tuning, et cetera. A correctly operating and correctly cycled handgun is totally disassembled. The first step is to carefully examine each and every part and component thoroughly for roughness and metal burrs left from the manufacturing process. A part or component may appear perfect to the naked eye but under five-power magnification, rough spots and metal burrs are clearly visible. The purpose of this close investigation leads to the goal that all bearing surfaces be made as rough-free and slick as possible.

*This custom-rebuilt PPC revolver was pistolsmithed by Austin Behlert. The target shows the gun's effectiveness.*

*Smith & Wesson Model 29 .44 magnum had been cut down by Behlert as a custom item in his New Jersey pistol shop.*

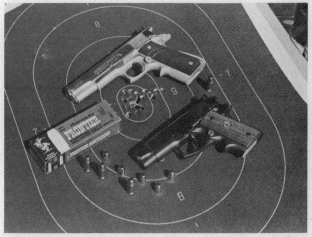

*Austin Behlert customized the nickel-plated .45 Model 1911 and the blued Colt Commander for target shooting. Frontier ammo is loaded with flat-nose Hornady bullet.*

*Austin Behlert also is the pistolsmith responsible for customization of this array of 9mm autoloaders, with a display of Frontier cartridges and Hornady bullets.*

The key point to remember is that friction is the number one enemy. The more friction is reduced, the more smooth the operating cycle. Each part must be allowed to function correctly without being retarded in its operation by friction. In addition, the timing of each step in the operating cycle is adjusted until each occurs at the exact split second for maximum efficiency. When friction has been reduced to near zero and timing is as precise as possible, the result is nothing short of remarkable in functional smoothness. The third and fourth phases of handgun work always include this step without exception.

The third phase generally is called semi-custom. The basic handgun is retained, as are most of the basic components. The difference is that some of the original parts and components are replaced with custom-made parts and components generally designed and manufactured by independent companies to increase operating efficiency or accuracy. Many such items are simply attached to the original gun, such as grips or a different type of sight. This is, perhaps, the most comprehensive phase once you leave the original gun. If correctly installed they add that personal touch to a handgun.

The fourth and final phase results in the fully customized handgun. In essence, the tuned handgun is carried past the semi-custom phase as far as imagination and money allow. As the name implies, full customizing uses many specialized parts and components, plus many components made specifically for a certain gun. It is a rare occasion when two guns are customized exactly alike, as there is almost invariably some deviation. It is not uncommon for such a gun to cost as much as $1000 — above the original price of the gun!

*Three-V barrel vise, wrench are recommended in text. Vise is attached to heavy plate atop upright for strength.*

On this semi-custom job by Ralph Walker, a low profile Micro sight has been installed on Colt Combat Commander. Auto has been satin-nickel finished. Sight also has been disassembled for satin-nickel finish. Front sight blade was left in original blue. Walker tuned entire action. Gun is clamped in protective no-mar vise jaws.

What does all this have to do with tools? Everything; for as the beginner starts at simple general repair and progresses to the full custom handgun, his tool requirement increases in direct proportion. Quality tools are expensive, hence the beginner must choose wisely or he will find himself in the position of having to work without a needed tool as his money is required to replace the cheap tools he purchased in the beginning.

Handguns, being shorter than rifles or shotguns, require less bench area, but the sturdiness of the bench should not be less. The most common mistake is not anticipating future bench area need. As the beginner progresses into the four phases, more work space will be required, especially for bench-mounted power tools. Always plan for expansion in laying out your work area; this includes proper lighting and electrical outlets, as well as bench area. Unless you stop working on handguns and take up needlepoint, you will expand!

The bench vise is a necessity in any phase of pistolsmithing. Some gunsmiths prefer a regular machinist vise, available in several sizes with four and six-inch sizes predominating in most shops. One pistolsmith acquaintance has a massive machinist vise I am almost sure is military surplus and designed to hold 155 howitzer barrels, yet he swears it is just the ticket. Personally I have always preferred the Versa-Vise marketed by Brownell's. It is of ample size and sturdy. However, its two main features lie in the fact that it can be rotated a full 360 degrees and that the vise jaws can be changed in seconds from horizontal to vertical. This allows positioning the gun in almost any desired angle. Regardless of the type of vise chosen, jaw liners made from wood, leather, lead, or even a section of carpet are easy to fabricate and provide non-slip protection for the gun.

A hand vise is a tool usually overlooked, yet it is the handiest thing around when working with small pins, screws and similar items. It can be hand-held while trying a pin or screw for fit, or the hand vise can be held in the bench vise for close work.

More guns are damaged by poor screwdrivers than all other tools combined. If you have the required skill, you can make your own using Solex steel, the finest tool steel available for such purposes. Such tools will last a lifetime with proper care. If you prefer to purchase screwdrivers, skip the local hardware store as these tools are not designed

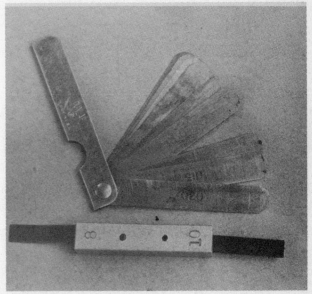

At top is a standard folding feeler gauge described in text. Beneath it is a special-made feeler gauge with go/no-go blades inserted into simple aluminum holder.

This tool made by Walker Arms is used to face off new recoil shields installed in the frames of some revolver models. End mill type cutter with a sliding insert is pinned to bore diameter range rod for proper alignment.

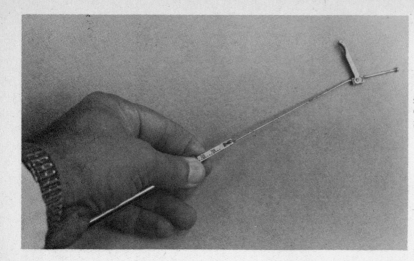

*This trigger pull gauge with an inner measuring marker is graduated to measure ounces of pull. It has been extended so the weight markings are fully visible.*

*These tools were specially built by Walker Arms for simpler removal of Colt-style ejector rod threaded bushings.*

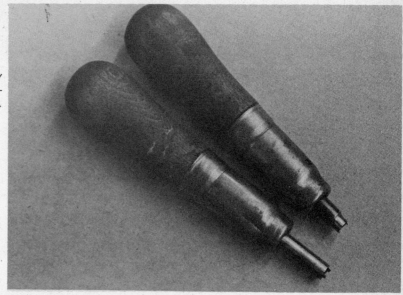

*Called the Versa-Vise, this bench model is shown in an upright position. It can be lifted up, turned sideways, then can be reinstalled on the bottom base rod.*

*These hand vises make pistolsmithing a great deal easier. Style marked with "1" is the standard hand vise which is described in the text. One marked "2" is mainspring vise.*

*Ideal for the pistolsmith's bench are these saws. "1" is a Challenger hacksaw; "2" is a deep-frame jeweler's saw; "3" is a metal bench saw. Purposes for all of the styles are described at length in this chapter's text.*

for gunsmith work and usually of less than adequate quality.

In my opinion, the two best screwdriver sets for gunsmithing are the Brownell Magna-Tip and the Chapman set. Each uses a single handle with interchangeable bits specifically designed to fit gun screws correctly. Replacement or extra bits are inexpensive and can be easily ground for special screws.

The next gun damaging culprit is the pin punch. Again, the use of only gunsmith-grade tools is the answer, not the local hardware store variety. Both Grace and Brownell's offer a good basic set that will get you started on the right road. The sets include those sizes most often used and you can add additional diameter sizes as needed.

The addition of brass, bronze, and plastic punches of various sizes and diameters, as well as shape, will come naturally as you progress. These are special punches for providing no surface marring of the metal. The Brownell three-punch wire-size set is excellent, as common punches in this small diameter are difficult to find. As small sizes suffer the most breakage and bending, each punch consists of three pieces: the main body, a screw cap, and a

replaceable pin. This greatly reduces the price, as only the pin is replaced if damage occurs. This set has proved so popular that it now is offered in a three-punch starter set.

The main problem in using pin punches — especially those of small diameter — is that few people use a starter punch. This is nothing more complicated than a pin punch with a short shaft. With it, you get the pin moving from its original position, then switch to the longer shaft of the same diameter to complete the removal of the pin. Simple as this sounds, most amateur pistolsmiths tend to use the long shaft from start to finish, then wonder why they break or bend the long-shaft, small-diameter pin punches so often. The whole purpose of a pin is to secure two pieces together and the longer the pieces remain together, especially under stress, the more securely bonded the pin becomes. The short-shaft starter punch simply breaks this bond and allows smoother pin removal without damage to the pin or the surrounding metal. It is one of those little things that make a professional.

The most versatile tool in a gunsmith shop is the file. While I do not hesitate to use power tools, nothing can ever take the place of the file in the hands of someone who

*Files are: "1", single-cut files; "2", double-cut files; "3" indicates three pillar files in fine, medium and coarse cuts; "4" covers two extra-narrow pillar files; "5" is a sight base file; "6" is triangular type.*

*From left: Two sets of needle files — fine and medium cut — are stored in wood block holder; needle file handle that locks onto file; clockmaker's file; three screw slot deepening files of different widths. Last is a steel burnishing tool that has been made with handle.*

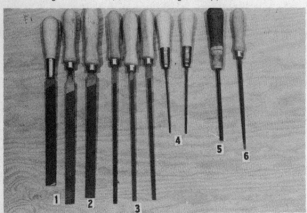

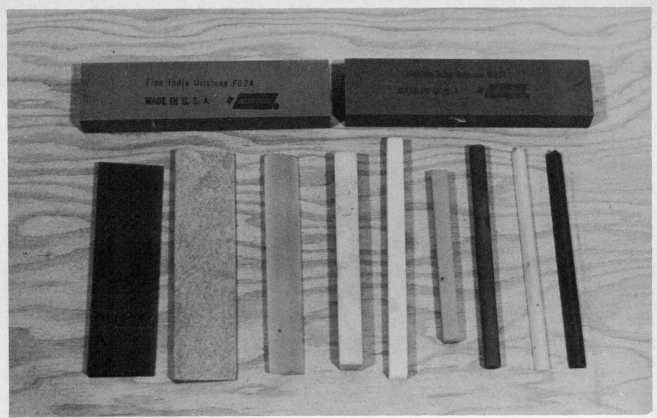

*At top are India stones in fine and coarse cut. Below are gunsmith's Arkansas stones. Black ones are extra-fine cut in surgical grade. Included are three knife-edge stones, three square stones of different cut, one round type. Last two on right are triangular in shape. A wide variety of stones makes gunsmithing easier job.*

knows how to use it correctly. Regrettably, you will find few gunsmiths today who know how to file, yet I have noticed that all top professionals invariably have had a large file selection at hand. Given a good selection, a top gunsmith can literally make any part of a handgun, rifle or shotgun. If the file will not do a particular job, he uses his files to create the tool to do the job.

Handgun work will not require the use of large files of hand milling machine size. Most of the work will be on small parts, hence the selection can be less in number, but not lower in quality. A good file, properly used and properly maintained, will give years of good service. The eight-inch file is about the maximum length needed with the six-inch predominating. The short four-inch length also is useful in handgun work. I personally prefer the single-cut file for the majority of work, as it removes a lot of metal in a hurry. Yet, with light strokes, one can almost duplicate the finer-cutting double-cut file for finish work. On each of these, carefully grind away the cutting teeth on one edge to make it "safe" which will allow you to file deep without the edge cutting the walls. If the walls of a cut are to be removed, you simply use the regular edge against the wall, thus deepening and also widening the cut.

Pillar files in fine, medium and coarse cut are the next most handy. These are long, narrow files of the double-cut style and probably the most common in regular gunsmithing work. Extra-narrow pillar files are simply shorter and more narrow for closer work. Unless you enjoy punching holes in your hands, always install a good, secure handle on each file.

Two sets of needle files — one for fine cut and one

medium cut — are absolutely necessary in gun work and especially so in pistolsmithing. They usually are marketed in a box containing a block of wood with holes drilled to receive the round shanks. To avoid breakage, keep them in the block and box. There is a special needle file handle that accepts the round shank and the cap is tightened to lock the handle in place temporarily. A couple of these will prove invaluable and allow more precise control of the file. Micro needle files are simply a smaller version, and while useful, are not an absolute necessity at the beginning.

Next on the file list is a set of screw slot files, three to a set; with each of a different file width. These cut only on the edge and are used to deepen the slots of screws that have become damaged. The clockmaker's file is somewhat like two knife blades back to back with the cutting edge on the sides. It is used to clean up the burrs in damaged screw slots, especially at the top of the slot. A sight slot file needs no explanation as it is an absolute necessity when altering or modifying the dovetail slot found on sights. A four or six-inch triangular tapering file, often called a rat tail file, is the last of the bare necessity file selection.

Stones are another necessity for handgun work and one never seems to have enough of them. A good bench-size Washita stone is basic in any shop. Next is a bench-size hard Arkansas stone; if you can afford the extra money, buy the black surgical variety, as it is the finest-cutting natural stone available. These two stones are not used for tool sharpening. Instead their flat surfaces are utilized to smooth parts such as the sides of a hammer. Use a light honing oil on the stone as the oil floats away particles of metal during removal. When finished, wipe the stone with a rag soaked in

*Russell's bench stones with honing oil from the same maker is a good beginning kit for the shop. Black stone is extra-hard surgical Arkansas stone; the lighter in color is Washita stone. Both are used to smooth up rough parts.*

mineral spirits or kerosene, then follow with clean rags until all residue is removed. Do not leave these two stones on the bench where parts can fall on the flat surfaces and cause damage. Use an extra Washita or man-made bench stone for tool sharpening.

Hand stones are those most often used in handgun work. India stones in coarse and fine grit will do all of the rough jobs and save a lot of time. Then switch to first soft, then hard Arkansas stones for the finishing work. Again the black extra-hard Arkansas stone will give the finest cut. You can buy a basic set of gunsmith stones which will include a variety of shapes. Add other shapes and grades as you progress. The square and the triangular are the two shapes most used and it is a good idea to keep a spare of each, as their edges receive a lot of use and wear.

Most stones are damaged by misuse and breakage either from excess pressure or by leaving them lying about on the workbench. A small multi-drawer cabinet with one stone per drawer will pay for itself in preventing breakage. As with the large bench stones, always clean the stone before storing it in the drawer. A dry hand stone cuts fast, but if you add honing oil, you will find the stone cuts more slowly, as well as floating away particles for that extra smooth surface you are trying to achieve.

Stoning, like filing, is an art in itself and only time, patience and practice can teach someone to do each correctly. The most common mistake is trying to rush through the job. If you work slowly and methodically with mild pressure, you will find you not only do a better job, but have absolute control of the amount of metal being removed and where that metal is removed.

The basic pair of pliers is the flat-nose parallel-action type, the jaws of which open the same amount at the rear as at the front. Purchase one standard type with serrated jaws and a groove running the length of the jaws. The groove is used to hold and secure pins and screws. Add a similar pair with smooth jaws to protect finished surfaces. The six-inch size is the most useful. Another parallel-action type is the common vise-grip pliers, in six-inch size. The primary difference is that the vise-grips can be adjusted until they lock on to the work and hold items such as pins and small parts steady somewhat like the hand vise. Buy one good pair for regular use, then buy a cheap pair to hold parts while heating them, as in spring making, et cetera.

Needle-nose pliers allow you to reach down into close places and secure a good grip on pieces and components. Purchase two, one with straight, long parallel jaws and one with curved jaws. While on the subject of reaching into small places, a pair of shop tweezers will prove to be both inexpensive and extremely useful.

Wire cutters or piano-wire cutting pliers are needed for cutting coil springs to desired lengths. However the special gunsmith nippers sold by Brownell's are equal in use, and have a lot of extra cutting power due to high-leverage linkage. This allows you to cut all sizes of spring wire and most pins! My pair is over ten years old and will still slice through metal that would be impossible with common wire cutters.

A gunsmith without several good hammers is like a bird without his tail feathers. He doesn't get far. However, the list of hammers most used is quite small. The most useful and most versatile is the crosspane hammer in four-ounce

*This set of lapping compounds from Brownell's comes in differing degrees of grit, each separately packaged.*

weight. In one form or another, it has been around about as long as gunsmithing. The face of this hammer is long and narrow, which allows the hammer to reach down into tight places as well as perform the usual duties a gunsmith's hammer requires. This narrow head also eliminates a lot of cussing when you are holding a small pin between your fingers and trying to tap the pin into a close place leaving fingers undamaged. The back end of the hammer head has flat sides somewhat like a blunt chisel. With this end, one can extrude metal with controlled blows to achieve a better fit or to take up slack. Once you use a crosspane hammer, you will find yourself using it for most all hammer needs.

A four-ounce ball-peen and an eight-ounce ball-peen hammer is next on the list and perhaps more readily identified, as these are used by gunsmiths who have never used a crosspane. The face of the hammer is similar but the back end is ball shaped and does have some uses that the crosspane cannot duplicate.

Next on the list is the non-marring, old, reliable eight-ounce rawhide mallet, which allows you to whack daylights out of something without marring the metal. Add one of the new non-marring hammers with interchangeable heads. One end may have a plastic head, the other a rubber head. A brass hammer of about five ounces should round out your basic hammer needs.

One tool I use as a hammer is really an adjustable automatic center punch with replaceable heads. You adjust the stroke desired, place it on the desired spot and push down. An internal spring and block is compressed, then trips to deliver a short, controlled blow. With the standard pointed head, it performs its usual center punch duties and with an extra head ground flat like a hammer face, you have a miniature hammer that can be used to begin driving in a pin in an awkward area. Once the pin is started, switch to a regular pin punch and hammer to complete the installation. Incidentally, with the pointed head in place, the tool can be used for stippling a surface area.

While most punches and hammers are used with the work held in a vise, a steel or brass bench block with a series of holes of various diameters will prove useful. The gun is held against the block and the pin being driven out enters one of the holes in the block. This allows the gun to be held sturdy and the pin is always down in the hole for retrieval rather than under the bench or somewhere else in the shop, as they seem to take wings and become lost. The bench block also serves as a small anvil.

A good hacksaw, such as the Challanger, will prove useful in many instances as will the small, thin-bladed metal bench saw. For handgun work, a jeweler's saw with a deep frame will see twice as much use. The small, thin blades are inexpensive and allow cutting in tight places with precision. The main reason most gunsmiths fail to use a jeweler's saw is simply that they try to make it cut like a hacksaw on the forward stroke. A jeweler's saw blade always should cut on the pull or backstroke. With work held sturdy and the correct blade chosen, you can cut the best of steel in tight, intricate cuts like a coping saw cuts wood.

A good one-inch micrometer and a good grade six-inch dial caliper will suffice for most measurement work. The dial caliper should be capable of internal, external and

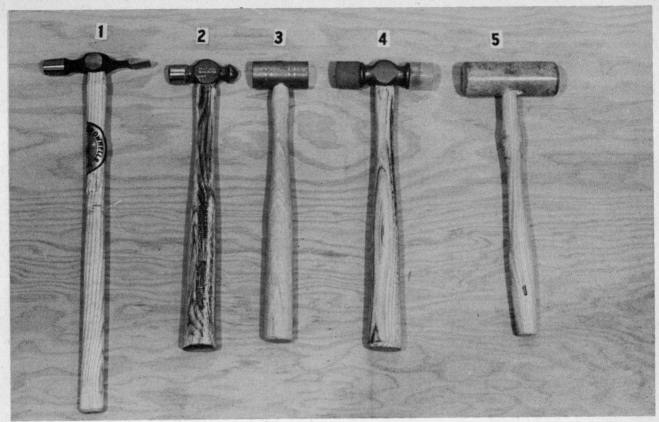

*Gunsmithing hammers are: "1", crosspane type; "2", ball-peen; "3", brass mallet; "4", rubber/plastic head; "5", rawhide type.*

depth measurement. A thread gauge, preferably in both inches and metric measurements, will aid in identifying handgun screw sizes.

One tool often overlooked is the hand steel burnisher. Even when a part seems as slick as greased glass, a few strokes with the steel burnisher not only will improve the smoothness of the part, but work hardens the part. It is one of those old tools that once was standard gunsmithing equipment, but through lack of training, has fallen into misuse. Even the best prepared surface ready for bluing can be improved with the steel burnisher to give a deep, glass-like finish to the surface after bluing.

One inevitable job in handgun work is the lapping in of parts by working them together with an abrasive between the two. In the past, this was done with a series of lapping compound dusts mixed with the handgun worker's favorite lubricant, which ranged from kerosene to 30-weight motor oil or even grease. It left a mess and a lot of it was guesswork or trial-and-error. Bob Brownell now markets several kits designed specifically for this purpose. They start at number 120 grit and go up to number 1200 grit which is almost the dust stage. No guesswork is involved. Each kit contains a series of small containers with the grit and type of lubricant specified. By making the right choice, you can choose one for fast cutting and work up to extra-fine grit for that glass-like smoothness. Even tough jobs like lapping aluminum frames and steel slides has its specific compound. An added plus is that the lubricating agent is cleaned easily from parts with no residue left to continue working once the gun is reassembled for use.

These are the basic or fundamental tools needed for handgun work with the exception of woodworking tools. As woodworking usually is confined to grips, most tools used for rifles and shotgun stocks will prove ample for handguns, with emphasis on the small palm-size chisels for inletting. Checkering is generally on the coarse side, about eighteen lines per inch. If you want to get into engraving, this is another ball game and your best bet is to refer to a catalog that lists these tools.

## JIGS AND FIXTURES

In the recent past, most handgun jigs and fixtures were available only through a handgun manufacturer. The top pistolsmiths made their own for personal use, which left the beginner out in the cold in both cases. In recent years, this has changed and now pistolsmiths are making their designs, special jigs and fixtures available to the public. While some sell them direct as a sideline to their gunsmithing, most have made them available through Brownell's.

One of the main jobs in handgun work is obtaining a crisp, smooth trigger pull. Assuming that work on various springs and pins, plus friction reduction, is completed, the stoning of sear engagement is the critical stage. The basic principle is to maintain correct sear and sear notch angles, while correcting any deficiency in the angles due to manufacturing, removing burrs and rough spots, plus any other feature that prevents that crisp, smooth pull. Proper let-off is often described as like breaking a piece of glass. It can really make a difference on the target!

The two components must have correct alignment,

*A good deal of work can be saved with the packaged handgun springs available from a variety of sources. They come in assorted sizes, shapes and strengths as ordered.*

contact, and spacing. On handguns with a detachable side plate one can see the amount of engagement and all other necessities, but if the gun does not have a detachable side plate the fun begins. One method of adjustment is to use special trigger adjustment pins. The parts are removed from the gun and a special screw takes the place of the hammer screw; another takes the place of the sear or trigger screw. The difference is that a precision-ground pin duplicating the original pin is on top of the screw. Each of the parts is placed over the respective extended pins, which gives the exact same alignment and contact as they would have if inside of the gun. With the parts in view, you duplicate hammer spring tension with a finger and the same for the sear or trigger. Viewed under a magnifying glass, or if you are wearing an Opti-Visor, one can easily see the exact amount of sear and sear notch engagement. Each can be removed and worked over with hand stones, then replaced on the pins and tried again and again until desired contact is obtained.

Another method involves the use of sear blocks. These are simply blocks of tool steel with holes drilled and the correct pins installed to duplicate spacing and pin diameter as in the gun itself. While some sear blocks can be used for gun models of the same frame size or receiver size, several blocks will be needed. The sear and sear notch stoning procedure is the same as for trigger adjustment pins.

Only a few years ago, commercial handgun range rods were not available, unless you knew someone in the service department of a handgun manufacturer. Again this has changed and Brownell's now offers them in calibers ranging from .22 Long Rifle to .45 Long Colt. Unless you have precision grinding equipment, it is better to buy them, as they are difficult to make correctly. A range rod, incidentally, is a rod that passes down the bore, precision ground to match the lands and grooves of the bore. With the cylinder locked in firing position, the range rod enters the front of the cylinder, thus checking the alignment of the cylinder and barrel bore. If it will not enter the cylinder, the cylinder obviously is not aligned and will shave lead as the bullet exits the cylinder. It is an easy tool to learn to use and indispensible for creating revolver accuracy.

Smith & Wesson revolvers lock on each end of the ejector rod, so a common cause of the cylinder binding

when it turns lies in the fact that the crane is bent. Brownell's offers a precision-ground jig with .0005-inch tolerance that takes the place of the cylinder. Once in place, with the crane swung up into lock position, it is easy to spot where the crane is bent and to straighten it slowly until the jig locks securely. With the jig removed and the cylinder reinstalled, there is no more binding of the cylinder due to a bent crane. Without the jig, it is strictly guesswork and experience to attempt to straighten the crane correctly. A similar useful jig is the Brownell Colt crane bushing tool. It fits over the end of the ejector rod and down into the cylinder to remove the crane bushing without damage to this many-threaded part. A ticklish job without the tool.

The Colt Model 1911 semiauto barrel bushing wrench has been around a long time, but Brownell's has added a new wrinkle to an already useful tool. The removal of the combination ratchet-extractor from the ejector rod of a Colt revolver is not the easiest task in the world and generally requires some type of rigging. The Brownell Colt wrench has a hexagonal opening which acts like a socket wrench when placed over the ratchet base, and the component is easily removed or reinstalled without damage on large-frame Colt revolvers. On small-frame Colts, the opening is not used. Instead on the opposite end is a slot and two tool-steel-grade screws mounted flush close to the slot. This slips under the ratchet-extractor and the screw heads engage the underside of the extractor cuts for the cartridges in the component. You can unscrew the component or reinstall it without damage with this wrench.

I doubt whether any other handgun has seen more customization, alteration or modification than the old M1911 semiauto. There are literally dozens of goodies that fit onto or attach in some form or fashion to customize this old lady. But somewhere along the line you run into several parts that must be staked in place. They are the grip screw bushings and the combination slide and safety spring plunger tube on the left side of the frame. Brownell's offers a tool for each staking job — they work easily and efficiently. The front sight is also staked into place, unless you choose to silver solder it there along with the required refinishing of the slide. Brownell's has a front-sight staking tool that firmly anchors the sight sans any silver soldering.

Barrel replacement on revolvers or the installation of

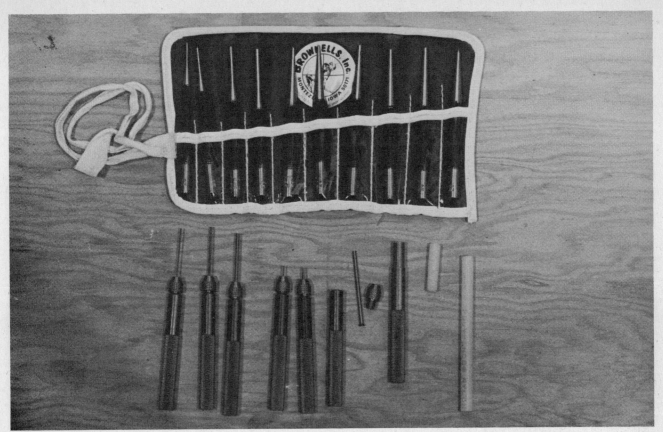

At top is Brownell's standard starting set of pin punches in a roll-up holder. Below (from left): three standard-length wire-size punches; two starter punches; starter with the cap removed and new pin ready to be inserted; combination brass and nylon punch, which screws into a single base. At extreme right is round plastic punch.

another cylinder seems simple, until you start to close the cylinder. Generally you end up with not one but several problems. First comes headspacing, which requires a go gauge. Once this is in place, you need two feeler gauges. One leaf of the feeler gauge goes between the headspace gauge and rear of the frame, while the other goes between the front of the cylinder and the rear end of the barrel. Some simply use one feeler gauge, as all cylinders have a bit of front to rear slack, but using the two feeler gauges and headspace gauge is the best procedure.

If you have a problem at the rear of the cylinder, a finishing chamber reamer can solve this phase of the headspacing problem. It is always a good idea to check with a no-go gauge or at least a full cylinder of brand new ammunition, rotating the cylinder to assure that there is no drag, but do not fire the gun at this point. Revolvers, almost without exception, use rimmed cartridges, so the fit here is more for proper clearance than headspacing, as is the case with rimless cartridges.

What about the front of the cylinder and its spacing with the rear of the barrel? If the space is too short, you will get powder and lead fouling build-up, resulting in a jammed cylinder. If there is too much space you will have trouble-free cylinder rotation but with quite a sacrifice in velocity due to the escaping gas. The trick is to find a happy medium, but always with the go gauge and feeler gauge at the rear to duplicate normal spacing. The old way was to unscrew the barrel and face off the end by guess and

experience. A few pistolsmiths are good enough to use a file and get a close fit.

The crew at Brownell's — and its field consultant staff of professionals — came up with the perfect answer. First, a steel rod with a detachable handle goes down the bore with an aluminum cone guide between handle and barrel muzzle. Next comes a brass section similar to a tube with the inside diameter matching the rod and the outside diameter matching the bore diameter. This is to assist in centering. The threaded end of the rod is the business end.

First, you screw on a ninety-degree barrel facing cutter and lock it in place with a simple tool. By pulling to the rear on the rod as you rotate the operating handle, your cutter faces the end of the barrel off exactly centerline of the bore and with absolute control of amount of metal removed. Once this is accomplished and the feeler gauge says you have the proper spacing, you take on the task of cutting the forcing cone at the barrel end. You have a choice between the common eighteen-degree cone or an eleven-degree cone. The cutter simply takes the place of the initial facing cutter. When the cone is complete, you then switch to the eighty-two-degree chamfering cutter. When all cutting is finished, a brass cone goes on next with lapping compound to finish the cone to be as slick as greased glass for maximum accuracy potential.

You have to use this tool only once to fall in love with it, as it makes a difficult task easy and results in a professional job. In addition to its obvious use with a new

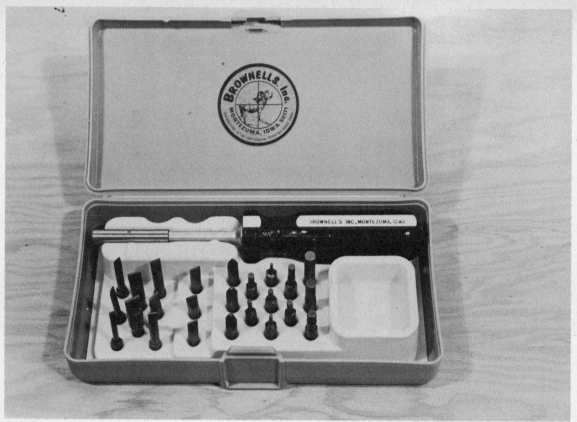

*Bob Brownell's Magna-Tip screwdriver set comes in this case, complete with open tray for screws. Blades can be interchanged to match the screw slot properly. A sign of poor gunsmith work is the mangled screw slot.*

barrel or new cylinder, it also is the answer to many revolver problems where the forcing cone is improperly cut with too shallow of a cone, or the cone is off to one side, or even to remove leading build up. If your time is money or you just want a professional job, I have never seen anything that will do a better job.

Good ignition is always important with any gun and firing pin protrusion is a key ingredient. In the past, the standard method of measurement was either a depth micrometer or a go/no-go gauge made in the shop. There now is a special firing-pin protrusion gauge available with accuracy to within .001-inch. Again, Brownell's came up with this little jewel. I had the opportunity to put the first one made to practical use during a trip overseas on a consultant job to a firearms manufacturer. It consists of only three parts: the body, the inner rod and the lock screw. You simply loosen the screw and, using a micrometer or dial calipers, set the inner rod to zero. Press the inner rod against the protruding firing pin until the face of the outer body stops against the face of the recoil plate. Lock the setting, remove the gauge and measure its overall length. By subtracting the original overall length when set at zero, you have the exact amount of firing pin protrusion — simple and accurate.

These are only a few of the special tools, jigs and fixtures available, to say nothing of the custom components for today's pistolsmith; items like special springs, spring kits to increase or decrease tension, sights galore, barrels, and many others too numerous to mention in this chapter. I heartily recommend that you purchase Brownell's catalog and the Gun Digest's new book of Gun Accessories and Services for additional information.

## POWER TOOLS

The one nearly indispensible power tool for the pistolsmith is the hand-held Dremel Moto-Tool, which is capable of saving many hours of tedious work, plus usually gives professional results. While several models are available, the best of the lot is the model 380 with built-in variable speed control from 5000 to 25,000 revolutions per minute. Its ball-bearing construction allows long trouble-free rugged duty. The model 381 kit contains the 380 tool, a carrying case and thirty-four different accessories for the tool.

The Dremel Moto-Tool easily can see twenty times the use of any other power tool due to its versatility. A full range of additional accessories will allow it to polish, grind, shape and even do micro milling using the high-speed carbide cutters. It would take an entire chapter to list all of its uses in handgun work and there still would be some not listed. About the best recommendation I can offer is the observation that it is a rare gun shop — professional or amateur — that does not use this particular tool in some way on almost every handgun. The more you use it, the more additional jobs you will find it capable of performing.

There is little use for an electric hand drill, but a good old-fashioned hand-powered egg-beater hand drill will see some use, when you have to drill out the stub of a pin in a close place and need extra slow drill speed.

A good bench-type drill press fitted with an Atlas or similar compound vise should be your first bench power

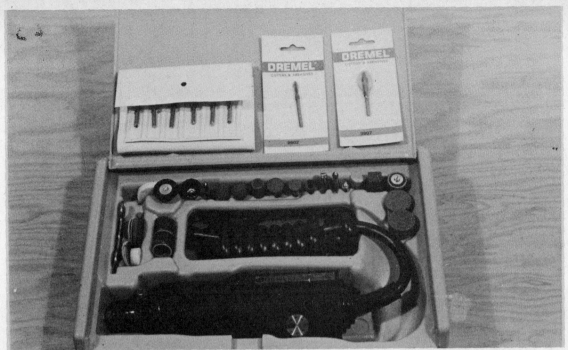

*The Dremel Model 381 MotoTool set is the first power tool recommended for the beginning pistolsmith. It comes with a variety of heads to do numerous jobs, as well as the additional accessories positioned on the top of lid.*

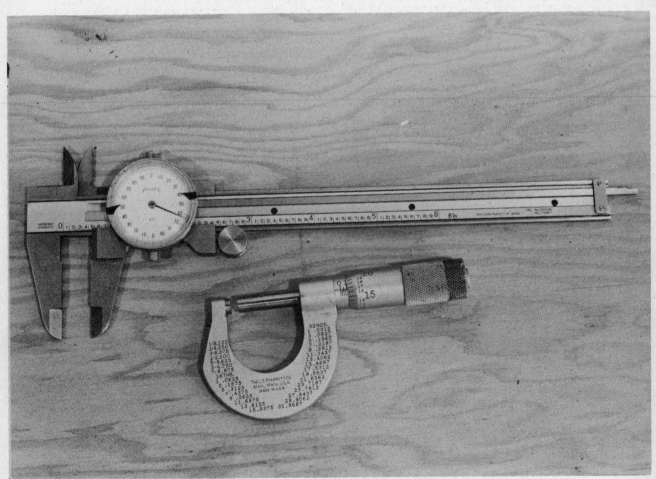

*Accuracy in determining measurements is the name of the game in pistolsmithing. The dial calipers at top of the photo, as well as the one-inch micrometer beneath will pay their way in day-to-day work in a gunsmith's shop.*

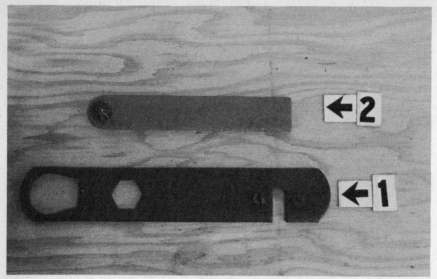

*"1", Brownell's Colt wrench has a Model 1911 barrel bushing removal wrench on the left end; the center hexagon opening is to remove Colt ejector/ratchet on large frame guns. Notch at the other end, with two screws perform the same function on smaller frames. "2" is grip screw bushing staking tool for Model 1911.*

tool. Chuck capacity should be from zero to one-half-inch. A bench-mounted drill press is more stable than the floor-mounted type and the extra cost of that compound vise will allow you to do precision drilling which is extremely important in handgun work. If you purchase a good one with thrust bearings and also roller bearings, you can do extra light milling work utilizing the compound vise. The only thing to remember is that it is not a vertical milling machine, but a drill press; so the name of the game is to feed the work slowly to the rotating milling cutter and not try to hog off a huge chunk of metal in one second.

A good set of numbered drills, Nos. 1 to 60, will serve the majority of your needs as most gun screws are based on number size drills. The fraction-size drills can get expensive for a full set, so purchase these one at a time on a need basis. Letter-size drills are seldom required and can also be best purchased individually as required. All of these are carbon drills and will do most of your work. However, sight installation — especially rear sights — requires constant use of specific drills and it is best to buy these special sizes as extras in cobalt drills which will be expensive but outlast common carbon type drills many times over. More taps than dies are needed for handgun screws, so purchase these as needed and in high-speed type only for maximum life and clean threads.

A good bench grinder is almost a necessity as you move up the knowledge ladder of handgun work. The only requirement is that it be equipped with roller or ball bearings instead of brass bushing-type bearings. The brass bushing variety can be detected easily even if the propaganda does not state what type bearings are used. With the grinder unplugged and wheels stopped, try pushing and pulling sideways on the grinder wheels. Ball or roller bearing-equipped grinder wheels will not give even a fraction of an inch, while bushing bearing style will have side play in the grinding wheels.

Put a coarse grit wheel on one side and a fine grit wheel on the other, both wheels of equal diameter. A grinding

*Indicated by "1" are two Ruger screw replacement style sear and hammer jigs, with ground bushing rod on top to duplicate hammer and trigger pin. In place on the gun, hammer, trigger are on outside of gun in plain view. "2" is a sear block for the same purpose. It is a metal block with ground pins inserted at the correct distance, alignment as in the gun.*

wheel dresser not only will true up the face of the grinding wheels, but will keep them uniform in diameter, eliminating wobble and erratic grinding. The Foredom Company markets a compact grinder that is reasonably priced and about the same size most often found in commercial pistolsmithing shops.

A power head with belt drive is inexpensive and handy, if you install a coarse wire scratch wheel on one side and a fine wire scratch wheel on the opposite side. These can be found at most hardware stores and can be the oil-impregnated brass or bronze-bearing type. If you cannot locate one, two pillow blocks with a shaft and a pulley in the center will accomplish the same thing.

An old polishing trick is to just let the metal lightly touch the coarse wire scratch wheel and the tips of the rotating wire will impart a soft-non-reflective sheen to the metal on parts such as the top of a slide to cut down glare when sighting.

A propane torch is fine for soft soldering and heating of springs and other parts but it is hard to beat an oxy-acetylene torch for maximum versatility. The common size is too large for most gun work, especially on handguns. One of the compact torches will prove more practical for close work in welding, silver soldering and other heating needs. With a torch and Kasenit compound, one can re-case-harden sears and similar parts easily. Always buy your case hardening compound, silver solder and soft solder from a gunsmith supply house, as there are numerous other types available that can cause problems. Those sold by the

gunsmith suppliers have been carefully compounded for gun-related use.

Barrel removal and installation for revolvers is almost impossible without a barrel vise and action wrench. Of the several brands on the market, most are designed primarily for rifle work; the Three-V barrel vise and action wrench is the most versatile and useful for revolvers. Making barrel-vise insert blocks to fit the contour of revolver barrels can be a chore, but if you use sheets of lead in the inserts along with rosin, the lead squeezes down to a tight fit thus eliminating literally dozens of special contoured insert blocks.

If you eliminate the machining of barrels in excess of six inches in length, the Unimat-3 lathe is a good choice. Maximum distance between centers of the little lathe is 6.9 inches, but it is a relatively inexpensive unit and capable of converting to a vertical drill press and vertical milling machine. Perhaps its greatest advantage is its compact size, where work space is limited. I would recommend that you purchase the instruction book for $2 before making your decision, as it illustrates the tool's uses and also its limitations. It is no piece of junk and fully capable of precision work within its size capacity.

In my personal opinion, the best overall choice for handguns is the Atlas six-inch lathe. Even fully equipped, the cost is far less than a standard ten or twelve-inch lathe with the usual thirty-six inches between centers. The six-inch Atlas is eighteen inches between centers, more than adequate for any handgun barrel, and I have used one to

*At bottom is Brownell's barrel facing and coning tool. At top is Brownell's range rod. "1" is operating handle with lock screw; "2", aluminum cone to align rod with barrel muzzle; "3", brass bushing with outside diameter matching bore for rod alignment; "4" is 11-degree cone cutter (assembly is pulled back and rotated while cone aligns with muzzle); "5", 18-degree cone cutters to handle from .32 to .45 caliber; "6" are 82-degree chamfering cutters; "7" is 90-degree barrel facing cutter for all calibers; "8" are brass lapping cones; and "9" is the range rod itself.*

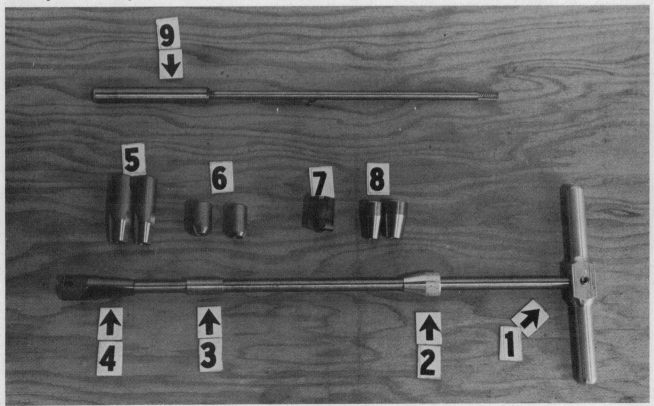

*Walker is very high on this Atlas six-inch lathe which has been bench mounted, with the three-jaw chuck and a Jacobs chuck on the tailstock. He contends that this is the piece of equipment most needed in professional gunwork.*

*Somewhat more complicated than the 6-inch Atlas model is this Myford lathe which is manufactured in England. It is designed for heavier work and, Ralph Walker feels, has more application in heavier industrial utilization.*

turn barrels in excess of eighteen inches by a little special rigging. At one time, I had both a six-inch Atlas and a ten-inch Clausing and found that I used the Atlas the most, especially on small parts, as is the case in most pistolsmithing.

The first one of these little lathes was manufactured over forty years ago and in the period since, all of the usual bugs have been worked out to produce a dependable, relatively inexpensive lathe capable of precision work. The lathe is thirty-four inches overall and twenty-four inches wide, including the motor assembly. In back gear you have spindle speeds from 55 to 300 rpm and in direct drive, from 430 to 220 rpm. Thread-cutting capacity ranges from eight to ninety-six threads per inch and one can purchase a set of metric gears if desired. Headstock capacity is 17/32-inch bore taking a 10 NS thread chuck and with a headstock taper to accept a number 2 Morse taper. Tailstock has a three-quarter-inch diameter bored for the Number 1 Morse taper with 1¼-inch travel.

The first thing a knowledgeable machinist notices is the absence of a quick-change gear box. Gears are hand-changed, using a diagram on the gear cover. All you sacrifice is a little time changing gears and you quickly get the hang of this by following the chart. If a quick-change gear box was added, the lathe cost would probably be about forty percent higher.

All of the usual lathe accessories are available such as a three-jaw chuck, four-jaw chuck, face plate, steady rest, follower rest, live centers, jacobs chuck that can be used in the headstock or tailstock, tool posts and boring bars in the conventional style plus a multi-cut holder. Most important is the milling attachment, which allows precision milling so important in handgun work.

The six-inch Atlas will do everything a larger lathe will do in handgun work and just as accurately. Accessories and even replacement parts are no problem. If your local dealer does not have them in stock, write to The Atlas Corporation, 2019 N. Pitcher St., Kalamazoo, Michigan 49007. Given proper care and maintenance, the unit will last a lifetime and is within the financial reach of the average person.

Calwell Industries at 603 E. Davis St., Lurling, Texas 78648, imports and markets the English Myford lathe which is the standard lathe of English hobbyists. The Myford Super 7 is about the size of the Atlas six-inch but available either nineteen or thirty-one inches between centers. Priced a bit higher, there are so many accessories that only their catalog can give a full listing.

Brownell's address is: Brownell's Inc., Route 2, Box 1, Montezuma, Iowa 50171.

*Brownell firing pin protrusion gauge is shown with inner section extended after measuring protruding firing pin. The measurement is made in this position, then a zero measurement, with inner rod flush, is subtracted to determine amount of protrusion. The lock screw secures inner rod.*

# Knowing How To Make Your Own Screwdrivers Can Save Time, Wear And Tear And Give You Tools That Will Serve Time And Again!

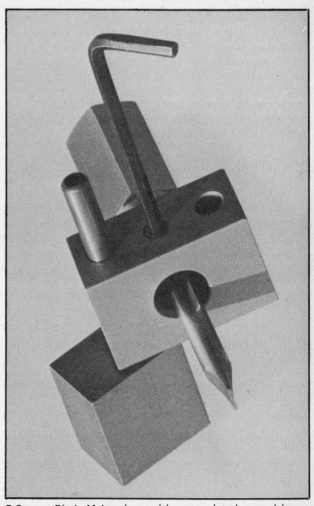

*B-Square Blade Maker, here with a completed screwdriver clamped in place for final touching up. With the hex wrench removed, the blade is pivoted against the grinding wheel, then lifted off, rotated to put the other hole over the pin, and the process is repeated, assuring parallel grinding.*

*Upper screwdriver has a ¼'' bit in a ¾'' aluminum hex stock handle. Smaller one at right has a 5/32'' bit in 7/16'' handle turned from brass rod.*

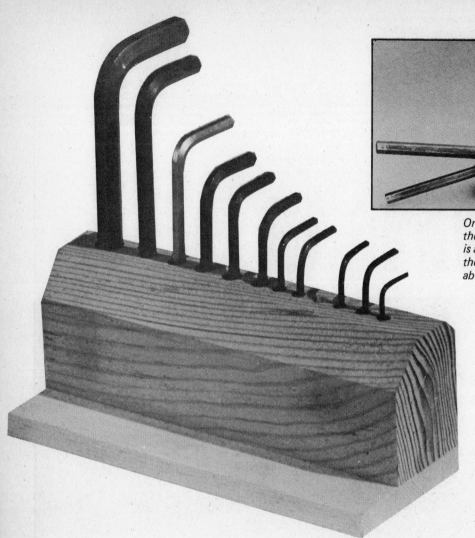

One solution to the problem of having the right size of hex wrench available is a pocket set such as this one with the seven most common sizes. It's about the size of a large jack knife.

Another approach, well suited for those who need and use all of the less common sizes, is a simple rack, with holes to accept each of the various sizes of hex wrenches.

**M**AGGOO'S ELEVENTH LAW of Universal Perversity states, "You can always find every size of hex-wrench except the size you need." I don't know about you but it seems that nearly every gadget I buy comes with one or more Allen-head wrenches and I've long since formed the habit of tossing all of them into one small drawer above the workbench, against the time of future need.

It came down to the point where I was endlessly burrowing among a peck or so of the little gizmos in hopeless quest for one exactly the proper size. If you attack a hex-head screw with a wrench that's just a bit too small, you're apt to round-out the corners and then all hell is out for noon. To make matters even worse, I have the unconfirmed impression that the metric system has its own progression of hex-wrenches, none of which quite match the native breed.

Finally, frustration conquered sloth and I spent a bit of time making a small rack of scrap wood, with a row of holes along the upper edge to hold at least one each of all the different sizes in the drawer. I used a micrometer to grade them as to size and tried to pick out ones showing the least wear and rounding of corners in each dimension. This

seems to be a helpful approach, assuming I don't mislay the little holding rack.

I have at least four sets of screwdrivers with assortments of interchangeable bits for handling a vast array of screw head dimensions and configurations. The two sets from Brownell's, Inc. (Route 2, Box 1, Montezuma, Iowa 50171) include a handle shaped like a conventional screwdriver, with a magnetic holder for the assortment of bits. The sets from Chapman Manufacturing Company (Route 17, Durham, Connecticut 06422) provides small spring-loaded ball detents on the side of each bit to hold them in the socket of the handle or extension and there's a tiny hex-socket set screw that you can tighten if additional solidity is needed. The Chapman bits also have a short serrated section at the end of the shank so that one can spin the screw into place with the fingertips, if it turns that easily.

The sets from both sources include bits in the full range of hex sizes, plus two or more Phillips-head or crosspoint types and an impressive array of slot-head bits in various widths and thicknesses. One of the Chapman kits — their No. 8320 — also includes a jeweler's screwdriver with two double-ended bits to provide for four different sizes of

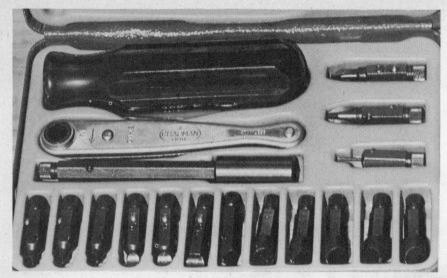

*Chapman kit includes universal handle, ratchet and extension, with bits from smallest hex through the slot-head and Phillips-head types.*

*An earlier screwdriver kit from Brownell's featured magnetic socket to hold assorted bits. Since the bits are six-sided, they fit nicely into the three-jaw chucks of electric hand drills. With a variable-speed, reversible drill, they make easy work of seating or removing screws.*

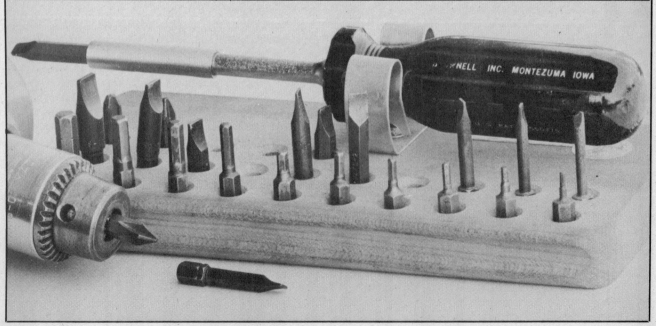

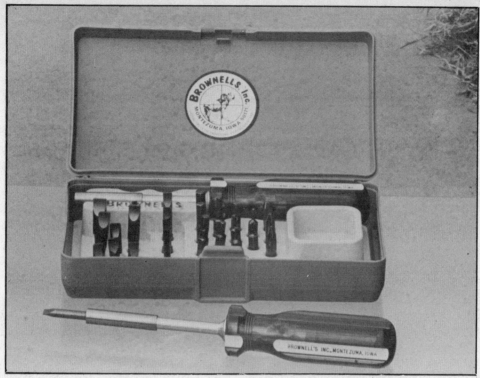

*Current pattern of the Brownell screwdriver set replaces the wooden block with a plastic rack and snap-top carrying case. The handle is big enough for hard jobs.*

those pesky tiny screws such as you may have to cope with in the temple hinges of shooting glasses, sunglasses and the like.

All of the slot-head bits in these sets are hollow-ground so that the sides are parallel rather than tapered in the manner of most "dime-store" screwdrivers. The hollow-ground feature tends to aid usefully toward preventing the bit from climbing out of the slot when pressure is applied.

In spite of owning a plethoric profusion of screwdrivers, I'm forever encountering some diabolical wee imp of a screw that has a slot that just won't accept any screwdriver or bit I can put my hands upon. Gunmakers seem to take a sadistic delight in dreaming up screws with head slots that are just paper-thin. As a result, even if you can find a blade

that fits, you're apt to snap it off before the screw loosens, marring the glossy bluing on the screw head in the process.

The small screws that hold the two halves of handgun stocks together present more than their share of difficulty. As a rule, they're countersunk below the surface of the wood so that a screwdriver that's a bit too wide will gouge the wood in an unsightly manner. If you go to the next smaller width, that's usually too narrow. Working a slot-head screw with an undersized blade is almost certain to leave the slot blurred and disfigured in a most painful manner.

I had often thought how great it would be if I could just make my own screwdriver, custom-fitted to the desired dimensions. Attempts to perform the operation freehand left little doubt that it required a gift I didn't have.

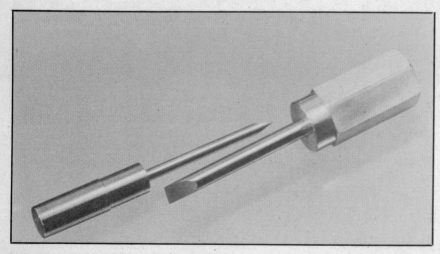

*The concave faces of the blades ground on the B-Square Blade Maker can be seen here, with sides about parallel to the depth of typical slots in most screws.*

Apparently, Dan Bechtel — the genial head honcho of B-Square Company (Box 11281, Fort Worth, Texas 76109) — must have felt there was a need for a systematic approach to such problems. Recently B-Square introduced their B-Square Blade Maker. It consists of a pair of gold anodized aluminum blocks. One positions a 0.250-inch diameter steel pin and the other has a hole in the center into which you can fasten the screwdriver or blank length of stock, holding it in place by tightening the hex-head set screw. There are a pair of 0.250-inch holes parallel to the center one and equidistant from it. By alternately slipping first one hole, then the other, over the steel shank, you can grind existing screwdrivers to precise specifications or, just as easily, form brand-new blades out of cold-rolled bar stock or lengths of drill rod.

The B-Square Blade Maker can be ordered direct from the firm at the address given. A diamond dresser bar, for smoothing and evening the grinding wheel is likewise available, or you can order the Blade Maker and diamond dresser together for a slight saving. It would be better to inquire as to the current price before ordering, in view of inflationary trends.

Since most grinding wheels are somewhat out of true, either as received or from extended use, the diamond dresser is a worthwhile investment. The small piece of industrial diamond is securely mounted on the tapered end of a steel rod. I found it worked well to chuck the shaft of small grindstones into the headstock of my lathe, putting

Inexpensive grinding wheels, mounted on ¼" shafts, are usually slightly out of round, but can be dressed to perfect contours with the diamond-tipped dresser from B-Square.

the dresser bar in the tool holder to hone the wheel to perfect circularity by means of several patient passes. A note of caution, here: Be sure to put paper beneath the wheel being dressed, so as to catch the emery dust and keep it from fouling the lathe bed. Likewise, avoid inhaling the lazily curling plumes of fine dust that waft up in your face, lest you get your lungs honed from the inside.

The B-Square catalog shows the Blade Maker C-clamped to the rest of a bench grinder. My grinder doesn't have the

Here the diamond-tipped B-Square dressing rod has been clamped in the tool holder of a small Unimat lathe to dress a grinding wheel of about one inch diameter. Note the buildup of abrasive dust on the lathe bed and take precautions to keep it out of the moving parts of the lathe. Likewise, avoid inhaling any of the fine, airborne abrasive particles!

sturdy cast iron rest like the one in the photo; just a lightweight affair stamped from sheet metal. Besides, I wanted the blades hollow-ground to a somewhat smaller radius.

I had a neat little shaft-mounted stone from Brownell's, about two inches in diameter by 0.625-inch in width, so I dressed that on the lathe, as described, and mounted it in the drill press. The Blade Maker was positioned in the drill press vise and the vise was fastened in place on the drill press bed with a C-clamp.

I cut some 0.250-inch cold-rolled bar stock to appropriate lengths with a hacksaw and dressed the ends smooth and square in the lathe. Lacking a lathe, the same step could have been performed by chucking the blank in a drill press or electric hand drill, then smoothing the ends with a flat file.

I find it's helpful to leave fine concentric rings on the end of the blank, going down to a visible dot in the exact center. The dot serves as a useful reference point when you're peering at the end of the blade with a jeweler's loupe later to make sure it's being ground symmetrically.

With the grinding wheel rotating at a fairly low-speed setting of the drill press, the stock removal was rather slow. The benefit was that there was no need to worry about overheating the steel from friction. I turned up a stout rubber band from the top of the workbench and stretched it from the rear of the Blade Marker to a handle on the back of the drill press bed to provide uniform but moderate pressure on the grinding operation. This approach seems to work well. You can go on about other chores about the shop, pausing to check the progress of the grind every few minutes.

With the blade blanked to the desired dimensions, I chucked the shank and used a progression of wet-or-dry paper in grades 240/320/400/600 to polish the shank. As the final polish, I applied some Happich Simichrome to the spinning shank, holding it on rifle cleaning patches. Simichrome is sold in small tubes, usually at motorcycle shops. It looks like wintergreen flavored toothpaste and it produces the slickest final polish of any medium I've encountered to date.

Having crafted a screwdriver blade, there remains the matter of fitting a handle to it in a suitably secure manner. I had a supply of hexagonal cross section aluminum bar stock on hand, measuring 0.750-inch across the flats. I cut it into short sections, using a Black & Decker metal cutting blade on the table saw and put them into the three-jawed chuck of the lathe for dressing and finishing. After truing-up the ends with a cutter bit in the lathe, it was a simple matter to round off the corners with a large, flat, fine-cut file held against the hex stock as it spun in the lathe. That was followed by a few wipes of 600-grit wet-or-dry and some Simichrome on a cleaning patch for a luster like polished silver.

A hole was drilled longitudinally in one end of the handle blank to accept the shank of the blade. Once it was fitted properly, a drop or so of Loc-Tite Stud 'N Bearing Mount was put in the hole and the shank pressed into place. Experience has shown that once this stuff sets up, it never comes loose. Should you ever need to remove it, you (might) loosen it a trifle by heating the parts judiciously with a propane torch.

There are several alternative approaches for making and installing the handle. You can grind a few tapering flats on the end of the shank and drive it into one of the wooden file handles with steel ferrules, such as are available in most hardware stores. If you don't envision a high degree of stress, a length of wooden dowel with a hole drilled in one end may serve acceptably.

Naturally, if you see a need for hardening and tempering the bit end of the blade, that operation is better performed before adding the handle. The exact procedure for hardening and tempering will depend somewhat upon the composition of the steel. If you're using drill rod stock, it seems to work fairly well to heat the blade end to a dull red with a propane torch or similar source, then quench it in water until cooled. Using 600-grit paper, polish one side of the bit down to bright metal and re-heat it to a color somewhere between dark straw and yellow brown (holding off before it goes to purple), quenching it as before. If that leaves you with a bit that's so brittle it breaks, perform the

*LocTite Stud N' Bearing Mount is a sealing medium that can be found in most auto supply stores. A drop or two will weld the bit and handle together with great strength.*

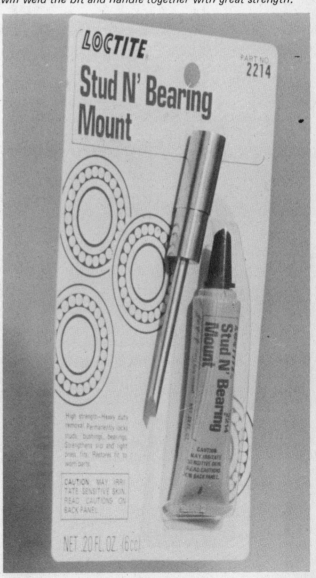

Another highly useful tool that's easy to make is the .45 auto tool discussed in the text. A short piece of 1/8" brass welding rod is rounded on one end and fastened into a handle with LocTite. Photo below shows how it is used for driving out the retaining pin for the mainspring housing. Naturally, in actual disassembly, the magazine would be removed!

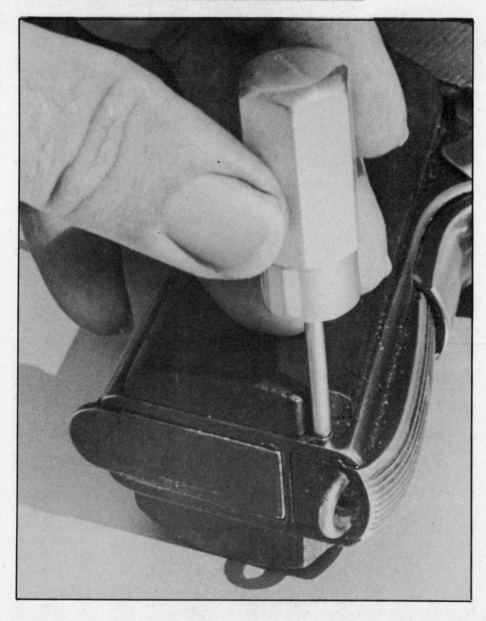

second quench somewhere between light straw and dark straw yellow.

If you're using plain old cold-rolled bar stock from the neighborhood hardware store, the procedures probably will require some amount of trial-and-error experimentation. The metallurgical properties of such material are not universally consistent. The problem is compounded by the fact that cold-rolled is readily available and drill rod may be hard to find.

If you have much occasion to disassemble the Model 1911 Colt auto, an extremely useful tool can be constructed by putting a short section of 0.125-inch brass welding rod into a handle and rounding the exposed end to a hemispheric contour. Such a tool is perfect for knocking out the pin that holds the mainspring housing in place and it's also handy for depressing the exposed end of the firing pin for removal of the firing pin gate. A similar tool, of smaller diameter, can be made and used to align the disconnector and sear from the right-hand side of the receiver before installing the sear pin from the left-hand side.

B-Square's catalog shows another item they call their Frozen Screw Jack that appears capable of coping with even the most stubborn situations. Priced at $25.95, postpaid, it consists of two steel bar crosspieces held together by a bolt and nut at each end. The upper plate that goes over the screw has a T-handled compression screw that forces one of the four supplied blade bits into the screw slot, holding it there against appropriate pressure applied by turning the T-handle. A small ratchet handle goes over the hex shank of the blade bit to apply torque for loosening the screw.

In nearly any stubborn screw situation, you can usually improve the odds for success by dousing the area around the screw head with a material such as Break Free or Liquid Wrench, allowing it to soak for a day or two before launching the all-out attack. I once had a pair of aluminum filter mount rings for a camera that were hopelessly hung up. I wiped Break Free all the way around the joint with a

*The tool shown on the facing page also can be used to depress the rear of the firing pin of the Model 1911 auto pistol, thereby permitting the gate to be slid downward for removal of the firing pin and spring. A similar tool, slightly smaller in diameter than the sear pin, can be useful in aligning the holes in the sear and disconnector in assembling.*

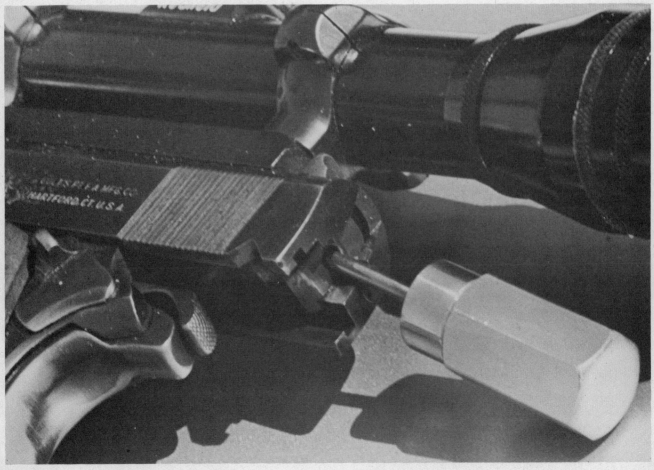

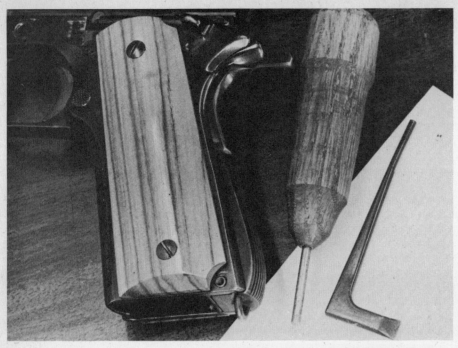

An earlier version of the .45 tool has its brass shank held in an oak handle turned on a wood lathe. The L-shaped device is a GI tool for work on the .45, combining a round-point punch and screwdriver.

Honing oil for use on the half-round India stone, a bushing wrench and punches are handy accessories for working on the Government Model.

fingertip, let it soak for a day and was astonished to find that they came apart with no more than moderate finger pressure. Don't overlook the possibilities of such an approach.

If you have occasional need to tap threads in drilled holes, B-Square's Tru-Tapper is one of the handiest items ever. The sliding shank is chucked into the drill press, the tap is installed in the chuck of the Tru-Tapper and the workpiece is clamped into the drill press vise and centered beneath the tap. Dip the tap in a bottle of Brownell's "Flute Juice" and it becomes an easy cinch to carve your threads at a perfectly precise ninety-degree angle from all around. If you've ever wrestled and sobbed, trying to perform this freehand, you're in for a real treat.

If it seems like a handy accessory, you might consider slotting the exposed end of a piece of bar stock and securing a coin of appropriate size into it, with a handle on the other end. This is a convenient way of coping with all of those coin-slotted screws you may encounter. If you don't care to use a penny, dime or nickel, a steel washer of the proper size probably will work even better.

Another unpleasant chore is the shortening of scope mount screws to keep them from protruding into the action to hang up operation of the bolt. Again, B-Square has a handy accessory with a threaded collar to hold the little screws during grinding. I've had good results putting the shank of the B-Square holder in the lathe chuck and rotating the entire assembly as I work on the exposed end of the screw with a grinding wheel in the Dremel Moto-Tool.

B-Square now has taps for metric threads and, Brownell is contemplating adding drill bits in metric sizes to their line in the jobber (short) length. Knowing where to find such things can be the other half of the fight!

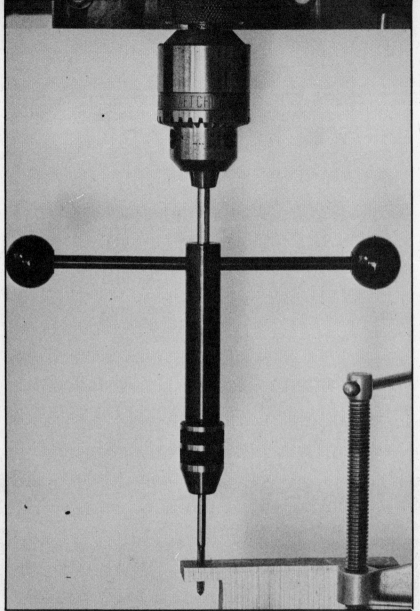

*B-Square Tru-Tapper has a sliding guide rod that attaches to chuck of drill press for precise alignment.*

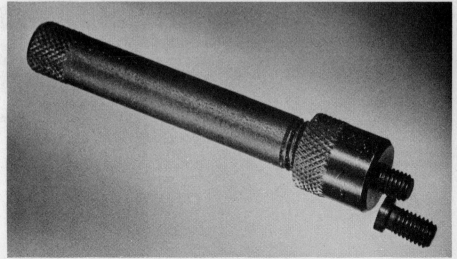

*B-Square holder makes easy work of shortening the shanks of screws used for holding scope mounts.*

# A
# MATTER OF

**J**UST AS it is helpful for a physician to have a more than passing knowledge of anatomy before he performs an operation, it is a basic requirement that the pistolsmith be familiar with the inner workings of the handguns on which he might be called upon to exercise his expertise.

While some revolvers seemingly have entered the realm of exotica and mystique on the basis of advertising and publicity, they remain basically the same as Samuel Colt envisioned them when he whittled his first model out of wood. The revolver is caused to function by pressure on the trigger activating a series of springs and levers. Automatics operate on the same general concept, except there are more complications. There invariably are more parts, most of them sliding under spring or gas pressures to feed fresh rounds from the magazine into the chamber, then extract and eject the empty case when the firing cycle is completed, feeding a fresh cartridge into the chamber.

# FUNCTION

## Chapter 2

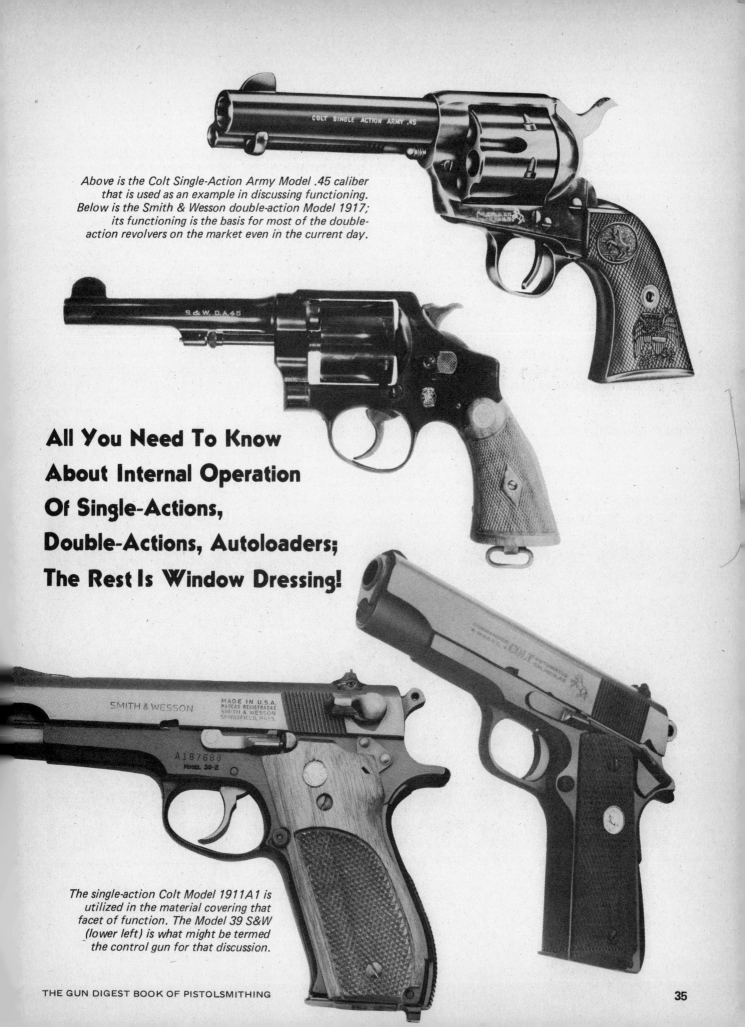

Above is the Colt Single-Action Army Model .45 caliber
that is used as an example in discussing functioning.
Below is the Smith & Wesson double-action Model 1917;
its functioning is the basis for most of the double-
action revolvers on the market even in the current day.

# All You Need To Know
# About Internal Operation
# Of Single-Actions,
# Double-Actions, Autoloaders;
# The Rest Is Window Dressing!

The single-action Colt Model 1911A1 is
utilized in the material covering that
facet of function. The Model 39 S&W
(lower left) is what might be termed
the control gun for that discussion.

## COLT'S SINGLE-ACTION ARMY REVOLVER

The oldest handgun still in popular use, of course, is the Colt Single Action Army model, with numerous variations being produced by other manufacturers. The single action is the simplest of today's handguns, since it has the fewest parts and, in spite of innovations, is the same basic gun that Sam Colt designed in 1836 for percussion ignition.

A look at the accompanying parts drawing of the Colt SAA should give you an excellent idea of just how the various parts work in relationship to each other; going through the drill of naming parts would be gilding the lily, so we'll get into the basics of functioning.

When the hammer is pulled to the rear by thumb pressure on the hammer spur, the functioning process already is under way. As the hammer rotates to the rear and downward, the foot of the hammer is rotating forward and up; this carries with it the hand, or pawl which is attached to the hammer by means of a pin.

As the hammer starts to rotate, the cam on the hammer's foot is engaged in the rear limb or extension of the bolt. Further pressure causes the bolt to pivot on its own pin, thus moving the bolt out of the locking cut in the cylinder.

The hand, driven upward by the hammer, comes in contact with the ratchet at the rear of the cylinder and begins to rotate the cylinder clockwise. While the hammer continues its rotation to the rear, the hand rotates the cylinder. The hammer foot lifts the rear of the bolt to its peak, at which time the spring action and the limb snap it over, the cam passing it. At this moment, the bolt spring drives the front end of the bolt upward, engaging the lock notch in the cylinder, stopping cylinder rotation.

With continuing rotation of the hammer, the hand continues through its own cycle. It brings pressure to bear on the ratchet which, in turn, rotates the cylinder the proper distance to align the next chamber in the cylinder with the barrel. When the cylinder reaches this alignment position, the bolt drops into the locking cut. This leaves the chamber in line with the barrel. Further rearward movement of the hammer under the shooter's thumb causes the trigger spring to force the trigger nose to snap into the full-cock notch. When the hammer is released, the trigger assembly is responsible for the hammer remaining in the full-cock position.

One must give some thought to Sam Colt's genius: As described, in the hammer's rotation cycle, the trigger nose has slipped past the safety notch as well as the half-cock notch. Old Sam planned it that way, of course. Had we chosen to stop the hammer at either the safety or half-cock position, the trigger nose again would have snapped into the

*From the left side, the Colt SAA hammer mechanism is seen with hand and hand spring which operate during cocking cycle.*

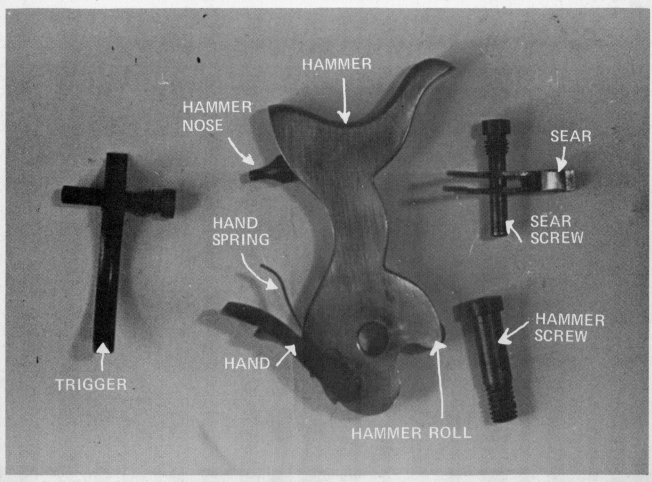

1 Backstrap
2 Backstrap Screws (2)
3 Balls (2)
4 Barrel
5 Base Pin
6 Base Pin Bushing
7 Base Pin Screw
8 Base Pin Screw Nut
9 Base Pin Spring
10 Bolt
11 Bolt Screw
12 Cylinder
13 Ejector Head
14 Ejector Rod
15 Ejector Spring
16 Ejector Tube
17 Ejector Tube Screw
18 Firing Pin
19 Firing Pin Rivet
20 Frame
21 Front Guard Screw
22 Front Strap Screw
23 Gate
24 Gate Catch
25 Gate Catch Screw
26 Gate Spring
27 Hammer
28 Hammer Roll
29 Hammer Roll Pin
30 Hammer Screw
31 Hand Assembly
32 Main Spring
33 Main Spring Screw
34 Rear Guard Screws (2)
35 Recoil Plate
36 Sear and Bolt Spring
37 Sear and Bolt Spring Screw
38 Spring
39 Stock—Left Hand
40 Stock—Right Hand
41 Stock Pin
42 Stock Screw
43 Trigger
44 Trigger Guard
45 Trigger Screw
46 Washer
47 Washers, No. 8 (7)

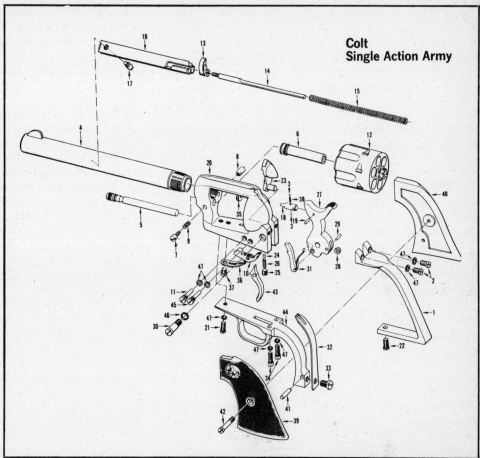

**Colt
Single Action Army**

corresponding notch to hold the hammer in the chosen position. It should be noted that both of these notches are undercut in such a way that, when engaged, they literally overlap the trigger nose. The result is that normal trigger pressure cannot cause the hammer to fall.

The gun now cocked, finger pressure on the trigger causes it to rotate about the trigger screw. This, in turn, moves the trigger nose out of the full-cock notch, leaving the hammer free. The hammer thus is driven forward by the mainspring, rotating on the hammer screw. The firing pin is driven with the spring force through the frame to come in contact with the cartridge primer, thus causing the round in the chamber to fire.

During the downward rotation cycle, the cam on the hammer foot comes into sharp contact with the bolt limb. However, a bevel on the bottom side of this cam forces the limb aside so it does not interfere with travel of the hammer.

During the same series of interactions, the force on the bolt limb creates pressure on the front of the bolt at the

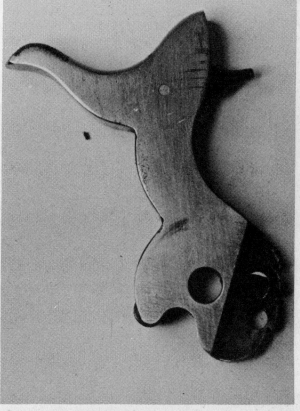

*On this Colt SAA, hammer is photographed so as to show the cocking and loading latches, hammer roll and firing pin.*

point where it engages the cylinder as the cartridge is fired. The firing cycle is complete at this point.

It may sound complicated, but, again, a study of the exploded view, or even disassembling your SAA and laying out the parts should help you to understand the interaction of each of the parts. As stated earlier, old Sam Colt showed his genius in the simplicity he employed.

While undergoing gunsmithing training at the Colorado School of Trades, I found that one of the available training aids was invaluable in understanding functioning, as well as helping to determine what was wrong with a SAA that was malfunctioning. This aid was nothing more than a steel block with pins properly installed so that the hammer, trigger and bolt could be placed over these pins and would be in proper functioning sequence. This setup enabled us to move all of the parts in their normal sequence and to observe the action and purpose of each. If the sequence didn't come off properly, that was where we were taught to start looking for the trouble. Needless to say, perhaps, if you are going into serious gunsmithing, such an aid can be invaluable and undoubtedly save hours of by-guess-and-by-gosh checking.

The only area in which Sam Colt may have overestimated the value of his design is in the safety notch of the SAA. It was designed originally so that six cartridges could be carried in the six chambers without fear of accidental firing. However, nearly everyone who has used a revolver for long has learned to load only five rounds and carry the empty chamber under the hammer.

Theoretically, when the Colt's hammer is in the safety notch the gun cannot be fired, but there have been instances, such as when a Single-Action Army model was dropped, that the firing pin did drop forward onto the primer resulting in an accidental shot. Considering the basic design of the SAA, there isn't much a pistolsmith can do to improve upon this situation. Hence the five-round load.

The half-cock notch was designed by Colt to offer a safe position of the hammer when the bolt has been retracted, thus freeing the cylinder for loading or inspection of the chambers. With the hammer in the half-cock notch, the bolt is disengaged and the cylinder can be rotated or spun.

In inspecting a stripped down SAA, one can see how the various parts are assembled. Again, the accompanying exploded view can be useful in this inspection. The mainspring, of course, is attached to the base of the trigger guard strap by means of a screw. The bolt spring is held in place by a screw beneath the trigger guard, while the hand is held in alignment in a groove by means of a flat spring that contacts the rear of the frame groove where it rides.

The SAA cylinder is mounted on the removable base pin by means of a bushing inserted into the cylinder, which is in direct contact with this base pin. This bushing is meant to position the cylinder in relationship to headspacing and cylinder gap with the rear of the barrel.

The ejector rod is spring loaded and the loading gate is held in place by a spring-loaded ball, which allows it to spring open or shut under pressure. A firing pin bushing is force-fitted into the front of the SAA recoil shield in alignment with the chamber, allowing the firing pin to protrude the proper depth to contact the cartridge primer for firing.

The Colt Single-Action Army model is probably the most copied handgun in history and it is the design from which other makers' revolver designs were evolved. Today, variations include coil springs, different types of firing pins and other so-called improvements, but the basic configuration doesn't differ that much from the handgun designed by Samuel Colt nearly a century-and-a-half ago.

## DOUBLE-ACTION REVOLVERS

There are far more variations in double-action revolvers than in the single-action models, but the basic designs remain pretty much the same. Rather than attempt to outline the variations, we decided to take one model and discuss it at length. A study of other models will show the similarities and differences, which the pistolsmith will grow to recognize as he becomes more deeply involved.

A typical example is the Smith & Wesson Model 1917,

*With the sideplate removed, this S&W Model 66 reveals the lock mechanism that is contained within the frame.*

Above: The double-action Model 36 Smith & Wesson has the hammer in the cocked position so that the pivoting action of the hammer, trigger on their respective pins is seen. (Below) Close-up photo illustrates working relationship between the rebound slide, the hammer, trigger, sear and the hand. The action is explained fully in the text.

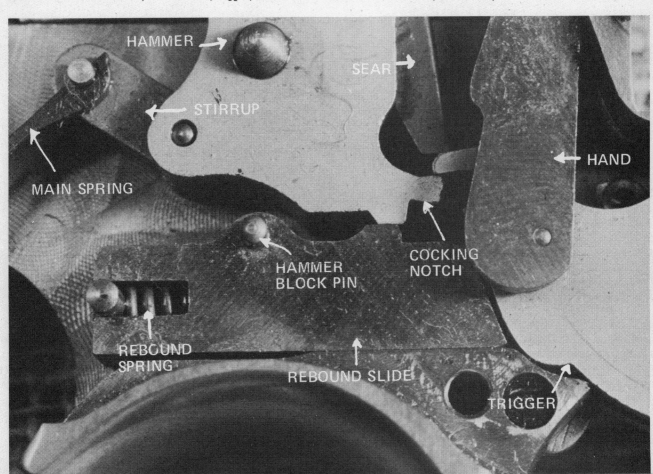

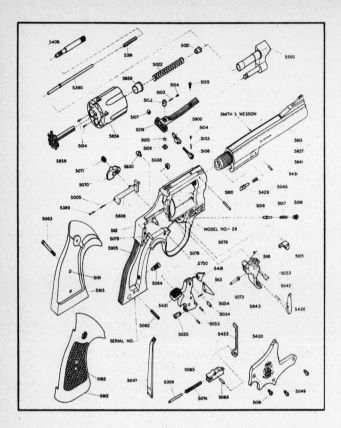

# SMITH & WESSON
## .44 Magnum Revolver — Model No. 29

| No. | Part | No. | Part |
|---|---|---|---|
| 5005 | Bolt Plunger Spring | 5118 | Hand Torsion Spring |
| 5014 | Extractor Pin | 5155 | Rear Sight Leaf Screw |
| 5015 | Cylinder Stop | 5191 | Escutcheon |
| 5016 | Cylinder Stop Plunger | 5192 | Escutcheon Nut |
| 5017 | Cylinder Stop Plunger Spr. | 5218 | Rear Sight Assembly |
| 5018 | Cylinder Stop Plunger Scre... | 5219 | Rear Sight Leaf |
| 5021 | Extractor Rod Collar | 5306 | Trigger Stop |
| 5022 | Extractor Spring | 5389 | Bolt Plunger |
| 5034 | Hammer Nose Rivet | 5390 | Center Pin |
| 5036 | Hammer Nose Bushing | 5391 | Center Pin Spring |
| 5042 | Hand Pin | 5409 | Extractor Rod |
| 5045 | Locking Bolt Spring | 5418 | Hammer Nose |
| 5047 | Mainspring | 5421 | Hammer |
| 5049 | Plate Screw, crowned | 5423 | Hammer Block |
| 5053 | Hand Spring Pin | 5426 | Hand |
| 5053 | Hand Spring Torsion Pin | 5429 | Locking Bolt |
| 5053 | Sear Pin | 5430 | Side Plate |
| 5053 | Stirrup Pin | 5431 | Locking Bolt Pin |
| 5053 | Trigger Lever Pin | 5500 | Yoke |
| 5054 | Sear Spring | 5608 | Bolt |
| 5055 | Stirrup | 5750 | Hammer Nose Spring |
| 5062 | Stock Pin | 5810 | Barrel Pin |
| 5063 | Stock Screw | 5843 | Trigger |
| 5064 | Strain Screw | 5856 | Cylinder, with extractor, pins and gas ring |
| 5070 | Thumbpiece | 5857 | Barrel, 6½" |
| 5071 | Thumbpiece Nut | 5858 | Extractor |
| 5073 | Trigger Lever | 5859 | Gas Ring |
| 5074 | Rebound Slide Spring | 5871 | Front Sight |
| 5078 | Trigger Stud | 5900 | Rear Sight Slide |
| 5079 | Cylinder Stop Stud | 5901 | Barrel, 4" |
| 5079 | Rebound Slide Stud | 5905 | Frame, with studs, bushing and lug |
| 5083 | Rebound Slide Pin | 5912 | Stock, right hand, target type of checked Goncalo Alves, with S&W monograms |
| 5085 | Rebound Slide | | |
| 5091 | Plate Screw, flat head | 5913 | Stock, right hand, target type of checked Goncalo Alves, with S&W monograms |
| 5102 | Rear Sight Elevation Nut | | |
| 5103 | Rear Sight Plunger Spring | | |
| 5104 | Rear Sight Plunger | 5930 | Frame Lug |
| 5105 | Rear Sight Spring Clip | 5934 | Front Sight Pin |
| 5106 | Rear Sight Elevation Stud | 5941 | Barrel, 8⅜" |
| 5107 | Rear Sight Windage Nut, | | |
| 5108 | Rear Sight Windage Screw | | |
| 5112 | Hammer Stud | | |
| 5113 | Sear | | |

which was built in .45 caliber for military use. Many of this maker's double-action revolvers in manufacture today feature the principles of this handgun. First off, some specifications: This is a breech-loading revolver, with a swing-out cylinder holding the six chambers for loading. The chambers are loaded with two half-moon clips of three rounds each, since the revolver was designed to fire the .45 Model 1911 military ball cartridge.

This is probably a good time to point out that the Model 1917 is obsolete, but there was a reason for choosing it: as one of the earliest double actions, it is basic and good for instructional purposes. All of Smith & Wesson's currently produced N-frame revolvers are based upon this design with only cosmetic and caliber changes made over the years.

There certainly should be no doubt among readers as to the difference between single-action and double-action shooting, but inasmuch as this particular revolver can be fired either way, the sequence is described well by the Department of the Army Field Manual FM 23-35 of 1953:

*In firing double action, pressure is applied to the trigger until the hammer falls, firing the cartridge.*

*In firing single action, the hammer is cocked by pressure to the rear with the trigger fully released. Pressure on the trigger releases the hammer which falls, firing the cartridge.*

In view of the simplicity of that explanation, we'll use details excerpted from the same field manual to describe the functioning of this particular model:

**(a)** *The lock mechanism is contained in the frame and consists of the hammer, with its stirrup, stirrup pin, strut, strut pin, and strut spring; the trigger, with its pin, the trigger lever, with its pin; the rebound slide, with its pin and spring; the hand, with its pin; the hand lever with its pin and hand lever spring; the cylinder bolt, with its pin, cylinder bolt plunger, cylinder bolt plunger spring, and cylinder bolt plunger screw; the latch, latch plunger, and latch plunger spring.*

**(b)** *The hammer and trigger are pivoted on their respective pins. These pins are screwed in place in the left side of the frame and then upset, and are supported on the right side by holes drilled in the side plate to receive them. The rebound slide is held in position by its pin and spring and the rear end of the trigger lever. The lower end of the mainspring fits into a slot in the frame while its upper end engages the hammer stirrup. The mainspring is stressed by screwing up the strain screw, which bears against the mainspring.*

**(c)** *The rebound slide houses the spring and slides on the pin against which the spring presses. When the trigger is released, after firing a shot, the rebound slide spring pressing against the rebound slide forces the rebound slide forward. The forward end of the rebound slide, pressing against the trigger lever, forces the trigger lever forward and returns the trigger to its original position. The hand being pivoted to the trigger by its pin is thus brought back to its lowest position. After firing, when the hammer is in its extreme forward position, the lowest projection on the hammer lies in the notch on the front end of the rebound slide. As the rebound slide moves forward, the hammer projection is forced out of the notch and onto the flat surface of the slide in the rear of the notch, thus moving the hammer back to its safety position.*

**(d)** *The revolver may be used either single action or*

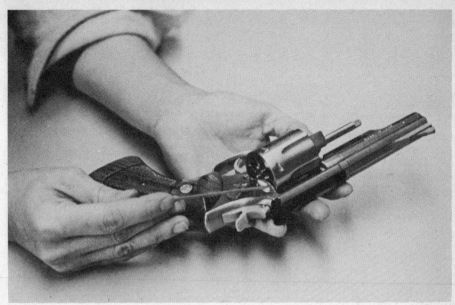

*Cylinder, with its six chambers, rotates upon, is supported by the central arbor of the crane.*

hammer to retract the firing pin for safe carrying.

In operation, the trigger movement disengages the bolt, then raises the hand to start rotation of the cylinder, while rotating the hammer rearward. During this phase, the transfer lever pivots to the trigger's rear. When the trigger is in the forward position, this bar keeps the face of the hammer from contacting the frame-mounted firing pin.

This effect may be achieved by the lever protecting the face of the hammer from the frame shoulder or the lever may retract a lug that normally acts as a connector between the hammer and the firing pin. Whichever system is used, they are effective as a safety device. Recent models that have incorporated the transfer lever in design include the Colt Mark III Trooper, the models designed and produced by the late Dan Wesson and the Security Six designed by Bill Ruger.

*The hammer block is visible in its recess in the sideplate. It rides on its pin, which is attached to rebound slide.*

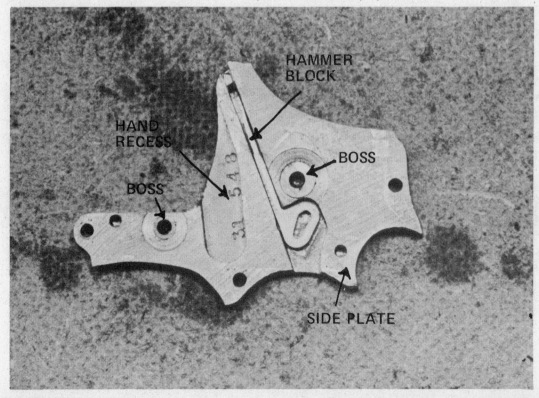

*Colt's Model 1911A1 has been produced for nearly seventy years. John M. Browning's design is the most popular and most copied of all of the single-action autoloaders. When one understands its function, changes are minor in others.*

## SINGLE-ACTION AUTOLOADERS

When one refers to the term, "automatic," the average shooter thinks of something complicated and tough to deal with. In reality, the so-called automatic pistol is not automatic at all. In reality, it is an autoloader. That means a new cartridge is seated in the chamber automatically; it still requires a pull of the trigger to fire the gun. A true automatic weapon is one that continues to fire so long as the trigger is depressed, not requiring a separate trigger pull to fire each round.

While the lockwork on the various types of autoloading pistols may differ, the actual theory of function remains much the same in the different designs.

In dealing with the single-action autoloader, we'll use as the typical example, the Colt Model 1911A1, which has been around for well over sixty years. In spite of its age, this design from John M. Browning is probably the most popular and most copied autoloader in the world today. To explain the functioning cycle, we again quote from the earlier identified Army field manual, since the pistol was designed originally for military use:

**a.** *The magazine may be charged with any number of cartridges from one to seven.*

**b.** *The charged magazine is inserted in the receiver and the slide drawn once to the rear. This movement cocks the hammer, compresses the recoil spring, and when the slide reaches the rear position the magazine follower raises the upper cartridge into the path of the slide. The slide is then released and being forced forward by the recoil spring carries the first cartridge into the chamber of the barrel. As the slide approaches its forward position, it encounters the rear extension of the barrel and forces the barrel forward; the rear end of the barrel swings upward on the barrel link, turning on the muzzle end as on a fulcrum. When the slide and barrel reach their forward position they are positively locked together by the locking ribs on the barrel and their joint forward movement is arrested by the barrel lug encountering the pin on the slide top. The pistol is then ready for firing.*

The photo above shows the Colt .45 Model 1911A1 in its field stripped condition. Below, the same pistol has been detail stripped. John M. Browning's genius is reflected in the simplicity of the gun's design, function.

**c.** When the hammer is cocked the hammer strut moves downward, compressing the mainspring, and the sear under action of the long leaf of the sear spring engages its nose in the notch on the hammer. In order that the pistol may be fired the following conditions must exist:

(1) The grip safety must be pressed in, leaving the trigger free to move.

(2) The slide must be in its forward position, properly interlocked with the barrel so that the disconnector is held in the recess on the underside of the slide under the action of the sear spring, transmitting in this position any motion of the trigger to the sear.

(3) The safety lock must be down in the unlocked position so that the sear will be unlocked and free to release the hammer and the slide will be free to move back.

**d.** When the trigger is squeezed the sear is moved, and the released hammer strikes the firing pin, which transmits the blow to the primer of the cartridge. The pressure of the gasses generated in the barrel by the explosion of the powder in the cartridge is exerted in a forward direction against the bullet, driving it through the bore, and in a rearward direction against the face of the slide, driving the latter and the barrel to the rear together. The downward swinging movement of the barrel unlocks it from the slide, and the barrel is then stopped in its lowest position. The slide continues to move to the rear, opening the breech, cocking the hammer, extracting and ejecting the empty shell, and compressing the recoil spring until the slide reaches its rearmost position when another cartridge is raised in front of it and forced into the chamber of the barrel by the return movement of the slide under pressure of the recoil spring.

**e.** The weight and consequently the inertia of the slide augmented by those of the barrel are so many times greater than the weight and inertia of the bullet that the latter has been given its maximum velocity and has been driven from the muzzle of the barrel before the slide and barrel have recoiled to the point where the barrel commences its unlocking movement. This construction therefore delays the opening of the breech of the barrel until after the bullet has left the muzzle and therefore practically prevents the

*In this photo enlargement, the hammer of the Colt autoloader is in the half-cock or safety position.*

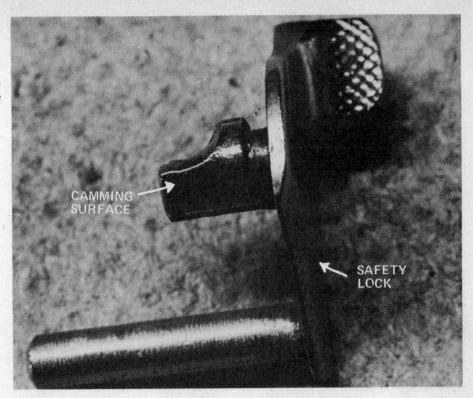

The Colt pistol's safety lock and camming surface are carefully machined. This is one of three safeties on gun.

CAMMING SURFACE

SAFETY LOCK

The safety lock, hammer and grip safety all have specific functions meant to make the 1911A1 the safest design ever.

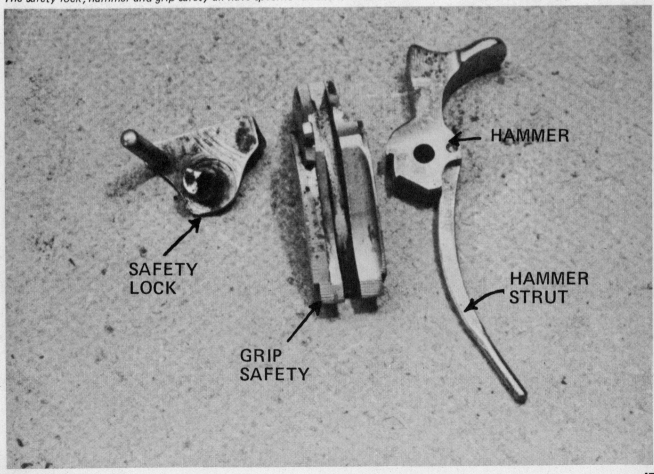

SAFETY LOCK

GRIP SAFETY

HAMMER

HAMMER STRUT

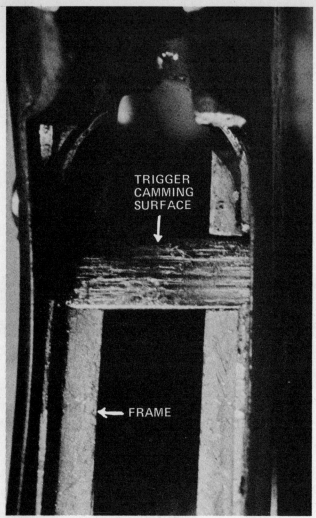

The back of the trigger, which rides on the sear, when trigger is squeezed releases hammer to strike firing pin.

As illustrated here, the gun's hammer strut extends down from hammer into mainspring cap in cocking action.

escape of any of the powder gasses to the rear after the breech has been opened. This factor of safety is further increased by the tension of the recoil spring and mainspring, both of which oppose the rearward movement of the slide.

f. While the comparatively great weight of the slide of the piston insures safety against premature opening of the breech, it also insures operation of the pistol because, at the point of the rearward opening movement where the barrel is unlocked and stopped, the heavy slide has attained a momentum which is sufficient to carry it through its complete opening movement and makes the pistol ready for another shot.

g. When the magazine has been emptied, the pawl-shaped slide stop is raised by the magazine follower under action of the magazine spring into the front recess on the lower left side of the slide, thereby locking the slide in the open position and serving as an indicator to remind the shooter that the empty magazine must be replaced by a loaded one before the firing can be continued. Pressure upon the magazine catch quickly releases the empty magazine from the receiver and permits the insertion of a loaded magazine.

h. To release the slide from the open position, it is only necessary to press upon the thumbpiece of the slide stop, then the slide will go forward to its closed position, carrying a cartridge from the previously inserted magazine into the barrel and making the pistol ready for firing again.

## DOUBLE-ACTION AUTOLOADERS

Probably the best-known double-action autoloader manufactured in this country today is the Smith & Wesson Model 39, so we will use this particular model for purposes of description and illustration.

As indicated earlier, the function of the double-action

and single-action differ little. The former can be fired single-action simply by thumbing back the hammer until it is in the fully cocked position, then squeezing the trigger, if desired. The double-action also can be fired with the hammer down, pulling the trigger until the hammer comes all the way back, then falls forward on the firing pin.

In the Model 39 — as well as with most other double-action designs — a part called a drawbar is attached to the trigger's upper limb and is positioned so a hook at its rear extends behind the foot of the hammer. This is while the hammer is down and the trigger forward. Drawing the trigger rearward to bring back the hammer causes the upper limb to move the drawbar forward. The drawbar thus contacts the hammer's foot, causing it to rotate forward on its pin; at the same time, the hammer is swinging to the rear. As the drawbar continues in its path of movement, the hammer moves into the full-cock position. During the same cycle, the drawbar moves the sear nose away from the path of the hammer. A cam surface moves the drawbar away from the hammer toe, allowing the hammer to drop forward under force of the mainspring, thus firing the round in the chamber.

With the cartridge fired, the auto's slide then begins to recoil to the rear. This causes the disconnector to cam downward under the rearward force of the slide's travel; the action disengages the drawbar from the sear, driving it out of the hammer's path. As with the single-action version, this movement allows the sear to engage with the hammer, as the slide forces the hammer to the full-cocked position. The trigger must be released to the forward position to repeat the sequence before another shot can be fired. Other than the sequence described above, the functioning of the double-action autoloader differs little from that of the single-action version.

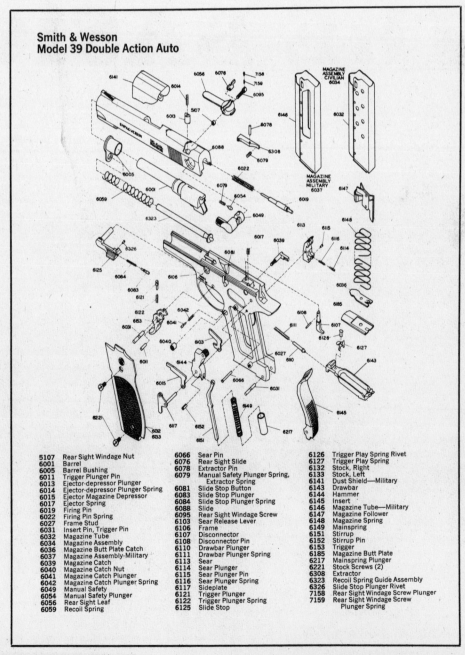

Smith & Wesson
Model 39 Double Action Auto

| 5107 | Rear Sight Windage Nut | 6066 | Sear Pin | 6126 | Trigger Play Spring Rivet |
|------|------------------------|------|----------|------|---------------------------|
| 6001 | Barrel | 6076 | Rear Sight Slide | 6127 | Trigger Play Spring |
| 6005 | Barrel Bushing | 6078 | Extractor Pin | 6132 | Stock, Right |
| 6011 | Trigger Plunger Pin | 6079 | Manual Safety Plunger Spring, | 6133 | Stock, Left |
| 6013 | Ejector-depressor Plunger | | Extractor Spring | 6141 | Dust Shield—Military |
| 6014 | Ejector-depressor Plunger Spring | 6081 | Slide Stop Button | 6143 | Drawbar |
| 6015 | Ejector Magazine Depressor | 6083 | Slide Stop Plunger | 6144 | Hammer |
| 6017 | Ejector Spring | 6084 | Slide Stop Plunger Spring | 6145 | Insert |
| 6019 | Firing Pin | 6088 | Slide | 6146 | Magazine Tube—Military |
| 6022 | Firing Pin Spring | 6095 | Rear Sight Windage Screw | 6147 | Magazine Follower |
| 6027 | Frame Stud | 6103 | Sear Release Lever | 6148 | Magazine Spring |
| 6031 | Insert Pin, Trigger Pin | 6106 | Frame | 6149 | Mainspring |
| 6032 | Magazine Tube | 6107 | Disconnector | 6151 | Stirrup |
| 6034 | Magazine Assembly | 6108 | Disconnector Pin | 6152 | Stirrup Pin |
| 6036 | Magazine Butt Plate Catch | 6110 | Drawbar Plunger | 6153 | Trigger |
| 6037 | Magazine Assembly-Military | 6111 | Drawbar Plunger Spring | 6185 | Magazine Butt Plate |
| 6039 | Magazine Catch | 6113 | Sear | 6217 | Mainspring Plunger |
| 6040 | Magazine Catch Nut | 6114 | Sear Plunger | 6221 | Stock Screws (2) |
| 6041 | Magazine Catch Plunger | 6115 | Sear Plunger Pin | 6308 | Extractor |
| 6042 | Magazine Catch Plunger Spring | 6116 | Sear Plunger Spring | 6323 | Recoil Spring Guide Assembly |
| 6049 | Manual Safety | 6117 | Sideplate | 6326 | Slide Stop Plunger Rivet |
| 6054 | Manual Safety Plunger | 6121 | Trigger Plunger | 7158 | Rear Sight Windage Screw Plunger |
| 6056 | Rear Sight Leaf | 6122 | Trigger Plunger Spring | 7159 | Rear Sight Windage Screw |
| 6059 | Recoil Spring | 6125 | Slide Stop | | Plunger Spring |

# Chapter 3

# A Look At THE BASICS

Revolver cylinders, as well as the barrel, always should be cleaned after each shooting session. Use the proper brush size for each caliber, making certain to coat the brush liberally with a good grade of solvent for the job.

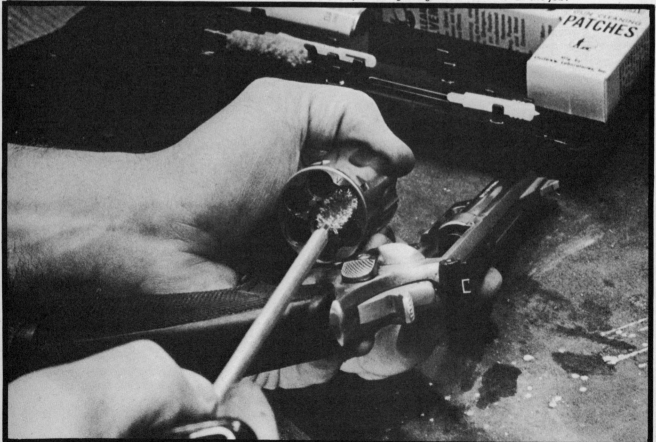

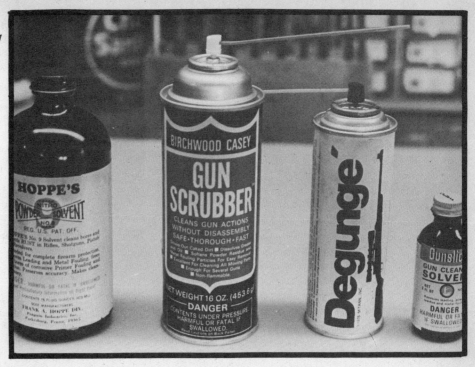

An assortment of typical cleaning solvents for firearms includes Hoppe's No. 9, which aids in detecting metal fouling; Casey Gun Scrubber uses high pressure to remove loosened particles.

# A Good Cleaning Often

# Can Solve Problems That,

# At First Glance, Seem

# Far More Complicated!

**W**HILE PISTOLSMITHING is something of a science and requires a good deal of study and knowledge, there are many problems that can be solved with a good cleaning of the handgun that appears to be damaged or in nonworking condition. Thus, the importance of a good cleaning cannot be ignored by the pistolsmith.

Unfortunately, many gunowners think that slapping a bit of oil on a gun whenever the thought occurs is enough effort to protect it. The rationale here is that, with today's modern technology and space age materials, little or no effort is sufficient.

To clean a gun properly we must accomplish three things. First, we want to protect it against rust. Second, the working parts of a gun have metal moving against metal so we must reduce drag for a smooth operation. Third, after firing any handgun, powder residue and corrosive particles build up in areas that, unless removed, can cause wear of parts and influence accuracy.

Even with all the different gun designs, sizes, calibers, etc., their basic function is to shoot. The three most important characteristics of any gun are reliability, durability and accuracy. All three can be greatly enhanced by proper cleaning and maintenance.

Let's deal with the problems of rust. Gun metal tends to rust without proper and regular care. One important consideration is how much cleaning and lubricating is necessary in your immediate locale. Hot humid locations such as Florida and Hawaii will rust a gun faster than a dry location such as Arizona, for example. The culprit is moisture combined with oxygen. It is wise to clean handguns regularly and provide a good rust preventive oil on them while in storage.

Merely handling a handgun can cause corrosion. Our fingerprints can leave acids and salts on the metal. The salts, when exposed to moisture, will begin the rusting process immediately. Remember, just moving from an outside location to an inside one can cause moisture to condense on metal surfaces and cause rust. Therefore, it is important that, after handling handguns, they should be wiped down thoroughly.

I use a G96 Gun Mitt which is like an oversize mitten.

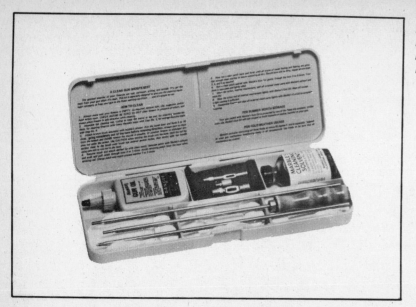

*Marble gun-cleaning kit contains a multi-jointed rod for rifle cleaning, but similar kits with handgun-length rods are available from this maker.*

*Durango cleaning rod comes in various lengths, caliber sizes. Rod is made of stainless steel, but sliding brass collar assures accurate centering in the muzzle during cleaning operation.*

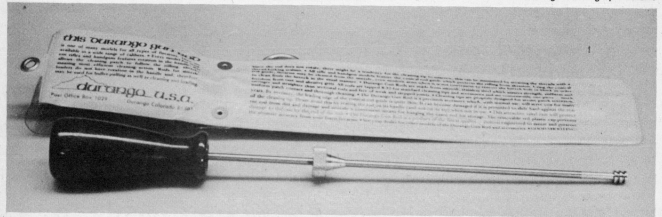

*Outers kit includes a swab, brass bristle brush, patches, patch loop and jag with the cleaning rod, plus a can of gun oil and a bottle of bore solvent.*

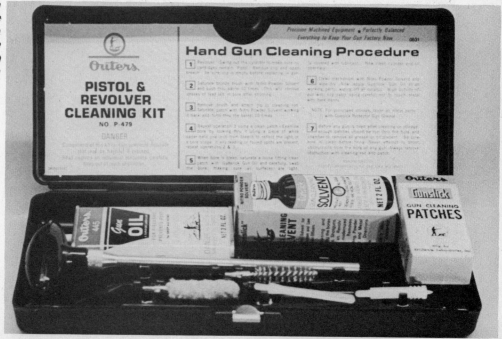

It's simple to use, and has rust inhibitors which will protect the gun.

Also, never store your firearms inside a soft case of the leather or vinyl type over any length of time. Moisture gets trapped in the case and only speeds up the corrosion process. I get ill when I hear of folks leaving their firearms in the trunks of their cars over periods of a week or more. If the trunk has a leak in it which traps moisture after rain, it is like storing the gun in a steam closet.

Actually, the ideal place to store guns is in a clean, dry location. One of the best ideas, in addition to a well lubricated gun during storage, is to keep a product called Hydrosorbent in the storage area right next to your guns. It is a packet of silica gel crystals which absorb moisture from the air. This product has been used aboard ship by the Navy for years and is both effective and inexpensive. For more information write to Hydrosorbent, Box 675, Rye, New York 10580. To reactivate the packets, simply heat in an oven to remove the moisture and return them to the storage closet.

The standard blue-steel finish found on the majority of handguns will not prevent rust. Stainless steel handguns such as the Ruger Security-Six or the Smith & Wesson Model 66 will resist rusting much longer than conventionally blued guns but they too require cleaning and maintenance. Although these two particular handguns are less likely to rust than the regular blued types, their accuracy and reliability may be reduced by metal fouling and corrosive particle buildups from firing.

If you have an old favorite handgun that is rusted, but otherwise functional, the Texas Gunshop, 299 Arapaho Central Park, Richardson, Texas 75080, offers a new plating process called Ni-Tex. This is a process of plating that results in a brushed stainless steel look that can be applied over just about any metal surface and is said to be rust resistant. The resulting appearance is impressive and it may give new life to guns that have been subjected to all sorts of harsh conditions.

When lubricating handguns to protect them from rust, remember that before they are to be taken to the field they should be cleaned and the protective lubricants may

*Here are four lubricants that incorporate molybdenum disulfide for reducing the drag between moving parts.*

*These multi-purpose compounds described in text are for use in cleaning, lubricating, preventing corrosion on steel, other metal parts.*

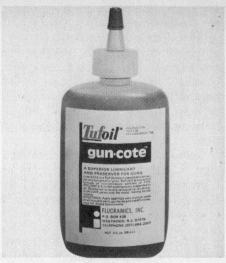

Tufoil Gun-Cote is another compound that lubricates and protects. It is made up with microfine particles of Teflon and Fluon in a permanent state of suspension and it works well.

Amsoil MP metal protector is one of the many compounds offered for lubrication plus rust prevention.

S&W Model 36 sideplate has been removed by loosening screws with properly fitted screwdriver, then tapping frame around plate with butt of the screwdriver until plate is loose. Never remove the sideplate by prying. Thus exposed, the internal parts of the gun are ready for cleaning, lubrication. Reassemble with care.

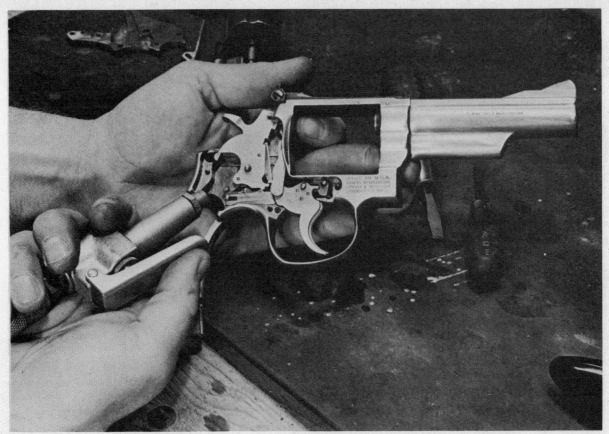

One of the fastest, most effective means of cleaning internal parts is to saturate the gun in solvent or kerosene, then use a compressor to blow out all foreign matter, drying the handgun at same time.

have to be removed. This is especially true in cold temperatures which may cause the lubricant to gum up and create malfunctions. Once back to the house, it is of paramount importance to get that rust-preventive substance back on the piece. It makes good sense to spend the time and effort to keep any handgun in the best condition possible.

The next important consideration is optimum reliability. This means each working part of the gun performs its assigned function to the best of its ability. This is accomplished more efficiently if the gun parts are clean and lubricated to prevent drag. Any time we have metal bearing against metal we need something that will reduce drag and continue to perform without breaking down under adverse conditions. I have found one of the best single lubricants to be molybdenum disulfide. It is excellent for reducing drag, does not break down in hot or cold temperatures and does, to a certain degree, act as a rust preventive.

On the minus side, it is difficult to remove from hands or clothing if used in a powder state and is about as attractive as mud, especially when it oozes out the bottom of the revolver frame around the trigger. It is available commercially from companies such as Dri-Slide, Perma-Slik, and RIG. When the molybdenum disulfide is suspended in a liquid it is simple to use and less messy than in powder form.

I recently have begun using a product called Break-Free on the working parts of guns. Although it has a Teflon base rather than the molybdenum disulfide, initial results have been just short of utterly amazing. It is much cleaner to use than the molybdenum-based products and also is an excellent rust preventive. Break-Free is relatively new to the market so for more information write to: San/Bar Corporation, P.O. Box 11787, Santa Ana, California 92711.

I think the least understood, yet the most important part of cleaning and lubricating pistols and revolvers is the proper removal of powder residue and corrosive particles left after firing the guns. This buildup, unless removed, will adversely influence accuracy, impair reliability, and destroy the gun itself. Granted, smokeless powder is much cleaner burning than anything up to its invention but it is not totally foolproof and can cause problems.

Most non-corrosive primers contain certain elements that can leave a residue causing a degree of harmful rust. Once in a while we come across ammunition with the older, corrosive primers. They contain potassium chlorate which loses oxygen upon ignition, leaving a residue of potassium chloride. The effect is similar to table salt; add a bit of moisture and the rusting process begins.

Lead fouling in pistols and revolvers is detrimental to accuracy. Looking down the bore, the fouling can be seen as darker streaks between the lands and grooves. Such

Chamber areas of revolvers are notorious for lead build-up. Area should be scrubbed well in cleaning cycle.

After running the cleaning brush and solvent through the bore, follow up with a patch that has been soaked in solvent, then finish this part of the job off with dry patch treatment.

fouling usually is quite prevalent near the rear of the barrel. It also builds up in the revolver chambers just forward of where the cartridge case mouth ends when the cylinder is loaded. Any leading must be removed, as it can actually cause the gun to malfunction. (How to remove this will be explained later in this chapter.)

Cleaning pistols and revolvers is not too difficult in most cases, unless metal fouling is present. Copper-jacketed bullets can cause metal fouling, although not as severe as the lead fouling. In extreme cases of metal fouling, metallic mercury – often called quicksilver – is an effective remedy. However, it is difficult and expensive to obtain. Another method of fouling removal involves an old gunsmith formula that works effectively. The formula includes 112 grains ammonium persulfate; 52

grains ammonium carbonate; 480cc distilled water; 720cc ammonium hydroxide.

To use, place the gun muzzle upward and plug the chamber with a tapered rubber stopper. Pour the solution down the barrel and let sit for about thirty minutes. This system works well, I find.

I do not recommend cleaning handguns using steel wool. When working on revolvers, steel wool and/or bristles from cleaning brushes may get caught between the ejector star and rear of cylinder, which can interfere with the cylinder lockup.

Birchwood-Casey's Gun Scrubber is a handy solvent and cleanser to have around. It is under a great deal of pressure and literally blows dirt and corrosion out of working parts which would otherwise be difficult to reach. It is sort of a combination airgun and cleaner. Hoppes' Cleaner No. 9 has been around longer than most. It contains an ingredient which will stain the cleaning patch a greenish-blue if copper fouling is present in the bore. If there is copper fouling, just let the pieces soak in the Hoppes overnight and the fouling will come out easily the next day. It is an excellent solvent, but does not have any rust preventives in it. Outers' pistol kits and rifle kits contain quality products and everything one needs is right there in one place. The same may be said for other gun cleaning kits such as Marble Arms.

To clean pistols and revolvers correctly, begin with a good solvent. If the gun is badly corroded let it remain in the solvent for twenty-four hours. It will make the job much easier. Clean the barrel using a cleaning rod and a patch soaked with solvent first.

After soaking the barrel, change from a patch to a solvent-soaked bronze or brass wire brush and run it through the barrel several times. Run another solvent-soaked patch through the barrel and finish with dry patches. Examine for metal or lead fouling and repeat the process again, if necessary.

On revolvers, this cleaning step will have to be repeated on the cylinders to clean thoroughly. Since gas escapes between the barrel and cylinder, powder residue and corrosive particles build up between barrel and cylinder. Clean this area carefully or functioning problems may develop. Examine the revolver frame just above the rear of the barrel, the firing pin channel, hammer nose and the hammer groove in the frame. These areas must be cleaned and all traces of buildup removed.

After all metal parts have been cleaned thoroughly, they should be dried with a lint-free cloth. On internal working parts of revolvers or the slide rails of automatics, I apply either a molybdenum disulfide solution or the previously-mentioned Break-Free. If the gun is to be stored, I apply a liberal coating of a good rust preventive such as G96 Gun Treatment. Do not store handguns in holsters, as this speeds up corrosion and may ruin the holster as well.

If you live in a cold climate, wipe off excess oils as they can gum up and cause sluggish operation. When returning the gun to a warm room after zero-type weather outside, moisture will build up on the metal so it must be removed and the gun re-oiled before storage.

In hot, humid climates handguns should be kept well-oiled during storage and wood grips rubbed down with either linseed oil or a commercial product like Stock-Slick. Be careful not to let linseed oil get into the metal working parts, as rust may ultimately result.

In hot, dry climates, dust or sand can get into the working parts. Before taking the gun out to shoot, wipe it down inside and out as oil and sand can cause drag and/or damage during the firing cycle. Wooden stocks will have a tendency to dry out. They should be wiped down regularly with either linseed oil or Stock-Slik.

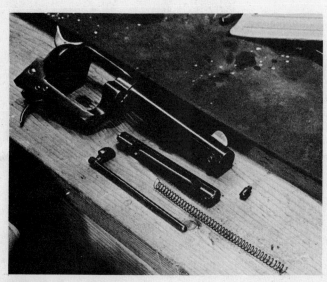

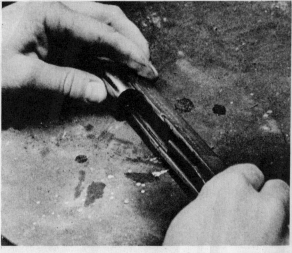

The ejector rod, housing and spring should be disassembled during cleaning of the Colt SAA, as dirt and grime can bind gun's mechanism.

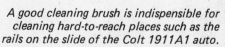

A good cleaning brush is indispensible for cleaning hard-to-reach places such as the rails on the slide of the Colt 1911A1 auto.

# Chapter 4

# SMOOTH IT

Pistolsmith Wayne Novak examines each part of a double-action revolver prior to the smoothing operation. Pistol is completely cleaned and must be in good functioning order before the smoothing process can prove totally effective.

**A**LTHOUGH RELIABLE, overall handling qualities, trigger pull, and general functioning of most of today's production handguns, can be improved simply by smoothing all bearing surfaces. Old shooters talk in reverent tones of these early ''smooth-as-glass'' production revolvers. Today, cost factors, inflation and increased pressure of heavy volume demands tend to prohibit pistol manufacturers from taking the extra time needed to individually smooth up each production gun to the point of perfection.

Many pistols such as the .45 ACP Government models were manufactured purposely with a certain amount of slop or looseness in an effort to make them more reliable as soldiers humped through the mud. Some current pistols are produced with built-in slop to aid in reliability for law enforcement agencies. With the increased popularity of combat pistol matches and target shooting, the desire for ever-smoother shooting pistols has come to resemble the legendary quest for the Holy Grail.

Smoothing up any pistol is not all that difficult. However, recognizing the truth of the old saying, that ''a little knowledge can be dangerous,'' there is a right way and a wrong way to go about smoothing up a favorite pistol. Smoothing, for the most part, is simply honing to glass-like smoothness all bearing surfaces. There are other considerations, such as lightening rebound springs in double-action revolvers, lightening hammers by removal of metal, and replacing certain parts with newer improved springs and so forth, but much of this is covered in our chapter on tuning and timing. Here we will look at the various tools and jigs used in smoothing, how to use them, and the importance of smoothing the various parts without altering their shape, possibly rendering the firearm unsafe.

To smooth any handgun, it is necessary to polish and, in many cases, buff various bearing surfaces to a glass-smooth condition. Combinations of stones, abrasive paper, lapping compounds, and polishing and buffing wheels are needed to accomplish the job efficiently.

A good polishing and buffing wheel setup is much faster than smoothing each piece by hand. But some hand honing still will be required. Polishing with the aid of a motor means removing metal rapidly in large amounts to erase surface imperfections, pits, scratches and burrs from the metal. The part being polished is subjected to gradually softer abrasives and softer wheels indicated by grit number identification; the lower the grit number, the more abrasive the grit and the faster the removal of metal. If the individual part has deep pitting or scratches it should be first draw filed or stoned before polishing. Neither extremely coarse nor extremely fine finishes are obtained

*This is a good polishing and buffing wheel setup with the motor supplying minimum output of one-half horsepower. A variety of grit wheels is needed for smoothing parts.*

normally by polishing, so this technique may be defined roughly as a process to remove metal.

Buffing is essentially a burnishing operation which displaces metal rather than removing it. We end up with a smooth, reflective, scratch-free surface by bringing the work surface into contact with sisal or cloth buffs charged with the proper compound or rouge for the job. Buffing sometimes called ''color buffing,'' is a misnomer. It simply means buffing to a high-luster gloss finish as the final operation. Heat created by pressing of work against the buffing wheel aids in this burnishing effect.

Probably the most common polishing wheel setup will include stitched muslin wheels running on a motor of at least one-half horsepower turning at 1725 revolutions per

# Step-By-Step Recommendations For Smoothing Up Your Handguns For Efficient Functioning

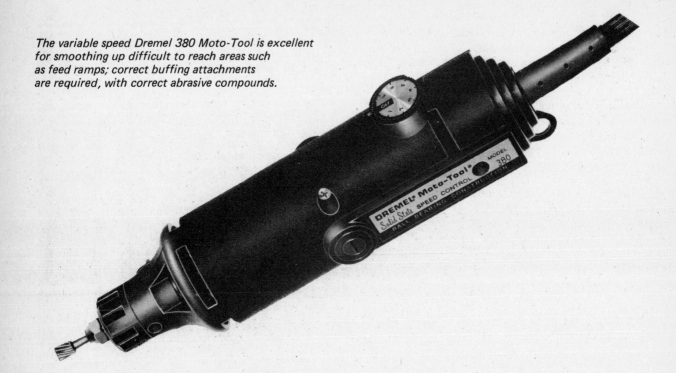

*The variable speed Dremel 380 Moto-Tool is excellent for smoothing up difficult to reach areas such as feed ramps; correct buffing attachments are required, with correct abrasive compounds.*

minute. This will give us a surface-feet-per-minute speed of 3795, adequate for most gunsmithing requirements. A good Baldour bench-type grinder/polisher is an excellent investment. I recommend at least one-half-horsepower output if much polishing and buffing is to be done. A variety of polishing compounds ranging from 140 grit through 400 grit will handle the rough through fine polishing requirements. Sax Corporation, 5657 Lauderdale Avenue, Detroit, Michigan 48209, and Brownells', Route 2, Box 1, Montezuma, Iowa 50171 carry the various polishing grits. Brownells' also carries a full line of polishing wheels and the Baldour motors as well.

Important to remember is that, as the wheel works, the grit face will begin to fill with removed metal. This is known as glazing and will slow the cutting action. The remedy is to face off the wheel by pressing a silicon carbide dressing stone against the face of the wheel, then lightly dress the wheel with more compound. This enables the wheel to do the work more efficiently and saves much effort.

I do not recommend polishing round screwheads on polishing wheels. (It often is necessary to polish these heads after someone has used the wrong size screwdriver to remove the screws and burred the heads.) Chucking them in a drill press and polishing with 400-grit wet-and-dry paper is one way to retain proper shape and polish them at the same time. Another ingenious and safe method is to chuck the

screw into the drill press. Take a small, soft piece of wood and, with the motor off, lever the screwhead down into the wood which will leave an indentation. Then, place a small piece of wet-and-dry paper into the indentation, turn on the press and lower the screwhead down into the recess of wet-and-dry paper. This works great and you don't have to worry about misshaping the head.

To buff each metal part to a mirror finish for drag-free performance, loose muslin wheels are used. Hard felt wheels also perform well for buffing, but the loose muslin spreads into every recess. Hard felt wheels must be trued absolutely for utmost efficiency and this can be difficult for the amateur. However, such felt wheels are excellent for buffing octagon barrels and other flat pieces. The buffs are used in conjunction with specially formulated siclo rouge, green chrome rouge (green chromium oxide) or royal chrome rouge (unfused alumina) to produce a fine finish without further metal removal. I prefer an eight-inch wheel turning at 3750 rpm, but even 1725 rpm will do the job. Pressing the individual pieces against the wheels produces heat. A container of water should be kept nearby in which to dip the piece as it becomes too hot to handle.

There are a few rules which should be adhered to when working metal parts on the wheels:

1. Never alter the original shape and contour of the part during polishing and buffing.

A wide range of Washita, Arkansas and India stones is necessary, if handgun smoothing is to be done with minimum problems and labor. Proper use and care of specific stones is discussed in the text.

Author reports Colorado ceramic stones are finest artificial stones he has found. They are excellent for final honing on most metal bearing surfaces.

| CROSS REFERENCE GRADE TO GRIT NUMBER | |
|---|---|
| Grade Number | Grit Number |
| E | 120 |
| D | 180 |
| B | 240 |
| 1A | 320 |
| 4A | 600 |
| 5A | 800 |
| 6A | 1000 |
| 7A | 1200 |

*Above: Author has cross-referenced the various grades of a commercial buffing compound with the type of grit that it carries. (Below) Silicone carbide and aluminum oxide are necessary for lapping .45 ACP slides for smooth operation. They range in grit from 120 for the former through the 1200 grit range which is in aluminum oxide.*

2. Never polish aluminum, brass, copper, etc., on a wheel used for steel. Particles from these metals will be caught in the wheel and can scratch the steel surface.

3. Improper selection of buffing wheels will result in reduced buffer life, excessive use of buffing compounds, increased direct labor, needless toil, and unsatisfactory results.

4. Polishing wheels should be kept in perfect balance and running true at all times.

5. Use only those polishing or buffing wheels designed for the particular purpose.

6. Always wear safety glasses.

7. Finish-buff each piece in the direction the individual bearing piece actually moves in the gun.

Make certain parts to be polished are cleaned first to remove rust, dirt, and other foreign matter. Cleaning dirty parts can result in depositing the foreign matter and grease into the abrasive compound on the wheels, or worse, having the wheels break them loose to fly at dangerous speeds into

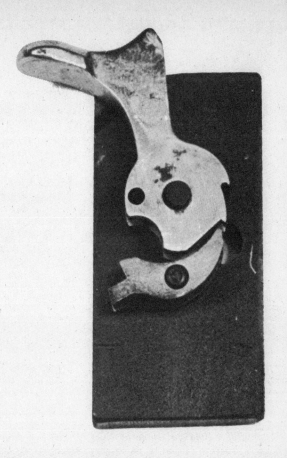

*Above: Tom Wilson sear block jig is useful in determining relationship of hammer/sear. This jig is designed for work with .45 Colt ACP. (Left)*

*The .45 ACP sear jigs above and at right are for polishing critical sear angles with proper stones. Jigs make the smoothing operation much faster and more accurate.*

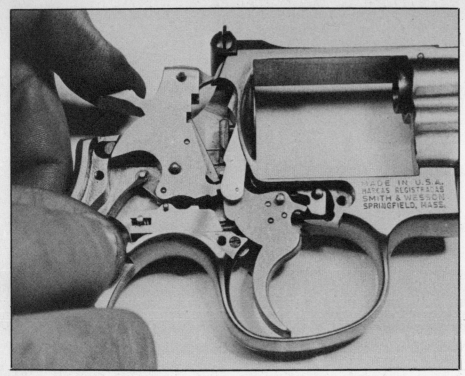

After cleaning the pistol in good solvent, each part is inspected for defects, wear. Parts then are placed back in the gun, checked for problems in the operation cycle. Such problems must be corrected before the smoothing operations can be started.

The trigger pull is checked, using the RCBS trigger pull gauge before smoothing begins, again upon finish of job.

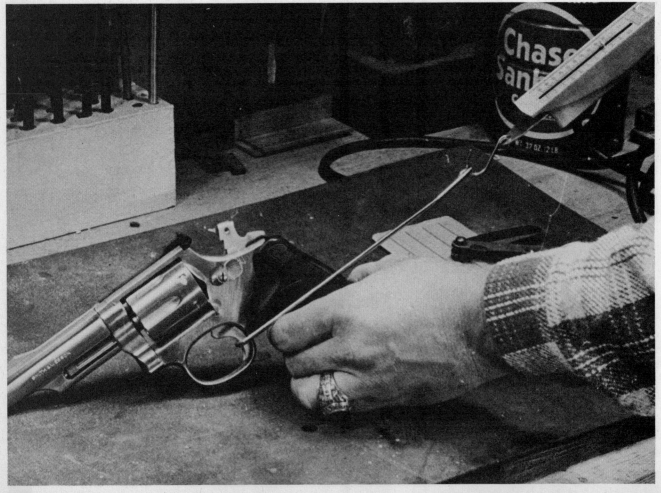

*Close-up of the bottom of the S&W rebound slide reveals rough factory machining, producing the problem of drag.*

*Part of the frame that bears against the bottom of the rebound slide has several visibly bright wear spots.*

your face. The use of a strip of leather on a wheel or belt dressed with talcum powder produces an excellent polish for parts. With the proper setup, it is especially good for polishing chambers.

Indispensable for pistol smoothing is the Dremel Moto-Tool grinder. Several models are available, but a variable-speed type is best for general gunsmithing work. Numerous available attachments are handy for gunsmithing Dremel's Brightboy abrasive and felt polishing wheels are excellent for getting into small areas of pistols not accessible to large polishing wheels. This tool will quickly become the most used in your shop, and works especially well to polish feed ramps and to bring chamber regions to a fine buff.

For parts polishing, you definitely need a good variety of stones. Probably the most used are two oilstones called the India and Arkansas. Another valuable stone is the Washita, coarser and faster cutting than the Arkansas. The Washita ranges in grades from the perfect crystallized and porous whetstone grit to vitreous flint and hard sandstone. The big thing to look for in Washita stones is the character of its crystallization which determines sharpness of its grit.

Good whetstones are quite porous, but uniform in texture, being made up of silica crystals. Solid or smooth-looking Washita stones should be avoided, as they generally have hard spots and will not cut uniformly. They range in colors from white to yellow or are red-streaked. A good Washita is an excellent fast-cutting stone.

Arkansas stones — harder and more dense than the Washita — are excellent for cutting purposes as well as polishing hard metals such as reamers. They are available in a number of shapes and sizes and are excellent for finish-polishing rebound slides and other pistol parts. The black hard Arkansas is the hardest in the Arkansas line and lends itself more to knife sharpening.

The India Stone actually is man-made and is manufactured by several companies. It comes in a number of shapes and sizes, all useful to the gunsmith, and in three grades or grits: coarse, medium and fine. The coarse grade is excellent for removing burrs in pistol work.

Good stones are expensive, can be broken easily if dropped on a concrete floor, and require care if they are to last. Stones must be cleaned and kept in oil. If left to the air over long periods of time, the stone tends to harden. A

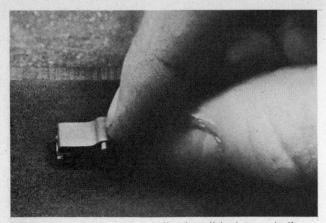

The bottom of the rebound slide is polished on an India stone. The piece must be kept flush with the flat stone to prevent rounded edges, altering the original contour.

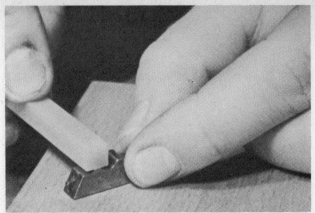

Careful stoning of the top of the hammer seat on rebound slide should be attempted only by an experienced gunsmith. Any alteration could cause problems in cylinder opening.

new stone should be left in oil for several days before being used for the first time. If you happen to have an oilstone that appears glazed, it can be restored by washing it in gasoline and wiping vigorously with a cloth. Treated properly, a good oilstone will last a lifetime.

Another excellent stone for the pistolsmith is the aluminum oxide type. These have excellent uniform density and excellent cutting properties. They work well for lapping and honing, but should be followed with good Arkansas stones for professional results.

There also is a line of flexible stones of a super-hard aluminum oxide impregnated in a flexible core. Such a stone can be bent almost double without breaking and is terrific for working in difficult to reach areas and around irregular shapes. They are extremely durable and quite inexpensive. Brownells' handles this line.

A variety of thin dowel rods is excellent for getting into small areas such as the inside of rebound slides of double-action revolvers. This area, if rough, can cause drag against the rebound slide spring. To smooth up this internal region, find a piece of thin dowel that will fit inside the area, cut a slot down the middle of one end for about a half-inch, insert the 600 wet-and-dry paper through the slot and wrap it around the dowel.

Another way to accomplish this is to wrap a bit of masking tape around the end of the dowel instead of cutting the slot. Leave a bit of extra tape hanging and tuck the wet-and-dry paper strip inside the tape and wrap. Be careful to smooth only the inside of the slide.

To do a professional smoothing job on both revolvers and autoloaders, lapping compound is required. Two types of compound are available that work well for the gunsmith.

Rebound slide spring bears against inside of the rebound slide; polish with wood dowel, 600-grit wet-and-dry paper.

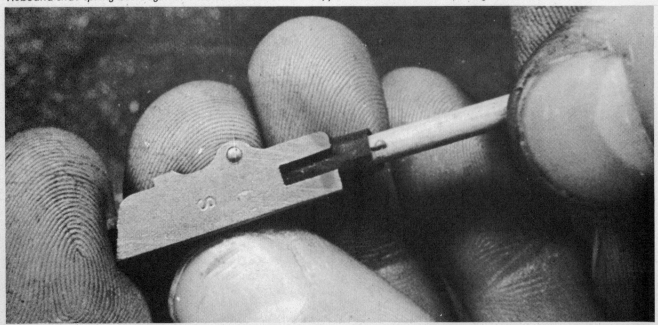

*The action can be made smoother by removing a maximum of two coils from the rebound slide spring. Check whether this has been done previously by counting the number of coils before cutting. Weak spring will cause malfunction.*

The first, silicone carbide, is the best for removing metal and roughness, especially in auto slides. Available in grits ranging from 120 to 700, this material breaks up into smaller particles as it is used, but the grit particles remain sharp and continue their cutting action. It cleans up well by washing the gun part in kerosene.

A word of caution, though, when working with silicone carbide: Particles can imbed themselves in softer metals like aluminum alloy frames such as found in the S&W 39 and 59s. It is intended for use only in all-steel guns.

The second type of lapping compound is water-soluble aluminum oxide. This abrasive compound is finer, running in grits from 600 to 1200. Since the particles break up into smaller parts, but do not retain their sharpness, they are ideal for working with aluminum alloys. This compound will break down and is not intended for heavy metal removal. However, it does do an excellent job for that super-fit needed in accurizing autoloaders and revolvers.

Not absolutely essential, but recommended, are pistolsmithing fixtures or jigs. These allow the pistolsmith to actually feel the engagement of bearing surfaces as he hones these surfaces. This is a blessing, as he can accomplish this part of the job completely without having to assemble the gun each time he removes a bit of metal to check engagement. It saves considerable time and results are more likely to be perfect.

One of the best, certainly the most used jig is the trigger pull pin set. This jig allows the pistolsmith to see the contact surfaces of the two bearing parts and polish and hone accordingly. The pins are mounted on the outside of the frame and thumb pressure is exerted instead of the normal mainspring pressure to check for properly engaging

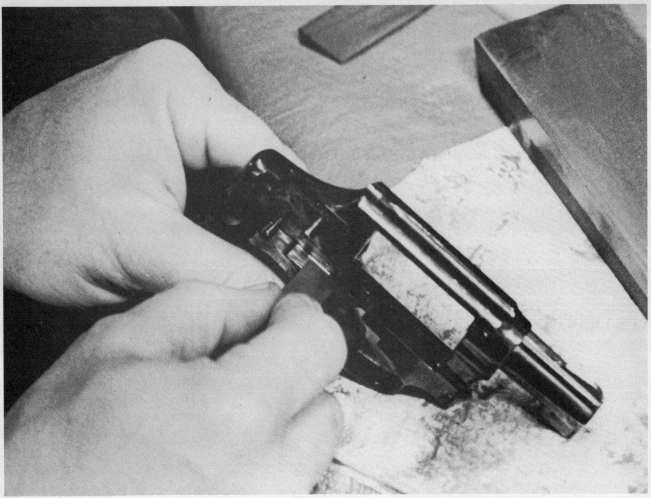

Surface of the frame where the rebound slide makes contact must be honed. For this, hard Arkansas stone is used.

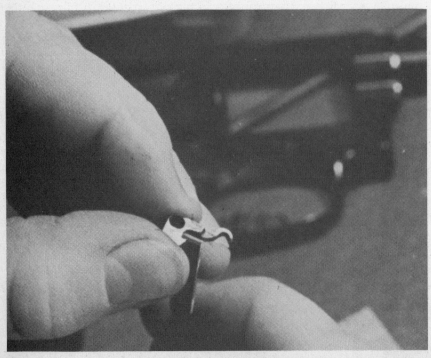

The cylinder stop should be honed with hard Arkansas or fine flexible stone. Care is required, as excess removal of metal or altered angles can affect gun's lockup capabilities adversely.

surfaces. They're available for a wide range of manufactured pistols.

A new sear block setup made by the Tom Wilson Company to determine hammer/sear relationships is another useful item. The hammer and sear are held in place on the jig in the same relationship they have to one another in the gun. It's a great timesaver.

The Wilson Company also offers a number of pistol jigs that allow the gunsmith to determine exact angles and put on a great polish accurately. I used the one for the Colt .45 ACP and was able to fit and polish a sear in a matter of seconds at the exact angles necessary. The resulting trigger pull was better and more crisp than anything I'd ever tried by freehand trial-and-error.

The first requirement in a professional smoothing job is to clean the firearm completely. I generally soak all metal parts in a container of kerosene for a day or two to loosen rust and corrosion. Lacquer thinner, dry cleaning liquid, or any good solvent such as Hoppe's No. 9 will loosen caked-on dirt and grime. Using an air compressor after removing the parts from the cleaning solution dries the parts and helps to blow any crud away. If no compressor is available, each part must be individually wiped down and inspected.

Another fast way to clean a gun for smoothing is to drop the metal parts in a boiling Oakite solution at the bluing tanks. It removes the dirt and corrosion in a hurry and saves much elbow grease.

If you attempt to smooth up the action of any gun with dirt and foreign particles still adhering to the metal

The hammer, trigger and cylinder stop pins should be polished with fine abrasive cloth or half-inch strips of worn 600-grit wet-and-dry paper. The pistolsmith also should check that the pins are not loose in frame, bent.

As another step in the polishing operation, the cylinder bolt should be carefully polished with hard Arkansas stone.

surfaces, you'll end up with unsatisfactory results. You will probably get the dirt caught between the surface you are polishing and the stone; scratches usually will result.

After all parts have been cleaned thoroughly, carefully inspect each bearing surface on each part for wear marks, burrs, scratches, pits or imperfections in the metal. All can cause drag and must be eliminated. By visually inspecting each part outside the gun, one can identify trouble spots we might not see if the part were actually in the gun. For example, the hammer on a double-action Smith & Wesson might be binding on the frame or bolt. When the hammer is inserted on its pin, we would not be able to see this drag problem.

When you see a drag spot on a part it is not enough simply to hone that individual piece. Something caused that drag in the first place and we must correct this influence to eliminate future problems. If the hammer is dragging, it might be caused by a loose hammer pin. So we dress the drag area on the hammer, and correct the loose pin condition.

After complete inspection of each part, we replace the parts in the frame. With the sideplate removed from the revolver, carefully inspect the cycle of operation of the gun to make certain there are no mechanical problems with the gun. One must pay particular attention to the trigger/sear/hammer/rebound slide relationship. Also, ascertain that the cylinder, hand, and stop are all working properly. It's a waste of time trying to smooth up an out-of-time gun.

After ensuring the revolver is timed properly, dismantle the gun to check each bearing surface for wear marks. They may appear as shiny spots, scratches or rough burrs. Run your finger along the edges of each piece checking for sharp edges. I found that, in the Model 66 S&W used in this chapter, the bottom of the rebound slide had several imperfections in the metal that caused drag against the frame. The bosses on the sideplate also revealed shiny wear spots that had to be stoned down. By polishing first with a medium India stone, and switching to a hard Arkansas stone, these blemishes were removed quickly.

It is vital that the stones come only in contact with the blemishes and the stones are kept flush with the work. We do not wish to round any corners or edges contrary to manufacturer's specs. Only the hard Arkansas stones should be used by the amateur so as not to go through any case hardening that is on hammers.

It's good practice to place each part that has been honed back into the firearm after oiling it lightly and checking for smoothness of operation. Since each handgun will have its own problem areas that can be smoothed up for a better performance, give them priority.

The double-action revolver rebound slide bears on the frame and much can be done here to greatly smooth the action. The bottom of the rebound slide and its left side should be honed carefully with a hard Arkansas. I also buff them on a 600-grit buffing wheel for a smooth, reflective finish. The buffs also help to burnish or displace the metal for drag-free operation. The inside of the slide also should

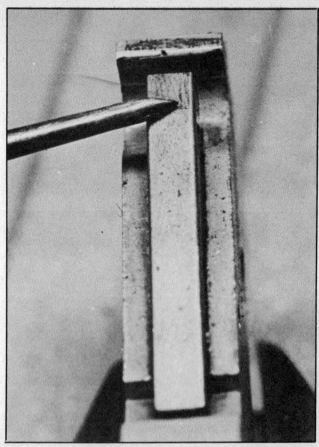

*Right: Sear is inspected for drag spots, scratches. Take care when stoning with hard Arkansas to polish only as needed for smoothness. Excess metal removal can result in soft spots, causing function problems. (Below) Boss areas on sideplate are polished with hard Arkansas stone to smooth drag marks that adversely influence operation.*

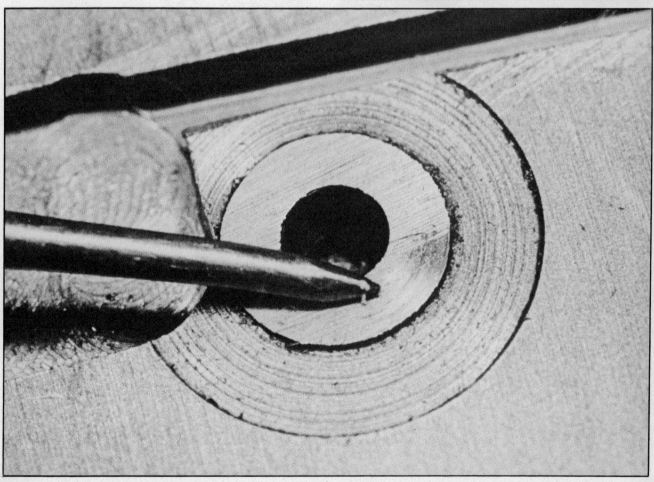

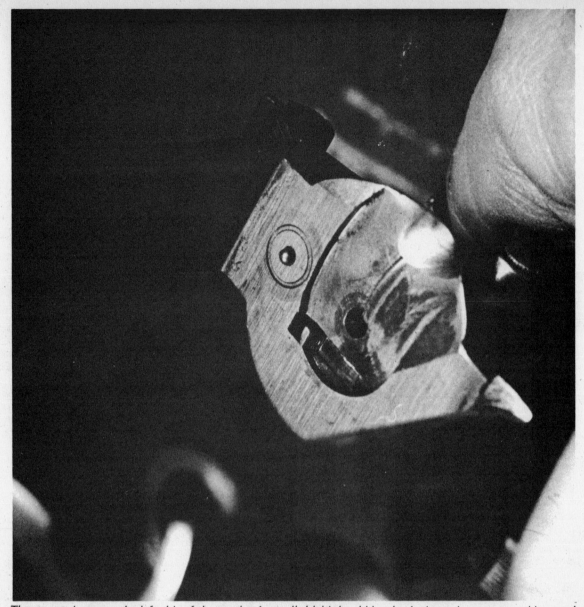

*The recessed area on the left side of the revolver's recoil shield should be checked, any burrs removed by stoning.*

be polished using the wooden dowel and 600-grit wheel as discussed.

Some like to cut a coil or two off the rebound spring to lighten the action, but determine how many coils belong on this spring in the first place. Someone else might already have cut off a few coils and your effort will only weaken the spring to the point the gun will not function properly. To determine how many coils belong on each spring check Brownell's *Encyclopedia of Firearms*.

The bearing surfaces on the frame where the rebound slide is located also should be polished with the hard Arkansas stone. Then check the cylinder stop. Carefully hone those areas that come into contact with its engaging surfaces. Care must be exercised here as excess metal

removal from the top of the stop will change the lockup. Just smooth the top and carefully bevel the edges of the stop to reduce drag as it comes into contact with the cylinder notches.

The cylinder notches also may require a bit of honing if drag spots are in evidence. Again, this must be done carefully to prevent lockup problems.

The hammer pin, trigger pin and cylinder stop pin also should be polished to reduce drag. This is best accomplished by taking a worn-out piece of 600 wet-and-dry paper and cutting it into half-inch strips. Then use a shoe-shine motion to polish each pin. These highly polished pins will greatly increase the smoothness of the action.

With smoothing almost completed, the gun lubricated and reassembled, the gap between cylinder and frame should be checked. (Below) Use feeler gauge to check this gap. S&W recommends Model 66 tolerance of .003 to .005-inch. The chamber area and front of the cylinder must be polished with great care to avoid changing critical tolerances.

After completing work on the three aforementioned pins, it also is necessary to polish the pin holes in the hammer, trigger and stop. Use either a thin wooden dowel with worn-out 600 wet-and-dry paper or there are thin pieces of porcelain available that will get into these regions. Be extremely careful not to enlarge the holes themselves or a sloppy action could result.

If you find the hammer hole has been enlarged or you have removed too much metal in your polishing zeal there is an efficient and fast remedy to bring the hole back to size. Lay the hammer on an anvil or some other flat metal surface. Take a half-inch diameter ball bearing and place it on top of the hammer hole. With a ball peen hammer give the ball bearing a good rap. Turn the gun's hammer over and again lay it flush on the flat metal surface. Repeat the same operation on this side. This procedure should close the hole uniformly, depending upon how much and how hard you rap the ball bearing. If you find you've closed the hammer hole too much, simply match the right size drill to the hammer pin and drill accordingly to reopen the hole to the right dimensions.

Carefully inspect the hand and its engagement with the cylinder ratchets. The hand is critical to timing, so we must be extremely careful to buff only and not remove metal from this area. The cylinder ratchets can become burred and should be checked and polished accordingly. Also check the hole in the frame where the hand moves in revolving the cylinder. Burrs in this region will cause rough functioning.

Assuming that the crane or yoke and cylinder pin are straight, we can lightly hit any bearing surfaces on a 600-grit buffing wheel.

The hammer stirrup pin that engages the mainspring should be polished as well as its sides that ride inside the hammer. The inside of the hammer also must be polished where it houses the stirrup.

The mainspring region that bears with the hammer stirrup can be polished with a round Arkansas. Hammer springs may be lightened for additional smooth action, but this is discussed at length in the chapter on tuning and timing.

Check the frame where the hammer goes through. Remove any burrs and polish the sides of the hammer. If there is case coloring on the sides of the hammer, make certain the customer will not object to this coloring being removed.

The sear also may be honed with the hard Arkansas stone, but be careful not to round any corners or edges.

The Colt SAA revolver bolt is critical to timing. Part of the bolt engaging cylinder notches may be polished lightly, edges beveled. Arrow indicates bearing surface on rear of bolt. This area has critical angles that must not be changed or altered. However, the sides of the bolt and bolt hole may be polished as explained in text.

CRITICAL BEARING AREA

Engagement of the trigger sear with hammer cocking notches is evident. Proper sear angle is critical and no type of alteration should be attempted here by the amateur.

Half-cock notch on this Colt SAA hammer is broken, thus influencing function, safety of the revolver. Fanning the hammer is almost certain to create this costly problem.

The point of a scribe is used to indicate where the bolt bears on the bolt pin. The sides of the bolt, as well as the bolt pin of the Single-Action Army Colt revolver should be smoothed with hard Arkansas stone during work.

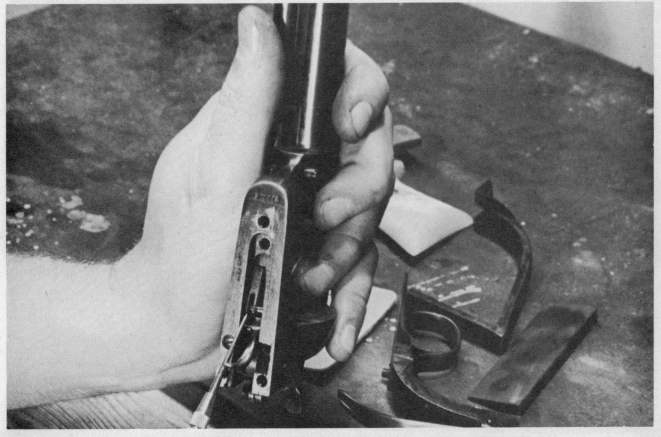

*The fastest, easiest way to polish the hammer, trigger, bolt pins is with a shoeshine motion utilizing exceedingly fine abrasive cloth.*

*The firing pin hole in the frame can become burred or peened in dry firing. This area should be polished with care not to enlarge the firing pin hole opening.*

Removal of any case hardening can leave soft spots in the metal; these will wear down bearing surfaces quickly and cause problems.

The cylinder ratchet pads may be polished. Also check the recess on the left side of the recoil shield; all burrs should be removed.

Next to be inspected is the space between the cylinder and barrel. Since the gun has been cleaned thoroughly and all leading removed, this is an ideal time to check for the proper gap tolerances between the two. Inspection also should reveal whether the throat is properly polished. Running a brass lap at this entrance will help prevent future leading problems.

After all bearing surfaces have been polished, replace them in the gun and dry fire it to check for any drag spots remaining. (Rimfire pistols, however, should not be dry fired.) Assuming you have removed all drag, lubricate all parts and consider the job complete.

Single-action revolvers require much the same procedure as the double-action. Begin by cleaning the gun completely and disassembling it to check for drag spots, imperfections in the metal, and that all parts are functioning properly. Again, it's a waste of time to try smoothing a pistol if it is out of time.

With the parts disassembled from the gun, check each for shiny spots, scratches, burrs, general wear. The parts most frequently requiring repair or replacement are the hammer, trigger and bolt. Check the bolt to determine that it fits into each of the six notches on the cylinder properly; repeat the cycle of operation when checking lockup on all six notches. Assuming the cylinder bolt fits all notches, examine it closely for wear marks. The top of the bolt may be polished with a hard Arkansas. The bolt's corners also may be broken with the hard Arkansas, if care is used. Sides of the bolt should be polished first with a hard Arkansas, and the bolt hole checked for size and movement on the bolt pin, then polished. Located on the rear tip of the cylinder bolt is a beveled area which comes in contact with the bolt camming surface on the hammer. Special care must be taken not to remove *any* metal from this surface, as it

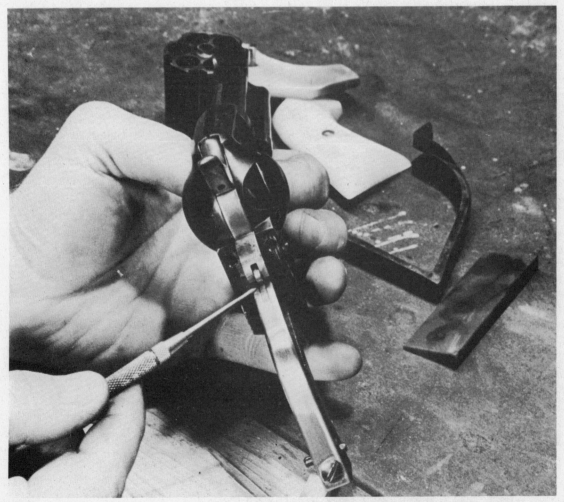

*The firing pin roll located on the rear of the hammer bears upon the mainspring. This roll should be checked for sharp edges or burrs or roundness, with appropriate action taken. Sides of the roll bearing on hammers should be polished.*

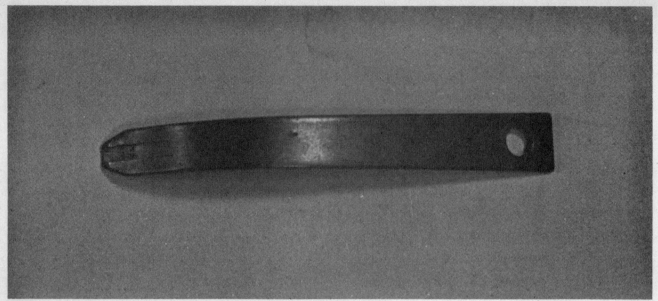

Mainspring for the Colt SAA has a recess at its tip that bears against the hammer roll. This may be buffed on the 600-grit buffing wheel, but care must be taken during the buffing not to overheat the spring and reduce temper.

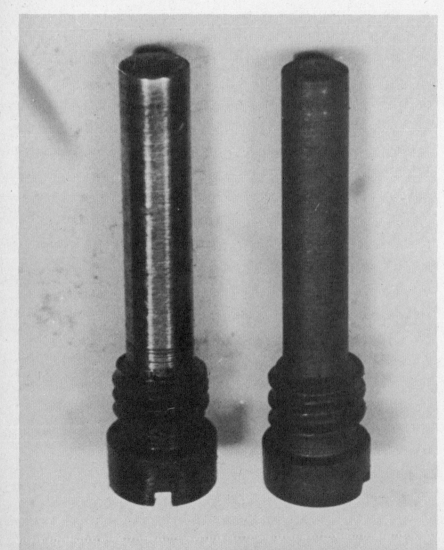

The trigger pin on the left has been partially polished for smoother functioning. The pin at right needs to have the factory bluing removed, as the coating can cause some roughness.

The bearing surface of the base pin bushing which contacts the cylinder should be checked for possible burrs. Any excessive removal of metal at either end of the base pin bushing will cause cylinder slop, creating gap problems.

can throw off proper timing of the revolver. However, any burrs may be removed and this area stoned carefully.

The trigger sear bears against the hammer notches. It comes from the factory cut to a particular angle that should not be altered. However, if one is careful to keep the original angles, this surface can be stoned with a black hard Arkansas stone. The original angles must be trued and buffed with extreme care that no metal actually is removed to influence the timing adversely. Sides of the trigger also are a bearing surface and should be polished with a hard Arkansas stone. The trigger pin hole also should be polished as should the trigger, bolt and hammer screws. These screws may be polished on a 600-grit buffing wheel or some good aluminum oxide abrasive grit can be used to lap the surfaces.

Check the sear and combination bolt spring where they bear on the bolt and trigger. The bearing surfaces of this spring may be polished lightly on the 600-grit wheel, but care must be used not to excessively heat up the spring.

The hammer surface which rides against the boss of the hand should be checked for both fit and roughness. If the hole is oversize, the ball bearing treatment discussed previously will correct it. If this area is scratched or burred, it should be stoned with the hard Arkansas. Check the hammer notches to see if cocking notches are all correct. Remedy for this problem is discussed in the chapter on tuning and timing.

Make an examination of where the firing pin attached to the hammer goes into the frame. This area can be damaged from repeated dry firing. The firing pin and frame hole may become somewhat peened and roughness result. The firing pin bushing may require replacement, if the hole is too enlarged.

The hammer roll located on the back of the hammer bears on the mainspring as the hammer is pulled back into cocking position. The hammer roll should be checked for roundness and fit with the hammer. Although it is possible to remove burrs or irregularities in the metal on this part, if

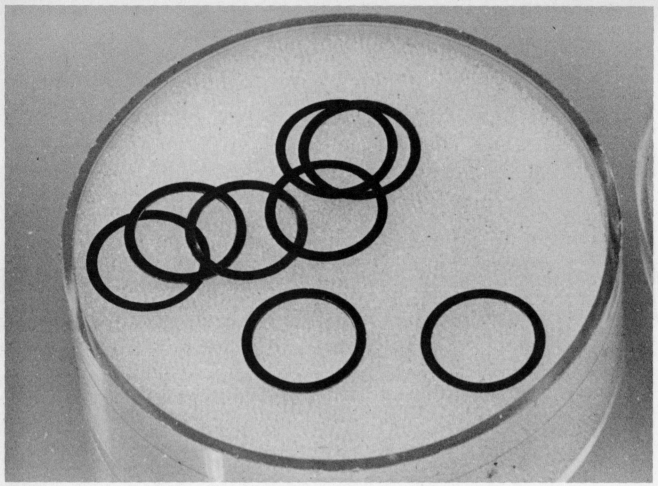

To eliminate cylinder slop, Brownells' markets end-shake bushings created by pistolsmith Ron Powers. Bushings, somewhat enlarged in this photo, are available in .002, .004 and .006-inch thicknesses to help solve the problem.

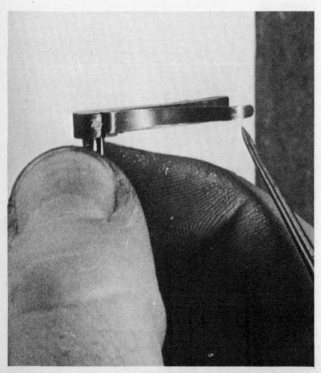

it is truly warped or out of round, replacement would be in order. The mainspring surface bearing on the hammer roll should be polished glass smooth. If a 600-grit buffing wheel is used, keep the part from becoming too hot.

Next, check the base pin for smoothness; it rides inside the base pin bushing. This piece can be chucked up in a drill press and polished using wornout 600-grit wet-and-dry paper, but extreme care must be taken not to alter the gripping area on the base pin.

The base pin bushing should be stoned at both ends to remove any burrs or scratches. Since this piece is cut to exact length, it is critical to not remove any metal; buff only. If too much metal is removed, bushing sleeves are available.

The hand should be checked for straightness, wear spots, and burrs where it contacts the cylinder ratchets. The original angles must be maintained, but careful polishing will help smoothness.

The cylinder ratchet pads also should be checked

*The hand should be checked for straightness, wear spots, burrs, where it comes in contact with cylinder ratchets. Hand spring may be buffed lightly where it bears on frame.*

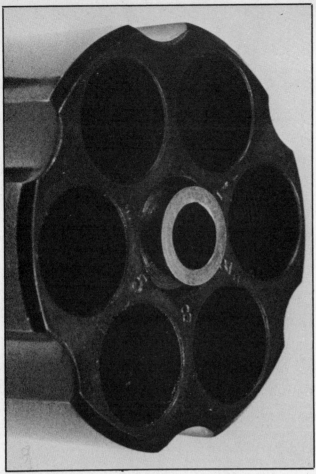

The bearing surfaces of the SAA base pin bushing should be checked for burrs, lightly polished to delete them.

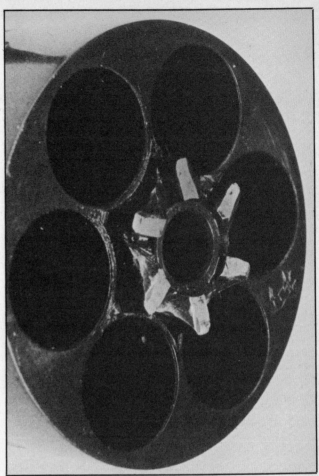

Colt SAA ratchet pads can become burred or peened, but any excess removal of metal can influence rotation of cylinder.

Barrel of the Colt .45 ACP autoloader should be polished where it rides inside barrel bushing during firing cycle.

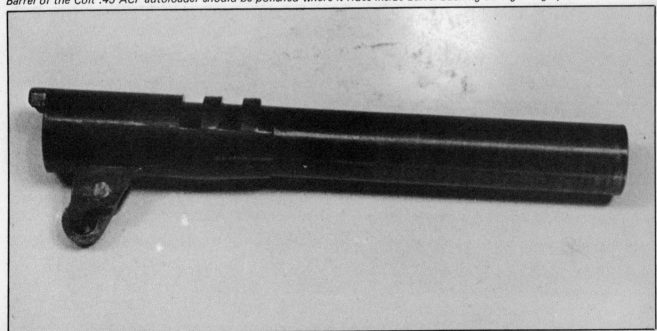

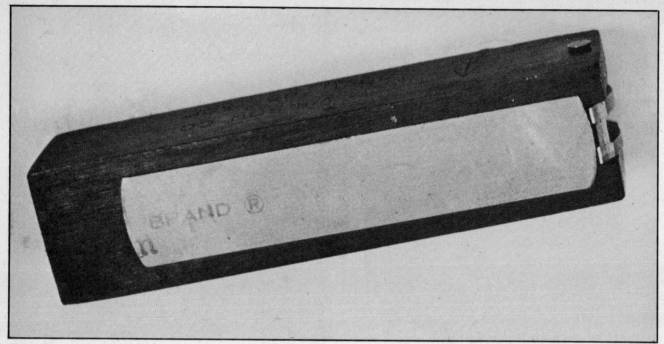

*Tom Wilson's sear block fixture makes polishing critical sear angles simple and is highly efficient. The sear is placed in the block and held in place with a pin. A shim is placed on top of the fixture. Instructions come with it.*

individually and polished. These pads can be battered badly, as they hit the frame during firing, resulting in deformation. This also can lead to excessive headspace problems as the pads are beaten down against the frame, causing cylinder gap in its relationship to the frame and firing pin. The hand spring should be inspected and replaced if worn or weak. It is possible to carefully polish the hand spring as it bears against the frame.

The ejection rod on the SAA Colt can become quite dirty during normal use and eventually become badly pitted. The rod should be checked for straightness and polished. The spring also should be checked. The ejector rod housing is the one part of the gun that generally is not removed for cleaning by the casual shooter and this is a prime area for dirt buildup. I would suggest running a wood dowel with 600 wet-and-dry down the inside and thoroughly polish.

Using these general smoothing techniques on a Colt SAA revolver should make a notable change in functioning; by honing the critical bearing surfaces the trigger pull will be

*One should lay the hard Arkansas stone on top of the shim and polish carefully, keeping stone flush with the block.*

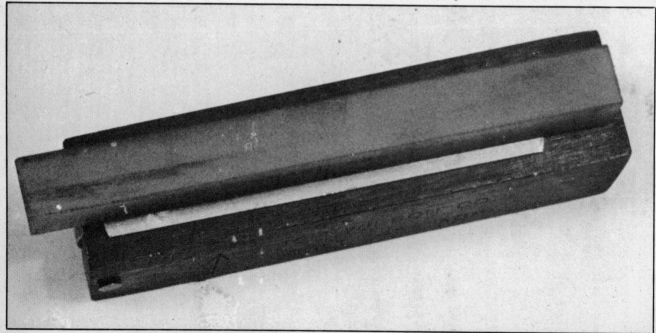

crisper, cleaner. To completely smooth up a SAA revolver as discussed should take an average of 1½ hours at a probable charge of between $35 and $50. If you don't have the experience and mechanical aptitude to tackle this job, it is better to leave it to the professional.

For smoothing an autoloader, the first bearing surface to check is that between the frame and slide. The interior slide rails are narrow and difficult to smooth with even small stones. Usually it is more efficient to use a good lapping compound such as silicone carbide or aluminum oxide. Remember, silicone carbide has a tendency to imbed itself into aluminum alloy as on the S&W 39 and 59 frames. It does work well in a Government Colt .45 ACP, all parts being steel. After lapping with silicone carbide, I soak the slide in solvent and relap with the finer aluminum oxide compound for resultant smoothness.

Both the internal and external surfaces of the barrel bushing should be polished. Since the outside of the bushing bears against the slide and the inside against the barrel, this part needs careful attention. A smooth bushing, incidentally, makes disassembly easier. The outside is polished using a light shoe-shine motion with 400-grit wet-and-dry paper and finished with 600-grit. The inside should be lapped with silicone carbide, cleaned in solvent and relapped with aluminum oxide. This mating between bushing and barrel is critical to functioning and accuracy and the time-consuming effort of lapping it in exactly will pay off with a superb fit.

The barrel should be polished with emphasis on that area where it rides inside the barrel bushing during the firing

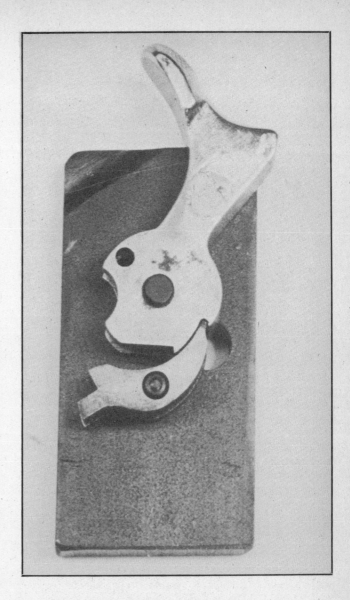

*Wilson's hammer/sear fixture for the .45 autoloader will enable the pistolsmith to check the sear relationship to the hammer in same manner as when aligned in the pistol.*

*Hole in the hammer/sear fixture allows one to view hammer/sear relationship on what normally would be the blind side.*

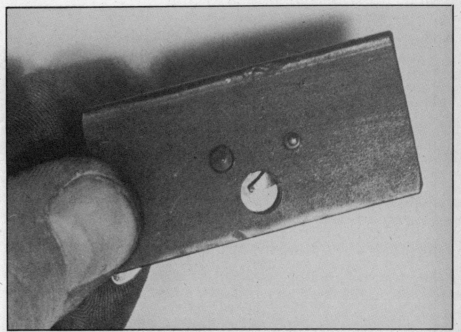

Bearing surface area of the slide stop of the Colt auto should be polished with abrasive cloth for smoothness.

effort should not be overlooked. The firing pin hole also can become enlarged in dry firing and should be inspected. Sharp edges can be removed from the firing pin, keeping in mind that to shorten the pin even a few thousandths can create protrusion problems.

The most important aspect in autoloader trigger pull is the hammer/sear relationship. Use of a Tom Wilson sear block enables the pistolsmith to view the hammer and sear on the jig in the same relationship they have to each other in the gun. Checking to determine how they mate up is a simple process.

We want the bearing surfaces of the hammer and sear large enough to insure safe, reliable operation, yet small enough to afford a smooth, consistent trigger pull. Mating

Feed ramp of the Colt .45 auto should be polished with Dremel Moto-Tool, Brightboy abrasive for proper feeding.

cycle. Special care should be paid to the locking lugs so as not to reduce this locking surface. We wish only to smooth these areas, not reduce or remove any metal. The feeding radius on the chamber end of the barrel should be polished for smooth chambering of each round.

The link attached to the bottom of the barrel with a pin, should be checked for burrs or scratches. The inside of the link hole may be polished, sharp edges and burrs on the bearing surface of the link removed with a hard Arkansas stone.

Remove the extractor to check angles and for any burrs. The frame should be checked for cleanliness. It may be lapped or polished using the wooden dowel and worn-out 600 wet-and-dry paper.

To polish a sear, one of Tom Wilson's new sear fixtures is extremely helpful. Wilson makes one for the .45 ACP that is virtually foolproof. With the sear correctly positioned in the jig, accurate polishing angles are guaranteed making a critical job a simple one. A final pass with a good hard Arkansas stone polishes critical angles to result in a fine trigger action. The trigger also should be polished, including the sides that bear against the frame and in the back which contacts the disconnector.

It is good practice to polish the firing pin, which can become pitted, corroded from certain primers, and even peened by being dry fired. Since a hung-up firing pin can result in the autoloader suddenly firing full automatic, this

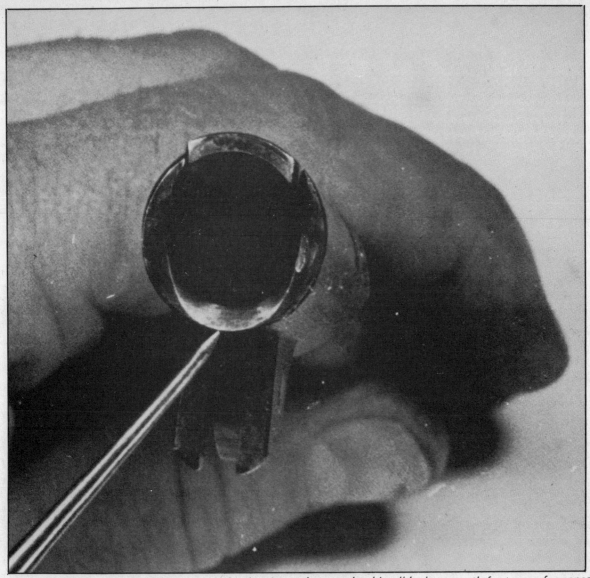

*The point of the scribe is used to indicate the chamber region one should polish glass-smooth for top performance.*

the two parts using the aforementioned jig makes an ordinarily time-consuming job simple and accurate. All parts are polished and pin holes smoothed up.

The sear spring should be checked for stress marks or undue wear. By bending the spring, we can alter the trigger pull to some extent, but caution should be exercised not to stress the spring itself. This is something best left to the expert.

The internal mainspring housing should be polished along with the mainspring cap. The spring itself should be checked for strength and straightness, as it can become bent and cause drag against the housing; if the spring is week, compression is decreased.

With the hammer, polish only the area on each side that bears against or close to the frame. Polish the hammer hole and hammer pin, then check the bottom of the hammer strut and polish its bearing surface.

Smoothing the frame's bearing surfaces was taken care of when we lapped the slide rails. However, the feed ramp on the frame must be polished so that there is no step or overhang between the feed ramp and barrel radius. This is especially necessary if wadcutters are to be fired with regularity.

The final area to be checked and polished is the top one-third of the magazine, as this bearing surface is important to overall functioning of the pistol.

Most of the smoothing operations mentioned in this chapter can be accomplished by the gun enthusiast who has some gun tinkering experience and is mechanically inclined. The novice can do much of the smoothing described, but should leave polishing or altering of critical sear and trigger angles to the professional. A beautifully polished part is a worthless piece of junk if critical angles have been reduced and the gun will no longer function.

# Chapter 5

# TUNING &

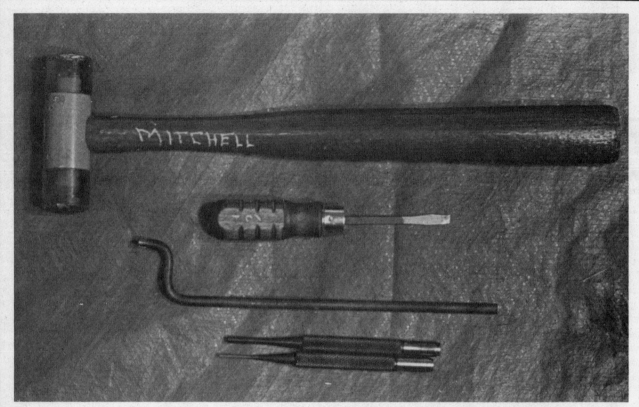

*Plastic and rawhide combo mallet for removal of revolver sideplate, properly fitting screwdrivers, a rebound slide spring remover and pin punches all are necessary aids for assembly/disassembly of handguns.*

THE .38 SMITH & WESSON Model 36 revolver — also called the Chiefs Special — is a compact revolver designed primarily for law-enforcement plainclothesmen who desire a small, light, easily concealed sidearm. The Model 36 with its two-inch barrel, built on the J-frame, is a five-shot revolver available in blued or nickel finish with optional round or square butt. Although there have been four design changes made in this firearm since its introduction, the gun is still basically a Smith, inside and out.

The basic statement often heard between gunsmiths — "If you can work on one Smith you can work on any of them" — is pretty much a true statement that reflects the good judgment of the manufacturer. Smith & Wesson has been successful with their double-action revolver design and have been far-sighted enough to incorporate much of the design principles in all their models, regardless of size or configuration.

A friend offered the information that he had bought his

Model 36 in practically new condition and almost unfired. He had fired the gun only a few times over the years, but had cleaned and oiled it regularly. He wanted to know whether I could smooth up the action, which he felt was a bit rough. As I examined the piece and checked it on single-action firing, then double-action pull, it was obvious the revolver was in need of custom tuning and timing, although mechanically it certainly would function.

Tuning and timing by hand can bring any revolver of quality to a point of ultimate smoothness and perfection. However, with rising labor costs, few firearms manufacturers could afford to spend the time and money on final handwork and still sell a firearm at a competitive price. As a result, most of today's revolvers require custom work by qualified pistolsmiths, if the gunowner wants the firearm to perform at its optimum potential.

If one desires custom tuning and/or timing performed on his piece, it will be fairly expensive. The reason is quite simple: The required work takes considerable time,

# TIMING THE REVOLVER

## The Techniques Used On This Chiefs Special Can Be Adapted To Other Models As Well

patience, experience and careful handwork. Much of the project means precise stoning of metal parts with a variety of abrasive stones most commonly referred to as Arkansas stones. Their purpose is to polish the various metal parts to a glasslike smoothness without removing great amounts of metal at the same time. These stones come in varying sizes and shapes as well as different grits or hardness to accommodate particular functions. Some of the softer stones are known as Washita stones. The softer stones are used to remove metal faster than with the hard stones.

One must be careful when stoning parts not to remove the case hardening on the hammer, sear and any other case-hardened pieces. Since the case hardening is approximately .005-inch deep, a light touch is required. Once case hardening is removed from any functioning bearing piece, the metal will wear down quickly and impair proper functioning. This could lead to extensive repairs by a competent pistolsmith with facilities for welding and case hardening not found in the general gun tinkerer's array of tools.

To facilitate working on pistols, certain tools are highly recommended and for particular functions, absolutely essential. Let's begin with a good vise. A four-inch vise is probably the best all-around for gunsmithing. Soft jaws are a necessary requirement of the vise when working on any pistol or longarm to prevent scratching of both wood and metal parts. Harris Engineering, Barlow, Kentucky 42024, offers soft jaws for both wood and metal work. I have used one set of Harris soft jaws for over a year and they are both efficient and durable. They not only prevent scratching, but hold the work firmly in the vise without slipping. And with the gallons of solvents, oils, kerosene, and what all spilled on them during this time, they've stood up exceptionally well.

However, a word of caution at this point: even though the Harris Soft Jaws are a gunsmith's boon, one must still be quite prudent when tightening down the gun in this or any other vise. Over-tightening can bend parts out of shape causing extra work or actual destruction to revolver cranes and cylinder alignment.

Exact-fitting screwdrivers for each different size screw are of utmost importance. Bunged up screwheads due to improperly used screwdrivers indicate the work of the gun hack. Marred screwheads on a revolver not only are unsightly, but reduce the value of a firearm by a goodly degree. If no screwdrivers are handy to fit that certain screwhead, it will be necessary to grind one down to fit it and finish by tempering it.

Rawhide or plastic mallets are necessary tools. A few firm taps on the backstrap of any revolver is the surest way to remove any revolver sideplate. Although you may have read this sage advice before, *never attempt to remove the sideplate of any revolver by prying it off!* If a sideplate does

---

*Course, medium and hard Arkansas stones are necessary for smoothing, honing parts, but require patience, experience, if your work on revolvers is to measure up professionally.*

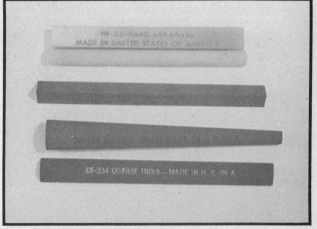

*Various bearing pins such as trigger and hammer pins must be polished for drag-free functioning. Shoeshine motion with fine grit cloth will aid in overall gun performance.*

happen to become bent, an expensive trip to the factory for the whole firearm will be necessary to repair it. By using plastic or rawhide, a gunsmith can use the force necessary without worry of scratching the gun. A mainspring clamp or a pair of long-nose pliers will come in handy for removing mainsprings. Oftentimes pistolsmiths will grind off the teeth on the pliers to aid in preventing scratching or marring external surfaces.

Assorted files ranging from the larger mill files to a variety of needle files always should be on hand. A gunsmith never seems to own enough screwdrivers or files. A necessity will be a good brush for cleaning the files. Without proper cleaning as the work progresses the files will clog up with metal chips and can cause deep gouges in the work — the file teeth must be cleaned regularly.

A ball-peen hammer and assortment of drift punches are essential ingredients for the pistolsmith. The drift-pins should be available in nylon and brass as well as good Sterrett stock. The ball peen hammer not only is the catalyst for driving out stubborn pins, but is excellent for peening parts to make them fit a little more snugly.

Feeler gauges and headspace gauges are invaluable. Smith & Wesson recommends for my friend's S&W Model 36 a distance between the cylinder and bolster or recoil shield of .062 to .064-inch. The corresponding difference between the cylinder and the barrel is .003-inch. To check your own revolver, when you know its factory-recommended tolerance, requires a trick more complicated than just shoving feeler gauges into the spaces. To check these two dimensions properly, measure between the cylinder and bolster or recoil shield first to determine headspace. The best way is to load the revolver with fired cases. To avoid

*This Smith & Wesson Model 36 with sideplate, cylinder and crane removed reveals many bearing surfaces that must be smoothed for ultimate single and double-action functioning. The techniques outlined here apply to other models, too.*

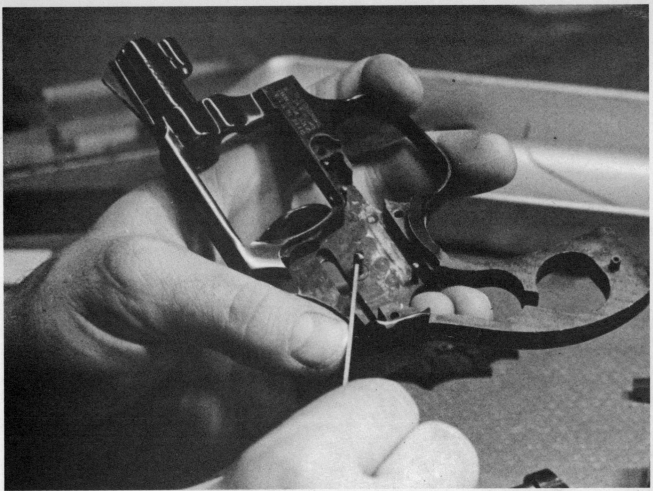

The hammer stud should be polished and checked with the hammer on the stud for exacting fit. If the stud is bent or worn, a loose hammer can result. Because of crucial fit, polishing of stud is done without any metal removal.

false readings, make certain there are no burrs on the cases nor around the firing pin hole. Also make sure the primers have not overly protruded on the test cartridges. After checking this reading and determining that the space is relatively close to the S&W recommendations of .062 to .064 we are ready to check the distance between cylinder and barrel. To get a true reading, it is essential that we keep the first set of feeler gauges inserted with pressure between the barrel and bolster. Although S&W recommends a distance of .003 between cylinder and barrel, a slightly larger measurement will not interfere with smooth functioning of this gun.

A J-frame yoke alignment gauge would be helpful while working on the S&W Model 36 if alignment work is necessary. This type of unique tool can be made on a lathe or purchased through Brownell's, Incorporated, Montezuma, Iowa.

Another essential tool for pistol work that may be relatively easily purchased from the above source is a rebound slide spring remover. This tool consists of a piece of 7/32-inch drill rod with a handle on one end and a slit at the other made with a hacksaw to a depth of at least one-eighth-inch. Heat the drill rod about one-quarter to one-half-inch back from the front tip and bend to an

approximate ninety-degree angle. Move the rod back another inch and heat and bend once again to a ninety-degree setting. This little gadget will save much time and energy in removing the rebound slide springs safely. Using just about any other method could result in having the spring fly out in unknown directions and places.

Many other specialized tools are available, including fitter's blocks, babbits for doing yoke work, etc., but for the most part we now have enough tools to handle simple tuning and timing of revolvers.

Probably the most important thing to remember about tuning and timing of revolvers is that the firearm *must* be in time before tuning and/or smoothing is attempted. This simply means that the timing chores come first and the tuning second.

Before getting into the timing aspects, we first must make certain the revolver is indexing properly. Indexing is a term used to describe proper alignment between the cylinder and the barrel at the cylinder's forward end and alignment of the chamber with the firing pin at the rear. A tool called a ranging rod is used to check for proper alignment. This tool can be nothing more than a polished piece of drill rod, but must be of a size to barely slide down the barrel and into the cylinder. The ranging rod should be

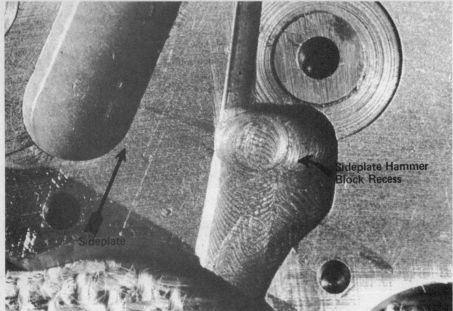

Sideplate Hammer Block Recess

Sideplate

The sideplate with the hammer block in the recess shows the travel cycle of the block and the necessity for polishing the bearing surfaces.

Sideplate

Hammer Block

ground to a sixty-degree taper on a lathe. The point on the end of the rod should meet the center of the firing pin when slid through the cylinder. Ranging rods can be ordered through Brownell's. However, on .357 magnums an ordinary piece of 11/64-inch drill rod is perfect for this caliber. Just put your sixty-degree angle on it by cutting it on a lathe and you have a valuable little tool for pennies.

In simple terms, proper timing is having the revolver cycle with no drag, the hammer cocks when it should (while the cylinder bolt is disengaging and reengaging when it should) and the hand contacts the cylinder ratchet at the proper time. Of course, all this is working together for a smooth cycle of operation. The main cast of characters in this function includes the hand, cylinder bolt, cylinder, cylinder notches, hammer, and trigger. Although this treatise involves the sequence of timing for the S&W Model 36, all Smiths are basically the same; the same principles extend to Colts and other double-action revolvers.

The timing sequence begins with trigger movement. As the hammer is pulled rearward, it cams the trigger back against the now compressing rebound lever spring. Simultaneously the cylinder bolt is disengaging itself from a notch in the cylinder moving in a downward position into the frame through a narrow rectangular hole. The critical part of this operation is that the cylinder bolt is drawn clear before another part — the hand — begins to attempt to rotate the cylinder. If the bolt does not clear before the hand begins its cylinder-turning function, there will be a noticeable heavy drag or catching sensation at the beginning of the trigger pull.

The second phase of the timing cycle is the hand which is attached to the trigger engaging the ratchet located on the back of the cylinder and rotating the cylinder a specified amount. It is obvious that the thin piece of steel known as the hand bearing against the cylinder ratchet is subject to extreme wear. It is important to know, therefore, what the size and diameter should be on the particular firearm you are attempting to check. For example, the Model 36 has a factory standard thickness of .072 to .074-inch. The end of the hand should be one of the first things checked when a gun is out of time.

In the next phase in the timing cycle, the hammer is approximately halfway back. The cylinder bolt is released by the trigger and the cylinder bolt spring pushes the cylinder bolt upward into the cylinder notch or the adjoining narrow groove next to the notch. As the hammer is drawn to full cock or at double-action dropoff, the cylinder chamber should be in perfect alignment at the rear with the firing pin and at the front with the barrel.

Naturally, this perfect coordination between the above-mentioned parts must function between each of the six cylinder notches (or five in the case of Model 36s).

Now that we understand what timing does for the cycle of the revolver we must know how to work on parts that are throwing the whole operation out of kilter. Most critical is the hand. It could be bent, worn thin, or the hand nose

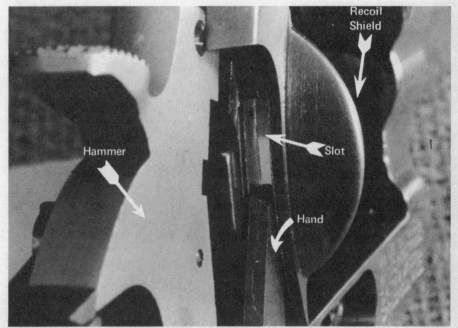

Hand must move between the slot in the recoil shield to contact ratchet and rotate the cylinder. If hand is worn or bent, gun may well become inoperable. Polishing inside of the slot will smooth the action. If slot is over-enlarged, an oversized hand can be ordered from the factory.

Cylinder stop must engage all of cylinder notches during the timing cycle. If the stop does not engage properly, hammer cannot be cocked on single-action, trigger cannot be pulled on double-action. Careful stoning or even replacement of the cylinder stop may be a requirement.

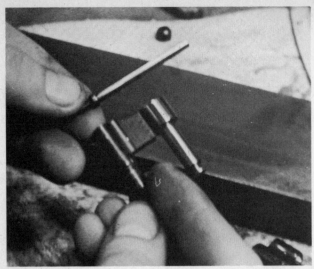

*A problem called cylinder cramp may be caused by a bent rod, center pin or an improperly aligned yoke. Bearing surfaces on these parts should be polished after each has been closely checked for its alignment, straightness.*

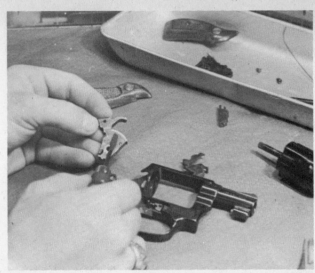

*The Model 36 shows a bright spot on the hammer meaning drag. Sides of hammer may be polished, but the camming surfaces are case hardened with little room for error. Many problems are solved by working trigger, not hammer.*

could be bent or deformed by improper contact with the ratchet. As mentioned, the J-frame Model 36 has a standard hand diameter of between .072 and .074-inch. However, an oversized hand measuring between .075 and .077-inch is available from the factory.

The oversize hand sometimes is necessary when the slot cut in the recoil shield has been worn and enlarged, causing problems with rotation of the cylinder. A word of caution: Sometimes when installing an oversized hand it may be a little too large for the hand slot. This means the slot needs to be enlarged by careful filing. If the hand becomes worn, the gun will not carry up properly and lead shaving problems will be much in evidence.

Another problem encountered in the timing cycle that is fairly common will be the cylinder bolt, or as S&W calls it, the cylinder stop, catching in a cylinder notch. When this situation occurs, you know it at once. The hammer cannot be cocked on single-action and the trigger cannot be pulled on double-action.

What is happening mechanically is that the cylinder stop is jumping back into the same cylinder notch it just came out of before the hand can move it to the next cylinder. The reason for this usually is due to the top of the cylinder stop having had too much metal removed at the bevel on the underside of the stop. Or it could be that, on a new stop, the top may be a bit too wide for the cylinder notches. In the latter case, carefully stone the sides to fit. However, when the point or bevel of a stop has been altered, a new cylinder stop is sometimes recommended.

A situation known as cylinder cramp also can influence the functioning of a revolver and throw the cylinder out of whack during its timing cycle. This can be caused simply by a leaded breech. In this instance, a good cleaning will

rectify the matter. However, it could be a bent rod, the yoke could be out of alignment, the cylinder could be too close to the barrel. It also could be that the hand is a bit too long for the cylinder.

There are many individual operations required in professionally smoothing up and tuning a revolver, but there are a few basic rules to keep in mind. First, never work on the hammer's bearing surfaces. The sides of the hammer may be smoothed and polished which causes less drag, but the camming surfaces are case-hardened, which means it is simple to get carried away and go through the hardening. This will cause excessive wear very quickly. Besides the thin case-hardening on revolver hammers, one should remember that the cocking notch on a hammer is only about .006 to .007-inch deep. So we correct problems by working on the trigger — not the hammer!

In tuning and smoothing, first take a look at all the internal parts of the gun, looking for worn spots which appear as shiny, bright areas on the individual bearing parts. To do this, we first have to remove the grips and then the sideplate. Remember, just a few gentle and repeated taps on the back of the backstrap and on the opposite side of the sideplate is the method used to remove it.

Start your examination by looking over the sideplate. The raised areas around the screwholes are called bosses, which prevent other bearing surfaces such as the trigger and hammer from bearing against the walls of the sideplate which not only would cause drag, but could easily cause malfunctions in the firing cycle.

After checking that it is not bent in any way, lightly stone the inner side of the sideplate, being extremely careful not to come in contact accidentally with the circular bosses. Make sure there are no burrs on the bosses,

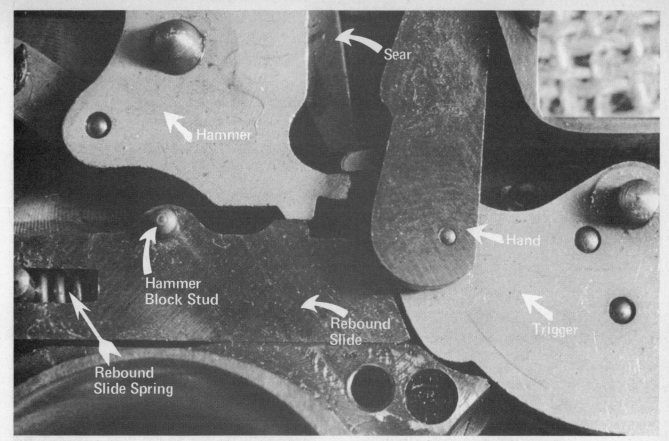

*Placement of the rebound slide requires that it be stoned carefully on left side, which bears against the frame; on the bottom, which also bears on the frame; on the right top side which contacts the hammer block. The top of the rebound slide also may be stoned, Mitchell says, but it must be done with extreme care not to remove much metal.*

also polishing the slot in the sideplate to reduce drag.

With the sideplate removed and the cylinder and yoke back in place, move the gun through its firing cycle to assure that all are performing their particular functions. To reduce drag in a revolver we must first discover exactly which parts are causing the problem. Although we want to smooth up all the parts wherever possible, we also must be conscious of the need for removing a minimum amount of metal.

One of the first things to look for through the dry-firing cycle with the sideplate off is whether the hammer is coming into contact with the cylinder latch. If so, the latch must be stoned down to allow the hammer to cock fully without touching the latch. Check also that the hammer isn't sticking on the hammer stud and that the hammer nose does not drag or stick in either the frame or the housing around the hammer when it is fully forward.

While examining the hammer, use this simple test: Hold the hammer forward with the back of your thumb while holding the trigger back at the same time. The trigger should be able to move forward slightly and backward without the hammer moving. This small amount of play is called wink. This play is necessary for the hammer nose to go far enough forward through the frame to strike the primer properly.

This play is allowed by the front angle of the hammer rebound seat to be at a slight angle to the bearing surface of the rebound slide. However, too much wink can affect the safety of the firearm adversely. Ability to judge what angle is proper should be left to the professional pistolsmith in most cases.

One other important factor in checking the hammer is to determine whether the tail of the hammer comes in contact with the rear leg of the bolt. This will prevent the cylinder from opening. To check this, simply push the thumb piece on the left side of the revolver forward and note whether it touches the tail or rear portion of the hammer. Again, we have to check for wink. If there is contact between the two, it is necessary to carefully stone down the top of the hammer seat. Great care must be exercised here as removal of too much metal could mean a whole new hammer or rebound slide being needed as a replacement.

Now take a close look at the hammer stud hole and hammer stud for close fit. Sloppy fit will produce a loose

All bearing parts on revolver frame should be smoothed to reduce drag. Frame area that bears against the bottom of the rebound slide is polished with hard Arkansas stone.

hammer. If this problem does exist, it will be necessary to use a special swedging tool to refit the hammer. However, it also gives us a reading on whether any drag exists between the hammer stud hole and the stud. We will want to polish the stud with 600 wet-and-dry paper. This is accomplished by cutting a few strips of 600 wet-and-dry into lengths slightly less in width than the stud. Using the paper wet, polish the stud with a shoeshine motion. All we want to do is smooth it up, not actually remove any metal.

When the stud is shiny, try the hammer on the stud and check for drag. If the hammer is loose on the stud, this could also lead to the hammer binding so care and experience are important. We also should be making certain the stud is not bent in any way as it could result in a problem known as overhaul. This means that the hammer cannot be cocked on single-action. This is due to the alignment between the stud and the frame spur bay which causes the hammer to disengage out of its cocking notch. If this problem does arise, it might be wise to send the gun back to the factory. However the method usually is corrected by filing the back of the spur bay at a new angle to the stud. This problem is mentioned to ensure one realizes that light polishing of the stud is the key to success,

The inside of the rebound slide houses rebound slide spring. A thin dowel, with 600 wet/dry paper, is used with the Dremel tool to polish the inside area of unit.

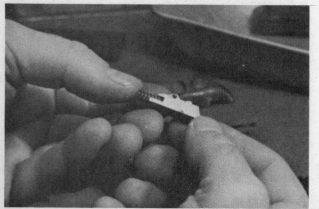

and a bit of overzealousness can necessitate expensive repairs that can be done only at the factory.

With only the sideplate removed, the next obvious step is to examine the hammer block. A safety feature of Smith & Wessons, the hammer block is important to the overall safety of the gun and should not be left out of the gun for any reason. Since this piece cams on a teat located on the upper right hand side of the rebound slide, some judicious stoning on the inner bearing surface of the hammer block should be done with a hard Arkansas stone to reduce drag.

The rebound slide should be stoned carefully on the left side, which bears against the frame; on the bottom, which also bears on the frame; and the right side, which comes into contact with the hammer block. The top of the rebound slide also may be stoned, but with great care so as not to remove much metal. Removal of too much metal could prevent the cylinder from opening.

The inside part of the rebound slide houses the rebound slide spring. With the spring removed, the inner part of the

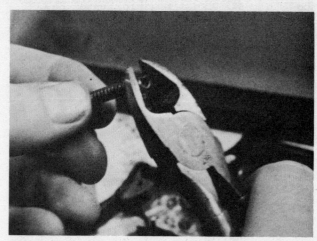

To smooth double-action pull, rebound slide spring may be cut down. Model 36 spring comes from factory with 17 coils. Maximum of two coils may be removed for function.

rebound slide should be polished carefully. The easiest way to do this is to use a small wooden dowel with 600 wet-and-dry paper. Wet with kerosene, the paper is held in place by cutting a thin slit down the middle of the dowel to hold the paper. It can be chucked in an electric drill and polished with care.

To really smooth up the double-action, a possible method is to remove a few coils from the rebound slide spring. Unfortunately, this bit of advice is rather widely known and few amateurs are aware of a couple of important problems before they begin cutting coils. For example, what happens if a former owner of the gun has already cut a few of these coils before he sold the gun to you? As protection against possible malfunctions in the gun then, one should know just how many coils are supposed to be on the original spring. The answer is seventeen. The number of coils ofttimes cut by competent pistolsmiths is no more than two!

I counted up the coils on the Model 36 in front of me and it did have the seventeen coils. I also had checked the pull on the gun several times before disassembly and knew that the coiled mainspring had not been previously altered, so I cut 1½ coils off the spring. This offered a notable smoothing effect on the piece.

When removing a rebound slide from a revolver, I use the tool described elsewhere in this chapter. However, a word of caution: To prevent the spring from flying out and possibly losing it or hitting yourself in the eye, it is a prudent move to place a towel over the entire piece after you have the spring under tension and are just about to remove it from the gun. If it does get loose, it doesn't go far and is a good safety practice.

The next piece to smooth up is the cylinder stop. Before polishing the top or ball of the cylinder stop, carefully insert the ball into each of the cylinder notches. If the ball is too loose in one or more of the notches, it probably will be wise to get a new cylinder stop. However, if there is a good fit in all notches, just break the edges of the ball and lightly polish the top to reduce drag.

A critical area on the stop that must be checked as well as polished is the front bevel on the cylinder stop. If it is too long it can cause the whole stop to go too low into the frame, causing the stop to stick. If this happens, the bevel and the point of the top must be filed down. If the cylinder stop does not hold the cylinder in place, the upper middle bearing piece under the front trigger extension may have to be filed down and polished. The cylinder stop should be viewed carefully and the gun cycled slowly to fully examine and determine a proper course of action as to any necessary file work outside normal polishing.

The mainspring on the Model 36 is a coiled type. It is very strong. A smaller tempered spring may be substituted which will produce a smooth pull. The trick is to use a spring of the same diameter but smaller gauge wire.

The mainspring stirrup holds the mainspring in place.

After removal from the frame, the stirrup should be highly polished on a buffing wheel with 600-grit compound. This will reduce drag. The spring also should be examined carefully when reinstalled to determine that it is not binding anywhere on the frame.

Careful work on the trigger is next. The front trigger extension which fits into the cylinder notch should be polished. The proper bevel on the trigger is important to the trigger pull. Careful stoning on the bevel can prevent the cocking notch in the hammer from jumping off the bevel on the trigger. Stoning at the proper angle is extremely important. The top bevel on the trigger also should be polished carefully. The bevel contacts the sear and should be as smooth as possible.

One of the last pieces to stone will be the bolt, which is located on the left side of the hammer. The hand or pawl should be checked to make sure it is not bent and that no burrs are present. Carefully examine the slots through which the hand fits to reach the cylinder latches; make certain there is also no drag.

With all parts now polished and checked, put either a good molybdenum-based powder or Break Free on the internal parts.

With the gun now reassembled and the pistol grips replaced (after insuring they don't drag on the mainspring) I dry fire the pistol approximately 250 times. The Model 36 I held in my hand was now a much smoother functioning pistol.

There are many other custom touches to suit personal tastes that make a gun even smoother, but for general smoothing and tuning, these are the general steps required. The operation requires two to three hours for a good pistolsmith to do the job right. However, the results often are amazing.

*Front bevel on cylinder stop must be checked, polished. If too long, it can cause stop to go too low into frame, causing stop to stick. If cylinder stop does not hold cylinder in place, the upper middle bearing piece under front trigger extension should be filed down, polished. (Right) Front trigger extension should be polished to fit into cylinder notch. Proper bevel on trigger is important to trigger pull, with proper stoning, polish.*

# Chapter 6

# You Can Be A
# JOINER

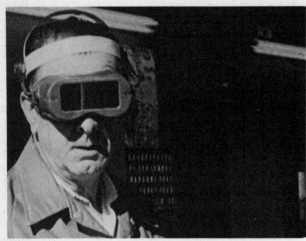

Proper welding goggles must be worn during welding to protect eyes against intense light and flying sparks, particles. Different types of welding require goggles made specifically for purpose. (Right) Both oxygen and acetylene tanks are held on a moveable cart by bands. The tanks should not be moved without safety caps, as a capless tank can become a projectile if it is dropped.

**A**NY NUMBER of pistolsmiths insist that they can do virtually all of the work required of them with a set of files. This no doubt is true for modern guns or those vintage models still high enough on the popularity scale that spare parts are readily available.

But when you get into some of the obsolete models, you have a problem. You either have to be sufficiently well trained that you can make replacement parts — usually with a file, I might add — or you should be able to repair the parts that are broken. The first method requires a lot of man-hours and the gunsmith may put in more time in making a new part than the whole gun is worth (if he charges by the hour what his expertise says he's worth.) It takes less time, of course, to repair a broken part, if possible.

In most instances, repairs of metal parts require a knowledge of welding, soldering and brazing, as well as the knowledge of which technique to use. Some of the latter

96

# There Are Various Methods For Joining Metals With Varying Degrees Of Success; This Chapter Tells How And Why

will be learned by trial-and-error, of course, but the first thing to remember is that any time heat is being used on any gun part, there is the problem of tempering and the ultimate stress on the metal, itself, when the gun is fired.

The barrels, cylinders, breech faces and, in the case of autoloaders, the slides, all have been properly heat-treated at the factory. If metal joining, using heat, is to be used in any such situation, rest assured that the specific part should be heat-treated again to return it to its original hardness.

There is no real guide as to what parts or areas can be soldered, welded or brazed without creating problems, but common sense is the usual denominator in such instances for experienced gunsmiths. For example, most of them know that you may be able to install a front sight with silver solder, but you would not do the same in an area over the chamber, where the metal's temper could be destroyed, thus weakening the part where the greatest stress may be experienced. At least, you don't do this unless you intend to heat-treat the piece again.

The piece to be soldered or whatever should be removed from the gun, too, to protect the other parts. I know of one instance wherein a less-than-professional gunsmith attempted to weld a part inside the frame of a revolver without properly stripping down the handgun. The result was that the flame softened all of the springs. In the end, each of them had to be replaced — but by another gunsmith, who deserved the name of professional.

No one is going to make an expert welder or solderer of you simply by telling you to read this book. It's an art learned by doing, but we may be able to give you some tips on what to do and what not to do that ultimately will save you some grief and could save a gun somewhere this side of destruction.

First off, let's take a look at the difference between welding and brazing.

**Welding** entails joining two metals of similar character and molecular structure. The surfaces of the two pieces are heated until they reach an almost liquid state, then the joining material — usually welding rod — is melted by contact with the heat from the two parts to be joined. Oddly, some experienced welders think that it is the heat from the torch that does this, but it's not true. With the

*The welding torch is lighted with release of acetylene gas. After firing torch, oxygen regulates proper flame.*

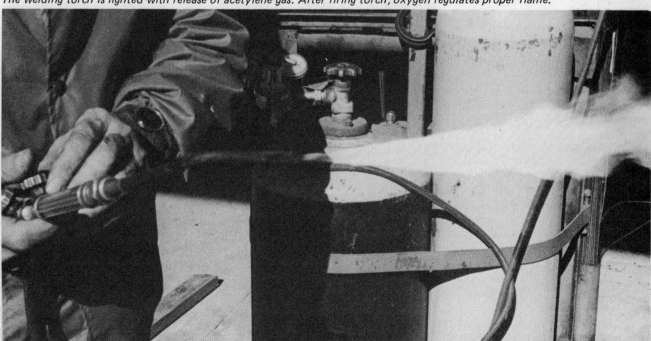

*Both the oxygen and the acetylene tanks have pressure gauges. Proper pressures must be adhered to if welding task is to be accomplished successfully, as well as with safety. Frequent checking of gauges is a good idea, too.*

three sources of metal all in a near liquid state, they tend to flow together to do away with the joint entirely, becoming one piece of metal.

When using an oxyacetylene torch in welding steel gun parts the metal is heated to approximately 3000 to 3200 degrees Farenheit for proper fusion of the two parts. During this heating process, when the metal has been heated to about 1500 degrees, the molecular structure of the steel is changed and the metal actually loses its magnetic qualities. This phenomenon is called "state of decalescence" and it is at this point that the metal is annealed, or "softened." Oftentimes pistolsmiths must anneal metal in order to successfully drill and tap slides for rib mounts.

**Brazing** also is a process for joining together two pieces of metal, but in this instance the edges of the pieces are heated enough that a filler rod of softer metal will melt, but the two pieces will not. The rod, usually of brass, copper or a combination of those and other ingredients, fills the space between the two pieces.

**Silver soldering** is used often in serious gunsmithing and, actually, is a sort of brazing process in itself. Silver soldering is used to repair numerous broken parts, which will not be taking great amounts of stress and also is a necessary technique with most gunsmiths for affixing sights of some types.

**Soft soldering** differs from silver soldering in that the former is just that — soft. For this work, an alloy composed largely of tin and lead is used as the filler material. This alloy requires much lower temperatures than any of the earlier mentioned methods and the strength of the resulting joint is considerably lower than in welds, brazed areas or joints that have been silver soldered.

Welding, for example, will approach or equal the strength of the two pieces of metal being joined, if the weld has been made correctly.

The tensile strength of silver soldering is reported to be in the area of 18,000 pounds per square inch (psi); brazing

with copper or brass will have a strength of about 15,000 psi; while the tensile strength of a soft solder weld is 4000 psi or less. Yet, each of these methods of joining metal has its uses and the gunsmith must determine which is best to use in a given situation.

Each of the techniques listed may require the use of what is called flux. This is a material which aids the melted joining material to flow more evenly and to provide a stronger joint. The problem here is to select the correct flux for the specific material being used. Manufacturers of the various rods usually will recommend the proper flux. There also are some materials that do not require the use of flux in joining. To use a flux in this situation means a poor joint when done, so pay attention at all times to the manufacturer's instructions.

Going back to the beginning to discuss welding a bit more in depth, keep in mind that only those surfaces along the lines to be joined should be heated to the point that they liquify. The heat should be contained and localized as much as possible. And keep in mind that the joining material, whether rod or wire, is not melted by the torch, but by the heat of the two parts you intend to join together. You'll know when the material is hot enough because if the heated area has not reached a high enough temperature to melt the filler rod, the material simply will not flow into the joint to fuse with the parts.

If you make the mistake of heating just the rod, it simply will flow into the break between the two pieces of metal, but will not adhere properly and there will be no strength under even minute stress.

The type of welding used by most pistolsmiths today is oxyacetylene, which utilizes a mixture of compressed oxygen and acetylene gas. To do any job correctly in pistol welding, you need to have the proper torch and tips for your oxyacetylene rig. There are several makers of these sets, all of which are adequate for the type of work you will be doing, but one concentrating on pistolsmithing would be wise to choose one of the miniature models that can be easily handled when working on small gun parts. Since these smaller models are more versatile, they can be used to better advantage in close work involved in pistolsmithing. Yet, they afford the degree of heat necessary for proper welding, et al.

When welding any steel part, it is important that the tip being used be large enough to handle the weld. Welding with a small tip on a large welding surface is difficult, as all of the area to be welded may not be sufficiently preheated. However, a good welder can use a tip that actually is a bit larger than needed and do a professional job. The key is moving the torch fast enough across the work without blowing the weld and melting the metal surface too quickly. When in doubt as to which size tip to use, a rule of thumb is to pick one a bit larger than necessary rather than one too small.

A gas/oxygen torch can be used, but I've found that the flame control on this setup is not what I would desire. This particular type of torch uses a solid chemical compound that generates its own oxygen. However, oxygen pressure is low and can't be controlled with any degree of success.

There's a good deal more to mastering welding than buying a torch and a set of goggles. Admittedly, the first welder probably had to teach himself, but chances are that some of his welds were pretty poor. There are a number of fairly good books on the subject, and they can give you the basics, but proper instruction on a one-to-one basis is the

*Each particular welding job requires the correct welding tip. Although possible to weld small jobs with an over-size tip, it often results in a poor weld. Tips should be cleaned periodically of slag with tip cleaners at right.*

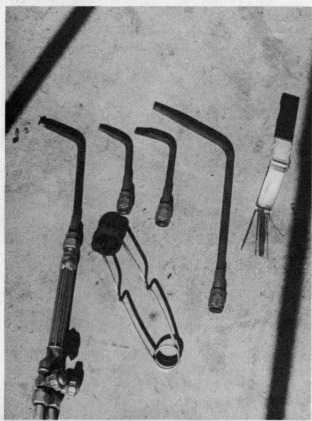

obvious answer. A number of states, including our own State of California, have colleges and junior colleges that offer night vocational courses. I can think of half a dozen welding courses available within comfortable driving distance of my own home, in fact.

In less progressive areas, you may be able to find a welder who is willing to teach you the job, if he doesn't think you're going to open up a welding shop next door to his. Even if you have to pay him for a few lessons, it will be money well spent.

Even with a degree of instruction, you should not go at any serious jobs until you're sure of your equipment and your own abilities. I'd suggest working on scrap at first, learning what not to do in joining your two pieces of metal.

Preliminary cleaning is a must, if you are to have a substantial weld. This means that the surfaces to be welded should be free of rust, plating or scale. In other words, you need bright metal. However, if a part has been broken, don't under any circumstances polish or grind the broken surfaces. These edges must fit together in their original conformation when welded! If there is rust, use a wire bush to remove it.

Any grease or preservative material should be removed from the entire part, not just the area where the joint will be welded. A good solvent and some elbow grease will do the job. If you attempt to use the welding torch without the oil being properly and totally removed, the result can be a hard residue that will affect your weld.

No welding job can be considered big in pistolsmithing. It's not exactly like welding seams in a ship's plates. Perhaps the largest job you'll ever do is to fill the rear sight dovetail on an autoloader pistol before installing a more modern sight. For this, I'd suggest a one-eighth-inch 3.5 percent nickel-steel rod. In fact I'd recommend this type of rod, although not necessarily the size, for all handgun work. This sort of job, incidentally, calls for a medium tip on the torch.

Before beginning such a job, of course, the autoloader should be dismantled, since we'll be working only on the slide. As explained earlier, it should have been cleaned thoroughly and a final dunking in a good solvent won't hurt.

I do not agree with the approach of one writer/gunsmith for running a puddle for a weld. Perhaps it is due to the fact that I was taught differently. However, even from my limited amount of experience with a torch running a puddle using a "circular motion" is one I've never heard of before. It is against common sense, and certainly not the most used method.

A right-handed welder — holding the torch in the right hand and working the weld from right to left — achieves a proper puddle using a half-circle or half-moon movement with the wrist. This method keeps the back of the puddle moving away from the flame, and with it the slag and impurities, leaving a perfect weld.

The important factors in running a perfect weld are keeping the work cherry red to the point of melting while adding welding rod. The puddle must be constantly moved to prevent the puddle from standing in one place. A full circular motion with the torch would blow the puddle back across the work just completed.

With the solvent dried, clamp the slide in your padded vise — taking care not to exert so much pressure that you

A piece of scrap metal is used to illustrate the normal right-handed welding method. Note position of the rod.

bend the slide — then light your torch, adjusting it for a neutral flame. We have to heat the entire dovetail area and this is done best by moving the flame in a small circular motion; don't just hold it stationary. As the bottom of the dovetail begins to heat up, the corner of the cut should begin to melt. As the metal thus liquifies, the edges may begin to fold down into the dovetail cut sort of like a cliff sliding down after a heavy rainstorm. At this point, use the torch to start melting the rod into the cut, using the back and forth series of overlapping half circles or crescents I described a few paragraphs back.

One should not attempt to fill the cut with a single pass. Instead, fill the bottom of the cut using the hand movement described, then lay another layer of the melted rod over that, continuing with this technique until the cut is filled and there is excess buildup above the plane of the side. While accomplishing this, you have to be certain that there are no holes left in the weld nor that slag has been allowed to build up. You don't want lines to show where the cut was filled either. This is accomplished with the overlapping series of crescents.

After the weld is ground level with the original material inspect the area carefully. Chances are, there will be a barely visible outline showing where the metal has been filled. If there are any holes or evidences of slag, these should be ground out with a Dremel Moto-Tool. The torch

and welding rod then should be used to fill these holes, then they should be ground down once more, reinspected.

One of the more common pistol parts requiring welding or building up is a revolver cylinder bolt or stop. A bolt that is too high in relationship to the cylinder notch will cause malfunctioning.

If this same bolt is worn causing it to pop up to catch the cylinder notch with not enough bearing surface, problems will also result. In either case the top of the bolt must be cleaned by hitting it lightly with abrasive paper, stoning it with a fine hard Arkansas stone, or cleaning it up on a grinding wheel.

Once the bolt is absolutely clean the top must be built up using the smallest welding tip possible. All techniques used in working large welding tasks are the same. However, working within this small area, it is critical that the entire diameter of the top of the bolt be heated to the proper temperature and the new weld be run, building up the entire surface area. Although only a few thousandths of an inch may be necessary it saves time and aggravation to build up the area a bit more than you think necessary. It is a simple matter to remove metal after checking for fit between the cylinder bolt and the cylinder notch until a perfect mating is achieved. However, if after welding the first time you find you haven't gained the desired new height on the bolt it becomes necessary to remove it from

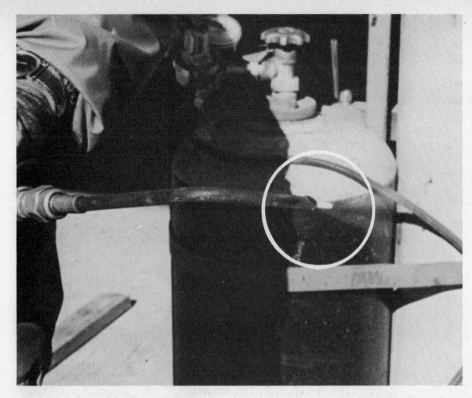

The proper length of the blue flame used in most gunsmithing chores is illustrated in photo, but holding flame near the tanks is not safe.

the revolver and set up the torch again.

The two pistolsmithing jobs described above should cover the parameters of the welding you'll be called upon to do in handgun work. Anything in between should be something pretty easily handled.

This chapter wouldn't be complete, incidentally, without some mention of safety for all of the techniques under discussion and this seems a logical spot in the text to bring it up.

Regardless of which technique is being used — welding, brazing or soldering — there are certain necessary steps to insure that you don't become a casualty. Welding, for example, requires that one wear dark goggles or a mask specifically made for this type of work. You'll also need welder's gloves, which have long gauntlets, to protect your wrists and arms from flying sparks, and a long-sleeved jacket that is heavy enough to retard the bits of molten metal that result from welding. I'd also suggest a heavy leather apron to protect the rest of your clothing and your body.

If you wear a welder's mask with its long hood, a lot of potential dangers will be covered. If you opt only for goggles to protect your eyes, wear a cap, at least, to protect your hair. The goggles can protect your eyes from the bits

Oversize bead on scrap metal shows the half-moon method of running the bead. If puddle is not moved on a continuing basis, slag will cause defects in the completed weld job.

Old front sight has been driven out of auto slide with small punch. Before a new sight is silver soldered in place, both areas must be polished, grease removed with sulphuric acid solution.

Soldering talc is rubbed onto slide surrounding the area to be soldered. Talc prevents solder from sticking to the slide, eliminates messy cleanup. It is not applied to the actual area to which the solder is to adhere.

of hot metal that spray up from your work on occasion. The dark lenses are designed to protect against possible damage to the eye's retina; the bright arc can burn this tender tissue.

Although brazing and soldering are less demanding, the dark goggles and heavy gloves should be worn when using these techniques, too.

Brazing, as we know it, utilizes brass or copper as a binding agent between the two pieces of metal and will be used in only rare instances in pistolsmithing.

Silver soldering is nothing more than another form of brazing, using silver as the filler agent. The joining method favored by most pistolsmiths, it is the technique that will be used in a vast majority of your work.

There are great similarities to the welding process. For example, one never should grind the matching surfaces of a broken part smooth, if they are to be silver soldered or silver brazed — whichever term you prefer.

The irregularities in the break will help in aligning the two pieces and, once soldering is done and the added metal

ground down to the part's normal level, it usually will offer added strength to the joining.

To prepare the two pieces of metal, the usual procedure is to clean the pieces with a light solution of sulphuric acid, then rinse them with clear water. All grease should be removed first, of course. After etching with the acid and rinsing, the surfaces to be joined should not be touched by the fingers, as the resulting salts can affect the final bonding.

Under usual circumstances, one of the pieces is clamped down for application of the flux to be used in conjunction with the silver solder. Although there are several brands available, I favor a product called Silvaloy. Be sure to apply according to the maker's instructions.

With a small tip on your torch, using a neutral flame, heat the break surfaces on the two pieces until the flux is fully melted. This is when you apply the silver wire to the area to be joined. The silver wire should melt almost immediately if it is to flow easily. Before it has an opportunity to harden, you can remove the excess material with a soldering brush. Once satisfied with the application, allow it to set and cool.

The other piece to be joined receives similar treatment. Then, when both of the pieces have cooled, fit the broken edges together, clamping them in such manner that the joint still is accessible for working. There should be silver solder on the broken edges, of course, but most of it should have been removed with the soldering brush. Thus, the rough edges still should fit together in proper alignment.

Apply torch heat only to the area of the break until the solder begins to flow. The solder from the two pieces should flow together and there should not be so much heat that the material begins to flow away.

Removing the torch, allow the joint to harden and, when it is cool, scrape off any excess silver solder. The joint should be strong and serviceable.

A secret to successful silver soldering is make certain that the solder covers the entire joining area of the two pieces of work. To best accomplish this add solder to one side of the work while keeping that side of the work at the proper temperature with the torch. After adding the proper amount of solder take the torch and begin heating the other side of the two pieces to be joined. This causes the solder actually to be drawn to the new source of heat, pulling the solder through the entire area of repair and creating a perfect bond. This same drawing technique also should be employed when brazing.

Perhaps the greatest single use of the silver soldering technique for gunsmiths is in attaching sights.

With the old sight slot filled by welding as described earlier, a new slot is cut and, with files, the sight is prepared for a perfect fit.

The first thing one should remember to do in this instance is to apply an anti-flux compound to the areas of metal, where we do not want silver solder to adhere. Removing excess solder could ruin the finish and mean a rebluing or replating job. The anti-flux makes removal of flux and solder simple once the job has been accomplished.

As described earlier, flux should be applied so as to be in contact with surfaces of both the sight and the slot, then a thin coating of silver solder should be applied with the torch and the silver wire. Again, the soldering brush should be used to remove excess material before it hardens, leaving only a thin coating.

If the sight was a tight fit to begin with, the added silver solder will make it even tighter. You can use a brass hammer to gently tap it into place. This may shave away some of the silver solder, but don't worry about this. Simply remove the slivers of silver and light your torch. Apply heat from the torch until the silver solder becomes

*The area to be silver soldered/silver brazed is carefully coated with brush-on paste flux. Front sight is coated, too.*

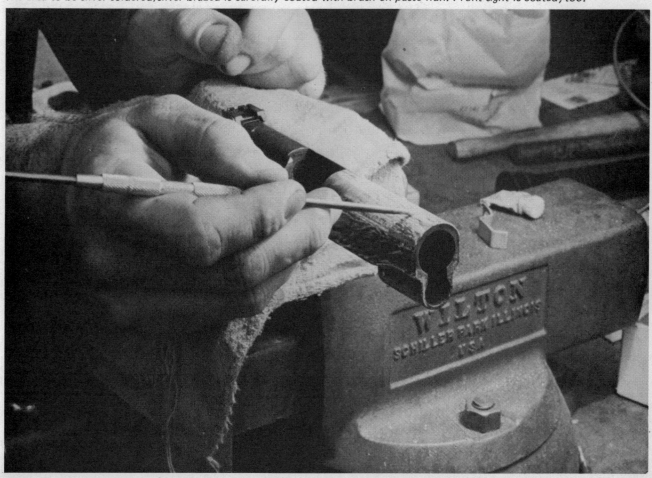

Using tip with proper neutral flame, Silvaloy silver solder is added for joining. To make certain solder covers entire area, torch will be placed on other side of sight; solder will run to heat source, insuring perfect job.

liquid, using your soldering brush to clean off the excess material, then allow the unit to cool.

Quite frankly, I can't think of a single instance in pistolsmithing wherein soft soldering — or lead soldering, as it sometimes is called — can be used to any advantage. Requiring less heat than silver soldering, the resultant joint usually lacks necessary strength if a handgun is to remain in service for any length of time.

The oxyacetylene torch used in welding, brazing or silver soldering can be used, but there are several much less expensive tools that can be used in this type of joining, including the common soldering iron. The best soft solder I've found has equal parts tin and lead, incidentally.

However, a discussion of this type of metal joining would not be complete without some mention of the techniques. Besides, you may find uses for soft soldering that I never have found. You know what they say about necessity birthing invention and all that. But if you are going to use soft solder, I'd give a lot of thought as to *how* you intend to use it. I know some gunsmiths who employ it to attach front sights on revolvers. I also know of one police officer, who drew his revolver one day to find that the front sight somehow had hung up in his holster lining and had remained there. Drawing down on a felon without a front sight can be a frustrating business at best!

As nearly as I've been able to determine that legend stuff

about the old-time gunfighters filing off the front sight to avoid holster hangups is the invention of fiction writers. If such a thing did happen, I suspect that the gunfighter was a professional backshooter, who practiced his trade at a range of about six feet!

Now that I've attempted to influence you as to the uselessness of soft solder in pistolsmithing, let's take a look at what it's all about.

Preparation of the two pieces of metal to be joined is accomplished in precisely the same manner as though we were going to use silver solder: the parts must be cleaned properly and one must be certain of a precise fit.

A number of soft solder fluxes are designed for use with softer metals such as brass, copper or aluminum. These are no good when it comes to joining steel and iron, however. It is imperative that you use a solid wire or rod in this type of soldering, taking care not to use the soldering wire that has a fluxed core. One should apply the anti-flux, of course, to the areas surrounding the actual section that will be soldered. As in silver soldering, each of the pieces of metal receives a coating of solder, then they are clamped together so the joint is as tight as you can get it. This will result in a thin joint, which is heated until the solder begins to run. The clamp should force out all excess material. The soldering brush should be used to whisk away any excess metal. As it melts at a comparatively low temperature, lead solder also tends to harden quickly, so this last step has to be accomplished rapidly.

Soft solder is available in wire, bars or rods, all of which are used in about the same manner, although there is a difference in price. Bar solder usually is the cheapest in relationship to its weight, but is not always as handy as wire or a rod in using.

Becoming popular these days is a technique called fusion soldering, which can be used for soft soldering or silver soldering, depending upon the compound you choose. This is a metal powder that is applied directly to the surfaces to be joined. Thus, it is not necessary to apply melted solder to the individual pieces. Instead, with the powder coating brushed on, the pieces are clamped together and joint heated until the powder melts down and begins to flow. Most gunsmiths have found this to be faster than using rods or wire and, from what I have been able to determine, the joint is as strong as any found in the techniques mentioned earlier.

This chapter on joining would hardly be complete if some reference were not made to the various epoxies and so-called magic glues being marketed today. They have found their place in gunsmithing work, of course, since they can be used to bond metals, and in some situations, offer even greater strength than the traditional methods of joining metal.

If you feel that you can use an epoxy for a specific pistolsmithing job, be certain to read the manufacturer's instructions, since each of them tends to differ a trifle in preparation. The two-compound epoxy is the oldest, with a resin being mixed with a hardening agent. The resin acts as the adhesive, while the hardening agent does just that: it hardens the resin. If you have too much resin, you may end up with a sticky mess that will never really harden. Again, read the instructions in the beginning, not after you've loused it up.

As for the cyanoacrylate agents — so-called magic or super glues — they do not require mixing, but they do need careful handling, as they tend to harden in a matter of only seconds. If you don't want to find your fingers attached to the job at hand, again follow the directions. These glues have amazing strength and can afford permanent bonding in a number of gunsmithing jobs, where you have little stress.

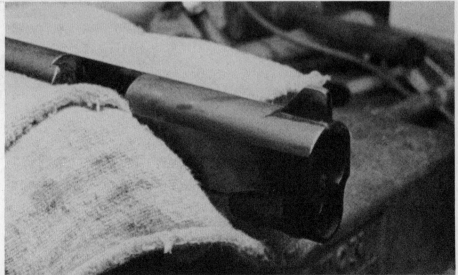

After the work has been allowed to cool, soldering talc is removed to reveal perfect mating of sight to slide with minimum cleanup needed.

Final stage of work is to degrease the area and cold blue around the sight. Gun is ready for assembly.

# Chapter 7

# TEMPER TOUGH

## The Basics Of Hardening And Tempering Can Be Accomplished With Minimum Gear

To harden and temper a screwdriver, one will need one of the hardening compounds such as Hard-N-Tuff, heat, water.

TEMPERING AND hardening of metals is a science that dates back through the ages to ancient times. In fact, the Romans allegedly knew the secret of tempering copper, but that knowledge has been lost in time and some contend that it died when Pompeii was buried under tons of lava with the eruption of Mount Vesuvius.

Then there's the legend about the village blacksmith who

I've found that electrically heated furnaces are the most satisfactory for heat-treating high-grade steels. This furnace derives its heat from a heavy low-voltage current passing through electrodes to resistance elements to produce uniform heat.

The so-called liquid bath is used commonly for heating tool steel for hardening. The molten substance is retained in a crucible heated by gas or oil. Advantages of the liquid bath lie in the fact that no part of the work can be heated beyond the temperature of the bath, which is maintained easily at the required temperature. While the submerged part is being heated uniformly, the finished surfaces are protected against oxidation during the hardening process.

The lead bath is not adaptable to high-speed steels, the bath will vaporize at about 1190 degrees Fahrenheit. If heated higher, can produce poisonous vapors. For this reason, don't use the lead bath without being certain to wear a protective mask and have good ventilation to carry away the fumes. The lead used must be free of sulfur and the best results come if the work is preheated before

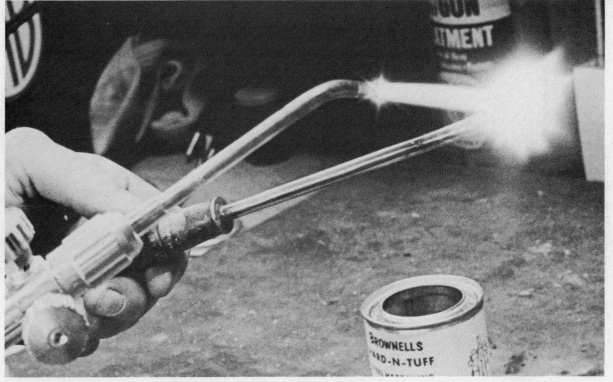

*For hardening with a torch, heating is begun back from the tip of the screwdriver and the area is heated then to a temperature of about 1400 degrees Fahrenheit or until the metal being tempered becomes a cherry red in color.*

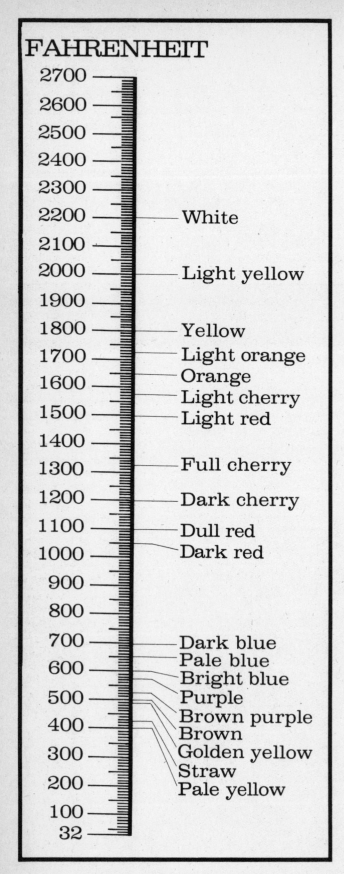

# FAHRENHEIT

| | |
|---|---|
| 2700 — | |
| 2600 — | |
| 2500 — | |
| 2400 — | |
| 2300 — | |
| 2200 — | White |
| 2100 — | |
| 2000 — | Light yellow |
| 1900 — | |
| 1800 — | Yellow |
| 1700 — | Light orange |
| 1600 — | Orange / Light cherry |
| 1500 — | Light red |
| 1400 — | |
| 1300 — | Full cherry |
| 1200 — | Dark cherry |
| 1100 — | Dull red |
| 1000 — | Dark red |
| 900 — | |
| 800 — | |
| 700 — | Dark blue |
| 600 — | Pale blue / Bright blue |
| 500 — | Purple / Brown purple |
| 400 — | Brown / Golden yellow |
| 300 — | Straw |
| 200 — | Pale yellow |
| 100 — | |
| 32 — | |

plunging it into the bath. For small work, some pistolsmiths use an ordinary bullet casting furnace.

Incidentally, uneven heating can cause defects in the hardening process. Usually, cracks from the corners of the work indicate the defect. If the part is not totally immersed in the hardening bath, soft areas and those that are overly hard may result. Carbon steels are hardened at temperatures of from 1350 to 1550 degrees Fahrenheit, while high-speed steel requires 1800 to 2200 degrees.

This treatise wouldn't be complete without some mention of the annealing process.

The reason for annealing steel — or "normalizing" it, as the term sometimes is expressed — is not only to soften it for machining, but to remove strains from the steel.

When annealing in a kiln, it is necessary that the work be enclosed in a piece of pipe or a metal box and that no air reach it during the heating process. This prevents the metal piece from undergoing oxidation.

The temperature for annealing should be just above the critical point, which varies with each type of steel. Low-carbon steels, for instance, are annealed at about 1650 degrees, while high-carbon steel is annealed at about 1400 degrees Fahrenheit. The temperature should be maintained long enough to heat the work thoroughly, but it is important that the steel not be heated beyond the decalescence or hardening point. Overheating inevitably causes coarseness in the metal.

In annealing high-speed steel, the metal is packed in the

*Developed to prevent scale, decarburization, pitting in heat treating is PBC non-scaling compound. It helps keep dimensions of parts from changing in heat-treating.*

pipe or iron box, but it is absolutely essential that the part not touch any of the surfaces of the container. Thus, the container is packed first with powdered charcoal. The size of the part determines the period of time that the work must be heated, the temperature maintained between 1470 and 1500 degrees Fahrenheit. The time may range between two to eight hours. The part must be cooled slowly. the best way is to shut down the kiln or furnace and allow the entire container to sit until it and the part inside are cold.

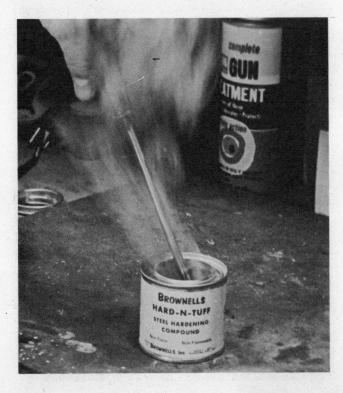

Chances are, you already know more about heat-treating than you really wanted to know, but this information will afford a better understanding of precisely what takes place, making it easier for us to accomplish the chores at hand.

Earlier, I mentioned critical points, so this may require a bit more explanation. The critical point for carbon steel is the temperature at which changes in the chemical composition of the steel take place during heating and cooling.

Steel at normal temperatures has the carbon content — the chief hardening agent — in a form called *pearlite*. When the steel is heated, a structural change occurs and the pearlite becomes *martinsite*, or hardened carbon. However, if the steel is allowed to cool slowly, the martinsite again reverts to the pearlite state.

When a piece of steel is heated to a certain point — that point depending upon the type of steel — it may continue to absorb heat without any notable rise in the temperature, although its immediate surroundings prove to be hotter than the steel, itself. This is the *decalescence point*.

Steel cooling slowly from a high temperature will actually increase in temperature at a certain point, although its surroundings may be more cold. This is termed the *recalescence point.*

According to scientific data, the recalescence point is lower in temperature than the decalescence point by from 95 to 200 degrees F. The lower of these points is not reached unless the higher point has been reached and fully passed.

These critical points bear a direct relationship to the hardening process for steel. Unless the temperature reaches the decalescence point so that the pearlite carbon is changed to martinsite, no hardening of the steel will occur. And unless the steel is cooled suddenly prior to reaching the recalescence, preventing transformation back to pearlite

*After heating the piece to cherry red, submerge it immediately in the hardening compound. Make certain the entire area to be hardened is submerged, left in the compound for at least a minute. Good fusing of the part with compound insures that hardening will result. Next, remove the part from compound and reheat until cherry red, making certain compound is fused with the metal.*

carbon, the hardening will not take place. The variations in the critical points require the need for heating different types of steels to varying appropriate temperatures for hardening.

The temperatures at which the decalescence point is reached will vary with the carbon content of the steel being used. Decalescence marks the correct hardening temperature for the specific steel, which should be removed from the heat when it is heated uniformly to the specified temperature.

Incidentally, there is a simple means of determining when the decalescence point has been reached. The steel becomes non-magnetic, although it will become magnetic again when it is heated beyond this point to the cherry red shade. A simple magnet can be used to determine the decalescence point, when a pyrometer is not available.

For simple heat-treating work, the pistolsmith usually needs equally simple equipment. Your torch is the basic tool, really. With that, you'll need a bucket of water, a piece of steel plate that measures about one-eighth-inch in

To draw and temper any hardened part, first polish it again, then reheat the tip, watching colors appear and begin to run. Just as the desired color is reached, quench immediately in water. Some gunsmiths use brine.

thickness, a can of light petroleum-base oil, the usual array of abrasive cloth and a sheet of asbestos on which to work.

Perhaps the simplest job you will do in tempering is a firing pin for an autoloading pistol. Most gunsmiths make these out of short lengths of drill rod, since working down bar stock can waste a lot of time. The problem with the firing pin is to temper it to be tough enough that it won't shatter when hit by the gun's hammer, yet it must be hard enough that it will make proper impact with countless cartridge primers for detonation without wearing down or becoming deformed.

With your torch fired up, you hold the pin in the flame set at neutral heat, which is indicated by a blue flame. It is best to use a piece of wire to hold the pin. If you hold the pin with a pair of pliers, the tool will draw away heat that should be going directly to the pin. The wire, being smaller, will not absorb as much heat from the flame.

The pin should be held so that the thickest part receives the most heat; in other words, the flame should be directed to this part, thus the heat will spread with some degree of uniformity. If you heat the smaller section of the pin first, it could even melt before the thicker part reaches the correct degree of temperature!

The pin is heated until it reaches a cherry red color. It then is plunged into the petroleum oil for several seconds. There probably will be a lot of smoke and sizzling, but

don't let this bother you. The pin then is drawn out and you return it to the flame until all of the oil is burned off. If everything is working correctly, you should have a well-tempered pin that will be good for thousands of rounds in the handgun on which you are working.

Although I've not used it personally, the lead bath is excellent for small parts such as the firing pin just discussed, extractors and other parts that might be subject to a lot of stress. I've been told the lead bath affords more uniform tempering than the direct flame method, but then again, I know gunsmiths who don't have much time for it. The choice has to be yours, but let's discuss it so you know what's available:

First, the lead bath method requires more equipment, namely an electric furnace for casting bullets. If you shoot as well as gunsmith — and I don't know a gunsmith who is not also a shooter of one kind or another — you probably have the furnace.

The part is quenched in oil as described earlier, but is not subjected to the burning with the torch afterwards. Instead, the firing pin or whatever small part we are treating is simply dropped into the molten lead in the furnace after being oil-quenched. Lead is heavier than steel, of course, so you'll have to use a piece of wire or maybe a bit of welding rod to shove the gun part down into the lead, itself. Otherwise, the steel part will simply float on top of the lead

*After quenching, remove the part and check the color of tempered area. Oftentimes, the desired color for proper tempering has been missed. If this is the case, the tempering operation is repeated.*

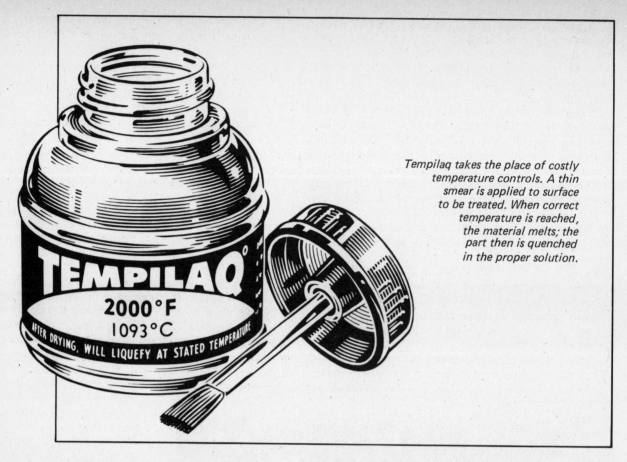

*Tempilaq takes the place of costly temperature controls. A thin smear is applied to surface to be treated. When correct temperature is reached, the material melts; the part then is quenched in the proper solution.*

just as wood tends to float on water. The heat control on the furnace, incidentally, should be set at about 600 degrees Fahrenheit.

The gun part remains submerged in the molten lead for about half an hour, then is removed and allowed to cool. When the part has cooled, any clinging lead can be polished off with little trouble.

With larger parts, the technique is basically the same, but in this instance, water rather than oil is used for a quench and the variations in color of the metal tells the pistolsmith when the correct tempering has been reached for a specific purpose. But let's take it from the top:

As with the smaller parts, the part is heated until it reaches the cherry red color, then is quenched in clean water. It is withdrawn quickly from the water, then a bit of steel wool should be used to clean at least part of it so that the bare metal is visible. The metal will continue to change color as it cools and, just as did the old blacksmith under his legendary spreading chestnut tree, we watch that change closely. When the correct color is reached for the desired purpose, the part again is quenched in water, but this time is left there until it cools completely.

The variations in color indicate definite temperature ranges and each of these ranges of tempering is good for specific parts or uses.

For example, when the color of the metal reaches a rich shade of blue, that means that the temperature has been reduced to about 560 degrees. This particular tempering is good for firing pins, as an example.

When the temperature is further reduced and the metal appears a deep purple, that means the head is in the 550-degree range. Most gunsmiths consider this ideal for hammers and triggers. Cooling more, the metal should take on a light purple, almost lavender shade, meaning it has cooled to about 530 degrees. This is the range favored by most custom knifemakers in tempering their blades for an excellent cutting edge.

When the temperature of the part has dropped to 510 degrees or so, it will appear to be a cross between purple and brown, the range favored for tempering welded areas such as sear noses, trigger noses and sear notches, to give you an idea.

When the color changes to a light brown, it has reached 490 degrees and by the time it has taken on a straw color, the temperature stands at about 470 degrees. Most gunsmiths favor this range for tempering bolts, various levers and rebound slides. Appearing even a lighter straw shade means the temperature stands at about 450 degrees, which is ideal for plunging the part into water, if it is a hammer face, firing pin head or any type of striking surface.

At 430 degrees, the part takes on a faint yellow appearance. As this tempering level results in an extremely hard part, it should not be used on thin metal.

The only problem with this technique lies in the fact that the smaller the part, the more rapidly it will cool, meaning that the colors will change quickly. Thus it may become difficult to strike just the right tempering heat as the piece is plunged into the water. As with welding, tempering and hardening require a lot of practice and I'd suggest that you perfect your techniques with scrap steel rather than the parts on an old gun that might not be replaceable.

Of particular importance is knowing what type of steel you are using, for the techniques differ a bit. For any alloy steel, oil should be used for quenching, while water is best for carbon steels. Hardening and tempering will result even if you reverse the order, but the results will be better if you stick to the rule-of-thumb above.

Casehardening also must be considered among the hardening techniques and serves a very special purpose. When accomplished correctly, it furnishes a thin but hard coating on the part that has been treated, while the metal beneath maintains its original degree of tempering. Casehardening is particularly desirable on metal that will be receiving continual wear.

The technique dates back centuries but the original method of using bone meal as an agent has been surpassed by more modern means. One may accomplish casehardening more easily and with less hassle, using only a torch and one of the commercially made hardening compounds such as Kasenit, which is available from most gunsmith supply houses.

To use this particular compound, one has only to heat the gun part to a deep red color, then dip it into the powder-like Kasenit. The part then is reheated with the torch until the powder melts and burns off.

If you do not like the initial results, it only requires another application or two to increase the degree of hardness. As has been suggested, you'll get best results if you simply follow the maker's simple instructions.

But again, I suggest that you do your learning on pieces of scrap metal before you try your newly acquired skills on a handgun of any great value. You'll learn by doing and it's better to learn slowly and correctly.

Since gunsmiths are called upon from time to time to do some hardening, tempering and heat treating chores he should also be aware of some of the common terms pertaining to steel.

1. Stress: The force acting on any structure.
2. Strain: A distortion or deformation caused by stress.
3. Tensile Strength: The ability to resist pulling forces.
4. Ductility: The ability to bend, be shaped, twisted, or bent without cracking or breaking.
5. Brittleness: The opposite of ductility.
6. Elasticity: The ability to return to its original shape.
7. Fatigue: The failure of metal when subjected to repeated and constant stress loads.
8. Toughness: The ability to withstand sudden shocks.
9. Hardness: The ability of the steel to resist indentation.
10. Compression Strength: Resistance to crushing.
11. Corrosion Resistance: The resistance to wear or chemical actions.
12. Steels

    Cold Rolled: Formed by rolling without additional heat.

    Low Carbon: Less than .3% carbon.

    High Carbon: Having minimum of .4% carbon or higher.

    Tool Steels: Ranging from medium to high carbon contents. Harder to machine but somewhat stronger due to higher carbon content. Also called cast steel.

    Brass: Red, 5 to 20% zinc, remainder is copper

    Yellow, 20 to 35% zinc, remainder is copper.

    Cartridge Brass, 30% zinc, 70% copper.

The following drawing temperatures may be used as approximations in determining hardness:

| Drawing Temperature (degrees F) | Rockwell C Scale | Impact Value (foot-pounds) |
|---|---|---|
| 300 | 63 | 19 |
| 400 | 62 | 22 |
| 500 | 61 | 23 |
| 600 | 58 | 28 |
| 700 | 53 | 41 |
| 800 | 50 | 58 |
| 900 | 46 | 75 |
| 1000 | 40 | 94 |
| 1100 | 36 | 113 |
| 1200 | 26 | 120 |

Drawing correct temperatures have been made easier by the development of a chemical now sold through Brownell's of Montezuma, Iowa, by the tradename of Tempilaq. It is available in a wide range of temperatures from 350 to 1550 degrees Fahrenheit. Simply use the Tempilaq in the temperature range suited for the tempering job and paint it on as a liquid from the bottle. Allow a few moments for it to dry and heat the work until the Tempilaq melts. Immediately remove the torch and the proper drawing temperature has been accurately and easily achieved.

In closing this chapter I think that the following chart given gunsmithing students from the Colorado School Of Trades will be very useful to the amateur and professional alike.

| HEAT TREATING | Temperature (degrees F) | Quench |
|---|---|---|
| **Hardening Temperature** | | |
| 1. Cold rolled | Bright red 1500 | Oil & water |
| 2. Low carbon | 1450 - 1550 | Water & brine |
| 3. High carbon | 1450 - 1500 | Oil |
| 4. Tool steel | 1450 - 1500 | Oil |
| 5. Brass | Work harden | |
| **Drawing or Tempering** | | |
| 1. Cold rolled | 700 | Air |
| 2. Low carbon | 300 - 500 | Air |
| 3. High carbon | 300 - 500 | Air |
| 4. Tool steel | 300 - 500 | Lead bath or sand |
| 5. Brass | Dark brown | Air |
| **Annealing** | | |
| 1. Cold rolled | 725 | Air (slowly) |
| 2. Low carbon | 725 | Air (slowly) |
| 3. Tool steel & High carbon | 725 - 900 | Air |
| 4. Brass | Dull red | Water |

# Chapter 8

# Why Won't It Shoot?

## The Diagnosis Of A Sick Handgun Is Necessary, Before One Can Effect A Cure

**W**HEN WE consider the incredible amount of time, testing, energy and expense required to produce a production line firearm for sale to the public and/or military, we expect it to be durable, reliable and accurate for the purpose for which it was invented.

Many of the new firearms today are designed and built with improvements over other previously built firearms utilizing original sound, basic principles. If a firearm is cared for properly and used for its intended purpose it often will serve its owner a lifetime. Unfortunately, these criteria are not always met by the average gunowner. Sooner or later these firearms require maintenance, repair, and/or replacement of parts by a competent gunsmith. Although the causes of a particular pistol failing to function are as many and varied as there are people in this country with those guns, the single biggest problem is most generally traced to one source; the owner. The overwhelming percentage of pistols on which I have worked have failed to work properly because the owner either failed to clean the pistol properly, if at all, tinkered with particular parts which should have been left to a qualified gunsmith, or mistreated the gun either through mishandling or using it for purposes never intended by the

manufacturer. This often is the case when an owner fires hot loads through his trusty sidearm which can ruin the piece or make it necessary to completely rebuild the gun for further use. When it comes to reasons why a particular handgun won't shoot at all or won't shoot with any great degree of accuracy, revolvers and autoloaders have their own specific problems. As mentioned, one of the major problems is due to improper cleaning. Since proper cleaning is discussed at some length in Chapter 3 of this tome, it does not bear repetition here.

No matter the type of revolver or autoloader brought into the shop for servicing, regardless of particular obvious repairs, the first requirement of the gunsmith is to clean and inspect it completely. Of course, the very first thing he must do is to check whether the gun is loaded. Although this sage advice is given by every knowledgeable person in the business, it is worth repeating. Even the best pro can get a bit lax, but sure enough, the first time he forgets he ends up with a hole through the ceiling, or worse, through himself.

Thorough cleaning is a must simply because it's the only way to determine the true worth of the gun's functioning. This step is followed by a complete inspection of each part and checked for wear. Special emphasis and examination of

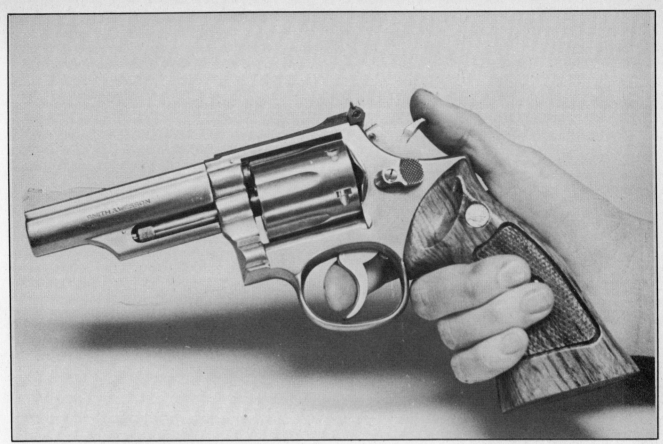

*When it comes to reasons why a firearm won't shoot, revolvers have their specific problems as opposed to autoloaders.*

traditional trouble areas peculiar to certain guns will save much time and effort. For example, revolvers most often fail to function due to cylinder malfunctions. It may be in the alignment, cylinder bolt, hand, crane, bushing, et al., but we must first check the cylinder rotation and lockup and start from this initial check. It would be convenient if I could simply list each problem a pistolsmith may encounter with each type of pistol, plus a cut-and-dried, simple list of steps to repair each one. However, this is impossible. There are too many different types of guns, too many variations in design principles for each.

Also, since a gunsmith will be frequently faced with having to repair a pistol with no source of replacement parts available for that particular gun, there are many instances wherein a gunsmith must use his own common sense and ingenuity to get the piece working properly and out the door again. This is what separates the professional from the amateur. Although I've never met two gunsmiths who accomplish a particular repair in exactly the same manner, there are certain guidelines most follow to complete general repairs. However, I don't know of any who would attempt to begin repairs without the initial cleaning and inspection of each part first. Keeping this bit of advice in mind, let's examine some of the most common

problems a pistolsmith will deal with in today's most common guns and some guidelines for corrective action.

Probably the most popular revolver ever made in this country is the Colt Single Action Army. Like all revolvers, it is subject to cylinder related problems. I came across one recently in dire need of corrective action. With the help of Clay Merrill, an experienced young pistolsmith with Saddleback Gunsmithing located in Dana Point, California, I managed to get the old Colt SAA back in shooting shape with a minimum amount of work, and with a lot of Clay's experience and own ingenuity.

This particular Colt obviously had been owned by a person who had shot it quite regularly, but cared little for the tasks of care and general cleaning. Close examination revealed that the forcing cone must have had extensive lead build-up at one time; obviously the build-up had become so serious as to cause cylinder rotation problems. The owner apparently solved this situation by removing the cylinder and running a file across the chambers. He not only removed the lead, but also managed to create a gap between the front of the cylinder and the rear face of the barrel that far exceeded safety limits. His amateurish use of the file was apparent, as there were low spots on each side of the forcing cone, but little metal removed from the center portion. This bit of stupidity meant that the barrel had to be set back and the forcing cone recut. (This repair is covered in a different chapter.

The cylinder could be moved by hand forward and backward on the base pin bushing approximately .200-inch. It appeared as though the gun had also had some very hot rounds fired through it which peened back to the front of the base pin bushing. This meant replacement of the bushing to cure the excessive headspace and the cylinder and forcing cone gap.

Merrill checked his inventory of replacement Colt parts and found the two base pin bushings he had on hand were too short to solve the situation. However, a bit of creative thinking quickly produced a working solution. Merrill took one of the new (but short) base pin bushings and inserted it into the cylinder. Using a depth micrometer with the base sitting on top of the ratchet pads he learned that the new bushing was .156-inch too short. Before measuring, he did face off the pads on a lathe to secure a true reading.

His plan was simple, but effective. He cut off a length of the old base pin bushing slightly longer than necessary, then set up the newly cut piece in the lathe and faced off both ends to square them. To cut the piece to the exact length required he painted on some Dykem and marked the piece for the proper length. Back in the lathe, it took only a few moments to cut the piece to exactly the length required.

Using a piece of flat steel, he placed the newly cut piece of base pin bushing into the cylinder and next, the new base pin bushing. After carefully measuring the two pieces inserted for proper length, he carefully placed the cylinder back into the Colt SAA frame to check for cylinder rotation. After a few checks and a bit of judicious stoning on each end of this two-piece bushing, he came up with a perfect fit. To insure smooth rotation, Merrill next stoned each end of the bushing to remove any burrs.

To keep the smaller piece of bushing in place against the bearing surface of the frame he now staked it in place, using a center punch. After checking cylinder rotation and determining the proper gaps at each end of the cylinder, he placed a live round in the cylinder and test fired the gun.

Merrill had completed more than just a simple repair task. He had done it without having to order a new longer base pin bushing which would have taken time to secure. He also accomplished the repair with minimum added expense to the customer, but most importantly, by completely checking the gun he found that it was in need

*With this Colt SAA barrel removed from the frame, the problem of the uneven cylinder/barrel gap is apparent. Someone obviously has attempted to remove lead fouling with a file. Expensive cure is to set the barrel back.*

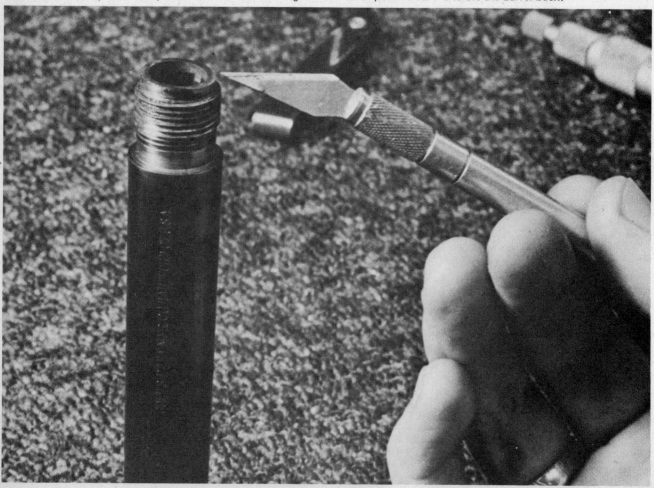

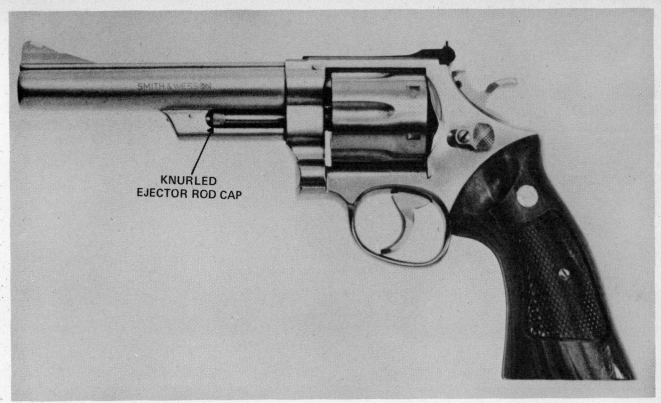

KNURLED
EJECTOR ROD CAP

*The newer Smith & Wesson revolvers have permanently attached ejector rod caps integrated into their design.*

of having the barrel set back. By just going through the normal check on the gun he had found additional work that would make the gun safer and more reliable for the owner.

In the case of the jammed cylinder syndrome, some older Smith & Wesson models, because of their particular design, seem to be the greater offenders. In this situation, the would-be shooter finds that the swing-out cylinder is jammed in place and refuses to open or to rotate. This problem can be caused by abuse, misuse or simple neglect, but usually can be remedied with minimum time and trouble.

Upon inspecting an S&W double-action revolver, one will note a knurled cap on the end of the ejector rod. This cap usually is screwed down tightly on the rod's threads, but there are times when it becomes loose through shooting. When this happens, the cap moves forward and jams against the gun's underlug, which is separated only fractionally. There is no such problem with current models, as the cap is formed as a part of the ejection rod.

Should this happen, the usual immediate action for freeing the cylinder is to pull the trigger rearward just enough to withdraw the handgun's bolt from the cylinder notch. The trigger is held in this position, while the cylinder is rotated clockwise by hand. (Clockwise, incidentally, is the opposite of the normal cylinder rotation cycle for the Smith & Wesson.) This action should result in the cap being

screwed back several turns on the matching threads cut into the ejector rod.

You may find this a trifle difficult and a hit-and-miss proposition, as it takes care and experimentation to draw the trigger back just enough to release the bolt the iota required to allow the necessary cylinder rotation, then releasing it to let the bolt snap back, thus retracting the hand so the cylinder may be turned. The trigger must be manipulated in this fashion for each movement to a new chamber and it may require two or three full rotations of the cylinder in this obviously awkward manner before the ejector rod cap has been screwed back onto the rod proper and there is sufficient space to allow the cylinder to be opened.

Once the cylinder has been opened, I'd suggest removing the cap and then degreasing and coating the threads with Loctite and screwing it down again. This can best be done with a pair of pliers, but I'd suggest using a piece of leather or heavy canvas as a pad between the jaws of the tool and the cap itself. If the bare jaws are used, they no doubt will leave ugly marks on the cap.

In some of the recently produced Smith & Wesson revolvers, gunowners also sometimes experience stiff cylinder rotation or perhaps the cylinder will not rotate at all. This invariably happens when the gun is loaded or when the muzzle of the gun is elevated.

This problem has been solved largely by the factory in current production guns, but it has been found to be caused

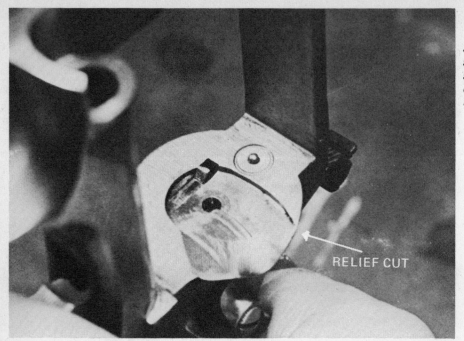

*Sharp edges of relief cut on left side of recoil shield can cause stiff cylinder rotation as rims of cartridges drag. Cure for this is to stone slight bevel, polish.*

RELIEF CUT

*Stiff cylinder rotation can result from fired primers dragging on burrs surrounding the firing pin hole. The remedy is careful stoning, polishing.*

← BURRS NEAR FIRING PIN HOLE

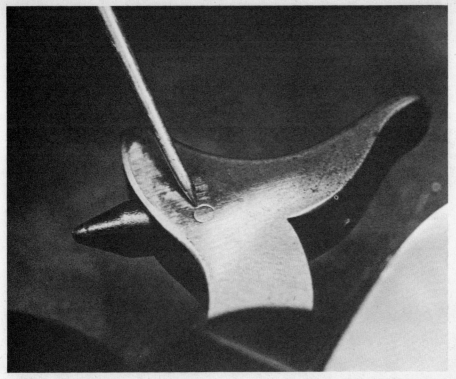

Left: On the Colt Single Action Army revolver, the hammer rivet should be center-punched, then drilled out with progressively larger bits, until the remaining metal can be driven out with a punch and a new pin installed. (Below) Smith & Wesson double-action revolver hammer uses a tubular rivet to hold firing pin in position. Removal can be accomplished in much the same manner as with the solid rivet.

by the sharp edges in the relief cut located on the left side of the recoil shield for the gun's ratchet.

Experimentation has shown that, when the muzzle is elevated, the cartridges tend to slide to the rear in their chambers. Thus, the cartridge rims snag on the lower edge of this cut when the cylinder is being rotated.

The usual remedy in this instance is to file or stone a slight bevel, then polish it smooth. Done properly, the cartridges then should ride over the polished spot with no further problem.

There also are instances wherein a cylinder may rotate freely when loaded, but becomes stiff after the revolver has been fired. The first thing to check for in this situation is the possibility of burrs around the firing pin hole. If they are present, it is possible that the fired primer in the cartridge is hanging up in these burrs. The simple remedy is simply to stone off these burrs. This invariably solves that particular problem.

Pitted firing pins also can create problems. This syndrome is particularly evident in older models in which cartridges with corrosive primers have been fired. In some models, what happens is this: When the firing pin becomes sufficiently pitted due to rusting and corrosive action, this produces excessive clearance around the firing pin's nose. Its shape and length often are altered to such a point that primers are pierced or, if the pin is too short, there is not sufficient striking force to ignite the primer and there is a resulting misfire. There have been frequent cases of metal from the primer cup being forced between the firing pin and the recoil bushing, thus rendering the gun inoperable.

I'd like to say the part is repairable, and in some cases it is, but a less expensive, less time-consuming cure is simply to order a new firing pin from one of the gun parts houses such as Numrich Arms in West Hurley, New York.

Removing the old firing pin and replacing it is no major chore, I've found.

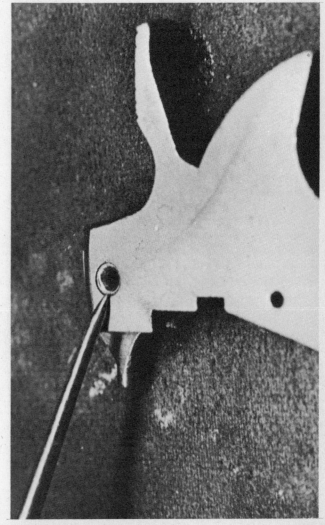

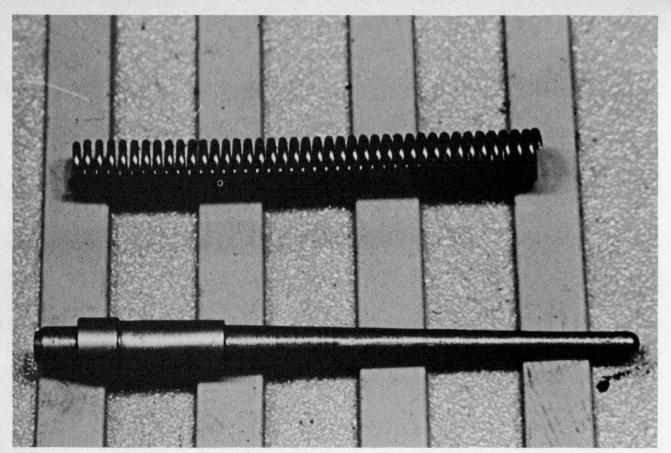

*Many surplus World War II 1911A1 Colt .45 autoloaders were subjected to dry firing in training. This often caused the firing pin head to become badly burred or peened, leading to the pin ultimately tending to jam in the firing pin hole.*

In the case of the Colt revolver, for example, one has to locate the rivet that holds the firing pin in the head of the hammer. This rivet is polished even with the hammer's walls and sometimes can be difficult to see.

Once its location is determined, the rivet is center-punched for positioning, then it is drilled out with increasingly larger bits until it is weakened to the point that it can be driven out with a punch. The new pin then is slipped into place and a new rivet installed. This rivet should be peened on the end to assure a tight fit. It should be finished down so it is flush with the side of the hammer, returning it to its original state.

In the case of the Smith & Wesson revolver and other models following that basic design, the firing pin is retained in loose fashion in the hammer's head with a tubular rivet much more visible than that of the Colt. The same general approach is used for the Smith & Wesson firing pin replacement: The rivet is drilled out, going through its center and increasing the bit size until the soft metal tends to collapse. It then is punched out. The new rivet and replacement pin are inserted and your punch is used to widen the rivet's bases until it fills the recesses in the S&W hammer.

At first consideration, one might think that solving firing pin problems with an autoloader would be more difficult than with a revolver. Such is not the case. In virtually every instance, the problem cure is more simple.

Autos, being available in hammer and hammerless configurations, thus have two different sets of problems. Since there probably are more hammer guns in existence today, we'll take a look at them first.

One of the greatest problems with a hammer-type auto's firing pin is in the gun that has been dry-fired a lot. If you have a World War II surplus 1911A1 Colt .45, this is a problem that is almost automatic, as it was part of the training cycle in those days to train shooters through preliminary dry-firing.

In this situation, the firing pin's protruding head usually becomes burred or even peened. Eventually, this protruding head begins to stick in the firing pin stop.

The easiest cure in this situation is to remove the pin, then use a light hammer to forge the relatively soft metal to its original factory diameter. This requires that the firing pin move freely through the firing pin hole. The protruding head then is smoothed up with stones, making certain the resulting radius equals the original proportions. To finish the job, the pin (sans firing pin spring) must be hardened again by methods described in the chapter on hardening and tempering.

Another frequently found problem involves a bent firing pin, which causes it to jam usually in the forward position. This has been known to cause what is termed a *slam-fire*: When the slide goes home, the protruding firing pin strikes the primer of the fresh round and causes accidental discharge. The dangers are obvious.

Equally obvious is the answer: Replace the bent firing pin with a new one. That's the best and most simple remedy. However, if such a part is difficult to obtain, the firing pin can be removed and carefully straightened, making certain it works smoothly in the action and is of proper overall length. Should it seem soft, reharden and temper as described in the chapter mentioned previously.

Another cause for a jammed firing pin can be the retracting spring, which can become twisted or even broken with heavy use of the auto. The obvious answer is to replace the spring. Other causes of pin jamming include the burring of the surface where a retaining pin passes through the firing pin. In some instances, burrs on the retaining pin proper can create the same problem. Whether on the retaining pin or the surfaces surrounding it, the burrs should be removed, the offending surface polished, then the item hardened and tempered, if required. Similarly, burrs around the firing pin hole can create firing pin jamming. In this situation, one has to ream out the hole, but extreme care must be taken not to cut the hole too large. If this mistake should be made, the easiest answer is to install an oversize firing pin.

Hammerless autoloaders, with rare exceptions, utilize a hollow striker-type firing pin, a lug protruding to engage the sear of the gun. A frequent problem involves this lug, which may become burred or even chipped. Welding is the usual remedy in this instance, but the lug also can be ground down and a new section silver-soldered in place. Should this type of firing pin break at the nose, welding can be used as the means of building up the tip, then filing and stoning the tip back to its proper configuration.

Keep in mind, of course, that if the firing pin is to prove serviceable, it will be necessary to harden and retemper the metal.

Most of this, of course, is predicated on the idea that replacement firing pins usually will be available. However, it is not all that difficult to make your own.

First, you need a piece of drill rod of equal diameter to the largest section of the pin. If there is no exact match, then pick rod that is the next larger size.

*Bent firing pins in autoloaders can jam in the forward position in the firearm's firing pin hole. This can result in a dangerous slam fire, pin hitting the primer.*

COLT SAA
FIRING PIN
BUSHING

Loose firing pin bushings in the Colt Single Action Army or copies can lead to problems, as discussed in the text.

Grinding down the rod to the size of the original firing pin can be a simple chore, if you have a lathe, but the next best thing is a drill press, rotating the rod as it is ground down. If you don't have any of these power tools, there is always the file, but if you're not working by the hour, you'll find turning out a firing pin by hand is less than profitable. I once spent something like nineteen hours while in gunsmithing school making a workable firing pin for a Remington rifle. The requirement there, though, was to do it entirely by hand. It came under the heading of Work Experience or some similarly popular term of modern education.

On the assumption we have a drill press or even a portable hand drill — the latter held firmly in a vise — the piece of drill rod should be chucked tightly into the drill. The length of the pin and a trifle more should be allowed to protrude from the chuck.

With the drill running at medium speed, a sharp file is run across the rod against the direction of rotation, using just enough pressure for a good bite. Using this system, and comparing the drill rod with the original pin from time to time, the new firing pin is formed. When the size and shape are correct, the pin is polished with abrasive cloth or paper, then the head is cut off, leaving a little extra metal for final fitting. Should the pin be cut too short, the only answer is to go back to square one and begin the entire procedure all over again.

In the event your new firing pin is for a model that requires small projections for proper operation in the gun, these can be silver-soldered in place after having been made from scrap steel. This, of course, is done after the pin has been hardened and drawn. In the event that the pin requires cut-outs for crosspins or retaining elements, these cuts are filed into the metal and the head shaped properly prior to the hardening/tempering process.

Another problem specific to the Colt Single Action

*If Colt SAA ejector rod is bent, a replacement may be made from drill rod measuring .250-inch in diameter.*

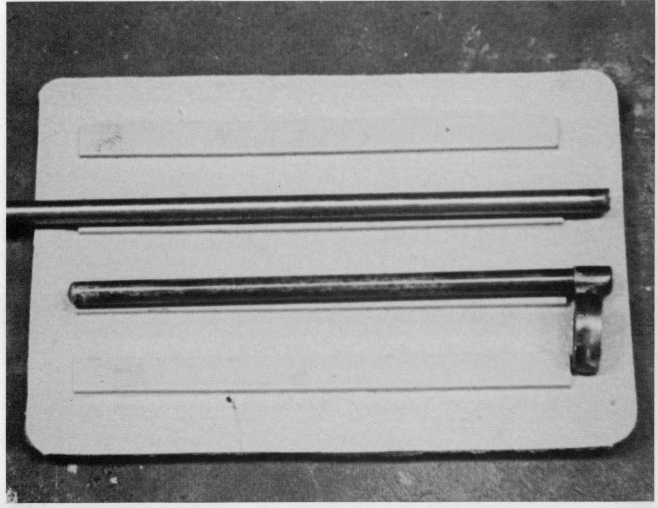

Army model — as well as some other guns that are close copies — has to do with the firing pin bushing. You can determine whether this bushing is loose by checking the recoil shield around the firing pin hole. If burrs are visible or can be felt with the thumb, stone them off carefully. If the firing pin bushing is only slightly loose, you can use a sharp punch to expand the metal on its outer edges and tighten it. This, however, is a temporary measure at best.

A more permanent cure is to replace the loose bushing with a new one. The bushing may be driven out, approaching it from the rear, with a punch somewhat smaller than the diameter of the firing pin hole. This is accomplished best with the frame clamped in a padded vise.

Fitting the new bushing is a bit more complicated. First, you have to remove the barrel so there is room to use a crimping tool. If a gunsmith does a lot of this type of work, he can make up a special tool from a piece of steel tubing. Simply file inner and outer bevels to fit, then reharden the steel so it will not bend on the edges or peen when in use.

Before the new firing pin bushing is installed, the hole in the frame into which the bushing fits should be cleaned thoroughly and degreased. It also is an excellent idea to degrease the new bushing. A liberal application of Loctite to both the hole and the bushing can assure holding the bushing in place permanently following repair.

Thus coated, the bushing is driven into place from the front. For this, most pistolsmiths favor a flat-faced punch, passing it through the barrel hole in the frame for straight-on contact with the bushing. When the operation is completed, the bushing should be seated to its full depth in the hole and should be flush with the recoil shield. If it protrudes above the recoil shield, this can lead to problems, but we'll get to that in a minute.

The newly installed bushing has to be crimped into place using the crimping tool fashioned from steel tubing. To do this the tool is aligned with the perimeter of the face of the bushing. The end of the tool then is struck with a hammer so that its edges cut into the recoil shield. This will force the lip of the bushing hole over the slight bevel on the edges of the bushing. A word of caution here: Care must be taken in positioning the crimping tool, for if it should be struck in off-center fashion, the resulting crimp can be crooked and the bushing seated at an angle. That usually means starting the whole job over again.

As mentioned earlier, if the bushing protrudes above the recoil shield, this tends to reduce the SAA's headspace to less than the required minimum for proper function. The protrusion also can catch on the cartridge rims and may result in cylinder jamming.

The remedy is to file down the excess material until the proper .060-inch headspace is achieved. If the bushing still is above the level of the recoil shield, it is wise to bevel, then polish the left side of the bushing so there will be no hangup of cartridge rims and thus no problem with cylinder rotation.

While it will not keep the single action from shooting, a bent ejector rod can lead to continuing frustrations. Replacement rods, with the necessary springs, et cetera, are available for most models. Frankly, I'd suggest such replacement as the easiest route, when it comes down to figuring what your time as a gunsmith is worth. There are those, too, who recommend a new rod be fashioned from drill rod, saying that the replacement usually is stronger and more durable than the original. True, but it does take a good deal of time.

The other resort, of course, is to remove the bent rod and straighten it. This usually can be accomplished by some diligent work with a soft hammer and a good deal of care not to batter the rod out of shape.

At the same time, it probably will be a good idea to replace the ejector rod spring. It may have become rusted or twisted, thus making it too weak to hold the rod solidly in its forward position. Again, replacement springs are readily available, or you may want to wind a new one of steel wire as outlined in the chapter on spring-making.

Another frequent ejector system problem involves the housing attachment screw which may have been badly abused. This short screw is somewhat fragile in that it is screwed into only a few threads in the stud on the single-action's barrel. These threads are easily stripped either through misuse or because the screw loosens during firing and the resulting battering damages the threads on either the screw or the stud. If the screw threads are damaged, the problem is solved easily enough: simply replace the screw. At the other extreme, if it is the threads in the stud that have been damaged, it may be necessary to weld up the hole. The solid metal then is drilled out and retapped to accept the new screw.

The stud itself can present a problem. If the housing does not fit tightly over this stud, there can be excessive wear. Sometimes, it is necessary to build up the stud with welding material, then file it down for a proper tight fit. In instances wherein the stud may have been broken off entirely, you can get a replacement barrel with the stud already installed or you can build up a new stud by welding, then file it down to its original shape. Of course, if you get carried away with your files and cut away too much metal, you're back in the same spot and have to do the welding build-up all over again. In some instances, it is possible to drill out what is left of the broken stud and silver solder a new stud into the hole.

The aforementioned probably cover the most frequent problems one will find in both autoloaders and revolvers, when it comes to a failure to fire or to function properly.

*Attachment stud for ejector housing may need repair or replacement. Silver soldering a replacement is simple, fast, but a new piece must be made on the lathe. Here the ejector bushing hole is being drilled in new barrel. Work has been set in a milling machine for accuracy. (Inset) New ejector housing bushing is midway through completion on lathe. It will be silver soldered in place. This job requires total accuracy to be done properly.*

When working on any double-action revolver, it is important to check for a phenomenon known as "push off." This is an initial check for sear engagement.

This problem usually is caused by amateurish attempts at a trigger job. The problem centers around uneven stoning on sears or hammer in order to lighten trigger pull. The test by the gunsmith involves pulling the hammer back to full cock, then with a medium amount of pressure using the thumb placed behind the hammer, pushing the hammer forward. If the hammer should fall with exertion of this gentle thumb pressure, immediate corrective action will be necessary to correct the problem by truing up the sear engagements.

Another quick check any pistolsmith should make while examining a double action revolver is to determine whether there is sufficient hammer spring tension to detonate the primers in the cartridge. There seems to be a tendency to attempt to create a silk-smooth action and extremely light trigger pull. The latter, in most cases, renders the handgun unreliable.

What actually is happening is that an amateur has worked on the hammer spring in his attempts to smooth the action to lighten the trigger; in reality, the spring has been so weakened by removal of metal or bending that it no longer meets factory standards for reliable operation.

If the spring does appear weak upon initial inspection — but does not appear to have been altered — the pistolsmith should check the strain screw setting. Corrective action involves replacement of the weakened or damaged spring with new factory springs or simply resetting the hammer spring strain screw to proper position.

# SIGHTS:
## Installation & Alteration

### Chapter 9

## Sighting Devices Are A Matter Of Personal Choice, But Installation Measures Are Basic

PISTOL SHOOTING and competition are enjoying a tremendous growth and popularity today. The recent founding of the International Handgun Metallic Silhouette Association (IHMSA) and the popular PPC competition have placed greater demands on sight manufacturers and pistolsmiths for more accurate, durable and reliable sights for pistols.

Since most pistols are designed as short-range shooters, solving the problem of long-range accuracy has brought about numerous design innovations and unique installation techniques in recent years. Some are quite good, and some are poor. Most expert pistolsmiths agree on two points: first, at present there is no perfect sight for all types of shooting; second, proper shooting techniques must be practiced by the shooter to record good scores at the range.

Armand Swenson, a top pistolsmith, passes on to new pistol shooters some sage advice given him by Jim Clark, one of the great shooters of all time: "The most important six inches in pistol shooting is between your ears."

Swenson urges competitive pistol shooters to dry fire practice at least five minutes every day. A good grip is

essential to accuracy. He teaches students to pull the gun back into the web of the hand between thumb and shooting finger in line with the arm. Learn trigger finger control so as not to disturb sight alignment. And watch sight alignment, not the target. Unless a pistol shooter learns and practices good techniques, he never will score well, no matter how good the sights.

Pistol sights generally may be broken down into two categories; fixed and adjustable. There also are various rib/sight combinations available, which will be discussed later. There is no shortage of choices offered by manufacturers today. Each has good and bad points. Fixed sights offer durability and can be extremely accurate. Adjustable sights are more versatile for shooting at different ranges and with varying loads, but subject to breakage and unwanted movement. The type of shooting, the intended use for the handgun, the particular loads the gun will be firing, the personal preference of the shooter, the adaptability of the sight to the firearm, even the weather conditions, all are factors to be considered in determining whether a fixed or adjustable sight should be installed.

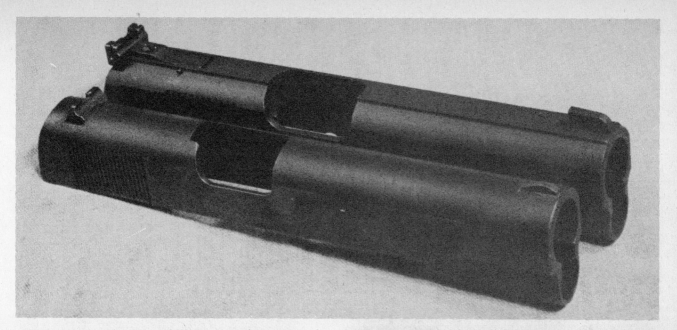

Pistol sights may be broken into fixed and adjustable categories. Both have strong, weak points. (Below) the fixed rear sight on the Colt Model P is created by milling out the topstrap. Although this arrangement is for a durable sight, it is not conducive to accuracy.

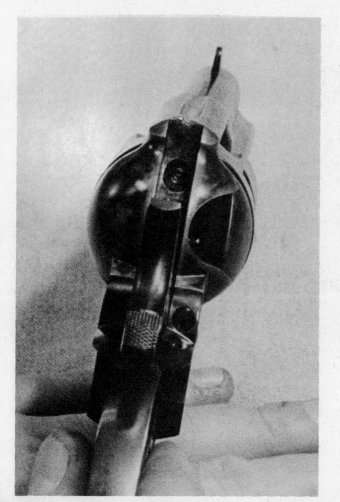

As a result of long experimentation, pistolsmith Armand Swenson prefers adjustable sights with the least amount of mass to withstand energy force created by gun recoil.

Adjustable sights seem more popular with today's competitive shooters, but can create certain problems for the novice shooter. An old adage states that, if you give someone an option, chances are he'll take it. Such options have resulted in beginning shooters using adjustable sights only to incur more problems than they solve. Oftentimes the new shooter will spend more time adjusting his sights for better shot groups than in perfecting his shooting style. In most cases, adjustable sights should be zeroed to the proper point of bullet impact, then left alone. It is recognized that most beginning right-handed shooters will shoot left and low; beginning left-handed shooters will shoot right and low. Adjusting the sights to compensate for

The fastest, most precise way for installing the S&W adjustable rear sight on a Colt .45 slide is with the use of a good milling machine.

After milling out, the auto slide is cleaned up to remove any burrs and to insure an exact fit of the sight.

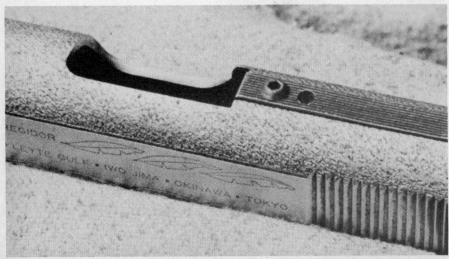

The back of the slide also must be cut down to accommodate a new S&W adjustable sight. Swenson redrills the factory sight hole for a 5/40 screw for better and more secure holding. Factory screw is 3/56.

Austin Behlert's Smith & Wesson replacement sight has 20 clicks of adjustment per revolution, which means the shooter has a total of 240 clicks for proper sighting.

this tendency only reinforces improper shooting techniques.

Adjustable rear sights certainly have their place in today's competitive shooting matches. There are many good reasons for their acceptance and popularity. Possibly the best, or at least the most popular, are the Smith & Wesson adjustable sights that have been around since the 1930s. Pinpoint accuracy can be achieved by fine-tuning the windage and elevation screws and reset for different ranges with the aid of a screwdriver. They adapt well to pistols such as the Colt Single Action revolver and the Colt Government 1911 .45.

The addition of S&W adjustable sights to these two venerable sidearms along with new and higher front sights makes a world of difference to the accuracy of either. If part of the sight should become damaged, replacement

One of the better fixed sights for the Colt .45 auto is manufactured by King's Gun Works. It is quite simple to install. After sighting-in a pistol with new sights, an index mark should be made on the sight and on the slide.

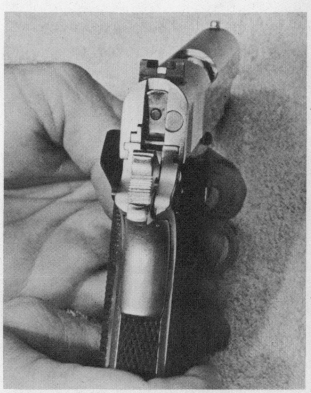

King's Tappan fixed sight provides excellent alignment picture. Same loads should be used in the handgun after sighting in, as bullet strike can shift accordingly.
(Left) MMC adjustable sight for Smith & Wesson Models 39 and 59 adapts easily, can be installed by pistolsmithing amateurs with the complete step-by-step instructions.

blades or other parts are readily available. And the aesthetically pleasing appearance of the S&W adjustable sights on a revolver topstrap or auto slide have made them a favorite of many of today's top shooters.

There are some other adjustable sight manufacturers that have brought a new meaning to accuracy in pistol shooting as well. One of the best is Miniature Machine Company, known simply as MMC Sights (210 E. Poplar, Deming, New Mexico 88030). This firm produces a wide variety of pistol sights consistently found on guns in the winner's circle. An important plus is that they adapt easily to most of today's better revolvers and autoloaders. They sit low, are quite light, easy to install, and are compact enough to reduce chances of breakage to a great extent. Their adjustable sights for the S&W Models 39 and 59 are excellent. A gross adjustment of 36 MOA (minutes of angle) provides nine inches each at twenty-five yards for both elevation and windage. And they are simple to install.

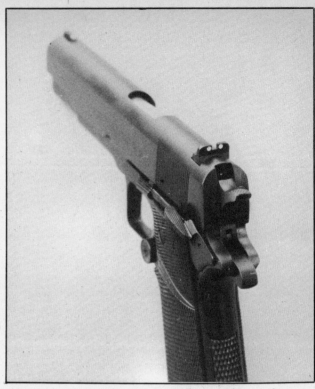

Behlert's new three-dot fixed sight for the .45 auto is finding increasing popularity in handgunning circles.

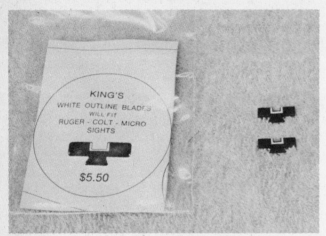

Replacement rear sight blades for adjustable sights are simple to install. These blades from King Gun Works are available in several variations for shooter's preference.

Austin Behlert of Union, New Jersey, also produces quality adjustable sights. His sights for Rugers and Dan Wessons have sixteen clicks each, with twenty clicks elevation on S&Ws per revolution (240 clicks in all). They offer a .110-inch notch width which aids in accuracy on longer-barreled guns. The Behlert sights, made of 4130 steel heat-treated to Rockwell 40, are quite simple to install and are compatible with S&Ws, Ruger Blackhawks, Security Sixes, Old Armys, all Dan Wesson models and the High Standard Crusader.

A popular adjustable sight for automatics is the High

Austin Behlert now manufactures a rib for handguns incorporating the new sight kit in S&W design.

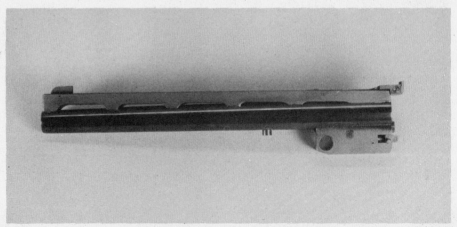

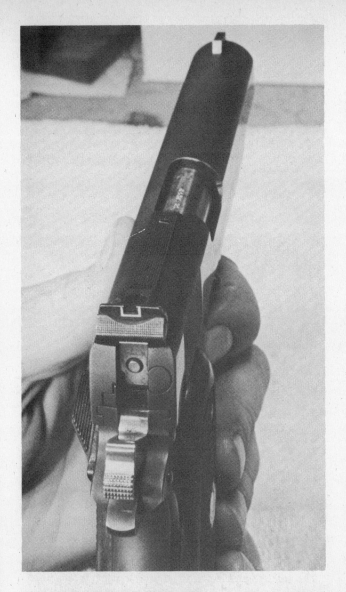

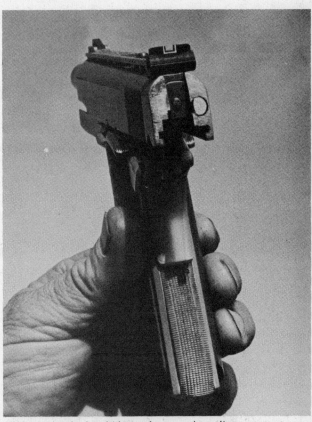

Left: Installed on the Colt .45 auto, the S&W adjustable sight offers a pleasing appearance. Note custom metal checkering that has been done on lower portion of sight.

Ribbed pistols should have the non-glare rib top to cut down on glare. The rib adds weight to the handgun, but many shooters insist it improves the handling qualities.

Rib installation often is more simple than individual front, rear sights. Bo-Mar manufactures rib arrangements for autos that fits the slide's contour. The unit is anchored to the slide with screws and with a dovetail.

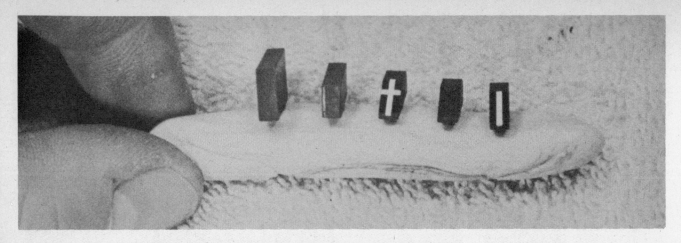

Front sights are available in several sizes, shapes, widths. Unramped sights can catch on a holster, clothing. This should be considered for police guns. (Left) Selection of sights is based on the best visibility factor. These are made by MMC.

Micro produced by Micro Sight Company. These sights also adapt easily and installation can be accomplished by the amateur. There is currently an installation performed by pistolsmiths using this company's products called Melted Micro's. This involves a process which contours the sight to the slide for both pleasing appearance and compactness.

Even with the many new innovations of today's sight manufacturers they would be hardpressed to beat the old King Target sights. These pre-WWII sights featured a chrome insert as part of the front sight to aid in reflecting light and are one of the better adjustable sights ever made.

And speaking of kings, King's Gun Works of Glendale, California, offers excellent adjustable sight blades for many of today's target pistols, as well as a complete line of other target pistol accessories.

Heavier sights for pistols are produced by Bo-Mar, which also produces a highly regarded rib sighting arrangement for both revolvers and automatics. Installation of the Bo-Mar rib actually is simpler than installing individual front and rear sights. It fits as a single unit and many shooters like the non-glare sighting plane of the matte-finished top. It does add weight to the gun, but some contend this improves handling qualities.

The greatest problem with adjustable sights is reliability. They can be bent or broken when treated roughly. Since they are subjected to heavy forces during firing, they may

With the replacement front sight held in place with the staking tool, a shear is placed in the fixture and one good rap with plastic hammer stakes new sight in place

This front sight staking tool from Miniature Machine Co. makes task of staking a new front sight a simple matter.

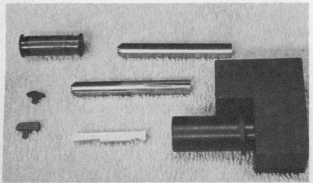

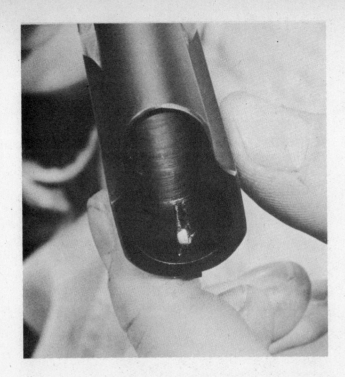

*Using the MMC staking tool, the new sight is staked in place on the underside of the new slide. The author feels that this tool is a good investment for time savings.*

can be counted upon to shoot in the same place each time, which is essential to law enforcement types.

There also are fixed sights that can be made extremely accurate. Generally they are sighted-in for target or combat shooting by starting with a high front sight. The gun is placed in a rest and shot-in by removing metal from the front sight until bullet strike is right on target at a set distance. Fixed sight pistols also can be made to shoot more to the left or right by removal of metal on either side of the fixed rear sight. However, it usually is better to tap the rear fixed sight left or right and re-stake permanently in place.

not always remain in perfect adjustment. Rear sight pins can shear due to strain during recoil. If the sight is made of aluminum to reduce weight, the roll pin hole can enlarge causing a loose sight.

Many of the aforementioned companies also manufacture fixed sights. Some fixed sights are nothing more than milled-out areas of the frame itself. Although this type is not as accurate as an adjustable sight, the assumption is that the firearm will shoot approximately where it is pointed; that at short ranges, in a real life defensive situation, they are adequate to accomplish the task. There is no question that they are stronger than adjustable sights, thus making them more reliable. And they

*After installation of the new sight, a touch-up with cold bluing finished the job. (Left) In installing the front sight, the use of soldering talc on the slide prevents excess silver solder from sticking to the slide. This can eliminate time-consuming cleanup work.*

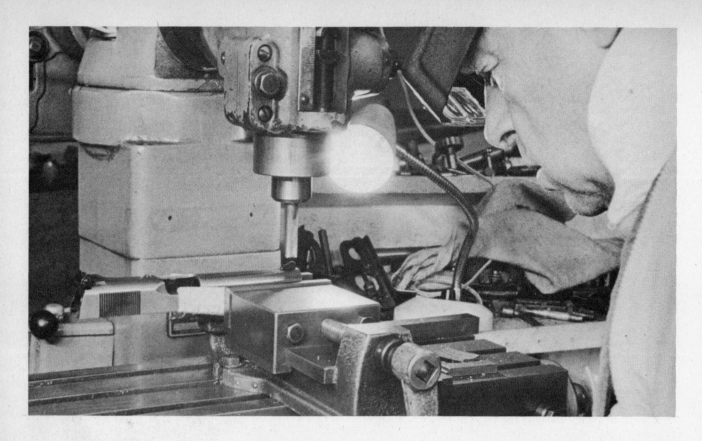

Armand Swenson sights in with adjustable sights that allow him to remove exactly the right amount of metal from the front sight to have the rear sight seated at lowest position and still be zeroed in. (Below) Swenson checks plumb of the front sight by seating the sight and slide in a mill vise, then ensuring the proper 90-degree angle.

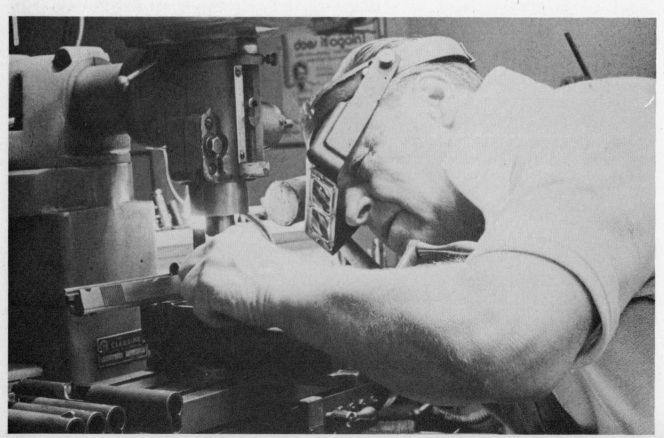

If you should be cutting on the rear sight, make sure you widen the side of the rear sight blade that you wish the strike of the bullet to move toward. In other words, widening the notch on the right side of the sight blade will have the effect of moving the strike of the bullet to the right. When attempting to move the strike of the bullet by altering the front sight, you must remove metal from the side of the blade in which you want the bullet to move also. For example, removing metal from the left side of the front sight will move the strike of the bullet to the left. After properly sighting in a good fixed sight arrangement on a pistol, the shooter knows that as long as he fires the same loads at the sighted-in distance, he can achieve outstanding accuracy.

There is a veritable plethora of front sights in all sizes, shapes and configurations available to pistol shooters today. Selecting just the right one to complement the rear sight arrangement is largely a matter of personal preference. It is important that the front sight displace light properly to make for a clear sight picture. The sight should be of the proper height to shoot accurately in the X-ring at a particular distance, wide enough to pick up easily through the rear sight. The front sight also should be narrow enough to allow strips of light to be seen through the rear sight on either side of the front blade, usually from one-sixth to one-fourth the width of the front blade.

Armand Swenson feels that a narrower front sight and rear sight combination, say .125-inch, is more suited to a young shooter that has the eyesight to quickly pick up the sight alignment, whereas an older shooter should have a wider rear/front sight alignment.

The determining factor is the sight combination that gives the particular shooter the best sight picture quickly and precisely in the best available light situation.

Installation of front and rear sights, whether adjustable or fixed, can be accomplished by the amateur in many cases. However, special tools and experience sometimes are necessary. If so, these jobs are better left to the professional.

Adjustable pistol rear sights for .45 autos need not

*The Colt Model P's accuracy can be increased greatly with the installation of Smith & Wesson J-frame adjustable sights. This operation, which requires a great deal of care, is initiated with the use of the milling machine.*

Pistolsmith Clay Merrill cuts a recess in the back of topstrap to accommodate windage/elevation portion of the new rear sight.

With the J-frame S&W rear sight fitted to the Colt's topstrap, removal of metal from the top of the hammer is necessary to clear the bottom of the sight.

discourage the amateur, if he chooses a sight such as the MMC. The dovetail may have to be modified, using a file, but if care and patience are employed it isn't much of a job. The sight must be disassembled before installation and the windage screw does have to be staked into the windage nut. A thin-bladed screwdriver will work as a staking tool. If the front sight also is to be replaced, it is a good idea to have an MMC staking tool. After driving out the old front sight, this tool is used to stake the new front sight to the slide. Professionals such as Swenson also silver braze the new sight in place.

Armand Swenson prefers to mill out a ramp about .040-inch deep for new front sights on .45 autos. He cuts a piece of solder and inserts it between the slide and the new front sight. The arrangement is held in place by a clamp. However, between the clamp and the sight a piece of paper is placed to serve as a heat dam. This prevents heat being drawn off by the clamp. Swenson then heats the solder from

the inside of the slide at the back of the front sight region.

As soon as the solder begins to melt, he moves the torch to the front of the slide region and the solder is sucked from one end to the other as clean and neat as a whistle. Not only is this an efficient way to accomplish this project, but it prevents excess solder from blowing all over the outside of the slide.

Swenson also uses another ingenious method of installing sights on .45 autos. After installation of adjustable rear sights and a new front sight that is purposely too high, he takes the gun to a range and elevates the rear sight as high as necessary to get the pistol to shoot accurately. He then checks the distance between the bottom of the rear sight and the gap to the top of the slide where the front sight ordinarily would sit on in its lowest setting. For this he uses a feeler gauge. If the gap is .047-inch for example, Swenson files exactly .047-inch off the top of the front sight. Then the rear sight can be reset

An extremely efficient method of silver brazing the front sight blank to the .45 auto slide is used by Swenson. He heats the area to be brazed from inside of the slide, starting at the rear and drawing heat to muzzle end. It is quick and eliminates excess solder cleanup. (Below) After Swenson silver brazes the new front sight in place and determines the exact sight height desired, he will serrate the ramp as aid to better, faster sight picture.

*The Eldorado front sight ramp from United Sporting Arms was chosen by Clay Merrill for Colt Model P. A colored insert will be epoxied in place after the ramp has been silver brazed to revolver barrel.*

to its lowest position on the slide and be exactly on target. It is simple, but highly effective.

When using an acetylene torch to solder on front sights, it is best to use a low oxidizing flame to reduce scale. This flame is recognized easily by its long yellow flame caused by less oxygen. Hot enough to run the solder, this setting reduces the chance of damaging barrels and slides.

Clay Merrill, in installing a United Sporting Arms Eldorado sight on a Colt Model P, first wedged a wooden dowel down the barrel before running the solder with his acetylene torch. His theory is that this dowel will be burned up when the barrel is heated. This produces carbon on the inside of the barrel, reducing any chance of scaling.

Whenever installing a front sight by silver brazing, it is a good idea to rub welder's chalk around the area adjacent to where the sight is to be soldered. The chalk should not come in contact with the area to be soldered, however. This procedure will prevent any excess solder from sticking to surrounding areas, thus necessitating additional cleanup.

There are times when a milling machine is necessary to install rear sights. Such is the case when installing a J-frame S&W adjustable sight to a Colt Model P revolver. The cut in the topstrap of the pistol should be slightly undersize and checked before final fitting. Exact alignment of the pistol in the milling machine is a must, if the sight is to align exactly with the front sight. Also, in this particular job, it is necessary to remove part of the top of the hammer as the rear of the S&W sight sits low enough in its ramp to cause problems.

When installing adjustable rear sights such as the S&W, it is a good idea to replace the factory shear pins with hardened drill rod of the proper diameter. Swenson cuts the

*Smoke issuing from the end of the revolver barrel is being caused by burning of a fitted wooden dowel before the silver brazing operation begins. The dowel burning during the operation reduces the possibility of barrel scale.*

New front sight on Smith & Wesson Model 29 is ready for installation of colored insert. Such sights can chip or fall out due to the heavy recoil of such a caliber.

This group fired offhand at 25 yards by gunsmith Armand Swenson is just under 1¼ inches, proof that a professionally accurized Colt .45 auto with a good sighting arrangement can produce outstanding accuracy. Of course, experience, good shooting techniques also are essential.

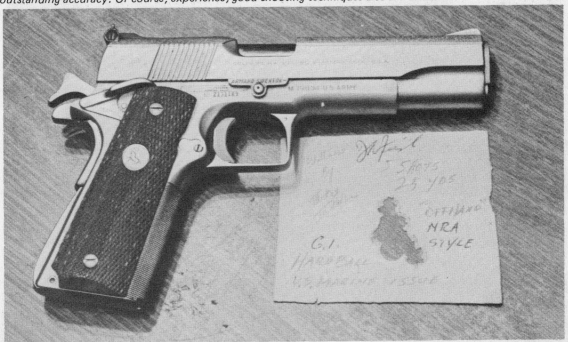

new drill rod shear pins with a dome shape at one end. Thus, when he hammers the new shear pin in place, the mass of the steel is forced into and around the shear pin hole to secure it in place. He also uses a 5/40 screw instead of the original 3/56 factory screw for a more durable arrangement.

Installation of sights such as the Bo-Mar requires a milling machine to cut away the original dovetail as well as part of the slide in order to have the sight sit as low as possible. This is a job for the professional and I do not recommend it be tried by an amateur.

Adjustable sights are secured either by dovetailing, staking, screwing, pinning, or silver brazing. More often than not, a combination of the above is used. Industrial adhesives also may be used in conjunction with the above methods. With the tremendous energy produced by the

firing, other methods usually prove futile.

Front sights can often be staked, pinned, silver brazed, and/or drilled and tapped for screws to hold them to the barrel. The larger the front sight, the greater the mass and the more holding surface is required to retain it in place.

Rib sights are simple to install. After driving out the original sights, only minor file work usually is necessary to fit the new rib dovetail to the existing slide. The whole arrangement then is screwed to the slide. The holes are predrilled. The bottom of the rib also is contoured to fit closely and securely on slides on .45 autos, for example. All holes, though, should be deburred and trimmed so as not to interfere with functioning. You also may wish to stake the dovetail blank or rear sight and file to a pleasing contour. Should there be a loose fit, one can dimple the inside of the slide's dovetail which will raise the metal for a tighter fit.

# The Question Of Restoration Versus Customization Gets One Answer Here!

## Chapter 10

# REBUILDING

This 1896 Mauser military pistol was turned over to the author with an inoperable safety mechanism. All metal surfaces were pitted deeply, numerous edges and contours had been obliterated by amateurish work with a file.

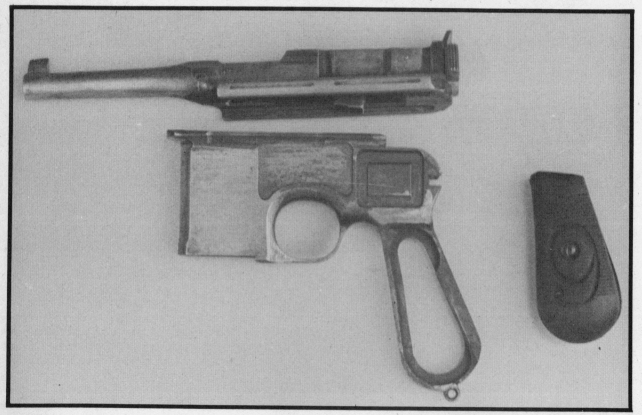

# The Junker

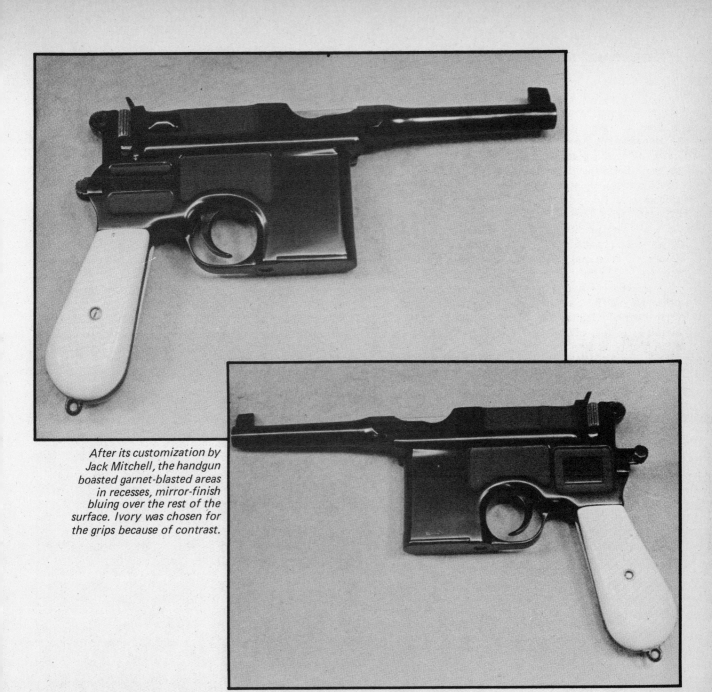

After its customization by Jack Mitchell, the handgun boasted garnet-blasted areas in recesses, mirror-finish bluing over the rest of the surface. Ivory was chosen for the grips because of contrast.

"**N**EVER DO any work on a gun that will lessen its overall value." That rule was preached more than once by gunsmithing instructors during my training at the Colorado School of Trades gunsmithing school. I'm sure this sage advice still is being heard at that and other serious gunsmithing institutions around the country. Any gunsmith found guilty of this practice would be branded forever as a gun hack not to be trusted with quality firearms.

A gunsmith earns his reputation by the quality of his work and, equally important, his honesty. Horsetrading for a firearm and getting a good deal is good business. Stealing a valuable firearm from some poor widow by paying her a fraction of the gun's true worth is the second fastest way I know of ruining a gunsmith's business. The fastest way is to take in work that will reduce the firearm's value. This is one

instance, incidentally, wherein the customer is not always right.

The best example of this doctrine occurred for me while a student at gunsmithing school. A fellow totally unaware of the value of a nice Browning Superposed shotgun walked into the school one day and requested that one of the students cut the factory thirty-inch barrels down to the minimum legal length. He knew nothing of hunting or the gun's value and simply wanted a man-stopper around the house for protection. After careful explanation to the fellow that such work would greatly depreciate the value of the shotgun, he still wished the work to be done.

The instructor informed him that he would buy the gun at a fair market price, but refused to cut the barrels of this fine shotgun. The customer departed quite angry, but the instructor was adamant in his refusal. He may have lost a paying customer, but he maintained the integrity of the school.

Knowing how to restore a gun expertly is an art almost unto itself. Knowing when is equally difficult. The key seems to lie in the ability to evaluate its condition initially. There are several good books available dealing with the subject of restoration. One of the best is the *NRA Gun Collectors Handbook*. This book lists three fundamentals for evaluating condition and value of a collector firearm: 1. What it is (constant). 2. Present demand (variable). 3. Condition (constant). We will deal with these factors presently using our test gun in this chapter as an example.

The NRA Gun Collectors Committee, working with other NRA-affiliated gun collectors associations, has put forth a set of condition standards that have been officially adopted by the NRA. These standards according to the NRA handbook are:

**Factory New** — all *original* parts; one hundred percent original finish; in perfect condition in every respect, inside and out.

**Excellent** — all *original* parts; over eighty percent original finish; sharp lettering, numerals and design on metal and wood; unmarred wood, fine bore.

**Fine** — all *original* parts; over thirty percent original finish; sharp lettering, numerals and design on metal and wood; minor marks in wood; good bore.

**Very Good** — all *original* parts; none to thirty percent original finish; *original* metal surfaces smooth with all edges sharp; clear lettering, numerals and design on metal; wood slightly scratched or bruised; bore disregarded for collector firearm.

**Good** — some minor replacement parts; metal smoothly rusted or lightly pitted in places, cleaned or reblued; principal lettering, numerals and design on metal legible;

*Improper use of the safety on the Bolo Mauser created a large burr on the camming surface of the gun's hammer.*

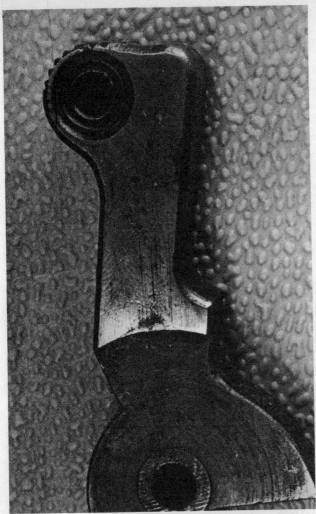

*Disassembly of the Mauser revealed interior parts as well as external to be quite rough. The hammer boss would require smoothing with the use of hard Arkansas stones.*

*This photo shows the lack of roughness after surfaces have been draw-filed, then polished with progressively finer grades of abrasive grit papers as told in text.*

wood refinished, scratched, bruised, or minor cracks repaired; in good working order.

Fair — some major parts replaced; minor replacement parts may be required; metal rusted, may be lightly pitted all over, vigorously cleaned or reblued; rounded edges of metal and wood; principal lettering, numerals and design on metal partly obliterated; wood scratched, bruised, cracked or repaired where broken; in fair working order or can be easily repaired and placed in working order.

Poor — major and minor parts replaced; major replacement parts required and extensive restoration needed; metal deeply pitted; principal lettering, numerals and design obliterated, wood badly scratched; bruised, cracked or broken; mechanically inoperative; generally undesirable as a collector firearm.

The key word in each of the above classifications is

"original," a major factor in setting standards on firearms in today's collector market.

The NRA evaluation table for firearms is essential to the world of collecting. It classifies guns into specific categories and helps establish a fair market value for firearms. But there are times I believe this grading system stifles creativity within the field of gunsmithing, inadvertently presupposes that one hundred percent factory original is the highest state of the art, and in many cases makes restored guns a poor investment.

My opinion may be regarded as a form of heresy, but let me explain. Since the NRA evaluation method is based upon original factory work, there are many cases wherein a gun is beautifully customized, but the piece is worth less because it is no longer original. And many times, a gun is restored carefully by an expert, but the resultant value can

Both photos illustrate the rough milling cut marks left by the factory in Mauser's manufacture. It was necessary to remove the marks and gouges, straighten and contour the design lines, then polish with a variety of stones and abrasive paper.

146

be far less than had it been left in its original condition. However, if the factory does the restoration work, a different value usually will be placed on the gun.

The decision to restore a firearm is best left to the expert. This is especially true in the field of antique and rare guns. In many instances, value of the piece may be diminished greatly or enhanced, depending upon the particular type of firearm, its rarity and condition. The particular individual or factory that performs the restoration also can be an important factor.

I feel it is a far better investment with many of the more recent production guns to customize rather than restore. In recent gun show visits, I have noted that restored guns have proved to be the most difficult to sell. The answer lies in the economics of the piece. Why would someone looking for a handgun valued at say $400 in mint condition pay $275 for one that has been restored, when he knows, with a bit of patience, he will find what he's really seeking? Almost without exception, guns of relatively recent manufacture that have been restored, no matter how expertly, are more often than not a very difficult item to

sell. But let me argue my case for customization with the particular gun we've chosen for this chapter.

While visiting a friend, the conversation inevitably came around to the topic of guns. Another fellow in attendance informed us that he traded for an old gun that day. Learning I was a gunsmith, he asked if I'd take a look.

His newly acquired 1896 Mauser pistol, in collector's terms, was a post-war rework (1920) manufactured to comply with the Versailles Treaty weapons limitation imposed upon Germany after World War I. Issued to the German police, the slightly less than four-inch barrel — including the chamber — was in 9mm and had fixed sights.

This pistol was one of the first and certainly one of the most successful autoloading pistol designs of the day. The original design, quality of manufacture, and mechanical soundness made it an immediate sales success and an international favorite. Today, this pistol is a highly valued collector item.

Using the NRA's three fundamentals for evaluating condition and value of a collector firearm, the first fundamental is: "What it is." By investigating the date of

*The deep pitting and overall poor condition of the Bolo Mauser is evident on the handgun's external surfaces.*

*Above: Essential tools for doing difficult polishing and contouring work on the Mauser include a variety of stones, selection of wet-and-dry abrasive papers, and wooden blocks for backing paper. It was slow, tedious labor.*
*(Right) The most difficult phase was the careful stoning of the recesses to remove mill marks, using wet stones.*

manufacture, the red 9, the fixed sights, we know that it is a post-war rework. This manufacture was quite rough when compared to the nicely finished pre-WWI models. As it was chambered for the 9mm Parabellum cartridge, finding ammunition would present no problem. Although rather clumsy and not the most comfortable gun to shoot, it does represent a landmark in autoloading pistol design.

The second of the NRA's fundamental questions is: Present demand. The 1896 Bolo Mauser is much sought by serious auto pistol collectors as well as by military collectors. The demand for good, representative pieces far exceeds the available supply, and as this supply continues to decrease, the demand quite naturally will increase, making this firearm a good investment even if purchased at today's market price.

The last NRA fundamental to determine is condition. Close examination of this particular Mauser revealed it to be NRA *fair*. The gun was inoperable, due to a faulty safety mechanism. Overall physical appearance not withstanding, the crude factory finish was quite rough. Worse, someone previously had attempted to remove with a file the deep

pitting which covered nearly all metal surfaces. That someone had been inexperienced and obviously lazy as he had only partially completed his dirty deed before giving up the task. Although he had damaged some of the contours, luckily he had not obliterated any lettering. The piece also looked as though it had been wire brushed; no bluing remained. One of the grips had been broken and amateurishly repaired.

After checking with several knowledgeable collectors, the value of the pistol was determined to be between $200 and $300. The new owner could leave the gun in its present condition. He could have it repaired, polished and blued and use it as a shooter. He could have it extensively restored. Or he could have it customized.

If left in its present condition, the owner would have an inoperable gun which would appreciate in value only slightly over a long period. He could have it repaired, polished and blued which would give him a shooter, but besides the cost, he would have a Mauser that was no longer original — at the bottom rung of the ladder as far as collector value was concerned. He could have the gun

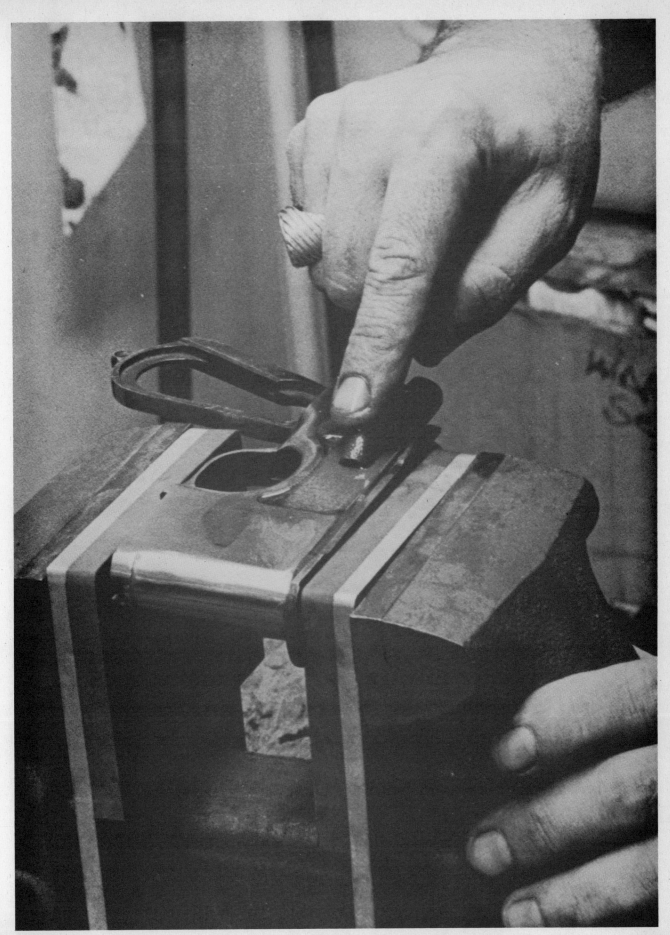

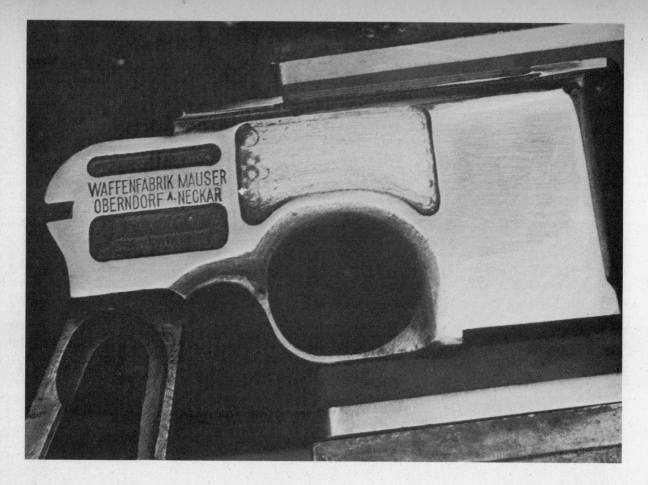

These photos illustrate two stages in which the recessed areas appear during the stoning and polishing processes. The author decided that the edges of these recesses would have to be recut for required clean and sharp appearance.

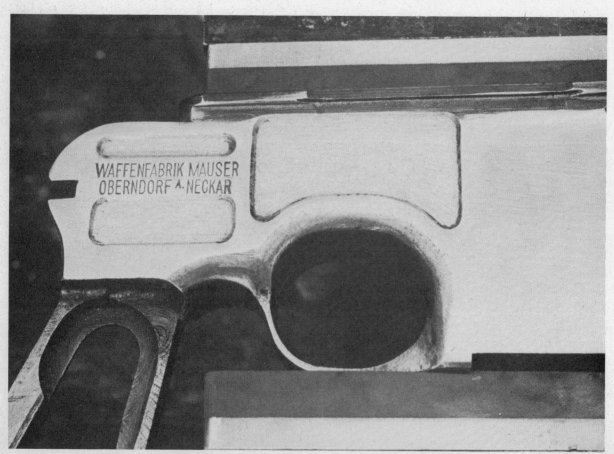

extensively restored, but this particular model, with its original crude factory finishing, would be a poor choice. Since the gun could not be sent back to the factory for restoration, finding someone qualified to do this work would be financially prohibitive. Even if expertly restored by a competent gunsmith, the Mauser probably would end up being classified as a counterfeit and certainly not a good financial investment for a collector.

The option left would be customization of the gun. Other than the repair of a few mechanical problems, the biggest task would be to create an aesthetically pleasing appearance without altering the original Mauser lines.

This last alternative appealed to the Mauser's owner, who had always wanted his own custom pistol. We agreed upon a price for the work and he decided to leave the custom design features to my discretion.

During initial takedown and inspection of the gun, I

remedied the safety problem. The safety was inoperative due to an extremely large burr on the hammer caused by improper handling. Stoning down the burr and using both India and hard Arkansas stones to recontour the damaged area was a relatively quick operation.

I reassembled the pistol and checked it for functioning. I found it to function well and operate reliably. The next step was to smooth all internal working parts. Smoothing steps for autoloaders are described in detail in another chapter.

My next task would prove my mettle. After considering how I wanted the gun to look, it was obvious that a great deal of hand polishing would be necessary. The Bolo Mauser has a great many recesses and contours that would prohibit the use of polishing wheels. Since the gun was so deeply pitted, draw filing would be necessary, but there are many areas on this gun that prohibit use of a file. These

With the frame approximately 80 percent polished, the edges of the recesses have been restored, while all of the pits and machine marks also have been removed. The author found the handwork hard, but results worth effort.

Further polishing on a Norton stone, then with varying grades of abrasive paper should bring surface to a mirror finish.

would have to be polished with a combination of stones and abrasive papers.

With this gun's unusual shape and design, I was trying to keep the customization simple, yet elegant. The first major metalworking requirement was to remove the rough milling machine marks. My first goal was to reach the pre-war quality plateau and proceed from there. My main concern during removal of the original factory milling machine cutter marks and the pitting caused by years of neglect was to keep all of the gun's original contours and design lines intact. As I began working on the metal parts, I realized I could actually recut some of the lines even more true than they had been made at the factory. With careful stoning, it would be possible to improve the contour areas at the top of the magazine region just below where it mated with the slide. Edges around the contours could be made even sharper as I suspect Mauser had originally intended them to be.

I've been told by experts that proper polishing of the metal surfaces of any gun is one of the most important prerequisites to top custom work. Such polishing takes experience and infinite patience. I began by using a file on all metal surfaces. With the numerous recesses on this pistol, though, there were many that prohibit the use of files. These areas, I found, would have to be polished first with India stones. Since a good file cuts metal faster, the requirement for stones certainly slowed my progress. Some of the recessed areas were so narrow that even using stones would not be possible. These spots would be polished starting with 100 grit wet-and-dry paper backed with small pieces of wood cut and contoured specifically for each recess.

I've found that experience is the only measure of knowledge for a gunsmith to know when to put down a coarse grit stone or abrasive paper and switch to a finer grit. If you don't remove the deep scratches and pits when you

*The ivory grips were ordered from Art Jewel Enterprises. They were fitted to the frame, but left oversize, thus allowing for further removal of ivory and metal during polishing of the frame, final contouring by author.*

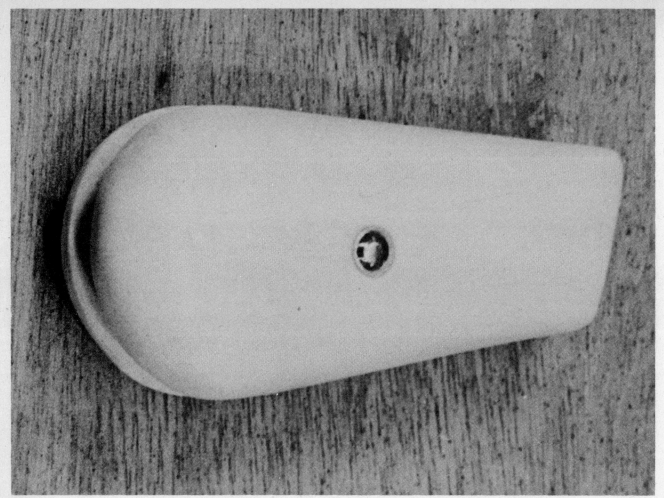

*These ivory grips have been fitted perfectly, final contoured to the Mauser pistol, a painstaking chore. (Right) Working with ivory should not be attempted without a mask and glasses, as ivory dust creates health problems.*

switch from 220-grit paper to 320, you'll have to rub that much harder and longer, accomplishing less. It takes a practiced eye and catching the work at just the right angle in the light to know when to switch to a finer grit stone or paper. The one step always included, no matter which stone or abrasive paper is being used, is to keep the work wet so the stone or paper can cut the metal most effectively. I use kerosene as a wetting agent.

The more time I spent polishing the metal surfaces, the more acute my determination that — with its unusual shape, many contours and the number of irregular recessed areas — when finished, the gun would appear clean, uncluttered and, hopefully, elegant. The many recesses were the most difficult to polish. Using India stones, hard Arkansas stones, and wet-and-dry paper ranging from 100 through 600-grit, I managed to polish most metal surfaces to a mirror finish. By the time I had the recessed areas to about a 500 finish, I decided to have them glass beaded.

The decision to have all recessed areas glass beaded was prompted by a desire to give the overall appearance of the gun more depth, thus contrasting the other mirror-polished surfaces, make it more distinctive and eye appealing.

To prepare the gun for the bead blasting process, all surfaces not to be blasted had to be masked off with tape. The tape was applied by fellow gunsmith, Wayne Novak. Two layers of tape were used to prevent the blasting from wearing through the first layer of tape and striking those regions that were to be mirror finished. Masking off this particular model required time, patience, and careful use of an X-acto knife to cut the tape right to the contour lines without scratching the surface below the tape. The slide was masked first, while masking the frame had to wait until the grips had been properly fitted.

I decided ivory grips should definitely be a part of this gun, as they would be perfect to highlight the deep blue-black finish of the metal. Ivory means class without fanfare; it is held in high esteem in the world of custom firearms and I hoped it would give the Mauser that elegant custom look I sought to achieve.

Since time was growing short to finish this gun, I shipped the frame to the Art Jewel Company, P.O. Box 819, Berkeley, Illinois 60163. Lee Smith, one of their top grip makers, fitted the ivory grips to the frame quickly and expertly and the frame and grips were back in my hands

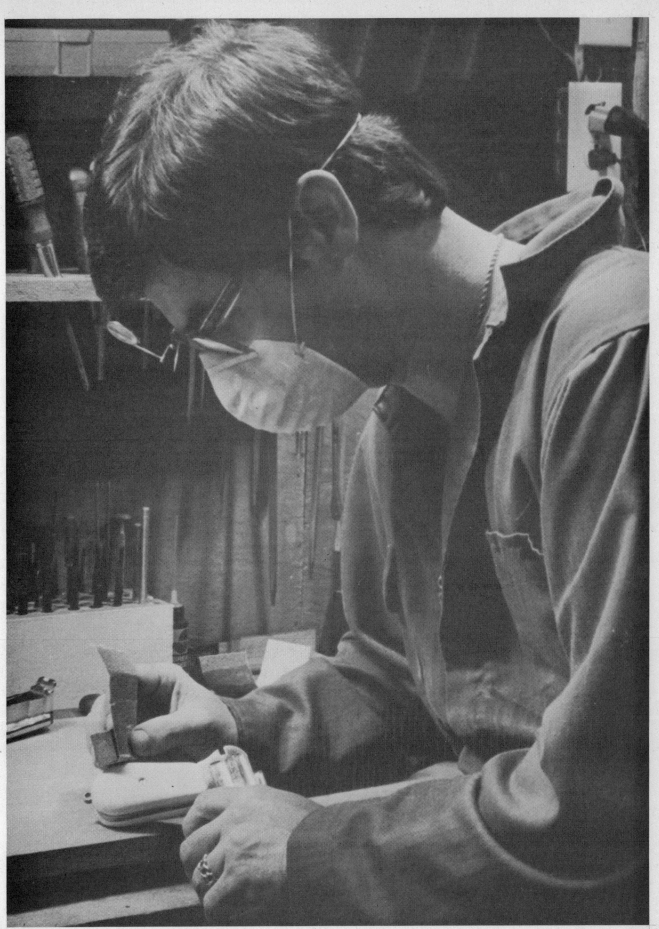

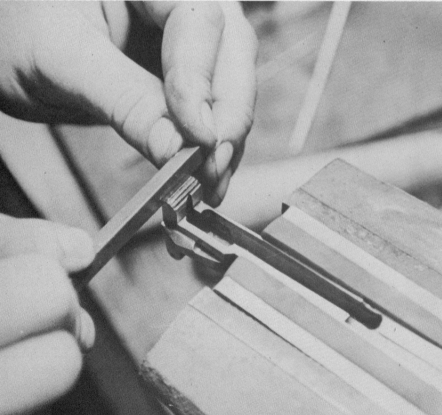

*Above: using royal chrome rouge on the buffing wheel produces a rich deep luster, revealing the characteristic grain of ivory. (Left) Serrated edges on bolt had been damaged, were deeply pitted. Wayne Novak recuts the lines with a triangular stone.*

*With most of the internal parts of the Mauser properly smoothed, they are checked in the gun for proper functioning; final smoothing follows.*

within a few weeks. Lee did not contour the grips, knowing I still would be removing metal from the frame, and final fitting at my end would be necessary.

If you have never worked with ivory, it's like carving a fine piece of French walnut. It is easy to work with and shape. However, the dust is extremely dangerous to the lungs and a mask and safety glasses always should be worn. Although the reason for the mask is self-explanatory, glasses should be worn to prevent the dust from reaching the eyes. Such dust can be quite irritating, so extreme care should be exercised.

Ivory not only carves well, but polishes to a brilliant finish on a buffing wheel. It can be burned so make certain to buff only lightly and do not overheat it. Over the years, ivory will have a tendency to shrink a bit and also to turn a soft yellow color, not unpleasing to the eye. In a class by itself, ivory is a good investment, as the world supply is quickly diminishing.

As mentioned, Lee Smith had left the grips slightly oversize, ensuring there was plenty of excess material to allow me the freedom to contour to any shape I had chosen for the Mauser. I began shaping each grip with 80-grit garnet paper and a piece of wood for backing. This helped to prevent ripples in the work as I removed material. Working with progressively finer grit garnet paper, I finished the hand contouring and polishing with 600-grit wet-and-dry paper used dry in this instance. It took only a few minutes on the buffing wheel to produce a deep luster and bring out the grain giving it distinctive character.

With all of the metal surfaces polished and buffed to their final finish the gun now was masked off completely. The Mauser was taken to Duncan's Gun Shop in San Marcos, California, where Pat Voight, an excellent gunsmith in his own right, examined the piece. Since I'm no expert in the beading process, I left the decision on which type of

grit to his expertise. He felt a heavy sandblasting grit was unnecessary, while fine glass beading would not give the gun the type of contrast I'd been working to accomplish. He decided to use a garnet grit somewhere between fine and medium. The actual blasting took only a few minutes. Duncan's has an excellent commercial blasting machine and Voight was able to give me exactly the right finish.

One of the final steps in the completion of this project was the bluing process. The Weatherby factory in South Gate, California, is within driving distance, so I called and made an appointment to use their bluing tanks. Wayne Novak and I made the trip to the factory and introduced ourselves to Chuck Murray, Weatherby's foreman.

He took us to the bluing room and Wayne Hudson, a fellow I was soon to learn is probably one of the world's top men in his specialty. Hudson has to be one of the big factors that has gained Weatherby its reputation as one of the top bluing centers in the world. The entire bluing process took slightly less than one hour. The results surpassed all my expectations as the Mauser has the deepest blue-black finish I've ever seen on a firearm.

With all major operations now completed, Novak and I assembled the handgun, checked its cycle of operation and test-fired it. We then gave it a thorough cleaning and the job was complete.

Whether or not this gun truly fits into the world of custom category can only be determined by that fraternity of gun collectors, shooters and experts who have final say on such matters. I had been apprehensive in the beginning of this project to customize a pistol that historically fits the collector category.

I learned a lot and had an opportunity to utilize whatever creativity I may possess. I believe the effort made the piece unique and more valuable than before. I hope it encourages others to try their creative energies and talents when the situation presents itself.

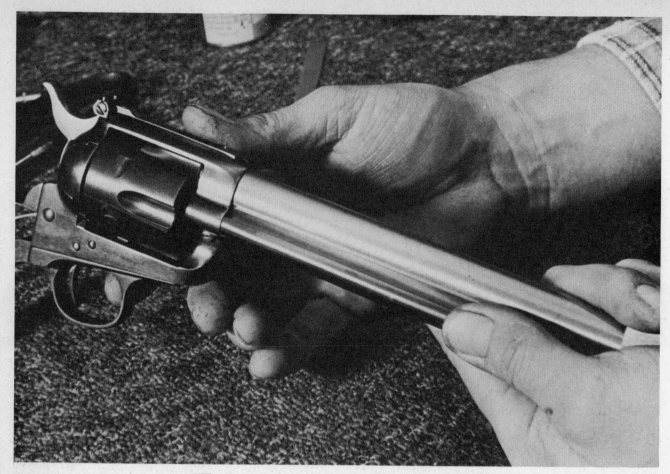

Colt Single Action with newly-installed 8-3/8-inch Douglas barrel fitted to frame and ready for new front sight.

## Chapter 11

# REBARRELING The Revolver

TWO IMPORTANT factors in rebarreling a revolver are access to a lathe and possessing the knowledge to follow all steps in completing the job. It is virtually impossible to teach one how to operate a lathe in the available pages of this tome, we must assume that the reader has a working knowledge of the lathe.

To do a satisfactory job of rebarreling, a number of steps must be followed in sequence; they are the same for all pistols, shotguns, and rifles. Before getting into the specifics of rebarreling the Colt single-action revolver, these steps are listed for clearer understanding of just how involved this job is, and one of the big reasons for it being one of the more expensive jobs in the field of pistolsmithing.

1. First, clean all parts thoroughly and take accurate measurements with a micrometer. Make a diagram of all

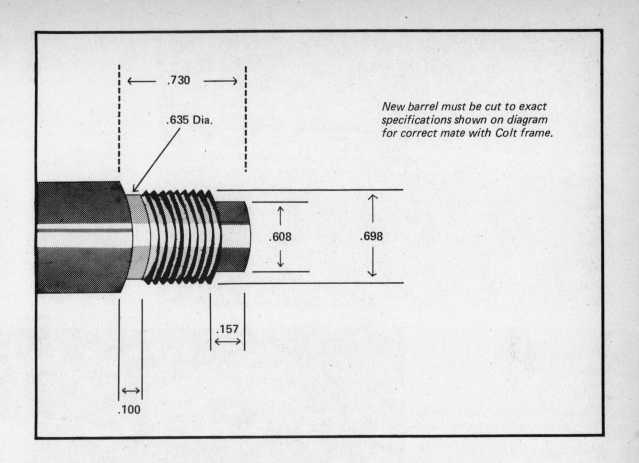

.730

.635 Dia.

.608

.698

.157

.100

*New barrel must be cut to exact
specifications shown on diagram
for correct mate with Colt frame.*

# There's More To This Project Than Just Screwing A New Blank Into The Frame!

*Thread pitch gauge indicates threads
on Colt barrel are cut twenty
threads per inch at sixty degrees,
in a vee configuration.*

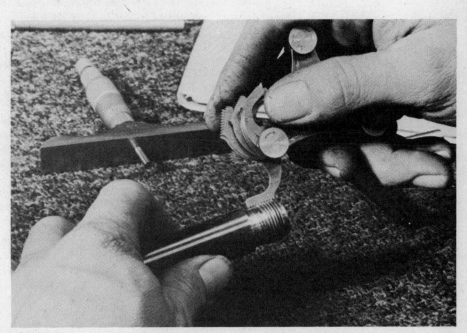

*Leather padded gunsmith action wrench makes separation of Colt frame and barrel relatively easy.*

*Frame is held securely and evenly in place by action wrench. Two adjusting screws enter and tighten from two directions, above and below frame.*

necessary measurements. Attempting to take measurements of a dirty gun could throw off the work enough to make all subsequent efforts futile.

2. Check for cracks or worn or damaged parts. If rebarreling a pistol with a used barrel, check for sharp lands with little or no pitting. There should be no bulges or rings inside the barrel. Since we will recrown the barrel as one of the last steps, minor dents on the muzzle present no problem. However, in most cases, rebarreling will mean fitting a new barrel to the receiver. Close scrutiny still is required, as it is possible to wind up with a new barrel with defects. It happens.

3. Open or enlarge the bolt face, if diameter of the bolt face is to be enlarged for a larger caliber. There are few pistols around with bolts other than Remington XP-100, so this step can be excluded in most pistol jobs. If working on a pistol such as the XP-100 Remington, it might be necessary to retemper the bolt face if it is too hard. This is accomplished by packing the lugs in wet asbestos. We would use a torch and heat to a medium blue color. (Further info is included in the chapter on tempering.)

4. Alter the bolt handle, if necessary. This could warp a bolt, so most often, a new bolt handle will be installed.

5. Heat-treat the action, if required, after all shaping, drilling and tapping have been done. Remove burrs from the tapping. This is not necessary with most pistols, but, again, is a normal progression in lathe work for other types of firearms.

6. Check the locking lugs for approximately eighty percent contact. This would be necessary in rebarreling the Remington XP-100. Contact is determined by using Dykem

*Powdered rosin or aloxite may be used between two lead blocks to prevent slippage as barrel is turned loose from frame.*

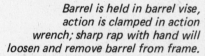

*Barrel is held in barrel vise, action is clamped in action wrench; sharp rap with hand will loosen and remove barrel from frame.*

on the lugs and working the bolt closed in the action, then removing it for inspection.

7. Measure the receiver for barrel thread extension and headspace measurement. This must be an extremely accurate measurement made with a micrometer. Remember to allow for the .002-inch crush factor during tabulations.

8. Cut new centers in the barrel with a piloted center drill .001-inch under bore diameter.

9. True the outside of the cylinder area by making a clean-up cut. This is an area that is most prone to chatter and should be watched closely.

10. Turn major diameter for threads between centers. The major diameter of the Colt SAA we will be barreling is .695-inch.

11. Make any required necking cuts; the Colt SAA has a .608-inch cut requirement.

12. Cut a forty-five-degree chamfer in the breech at the end of the barrel. Our Colt does not require this particular step.

13. Thread and fit the action by hand to a class 4 fit. (A class 4 fit is best described as snug, but not permanent, which is accomplished with special tools.)

14. Contour the barrel, if necessary. (Again, our barrel does not require this step.)

15. File and rough polish the barrel.

16. Set the lathe's steady rest on the cylinder section or threads, then face the thread extension to required length, using a depth micrometer. Cut the forcing cone if required.

*New barrel is chucked in lathe for threading operation. Colt Single Action frame requires threads be cut twenty threads per inch.*

*Thread extension is faced to required length, relying on careful, frequent measurements with depth micrometer. Step requires considerable lathe operating skill to match exact headspace dimensions of new barrel.*

*Before tightening new barrel to Colt frame, .002-inch crush factor must be computed into machining work to insure correct cylinder to barrel gap. Calculations and lathe work are not a job for the home tinkerer.*

With our Colt we can use Brownell's new throating device and complete the job by hand. The forcing cone, or throat, is that area of the bore at the cylinder end of the barrel that is tapered to allow easy and reliable entry of the bullet from the chamber into the barrel.

17. Rough the chamber to proper depth, using three-eighths-inch maximum cuts. (This applies more to rifles than pistols and is not necessary with our test gun.)

18. Finish chambering and headspacing are accomplished with a finishing reamer. The neck and throat also may be finished if necessary. Here we would check with a *go* gauge, measuring with a depth micrometer.

19. Polish the chamber and the round feeding edge with both 400 and 600-grit wet-and-dry paper. This is a must for smooth feeding and easy ejection.

20. Fit the barrel to the action. In the case of the XP-100 we would have the bolt in the action to prevent crushing of the receiver in the barrel vise. The bolt, however, should not be completely closed. Extremely important is that the gunsmith remember to put a good

lube or grease on the barrel threads to prevent seizing in the action. More than one gunsmith has lived to regret this extremely important step, when he attempted to remove the barrel.

21. Back off the barrel vise and the action wrench.

22. Check the bolt for free travel. The bolt must close without hitting the end of the barrel extension. (This does not apply with our SAA pistol.)

23. Check headspace with the go and no-go gauges. Many pistolsmiths use a live round for this check, but it is not a good practice.

24. Mark the extraction location, if required. Allow approximately .010-inch on the extraction slot. However, test fire the gun first.

25. Punch an index mark on the barrel and the frame. It is a good idea to clean the barrel thoroughly at this point.

26. Stamp the caliber on left side of the new barrel. On a rifle, the number must be above stock line. This is Federal

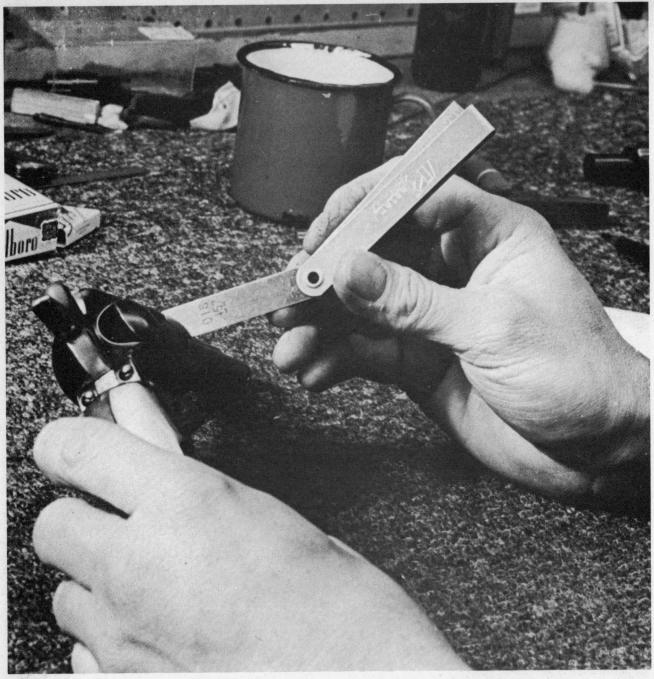

*Feeler gauge is used to measure correct cylinder to barrel gap on assembled frame, barrel and cylinder.*

law. Naturally, you will X out the old caliber if changing calibers.

27. Cut and crown the barrel muzzle at this point. Always leave the barrel approximately a quarter-inch longer than minimum legal length, when the customer wants a minimum legal length barrel.

The preceding twenty-seven steps are standard procedure within the gunsmithing field in barreling actions. It would be terrific if everything always went smoothly simply by following the instructions to the letter. But in gunsmithing and more specifically, pistolsmithing, some unforeseen factor always seems to poke up its ugly head. Such problems can be solved only by experience and a lot of common sense.

Many other factors are involved in rebarreling a revolver. First, seldom will the firearm be free of other problems. If the pistolsmith misses such a fault, he could end up with a lot of wasted time and effort for his barreling task. For example, if the frame should be bent before the new barrel is set into the revolver's action, it could throw off the barrel-and-cylinder gap. And, since many revolvers that come across the pistolsmith's bench have seen long and hard use, a bent frame is not all that unusual.

As I watched Clay Merrill, a fine gunsmith, go through the rebarreling process for the Colt Single-Action, I was impressed with his technique. He first checked out the Colt for broken or worn parts with an extensive inspection and cleaned the gun for accurate measurements.

Clay removed the old barrel using an action wrench with leather-padded jaws of his own design and manufacture. He also took the extra time to cut the wrench to mate perfectly with the Colt frame. Using proper size lead blocks to cushion the steel and hold it still, breaking the old barrel loose from the frame was a simple, but safe and efficient way to accomplish this task.

I cannot understand anyone using the old put-a-hammer-handle-through-the-cylinder-housing-and-bust-her-loose routine. Although this method has been called an accepted method of removing barrels from frames by one so-called expert, I think it's pure stupidity. Utilizing such a method means you are using a round piece against a flat surface with the distinct possibility of exerting extreme pressure to one specific area of the frame.

An action wrench of the proper size is indispensable to any pistolsmith worth his salt. Using a hammer handle can easily lead to uneven strain on the frame that can't be quickly or easily remedied. A warped or bent frame could mean a trip back to the factory for expensive repairs. The proper size action wrench eliminates this possibility.

Whether using lead or wood blocks specifically cut for a barrel, a bit of powdered rosin sprinkled on the blocks will aid in holding the barrel and keep it from slipping. If the blocks have been used several times and begin to enlarge a bit, place a strip of aloxite between the blocks and the barrel. Aloxite acts as a shim in this case and will help hold the barrel in its proper position for removing the frame.

The plan was to install an 8-3/8-inch Douglas barrel in

*Barrel chamfering is facilitated with Brownells' pistol chamfering tool, shown inserted in rear of barrel. After intial cutting with precision reamer, brass lap is used with fine abrasive for final polish.*

.44 Special on the old frame. With the barrel set up on the lathe, we first cut the .730-inch shank length, turning the major diameter of .698-inch. The sixty-degree V-type threads are cut at twenty threads per inch. After cutting the threads to the minimum diameter required, Clay Merrill screwed the frame onto the barrel to check for fit.

A good tip to remember is that, when the lathe operator thinks the threads are deep enough, he can run a file lightly over the barrel turning in the lathe. This takes the top of the threads off just enough to get the barrel to screw into the frame.

With the barrel threads cut as described, Merrill cut the throat into the barrel using one of Brownell's new throaters. The amount of throat cut into the barrel is an equal proportion of clear cut to the rifling cut. The correct angle of the cut is approximately ten degrees.

At this point, the barrel is mounted to the frame at its proper tolerances — including the .002-inch crush factor — with the aid of a properly fitted action wrench and the lead blocks. The cylinder is inserted into the frame and all dimensions rechecked. In this instance, the gap between cylinder and barrel was .005-inch and cylinder to frame relationship proved to be .003-inch.

There often is more to rebarreling a Colt single-action revolver than just cutting a barrel and fitting it to a frame. In this instance, it would be necessary also to refit the old ejector rod housing to the new barrel. This would require drilling a hole in the barrel to accept an ejector tube screw button or anchor. Since the thickness of the barrel is .160-inch, the hole could be no deeper than .080-inch. It is unsafe to drill in excess of one-half the thickness of a barrel. The ejector rod housing would have to mate perfectly to the barrel and also to the frame. There is little margin for error.

*Eleven-degree chamfer angle cut with reamer tool is visible through frame. Correct angle cut eases bullet entry into barrel and reduces potential bore leading problems while shooting.*

*New Douglas bull barrel had to be fitted with ejector tube screw button and mated to ejector rod housing before installation on Colt frame. Depth and location of button housing are critical to safe operation of handgun.*

Merrill silver soldered the button to the barrel. He assembled the ejector rod housing to the pistol and checked for functioning. With the barrel and ejector rod housing fitted and installed to specs, he was ready for the final steps in the rebarreling procedure.

All that remained would be to stamp the caliber on the new barrel and make an indexing mark. He also would install a new front sight, but that is detailed in another chapter. The final step was to test fire the gun, then examine it and the fired cartridge thoroughly to check for any problems, real or potential.

This type of work usually requires experience, expertise, and equipment not normally at the disposal of the amateur.

Even if all the proper steps and procedures are followed, adhering to factory specifications, rebarreling still is one of the most critical of pistolsmithing jobs.

Good practice: Gunsmith Clay Merrill gives Colt Single Action Army revolver a thorough cleaning and examination before beginning any repair/restoration work. Gun proved to have developed several faults.

# Setting Back A Barrel Can Improve Your Revolver, Saving The Cost Of A New Barrel!

**S**ETTING BACK a barrel in a pistol or rifle is a fairly routine operation for a competent gunsmith. This procedure can save the customer the cost of a new barrel and done properly, will effectively solve many problems in cylinder/barrel gap relationships in revolvers. Using a lathe, set-back involves refacing the breech end of the barrel to the desired length, requiring removal of a corresponding amount of metal from the barrel shoulder. There are other considerations, but they will be discussed in detail regarding our test gun, a neglected Colt SAA revolver.

This particular revolver is a good example of Murphy's Law: "If anything can go wrong, it will." It also perpetuates the theory that on-the-job training is the only way to learn to be a competent gunsmith. Our Colt not only needed to have the barrel set back, but numerous other functions also would have to be corrected to bring it back within factory specifications.

Gunsmith Clay Merrill could tell immediately that the Colt SAA revolver he was examining would require the barrel to be set back. With just a cursory glance at the gap between cylinder and barrel, it was obvious that the factory-recommended cylinder/barrel distance of .005-inch had been greatly altered in previous gun butchery. Checking with feeler gauges revealed an average distance of .013 and .018-inch at one point. Fixing this old shooter would be a major undertaking.

The apparent reason for the excessive cylinder/barrel gap was the uneven and amateurish use of a file. The previous owner probably encountered heavy leading at the breech end of the barrel and attempted to remove it by filing. He increased the gap and also filed carelessly creating an uneven gap as well.

Examination of the cylinder revealed excessive cylinder movement. The cylinder ratchet pads were deformed badly due to the cylinder moving back against the frame during recoil. The base pin bushing also would have to be replaced or repaired to help correct this cylinder slop. This gun had obviously had some very hot loads fired through it.

The final serious discovery made by Merrill showed that the Colt's frame was slightly bent. If not corrected, any attempt to refit the barrel to the frame would prove unsatisfactory. Fortunately, Merrill had the experience and the proper tools to straighten the frame. Thorough examination of the firearm and the experience of knowing what to look for had saved Merrill much aggravation and the customer extra expense.

Clay's first step with the Colt would be to repair the cylinder movement. The existing base pin bushing had been shortened by its contact with the frame during recoil. This bushing was faced off at both ends on a lathe and placed back into the cylinder to be measured with a depth micrometer. Merrill then found an old bushing in his

Close examination of gun indicates cylinder ratchet pads had become peened, deforming them out of factory specifications. First step in correcting problem is chucking cylinder into lathe, below.

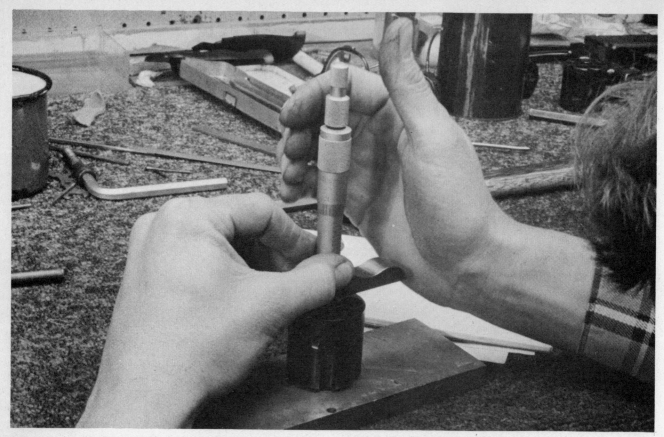

Base pin bushing was peened out of shape causing considerable cylinder slop in old Colt. Gunsmith faced off each end of bushing and measured with depth micrometer to determine length of additional bushing piece to eliminate problem. This work was done before setting back barrel.

Smooth functioning of Colt was restored by facing off cylinder ratchet pads and lengthening base pin bushing.

The amateurish file work done by previous owner was visible, leaving excessive and uneven barrel gap.

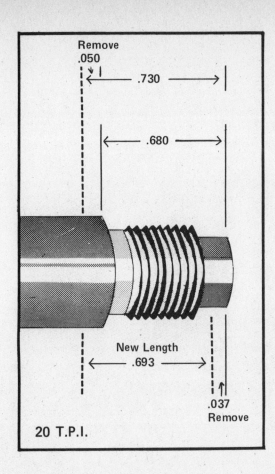

Remove
.050

.730

.680

New Length
.693

.037
Remove

20 T.P.I.

inventory and cut off a piece to mate with the other bushing in the cylinder. The cylinder ratchet pads were faced off on a lathe and the bushing and additional bushing piece were given a final fitting.

With the frame straightened, the base pin bushing repaired, and necessary measurements taken, Clay made a complete diagram on a sheet of paper for proper barrel set-back. All measurements and accompanying cuts made on the barrel would be critical to the set-back and must be made before placing the barrel on the lathe.

Merrill had removed the barrel from the frame earlier using his action wrench, lead barrel blocks, and a barrel vise. After examining the bore and deciding that the barrel was worth setting back, he carefully studied the diagram and the formula used to determine how much cutting would be necessary on the lathe. The formula is not

*With barrel chucked in lathe, metal straight edge assists machinist to maintain correct tool bit angle. Here, breech end of barrel is about to be faced off after new barrel shoulder has been cut to specifications.*

*Square India stone is held to breech end of barrel, intended to eliminate cutting marks after facing off.*

difficult, but it is important that crush factor and desired cylinder/barrel gap be considered.

Since the front sight must align perfectly in relationship to the rear sight, the first determination is how many complete revolutions would be necessary to make the barrel fit into the frame with proper gap and sights in proper alignment. Clay used his thread pitch gauge and determined that our Colt had twenty threads per inch. Dividing twenty into one inch gives us .050-inch. This means that one complete revolution of the barrel would set the barrel back into the frame .050-inch. It would be enough to correct the excess gap that existed.

Other measurements would have to be considered in completing the formula. The existing shank length — distance from barrel shoulder to breech end of barrel — was .680-inch. We would now add .018-inch (greatest amount of gap presently between barrel and cylinder) to the .680-inch to arrive at .698-inch. Since we must allow for the desired amount of barrel/cylinder gap for the Colt SAA

pistol of .005-inch, we subtract this figure from .698 and are left with .693-inch. This is the new shank length we need.

Knowing that setting the barrel back one revolution will increase the shank length by .050-inch Merrill realized he should cut .048-inch from the shoulder. The remaining .002-inch is the crush factor that must be considered when we use the barrel vise and action wrench to fit the barrel back into the frame.

With the new shoulder cut on the barrel, it is set back into the frame an additional .050-inch. The present total gap had been measured as .018-inch, or .013 longer than factory recommended tolerance of .005-inch. So we now had to achieve the proper gap by subtracting .013-inch from the .050-inch set-back; we knew we had to cut and face off the breech end of the barrel a total of .037-inch for a proper gap tolerance.

Merrill set the barrel up on the lathe and cut the shoulder accurately lengthening it .048-inch. He removed

New throat is cut into breech end of Colt barrel using throat cutting reamer. Polishing will follow.

With new throat cut and polished in breech end of barrel, frame and barrel are reassembled with correct set-back and gap.

As Colt barrel was shortened, ejector rod housing must have .050-inch removed to match shorter barrel.

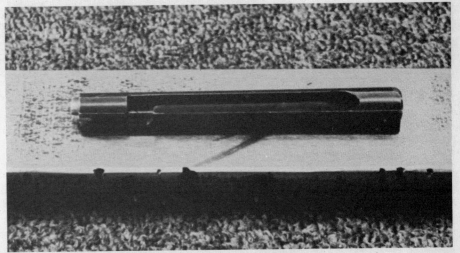

.037-inch from the breech end of the barrel, making certain it was faced off squarely. He then removed the cutter marks with an India stone. Before the barrel was screwed into the frame and checked for fit, Merrill greased the barrel threads. Forgetting this important step could result in problems in attempting to remove the barrel from the frame again.

With the barrel reinstalled in the frame, Merrill reassembled the gun and checked all measurements for accuracy. The next step was to use a throat-cutting reamer to rethroat the breech end of the barrel for smooth and efficient entry of the bullet. Polishing this area with its ten-degree angled cut would help reduce leading problems. After checking each measurement Merrill's next task was to mate the ejector rod housing to the barrel and frame and shorten the ejector rod.

Since the barrel had been shortened in its relationship to the outside of the frame by .050-inch it would be necessary to shorten the ejector rod housing an equal amount to avoid cylinder rotation problems. Turning this part in a lathe proved to be a problem, so Merrill used a quarter-inch piece of drill rod as a mandrel and held the housing to it

with a set screw. Cutting the .050-inch length thus was accomplished with little difficulty. Merrill shortened the ejector rod enough that it sat flush with the inside edge of the frame and the set-back was almost complete.

The pistol, completely reassembled, underwent a thorough examination to check functioning and all critical tolerances were measured. The gun passed all tests with flying colors. It needed only to be test fired and cleaned.

Merrill had done a first-class job of bringing the pistol back to top condition. The frame had been straightened, the cylinder movement eliminated, the barrel set back to recommended tolerances, the ejector rod housing shortened and fitted to barrel and frame, and the ejector rod also was shortened to fit in the housing and flush against the frame. All work had been checked and appropriate parts polished.

This phase of pistolsmithing is best left to the professional. An amateur, even with knowledge of how to run a lathe and a little bit of gun savvy would have run smack into Murphy's Law had he tackled this project. Fortunately, there are experienced gunsmiths around and it is the wise gun enthusiast that seeks them out when professional services are required.

*Section of ¼-inch cold rolled steel was used as mandrel to cut back Colt ejector rod housing on lathe.*

Barrel and ejector rod housing have been set back to correct specifications, requiring that ejector rod itself be shortened to prevent contact with cylinder during functioning of revolver, as shown above. After reassembly, below, standard procedure requires gunsmith to check handgun's operation with dummy rounds.

# Chapter 12

# What To Do
## ...Or How To Solve

MARK TWAIN once made the observation that everyone talks about the weather, but nobody does anything about it. There seems to be some sort of parallel among handgunners: Everyone talks about headspace, but in listening, it soon becomes obvious that a lot of these shooters don't really understand the meaning of the term.

Headspace is a bit difficult and technical to define. The type of cartridge case is a determining factor in measuring headspace accurately. There are rimmed, rimless, belted,

and the rimless, taperless pistol cartridge; and each has its own set of criteria to determine headspace.

Rimless cartridges obviously have no rim. Neither do they have any shoulder or other design features to stop the cartridge and hold it at the right spot in the chamber. The chamber must be cut to exactly the right depth so that the mouth of the case contacts the end of the chamber solidly. Headspace measuring is accomplished from the breech face to that square shoulder in the chamber which corresponds to the case mouth.

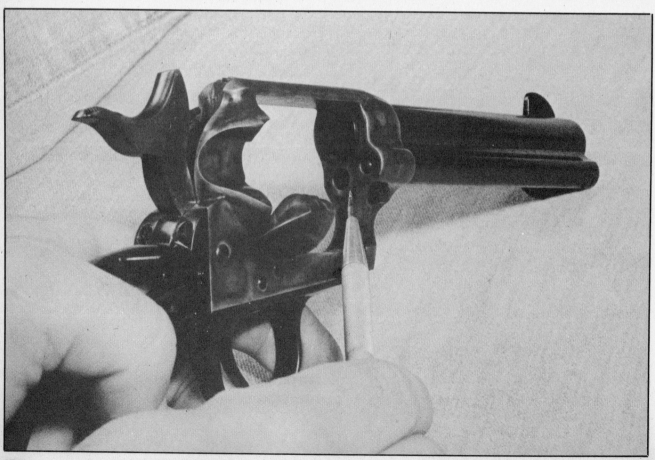

# About Headspace

## One Of Gundom's Least Understood Problems

The majority of revolver shooters don't seem to realize that there can be an excess headspace problem in that favorite handgun, yet this is one of the chief reasons for the over-standard gap between the cylinder and the barrel, which can mean gas loss and affect accuracy or cause erratic groups.

In revolvers with swing-out cylinders, the position of the cylinder as it applies to the gun's recoil shield is controlled by the collar located at the front of the cylinder; it must bear against the matching surface on the crane. Serving the same purpose on the Colt Single Action Army model — and the close copies of same — is the base pin bushing, which extends the full length of the SAA cylinder. In such solid-frame handguns, the surface bears on the gun's frame.

Should this collar become badly worn in a crane-type gun, it allows the cylinder to move forward. As the gun is fired from this point on, the surface continues to wear, causing the collar to be set back even farther, increasing the problem.

Recoil, of course, is one of the villains in this continuing sequence. With each shot from the revolver, the case of the cartridge is moved backward by the force of exploding gases, thus driving the cylinder forward to collide against the headspacing surface. Such wear, on a continuing basis, causes the gap between cylinder and barrel to be reduced, creating looseness. In really extreme cases, the wear can be so great that the cylinder ultimately begins rubbing against the end of the barrel as it is rotated or fired.

If a gunsmith is not checking for this condition, it can be overlooked. Measuring the gap between the cylinder and the barrel with the usual feeler gauge tends only to push the cylinder rearward, thus giving a false measurement. Actually, it becomes necessary to establish correct headspace for the proper gap between cylinder and barrel. So one should measure the actual headspace on the gun — especially if it is used or has undergone a good deal of firing. This is accomplished best, I've found, by using fired cartridge cases to load all of the chambers. The cases should be checked individually before loading to determine that there are no protruding primers and that there are no burrs surrounding the firing pin hole.

The gap between the case heads and the recoil shield then is measured, using the feeler gauge. The measurement

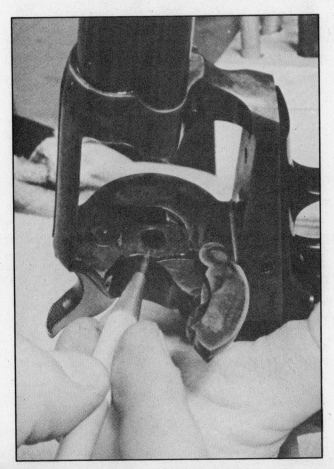

*Photo on opposite page and at left indicate areas of Model P Colt frame which are bearing surfaces to base pin bushing. Hard use and heavy loads can peen bushing length down to create headspace problems.*

*Nominal specifications for the .45 ACP brass and chamber call for a case length of .899-inch length overall (LOA). This Bar-Sto precision gauge has .899 stamped denoting distance from chamber ledge to barrel extension, for reference.*

*Here, a load is pressed into the chamber and the head can be seen to be some few thousandths short of being flush with the barrel extension.*

should not be more than .008-inch. Keeping the cylinder block fully forward, with the feeler gauge in place, you can use a second gauge to determine the accurate measurement of the gap between cylinder and barrel.

The cylinder-barrel gap should be at least .005-inch, with the cylinder held forward. This space is necessary to prevent any binding of the cylinder. It's also the ideal space when the cylinder is being rotated double-action for a second shot. In this situation, the cylinder has been driven forward by the firing of the initial round. This leaves the head of the cartridge case against the recoil shield. In this instance, the gun can be made serviceable by insuring that the minimum .005-inch barrel-cylinder gap is established,

but if you want to be assured of proper headspace, this must be extended rearward on the crane, if a swing-out cylinder, or in the frame if it is a solid-frame revolver, or it must be extended forward on the cylinder itself.

If you are dealing with a single-action revolver, one method of correcting the gun's headspace is to turn a new base pin bushing on a lathe, making it from quality tool steel and being certain it is hardened properly.

In the case of double-action guns there are varying methods, and on obsolete or foreign handguns they may vary considerably. You may have to experiment to determine exactly what is required to correct a headspace problem. In some cheap models, you'll find there are no real provisions for correcting headspace.

In the case of the Smith & Wesson double-action family of revolvers, proper headspace is dependent upon an integral gas ring extending from the center of the cylinder. The face of this ring bears against the crane and it is in this area that excessive headspace corrections must be made.

Some gunsmiths tend to take the easy way out and simply peen this gas ring, expanding it so to speak. Others will solder a thin steel washer onto the front of this ring, thus absorbing the extra space. But the most permanent correction is to counterbore the front of the revolver cylinder, then install a bushing made of hardened tool steel to replace the factory-installed gas ring.

In correcting excessive headspace in Colt's double-action models, a steel washer can be soft-soldered onto the flat face of the cylinder collar. I recommend soft solder, because it requires less heat and the job can be done without heating up the entire cylinder, which would require rehardening. I know of several gunsmiths who favor silver solder for this operation, but they have become experts at accomplishing the job in record time, before the entire cylinder becomes heated. With soft solder, the joint will hold well and there usually is not enough wear and tear in the area to break the joining. One can determine just how thick the washer should be by using a feeler gauge between the cartridge case heads and the recoil shield while the cylinder is full forward. Thickness of the required washer

for regulating the correct headspace is the difference between the gaps in the two.

Another method of correcting the headspace problem in Colt double-actions involves the use of a lathe. One first counterbores the front of the cylinder around the axis hole to a depth of one-quarter-inch. This allows one to install a new bushing of tool steel that can be soldered into place, or it can be tapped and screwed into position. Once installed, this bushing then is faced off to provide the correct headspacing length.

Headspace in the autoloading pistol is a whole new problem, with a whole new set of requirements for correction. One of the first problems lies in the fact that the casual shooter may not realize that he has a headspace problem, unless it reaches such proportions that he has a case blowout and fragments of brass are thrown out through the ejection port. This, of course, is the extreme case.

If the autoloader has a long, thin firing pin as is the case with the Colt family, the Brownings, Smith & Wessons, and a number of European-built models, the problem usually will be less obvious. In fact, to the occasional shooter it may not seem a problem at all. This is due to the fact that the firing pin will protrude far enough through the firing pin hole to ignite the primer in the cartridge case. I've seen guns with as much as one-eighth-inch excessive headspace that still operated with no apparent problem. However, in

This Colt Single Action Army revolver has had cylinder, base pin and base pin bushing removed to check wear. In extreme cases, cylinder may actually rub against end of barrel, a typical headspace problem.

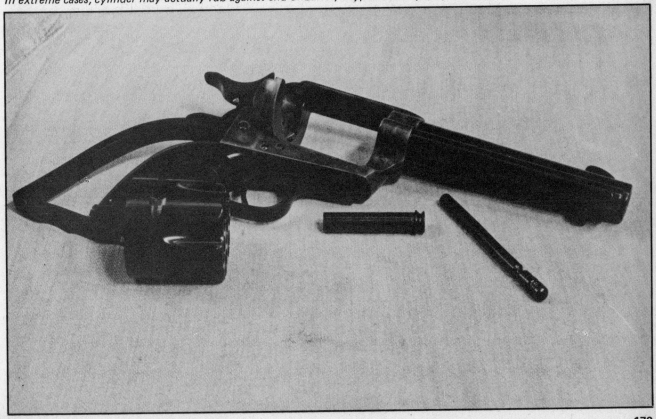

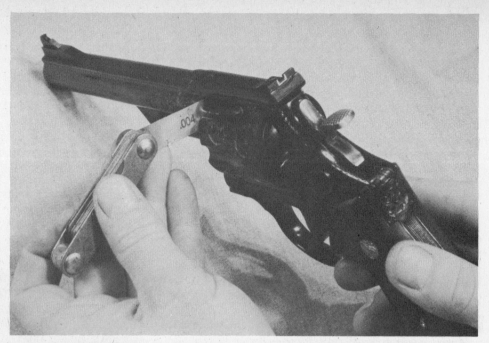

*Factory specifications call for barrel gap of .004-inch on Smith & Wesson Model 29, as indicated at right. Below is simulated problem of cylinder rubbing against breech end of barrel; incorrect head space.*

most instances, an autoloader that has sufficient firing pin length to fire the cartridge in spite of its excessive headspace usually will show the same signs as excessive chamber pressure. Inspection will show that the cartridge primer is badly flattened; it may even be perforated. The headstamp on the case rim may have been flattened by its contact with the face of the breech; the primer pocket and the case head itself may have been expanded in shooting. In some cases, the case head may become badly damaged or even ruptured.

What happens is rather simple in this instance: When there is excessive headspace, the cartridge case is driven rearward with the same force that the bullet is driven forward through the barrel. This is because the head of the cartridge case is not being supported properly by the face of the slide breech. The case's head, slamming backward at such high speed and with such force, collides with the slide and distortion is a natural result.

In those models that have shorter firing pins or, at least, less protrusion, excessive headspace often will result in a misfire.

All of which brings us to the question of what to do about excessive headspace in an autoloading pistol. In some cases, the barrel and chambering may be the offender. If you have spare barrels for the pistol, I'd suggest trying the others. If the headspacing is not an extreme problem, one of the spares may fit in such a way that the headspacing problem is largely solved.

But that's the simplest answer of all. The next logical step is to ream out the front of the chamber on a lathe and install a bushing. This bushing, short in length, is cut with a chambering reamer until the depth of the chamber is correct and holds the loaded cartridge in the proper position for proper headspacing.

In some instances, one may find that the walls of the barrel are sufficiently thick that it is possible to bore out the entire chamber, then install an entirely new sleeve with a new chamber of proper dimensions. However, there is a chance that this particular method, while perhaps less complicated than the bushing answer, will weaken the breech of the barrel.

An alternative is to reline the entire barrel with an insert, but this is logical only if the original bore is in such bad shape that the liner is a necessity. In most instances, it's cheaper to buy a new barrel. However, in case the new liner should be installed, it then is rechambered to the proper depth for the correct headspace.

There are other alternatives, most of them expensive if you are paying a gunsmith to do the work; and if you are the gunsmith, your clients probably will have a fit when they find what your time and expertise are worth. One approach is to build up the locking lugs by welding, then recut them so that when the barrel moves to the rear in conjunction with the slide, the excess chamber depth is eliminated. This, however, takes careful work if it is to be successful.

Headspace gauges, made especially in handgun calibers,

*Tolerance allowed between S&W Model 66's bolster and cylinder is .012 to .014-inch. Feeler gauge is slipped behind fired rounds which have been checked for protruding primers and/or burrs, avoiding false reading.*

are the easiest method for determining correct headspace, but an accurate vernier caliper or a depth micrometer with readings up to an inch can be used with little trouble.

As an example, determining the degree of headspace in the Colt autoloaders requires that one measure from the hood to the headspacing shoulder of the chamber. The hood, if there is any doubt, positions the barrel, engaging the face of the slide breech. This measurement then should be compared to the proper headspace dimensions listed as minimum and maximum by the factory references. If the depth of the chamber is greater than the maximum listed, the autoloader probably suffers from excessive headspacing. Incidentally, the same general method is used to determine headspacing in most copies or variations of the Colts being made abroad today and often imported into this country. The method also will suffice for measuring headspace in the autoloaders in the Browning line.

Autoloaders chambered for bottleneck cartridges present a challenge, when it comes to headspace measurements. The easiest method of measurement is with headspace gauges, of course; however, an adequate determination can be made with the use of small circular shims, which should be no more than .002-inch in thickness. Using thick grease or some temporary adhesive such as double-sided Scotch tape, adhere the first shim to the head of the cartridge in the chamber, then add more shims, one on top of the other, until the gun will not go into full battery when the slide or breech, depending upon the model, is moved forward slowly and with care. If you are using the double-sided tape, be sure to include its thickness when measuring the shims being used. If heavy grease is used, this coating becomes so thin that no additional measurement qualification is necessary. However, the shims may tend to move about or fall off if care is not taken. Personally, I prefer using the tape.

When enough shims have been added that the gun will

*Components of S&W revolver below are not in correct assembly sequence. Scribe is indicating gas ring which bears on frame, critical to headspacing of popular Smith & Wesson family of double action revolvers.*

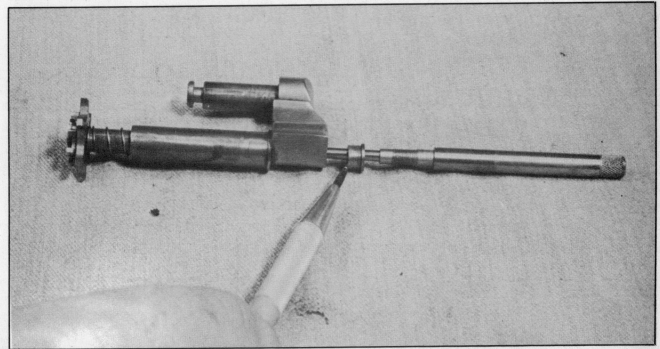

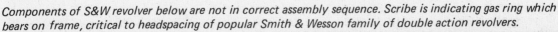

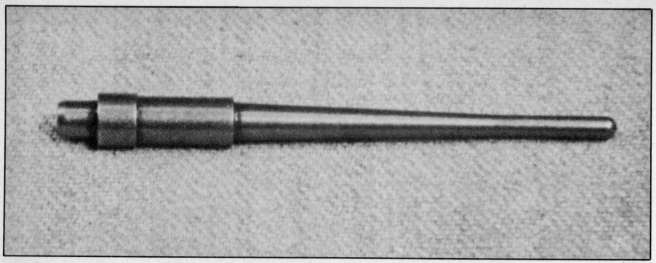

*Long firing pin design of venerable Colt Model 1911 caliber .45 automatic, may protrude through firing pin hole to ignite primer despite excessive headspace. Clue to this problem is revealed by deformed or flattened cartridge primers. Text describes additional indications of headspace problems in autoloading pistols.*

not go into battery by just the slightest margin, the total thickness of the shims — and the tape, if you are using it — should tell you the approximate measurement of the excess headspace for this particular autoloader. The measurement, incidentally, will vary from cartridge to cartridge, if those of different manufacture are used for testing. One must find a happy medium in this situation. In other words, one should not adjust headspace to the point that the gun will handle the cartridges of only a single manufacturer. As mentioned before, in most autoloaders, the maximum headspace allowable without problems is .006-inch more than the length of the standard cartridge case.

So much for the problems; but what are the remedies?

Taking the bottleneck cartridge auto first, if the barrel is screwed into a barrel extension — as is the case with the Luger, for example — set the barrel back one additional thread, thus turning it deeper into the barrel extension. The

chamber then is recut to the necessary dimensions.

In those models that do not have the barrel screwed into the receiver or a barrel extension, the usual remedy is to bore out the chamber, then install a bushing. Into this the new chamber is cut. For minor corrections, one also can build up the face of the gun's breech with shim stock that is soldered on.

To install an insert bushing in the chamber, one normally cleans the chamber with a degreasing agent, then drives the insert into place until it is solid against the original headspacing shoulder. With some models, it is a good idea to make the insert bushing a trifle long, then ream it down with a chamber reamer in the appropriate caliber until the new chamber depth meets the specifications for the caliber.

In some cases, the excessive headspace may be so minimal that it would be impossible to insert a bushing to

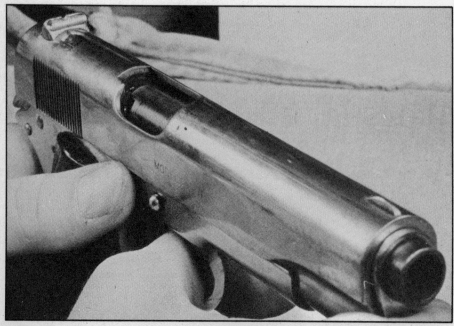

*One result of excessive headspace in autoloaders may be distortion in slide breech area. As round is fired, case is driven back against breech with same force that bullet is driven through barrel bore.*

absorb the difference. In this instance, the normal practice among pistolsmiths is to deepen the chamber enough — usually one-eighth-inch or more — so that a bushing can be driven in to the proper depth. This requires reaming out the chamber with the reamer for the caliber involved. You also will need a bore-riding pilot or jig to assure that the hole is drilled perfectly straight and in proper alignment.

To accomplish all this, first measure the depth of the original chamber. After adding the length of the chosen insert to the length of the cartridge case, attach a stop to the drill so that the depth will be no more than the added dimensions of insert and case.

The barrel, of course, should be held firm in a padded vise, then the variable speed drill should be run at the slowest possible speed, using a good deal of cutting oil. When the chamber has been deepened to the prescribed depth, it then is cleaned and degreased with a solvent. The depth is checked again by measuring, then the bushing should be driven into position. For this, I recommend a brass or aluminum alloy rod that will barely fit into the chamber. The soft metal will not damage the bushing as it is being forced into place. If you have figured your dimensions properly, the gun now should be reassembled and test fired. But before testing, check the headspace once again with your gauge to be sure all has been accomplished correctly.

There are instances wherein some gunsmiths I know favor bushing the entire chamber, a job that can be done with a drill press and tooling, but one must be careful in this approach, as there are a number of the larger bore autos that utilize barrels with thin walls. Most of the .45 autos, for example, fall into this category.

To use this technique, the pistolsmith first must drill out the auto's original chamber, going one-sixteenth-inch deeper than the original depth of the chamber. The new chamber bushing, one turned to the necessary specifications, is coated with soft solder and allowed to cool. The walls of the barrel's chamber also are coated with soft solder. The barrel should be relatively warm, the solder in a semi-fluid state, at the moment the bushing is driven into place. As always, one should ensure that the bushing is driven to its full depth in the chamber recess.

Then the entire unit is heated just enough to assure that the solder is melted and has joined the two units — barrel and chamber bushing — properly. If there are any apparent gaps at the joining on the rear, they should be filled with solder, too. When cool, it will be necessary to cut the new chamber, shape the feed ramp and clean up the breech, all relatively simple chores. The excess solder is removed with scrapers and wire brushes.

Those are the basics. Needless to say, each model will have its own idiosyncrasies so far as design and resulting innovation on the part of the pistolsmith are concerned. Perhaps the best way of learning what to do with an unfamiliar handgun is first to understand how it functions and what parts tend to react upon others. By this simple progression, the needs for adjusting headspacing should become relatively simple.

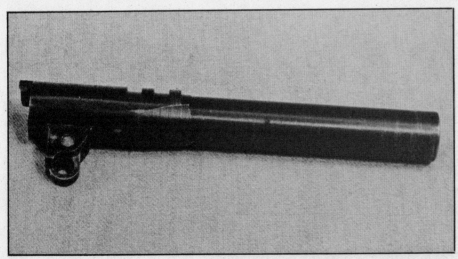

*The simplest and often cheapest solution to autoloader headspace problems may be a new barrel.*

*Invaluable tools for the gunsmith struggling with headspace problems include dial calipers and an accurate depth micrometer.*

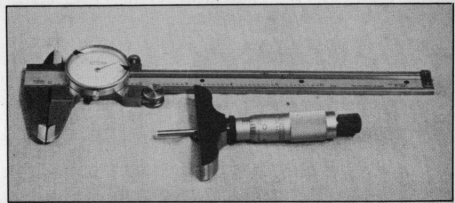

# THINGS FOR SPRINGS

## Chapter 13

SPRINGS HAVE been a necessary part in the functioning of just about every firearm ever built. They are a necessary part in handguns, as well as rifles and shotguns. A vast array of different sizes, thicknesses, and types of springs are used in gunsmithing repair.

The fastest and most economical way to replace broken springs is to purchase either replacement springs, or spring stock, whether coiled springs, V-type trigger return springs, flat-type trigger return springs, or flat-type hammer springs. Buying spring stock or replacement springs will save time and money, also aggravation. One never knows whether the spring is perfect until it is tried in the firearm. If the gunsmith has done a perfect job of springmaking, the firearm functions. If not, the spring shatters and you have to start from scratch again.

Basically, to make a flat spring we must first form it. It is shaped by polishing and drawfiling the metal to proper size and shape. All filing and polishing is done longitudinally with the grain of the metal (never across the grain). The spring stock next is tapered from the center toward the tip. We then heat it and bend it by heating to a cherry red. The spring is reheated and again bent. We heat it once again using a shim.

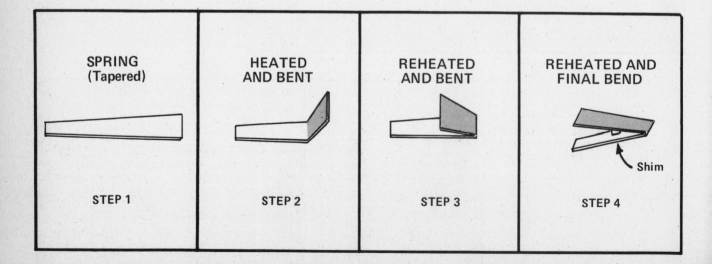

| SPRING (Tapered) | HEATED AND BENT | REHEATED AND BENT | REHEATED AND FINAL BEND |
|---|---|---|---|
| STEP 1 | STEP 2 | STEP 3 | STEP 4 — Shim |

# Buying Replacement Springs Is The Easiest Route, But If Not Available, Here Is How To Make Them

The spring now must be annealed or normalized by heating to a cherry red and allowed to cool. It then is reheated to a cherry red again. When again cooled, we place the spring in the gun and check for size. Important: Do not put any tension on the spring at this point. The spring is removed from the firearm and hardened at between 1550 and 1600 degrees Fahrenheit and quenched in oil.

The spring now is tempered at 925 degrees F for approximately thirty minutes in an oven or kiln.

Although we could use a torch, it is much more difficult and not as positive. During this phase, the temperature is raised very slowly. Now we place the spring in the gun. If it is a good spring the gun functions. If the steps were not followed correctly the spring shatters and we start all over again.

To make a spring properly, we must begin with steel that has the necessary elasticity properties. Good spring steel material should have the following: carbon

*Steel for making springs must have a high carbon content. A fast check method is to hit the metal on a grinding wheel. A large shower of sparks indicates the necessary carbon content. Drill rod is excellent for springs.*

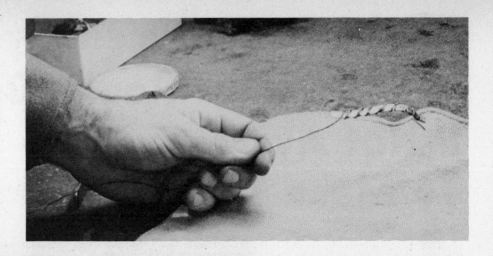

0.45-0.55%; manganese 0.50-0.80%; phosphorus 0.03-0.04%; sulfur 0.03-0.04%; chromium 0.80-1.10%; and vanadium 0.15-0.18%. Springs should be made from high-carbon steel. A quick method of determining the amount of carbon in a piece of steel is to lightly touch the end of the steel to a grinding wheel. Good carbon steel will literally shower sparks as it comes in contact with the grinding wheel. To properly make a spring the steps include hand forging, filing, polishing, heat-treating, tempering, and a final polishing.

We begin by bending the spring. This is done in stages and the metal must be reheated each time as described above. We use the heat from a furnace set at 1450 degrees F. Maximum temperature for this operation is 1550 degrees F. The spring should be placed near the furnace and allowed to heat slowly before actually putting it into the furnace. The spring is removed after it has reached the desired color and then is bent the first time. In each bending, do not allow the steel to drop below the cherry red color. After each bend, the spring is allowed to cool in a container of lime.

By heating and bending in this three-step series, we are attempting to prevent the steel molecules from being damaged which would cause fractures. After the spring has been forged and bent, it must be polished and checked for proper size and shape. It is extremely important that all scratches and file marks have been removed at this time.

During each phase of springmaking it is important to polish the spring without heating the metal. Polishing eliminates stress marks in the metal. Heating the metal would risk changing the molecular structure of the steel

*Spring tempering is accomplished here with oil bath. Oil should be heated before immersing the heated spring. (Right) After heating and bending steel to the desired shape, it is immersed in container of lime to allow slow and even cooling.*

and hence destroying any chance of making a perfect spring.

The next two steps involved in making a spring include hardening and tempering which must be accomplished precisely or the spring probably will fracture. Here, different methods may be used, depending upon the equipment at hand. An old gunsmithing practice to harden and temper springs is to use the lead bath described in the heat treating section. Before immersing the spring in the lead bath, it is coated with alcohol and chalk to prevent the lead from sticking to the part. An amount of charcoal is placed over the lead bath to prevent oxidizing. Preheat the spring to about 850 degrees F and submerge it in the lead bath which should be at a

temperature between 1350 and 1400 F.

Since the steel spring will float on the heavier lead, it must be held under the lead with tongs to allow the spring to be heated uniformly throughout. With the spring properly hardened, it is ready for tempering.

If the metal is to be tempered by the oil bath method, the spring should be immersed into the oil with the spring pre-heated to a temperature of about 300 F or the oil heated to a temperature of about 700 F. Do not plunge the hardened piece into oil while it is cold. When using the oil bath to temper a spring it is a good practice to swirl the spring in figure-eight motions while it is immersed.

Another method of hardening and tempering springs

In plunging heated spring into oil bath, swirl the spring in figure-eight motion in oil. Do not rest spring on bottom of container. The spring is held here by a piece of piano wire. (Below) Coil spring is being made with special spring winding tool and piano wire. The tool is adjustable for sizes.

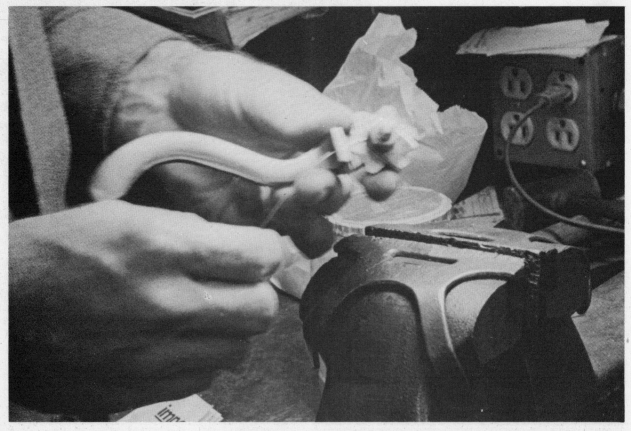

which may prove easier for the gunsmith with limited equipment is a technique described in Bob Brownell's *Gunsmith Kinks*. John Frazier, a gunsmith who has made several thousand springs quite successfully reports: "Heavy V-springs are best forged and finished-filed and ground to shape. Be sure all lines are absolutely true and all tapers are similar to a 'buggy whip.' Beyond the end of the taper of one leaf, leave part of the original steel

size, this to be used to hold the spring while hardening to prevent heat bleed-off if the spring itself were held with pliers.

"In a dark or unlighted corner of your shop, heat the spring until it just shows red color and quench.

"Then, take a regular quart motor oil tin can and with a hammer, pound in one side of the can making an indentation deep enough to hold the spring – which is

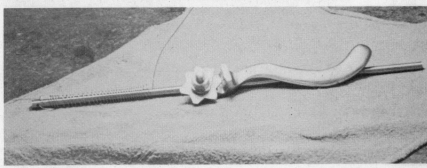

After drilling a hole in a piece of drill rod for a mandrel, it is set up in lathe, using slow back gears for easy winding. (Right) After the wire is wound on mandrel of proper diameter, proper length must be determined for fit of spring in gun.

now filed or ground to final exact shape and dimensions.

"Place the spring in the indent in the can and cover it with regular motor oil. With your torch, set the oil on fire and let it completely burn up. Then throw in a handful of dry asbestos over the spring to keep it dark for a couple of hours. The spring has now been properly tempered and heat soaked. You either have a spring or you don't. A complete compression in your vise will darned soon tell you."

The above method sounds excellent. It should be mentioned, however, that when burning off the oil that the spring should not be at the bottom of the container which may cause weak spots in the spring.

The spring is final polished and checked closely for any cracks.

Helical springs or coiled springs may be purchased from gunsmith supply houses in different widths to cover just about any replacement job. In this instance, it is simple to check the broken spring for its number of coils per inch and the diameter of the spring material. Having found the proper replacement material, the job requires only cutting the spring to proper length and replacing it

in the handgun.

If helical spring stock is purchased in a roll without the coils already made, the gunsmith must coil his own wire. He will need a mandrel of the proper diameter on which to wind the spring to match the number of coils and diameter of the original. There are many ways to coil a spring, but if the gunsmith does not have a regular springmaking mandrel, Howe, in his *Modern Gunsmith*, suggests, "Hold a long, threaded bolt in the vise. First, drill a small hole in the end of the bolt and then screw on the nut to such a distance that a hooked tool can be placed over the bolt. Place the wire in the hole, and with the tool in place, screw up on the nut, allowing it to follow the thread on the bolt. When enough is wound, file off the end of the wire in the hole and release the spring, which can be screwed off the bolt. Springs of almost any coil, but not of 'almost any diameter' may be made in this way."

Since the number of spring diameters and numbers of coils per inch is quite extensive, I recommend purchasing pre-coiled helical springs from an outlet like Brownell's. It saves hours and heartburn.

# Chapter 14
# ACCURIZING THE .45 AUTO

## If You Want A Professional Job Done, You Go To A Pro, But Bob Day's Techniques Can Be Used In Your Own Shop

"A N ACCURACY job is nothing more than removing all the built-in factory clearances that are necessary to a military pistol. With those clearances removed — making everything zero-zero again — you have your accurized pistol. It's as simple as that."

Pistolsmith Bob Day was doing the talking on his favorite subject: accurizing Colt autoloaders.

As it turned out, there was a bit more to it than that, including a good many hours — and days — that elapse between removing the magazine as he starts to strip the gun down and test firing the accurized version on the range.

This chapter involves a Colt MK IV .45 Series '70 (serial number 70G34084) in a step-by-step accurizing by Bob Day.

Bob Day is owner of the Powderhorn, a gun shop only a little removed from Lackland Air Force Base in San Antonio, Texas. His retail store is well-rounded in all phases of the shooting sports but does tend to lean a bit toward handguns and muzzleloaders. Day's first and second shooting love affairs come to the front here. He is heavily stocked in reloading components, and there is another fulltime gunsmith for repairs, since Day is far too busy to work on day-to-day customer repairs. But it is in this shop that Day Arms Corporation work is done.

Day spent more than twenty years in the Air Force. He underwent basic training at Lackland then was shipped to Ellington Air Force Base in Houston, where he performed the assigned duties of an electrician.

After numerous assignments, he spent two years with the Air Force Detachment at California's Point Mugu Naval Air Missile Test Center. It was there he became interested in gunsmithing, reading everything he could get his hands on to learn all he could on the subject. He wanted a deer rifle and couldn't afford one, so he bought a Schmidt-Rubin 7.5x54mm and made a deer rifle with the aid of a fifty-cent

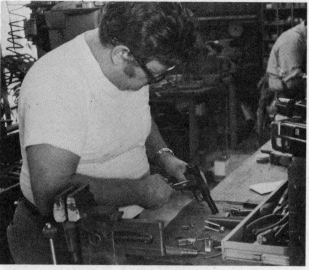

*Above: Bob Day, one of the nation's best-recognized gunsmiths, strips a Colt Mark IV preparatory to start of accurizing. (Below) He checks the magazine for cracks at the rear edge of the feeding lips, a trouble source.*

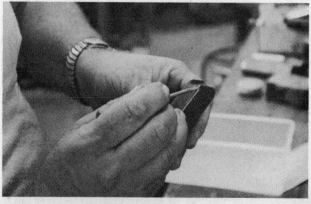

vise clamped to his wife, Betty's, sewing-machine table.

It turned out so well (this was in 1957), that he converted thirty-five more for sale by simply cutting off barrels, crowning, doing a little stock and trigger work; all things an amateur could do to a military rifle. Bob Day still has that Schmidt-Rubin and on occasion takes it hunting for old time's sake.

Transferred to Holloman AFB near Alamogordo, New Mexico, he bought a walnut plank and turned it into a stock for his Schmidt-Rubin by copying an Anthony Guyman ad in the *American Rifleman* for style.

Pistol shooting came about by his being on flying status and having to qualify annually. A bragging session caused him to take it up seriously following the challenge that, if he was really that good, the base pistol team sure could use him. To save face, Day started to shoot competitively. This led to more tinkering with pistols than rifles.

Day competed in the All Air Force Pistol Matches in 1957 with the Air Research and Development Command (ARDC) team.

His team won the service pistol championship and went on to the National Matches at Camp Perry.

At the Lackland match, he won his first leg toward Distinguished; at Camp Perry he got the second.

During this initial Lackland experience, he toured the Air Force gun shop and was so impressed he knew he had to become part of it. Day succeeded in getting a trial assignment, then was accepted and transferred to the gunsmith shop effective January 1, 1960.

His goal then was to become the Chief Gunsmith for the Air Force Pistol Team. His second goal was to become Distinguished with the pistol. And his third goal was to break a 2600 score.

He accomplished them all.

The third leg and Distinguished came in 1960; he was made non-commissioned officer in charge of the Custom Pistol Section servicing the All Air Force Pistol Team in 1961; and scored his 2600 in 1967.

Bob Day was in charge of the Air Force Marksmanship Research and Development Section from its inception to his retirement in 1969.

Now you know who Bob Day is, so let's talk about how he accurizes guns.

In our step-by-step accurizing job, the first thing he did was remove the magazine and pull back the slide to make sure the gun was unloaded. It was only a moment until he had the gun stripped completely.

"There is nothing to an accuracy job that can't be done by any man with a file and a hammer at home," he insists.

Thorough is a totally inadequate word when used to describe the way Day went over each piece as he stripped the gun, searching for any part that might need replacing. This included springs which were checked for kinks or any abnormality. The recoil spring plug got a quick going over with a bearing scraper to take off the sharp edges and the possibility of a burr, so when the recoil spring is relaxing inside, it can do so smoothly.

As he checked the barrel carefully, he removed the link pin and link, pointing out that this link would not be used in the finished gun.

Each of the parts was placed in a small plastic container

This is what the Mark IV looks like after it has been totally disassembled by Day in his San Antonio shop.

An early step is close examination of the recoil spring and the plug of the autoloader. (Below) Day inspects the Colt's barrel to determine whether there are any problems. He insists what he does can be done in a home workshop.

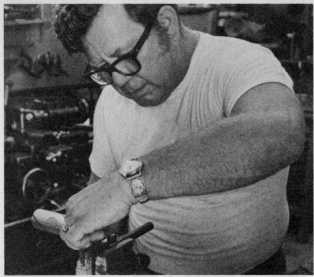

With the barrel assembly held in a padded vise, Bob Day knocks out the link and the link pin with his punch.

Day inspects the special Colt Match bushing that will be installed in the Mark IV to replace collet-type bushing.

With the unit held in the jaws of his well padded vise, the gunsmith carefully files the corner of the extractor.

With the extractor corner filed to Day's specifications, it then is buffed to remove any burrs, make it smooth.

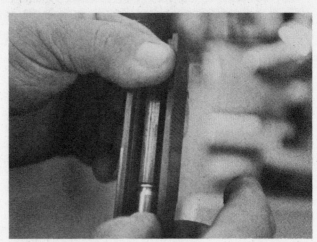

Holding the extractor in the frame, Day uses his test cartridge to check smoothed-up extractor for function.

Day also polishes the recoil spring guide in each auto.

With the recoil spring guide properly polished, Bob Day inserts the guide into the spring to inspect proper fit.

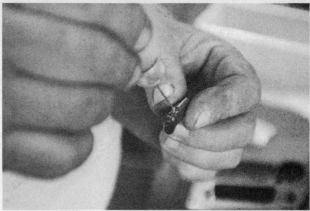

Details are important, the gunsmith contends. He checks the magazine catch for operation, then oils it carefully.

as Day decided it was usable. The slide stop pin was miked and declared within specified tolerances of .198 to .200-inch diameter. Day uses the smallest diameter pin possible in his fresh accuracy job, sometimes even .197-inch, because this allows the gun to be brought back to pristine (a favorite word of Day's) condition by doing little more than tightening the slide and replacing the slide stop pin with a larger one.

Removing the Colt collet-type bushing from the barrel, Day commented that, so far as he is concerned, it isn't suitable for accuracy and will be replaced with a special oversize part. This special bushing is oversize on the skirt and undersize in the barrel hole so the skirt has to be fitted to the slide and the hole to each individual barrel.

Talking about zero tolerances, Day took exception to a negative comment as to the reliability of an accurized gun. He said under extreme conditions, such as falling in a mud puddle and hiding there for four hours, the mud and silt might keep the gun from functioning but under conditions of normal use and care, Day considers his accuracy jobs totally reliable; possibly more so than an issue gun, particularly if the auto is tuned to a particular type of ammunition.

With the extractor, firing pin, firing pin spring and firing pin stop out, he inspected each. The extractor hook was checked for burrs or possible breakage, as was the firing pin stop. Day said he had seen only two or three broken in half but had seen lots that were cracked — some that had fired thousands and thousands of rounds without any problem. However, if a cracked firing pin stop is found, he changes it.

He carefully inspected the firing pin and spring for missing or broken coils in the spring. He pointed out that this spring can go on in only one direction. If it isn't tight, it is on backwards. His reason for carefully checking the spring, he told me, is that sometimes a coil can break off and jam the firing pin at the most inopportune time.

With a little file, Day rounded off the extractor's sharp shoulder. He said this would allow ammunition exceeding factory tolerances to be gripped. "And this does happen," he added. "I want the extractor so smooth that, when a

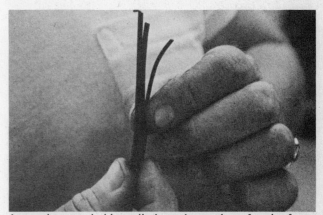

As another step in his preliminary inspection of each of the gun's components, gunsmith looks over the sear spring.

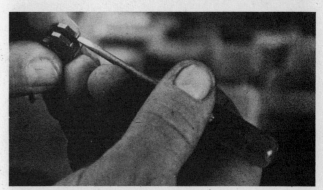

Day uses a small screwdriver in inspecting hammer locks.

*The gunsmith sometimes is not happy with grip bushings and removes the originals to replace them with new ones.*

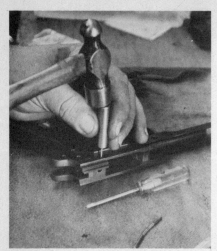

Using a small punch and a ball-peen hammer, ejector is removed from frame.

Working with care and precision, Day puts new dogleg in slide stop and safety plunger spring of Mark IV.

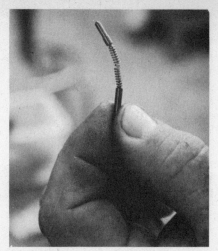

This is how the spring looks after Day has given the unit an extra kink.

round does feed a little hard, the extractor won't keep it from going in."

After filing, the part was buffed for complete smoothness. It also was noted that this particular part was much too loose; that it needed a bit of resistance. So it was fitted properly by bending slightly on the rearmost area. This gave it positive extraction pressure, regardless of rim diameter. Bob Day prefers bending the rear over the front where excessive pressure might be achieved.

The finished extractor was checked with several dummy rounds and pronounced ready to use.

Day polished the shank of the recoil spring guide and checked it assembled to ensure there was nothing to drag or hang up.

The magazine catch was pulled out and checked along with the spring. Sometimes, according to Day, bluing-salt residue remains in this hole, and being highly corrosive, can jam it up. There is no modification here, unless he is going to utilize his .22 Day Conversion Unit. If this is to be, Day

breaks the corner slightly, grinding it off, as it sometimes interferes with the .22 magazine.

A note on Day's .22 Conversion Unit might be in order. It is made entirely by Day in his shop and converts any .45 or .38 Colt autoloader to a .22 target pistol in seconds. No tools are necessary and it changes back to center-fire just as quickly.

X-ring accuracy at fifty yards is guaranteed with this .22 Conversion Unit, which makes it possible for competitive shooters to use the same gun for all their shooting. There is only one trigger pull and one grip to get used to. The unit is made up with a Douglas premium-grade barrel which is stationary and is equipped with fully adjustable target sights.

Some grip safeties, Day has found, show signs of factory fitting, others don't. This one had obviously been hand fitted at the factory. All Day did was smooth up some edges, as he is a fanatic on no burrs.

The sear spring was next to catch his eye as Day showed

Again using his padded vise, Bob Day disassembles the main spring housing.

Day removes the factory front sight from the slide of the Colt Mark IV.

The sharp edges are removed from the locking recesses in the auto slide.

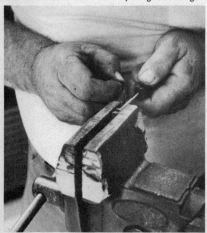

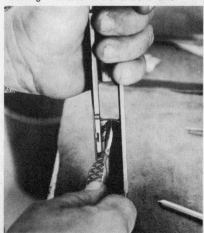

how they come bent in all sorts of different shapes from the factory. Since he knows about how it should look when his trigger job is finished, he made the initial changes. He also chose to grind off about .020-inch from the side to make certain it would clear the grip safety. Sometimes a burr, he said, can be built up with use allowing it to catch. With this relief, there is no danger of a burr catching and causing the trigger job to go bad.

The trigger needed a stop, so it was put aside temporarily, as Day noted that, when finished, the trigger would receive a bit of extra polishing. "One of the few concessions I make to cosmetics," he added.

The hammer and sear on this particular gun passed Day's intense inspection.

The disconnector on this gun was smooth and well polished. Sometimes Day will modify them a bit because, as the gun is cycled, it wears and sets up a reaction known to competitive shooters as "disconnector click," which has ill effects on an otherwise fine trigger pull. To correct this, he

Using his electric-powered stippling tool, the gunsmith stipples the front area of the autoloader's steel forestrap

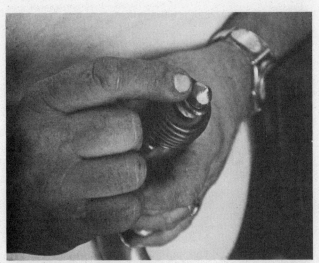

Pistolsmith Bob Day developed this stippling tool for use in his own shop, reducing the time required for the job.

After stippling, it is necessary to clean up the gun's main spring housing, using files chosen for the work. (Below) Day wears protective goggles in welding the head space extension. He is adding metal for an improved fit.

stones the sharp edge to make it round, but only on the front. To work the back would be for cosmetics only, and Day doesn't believe in it. If it will benefit the shooting capabilities of the gun, he does it; if not, it's a hands-off situation. Absolutely nothing is done for looks alone.

Frequently, when the grip screws are backed out, the bushings in the frame come with them, so each one has to be checked carefully. Often he replaces them.

Now it was the ejector's turn. It was removed with care so as not to break off one of the legs. The pin was put back in place so the hole wouldn't collapse during the peening to follow later.

The thumb safety and slide stop plunger and spring were removed. There is supposed to be a dogleg in the spring sufficient to keep it from jumping out when the safety is pulled out. A more positive dogleg was set to make sure it would stay as it should.

The main-spring housing was disassembled by putting a punch in a vise and pressing the main spring and pulling out the retainer pin, then gradually releasing the pressure on the

In welding the head space extension, gunsmith is careful in selecting the type of flame he uses with his torch.

In welding the recoil lugs, more metal is added with the torch so that there will be closer tolerances when done.

Photo illustrates manner in which additional metal has been added to the head space extension and recoil lugs. (Below) Again using his torch, Bob Day anneals the part of the barrel that was welded earlier in the sequence.

Using his ever-present file, gunsmith removes the sharp edges on receiver rails. Note stippling on the grip area.

Bob Day insists that most of the work he does in job of accurizing an autoloader can be done with files, stones.

In taking the side play out of the slide, the gunsmith uses a vise to squeeze the sides a bit closer together.

*After the sides are squeezed properly, Day again goes at the rails with his file, cutting metal for good fit.*

*The shiny area on the slide shows where metal is removed.*

main spring. Each was checked thoroughly: housing, main spring, the hole. Each was inspected for smoothness, burrs, anything that might cause binding or hesitation. The inside of the housing was polished to be safe. Then this grouping was declared ready.

The safety lock on this gun had been bearing heavily and required a good deal of fitting.

On the subject of accuracy jobs, there is only one with Bob Day. If the shooter orders the complete job, he gets the same work whether it is for target or field use. The only difference is the sights.

"I can tighten a slide and do a lot of nit-pickin' things, but not help the gun all that much — and I tell the customer that." Day said such a job wouldn't improve accuracy ten percent, except that it might help between the ears, since the gun doesn't rattle as much. He pointed out again that he doesn't waste time on cosmetics. "If it doesn't benefit the shooting qualities of the gun, I don't mess with it."

Day feels oversize safeties serve a definite purpose and he usually builds up the safety on his accuracy jobs. The only fault he finds is the price. Pistol work is a labor of love with Bob Day and he keeps his prices to the bare minimum so as not to price an accurized pistol out of the reach of anyone really wanting such a fine handgun.

As Day prepared the slide, the initial step was to barely break the edges of the locking recesses in the top of the slide — the rear edges only; all three of them. To do any work on

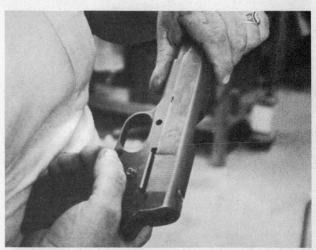

*Day pauses in his labors long enough to check the fit of the slide to the receiver. Fitting is a continuing job.*

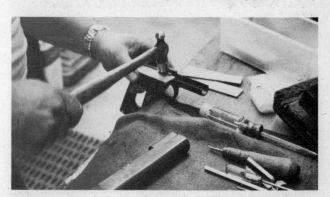

*Set up to peen down the rails on the receiver, Bob Day uses the corner of his smithing bench to hold the unit. Note that rails are protected by soft material so that there will not be peening marks on the metal of the gun.*

*The slide of the Mark IV is beginning to take on custom look, as the Texas gunsmith holds it for his inspection.*

After peening down the rails on the receiver, the gunsmith uses one of his files to true worked-over rails.

Bob Day has found that, for perfect fit, it also is necessary to true up the underside of the slide rails.

The gunsmith puts himself into feel of fitted parts, as he concentrates on the way the gun feels in his hands.

the front is a waste of time, because they don't touch anything, he said.

When asked where he learned all this he said, "At the Air Force Marksmanship School. Many of the basic principles of accurizing .45s and .38s were already established. A lot of refinements have been added but most of the basic principles were already there."

Day credits Robert L. Roripaugh as the man who understood more about the .45 than anyone he had ever met. Day worked for three years with him. Sometimes when Day had thought of what seemed to be a terrific discovery, he would discover Roripaugh had figured that out a long time ago.

"He's the one man in this world I have to take my hat off to," Day reflected.

"I don't believe, if John Browning were alive today, he would be a bit surprised at what we are doing. In fact, he did exactly what is being done now, in principle, because basically an accuracy job is nothing more than removing all the built-in factory clearances that are necessary in a military pistol. With those clearances removed — everything

zero-zero again — you have your accurized pistol. It's as simple as that."

The subject of hardball ammo in a Colt Gold Cup came up, with the common thinking that such ammunition will tear it up. In a test done by Skeeter Skelton several years ago, five thousand factory hardball rounds, furnished by Federal, were fired through a Gold Cup with no visible damage whatever. The gun held up flawlessly.

"The gun that enabled me to shoot well enough to make the ARDC pistol team in my first year of shooting, was an out-of-the-box factory Gold Cup. Not only did I shoot well enough to get on the team and to Lackland's All Air Force Matches and Camp Perry as well, but this gun was used to shoot two of my three legs on the Distinguished.

"This out-of-the-box gun did double-duty for everything: hardball, three-gun aggregate, wadcutters, handloads, or whatever I could get my hands on. It is probably better than most of the guns being touted as accurized."

Bob Day likes the pre-70 Series Gold Cup better than the current model, because he has little confidence in the

With his indispensable file, Bob Day cleans peen marks from receiver top.

Careful filing also is the means for removing excess weld from the barrel.

Inside of the slide must be measured to establish the length of the auto's head space unit, according to Day.

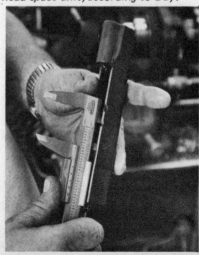

Micrometer carriage stop is used in cutting the head space extension to the proper length, using the lathe.

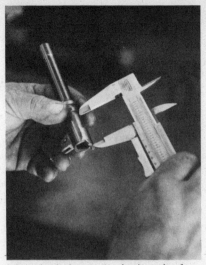

After the lathe work, the length of the head space extension is checked once again with Vernier calipers.

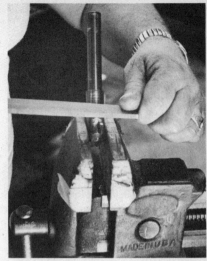

Extra metal was added to the lugs in welding. Now some of it is removed for an improved fit, using the file.

Using special facing jig, gunsmith cuts side of head space extension, using file to attain proper width.

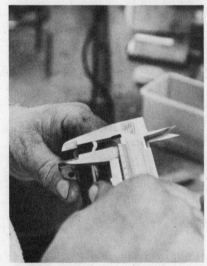

Gunsmith uses his vernier calipers to measure the width of the head space extension after filing down the side.

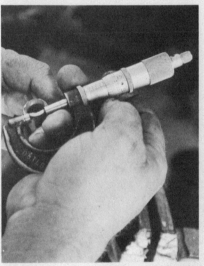

Additional checking on width of the head space extension is accomplished with the use of standard micrometer.

new collet-type bushing. The old Gold Cup had a bushing set up with double bearing bands inside the bushing, fore and aft, with a bevel cut in the base of the bushing where the recoil spring presses, and that area of the recoil spring plug was also beveled. Each time the gun went into battery, the bevels fitted together and kept the bushing tight.

Checking the hammer and sear pins for any obvious undersize, he said there was nothing else to watch for here.

Bringing into play what is best described as a miniature jack-hammer, the front of the receiver and the main spring housing were stippled. This is the same tool he's been using for years. "The carbide point hasn't been sharpened since the day I made it," Day said with a grin.

"There is absolutely nothing that has to be done to accurize the .45 that can't be done with the most common of hand tools and end up with a job just as good as one done with all kinds of elaborate tools.

"Everything can be done by hand and I have done everything by hand, with a hammer, pliers, screwdriver, punches, and a file."

Often someone will remark he could do that if he had the tools to do it with. With the exception of a welding torch, Day insists everything else can be done by hand.

In his beginning years as a gunsmith, Bob Day was forced to do everything by hand; he had no power tools of any kind. He used as an example his learning to fit the head-space extension. He said he would weld it up, fit it to an old slide, show it to his teacher and be told it was a good job, but could be better. With that, the teacher would file off all the weld and hand it back with the comment: "Do it again." It was done over and over, until it was good enough for the instructor then on to the next step.

At that moment, Day was welding on the head-space extension using ten pounds of oxygen and five pounds of acetylene with a number 2½ tip on the torch. He added length and width to the head-space extension and also built

*Holding the unit, the San Antonio gunsmith shows the manner in which the head space extension fits the slide.*

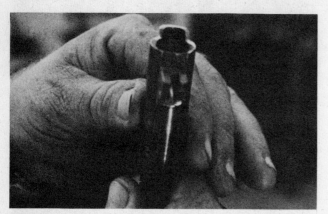

*Day displays the finished head space extension in photo.*

up the lugs on the bottom of the barrel.

For this he uses high-carbon spring wire from an old .45 magazine. He has found, over the years, that this substance gives the best possible weld approximating the original steel in the barrel for hardness and durability. When finished, according to Day, this weld is equal to or superior to the original barrel.

Ordinary mild steel welding rod will not stand up to the battering the average .45 receives. The weld beats out and the gun will lose accuracy quickly, according to Day.

In welding with high-carbon spring wire, Day usually gets the base metal almost to fluid temperature, then turns the torch onto the spring wire, melts it and lets it drop into the base metal. He then heats the two together to cause it to puddle. Building the puddle first then putting in the spring wire doesn't work too well in Bob's opinion.

He uses a flame on the torch that is slightly excess acetylene and drops a puddle on the right side of the head-space extension then a bead across it to a final bead on the other side. He added .080 to .100-inch of metal to the lugs.

After the barrel cooled the weld was polished from the chamber area. He then came back with a torch and heated the entire thing, including the barrel lug, playing the flame around, not holding it in any one place, and carefully watching the color change in the barrel. From a purple to blue then bluish-purple then to a dull gray.

When all of the metal is back to the dull gray, Bob Day

removes the heat and lets the barrel cool normally by itself. Incidentally when high-carbon spring wire welded to the barrel doesn't receive the heat evenly, it can, and usually does, form small pockets of extremely hard metal. They are so hard they will knock the teeth off a file!

Back to the slide, Day eased off all the sharp edges where contact would be made, using file work. He does not like lapping compound and seldom uses it.

"The only place the slide has to fit perfectly, or nearly so, is at the point where it is in battery position. If all the side play and vertical play is out of the slide in that position, the gun will shoot as well as it can be made to shoot," Day says. "This one is a little tighter than I want it to be, so we'll go a bit further in fitting. When finished, it will fit so close that when the slide goes into battery it will actually 'ring.' It will be that solid.

"I have my own way of doing it, and I've been doing it

*This was Bob Day's first stocking job. He copied design from an Anthony Guymon advertisement in American Rifleman.*

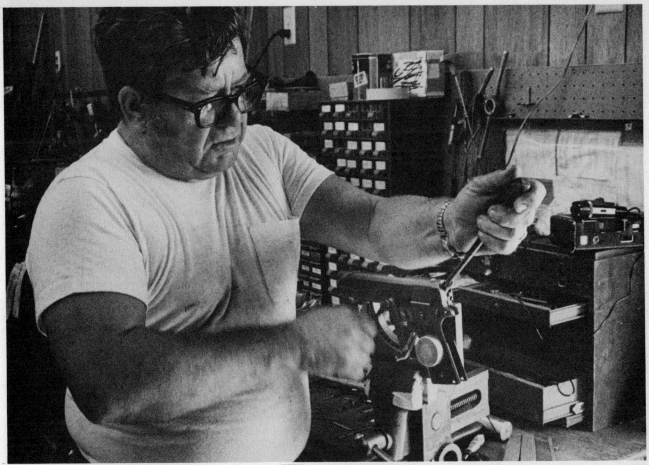

In his San Antonio gunsmithing shop, Day uses this lug cutter which was designed by another smith, Bobby Trapp.

for a lot of years. I've been fortunate in that the men I was building guns for were among the finest shooters in the United States and I was virtually married to those guns for years on end. And I got to see what the gun did on the very day it was accurized by me until the man retired or quit shooting — how it held up — and that was the big secret. I knew how to build a gun for durability. Those men were shooting world and international records. You don't fool around when you give them a gun. Any one of them was good enough to take a gun to the range, shoot five shots

through it, bring it back and throw it on the desk saying, 'that gun don't shoot,' and know he was right."

One of his shooters shot a Hammerli free pistol with the trigger set so light that, when the muzzle was elevated more than forty-five degrees, the weight of the trigger would cause the gun to fire. Yet that shooter could actually feel the trigger creep when he was shooting this pistol. This same shooter was so good he could call his shots within a half-inch at fifty meters.

Day places a bar in the receiver to peen the rails down,

After the lugs have been cut, they are rough and carry numerous burrs.

Day cleans up the burrs, excess weld between lugs with a knife-edge file.

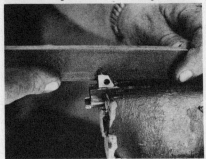

With lugs shaped properly, unit now is ready for link, pin installation.

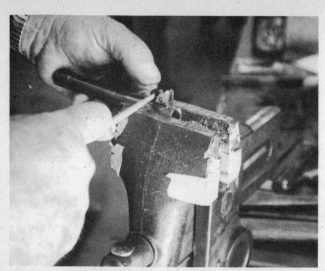

The Texas pistolsmith next fits link into rebuilt lugs.

The link in place, slide stop is fitted as next step.

Feeding ramp on the barrel is cut, using a power tool.

thus removing vertical play in the slide. Horizontal play already had been removed at this point. This bar is of hardened steel ground to .118-inch thickness. The rails are peened against it to remove the vertical play. This is a matter of experience, since there is no way to measure it. From here, Day went to a .117-inch bar for the first .75-inch, peening and filing to perfect fit.

"Accurizing can be told to someone but it is still experience and only experience that gives the ability to do a good job. Some gunsmiths claim high-falutin' secrets," Day said. "The only secret they have — and what they are trying to keep from their customers — is that they aren't nearly so smart as they want the customer to think."

Day feels there are no such things as secrets and he was willing to tell or show anyone what he did and how he did it. "Experience and hard work get the job done," he said, then added, "To be good at custom pistolsmithing it almost has to be a labor of love."

Incidentally, he has found that it usually takes three or four hours to fit a slide, once you really know what you are doing.

When the rails are pulled together they lose their original configuration and must be filed back to shape. Here Day did a bit of lapping, with a German-made compound. He cautioned this was an area where someone might get carried away and, by trying to make it look pretty, could ruin it.

He cleaned up the holes as sometimes they can become distorted during the peening. He then refit the ejector and pronounced the receiver and slide finished to the point they would ring if put together.

He revealed one secret he had never shown anybody else: he measured the inside of the flat between the rearmost surface of the rear locking recesses and the breech face — 1.320 inches — then went to the lathe (pointing out this could be done by hand) and fit the head space extension to this measurement. He finished it with a file, pointing out he would find out in a hurry if he had left any hard spots.

He then finished off the excess weld on the front of the lugs, bringing them back to their original configuration.

Fitting the sides of the head-space extension, where it was welded up, was done with a handmade gadget of his

Another file is used in initial deburring of the barrel.

Buffing wheel is used to polish exterior barrel surfaces.

Pistolsmith uses an aluminum oxide wheel to remove the excess weld material from the inside of chamber mouth.

Dremel buff is utilized in polishing the auto's chamber.

own design. This tool is made so that when the file hits the rollers he knows the head space extension is where he wants it. Speaking of the tool, he said it took a long time to work it out and, though it appears simple, extreme finesse was required because of the precision involved.

Day then took what he called a "work bushing," a plain old GI bushing, for barrel fitting on the head-space extension. The desired fit is for the barrel to go back into the head-space extension area and up into battery without interference but with zero clearance. This one was nearly correct and took only the tap of a mallet to bring it into battery. Three light strokes of a file fitted it perfectly.

There was no fore and aft play. Day contends there are only two other gunsmiths in the country who fit head space this perfectly. Others claim it isn't necessary. But Bob Day is convinced it is only by going this route that he has been able to get the durability he expects from each accuracy job.

Bob Day's aim, what he expects of his work, is simple: when an accurized gun goes out of his shop, the average competitive shooter should be able to use it for the next ten years without doing anything to it except maybe a trigger job. And if the shooter will take care of the gun that's all that will be necessary, based upon history of Day's efforts.

Day likes his guns kept oiled well and often. With the slide back, he recommends a drop or two on each rail and on the muzzle end of the barrel so it can work back under the bushing. Close the slide and place a drop or two on each

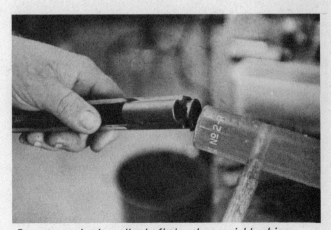

Day uses a plastic mallet in fitting the special bushing.

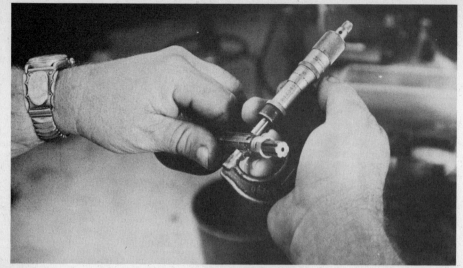

*Reamer is adjusted to ream special bushing so that it will match barrel.*

*Bob Day accomplishes the final hand fitting steps on bushing for Mark IV.*

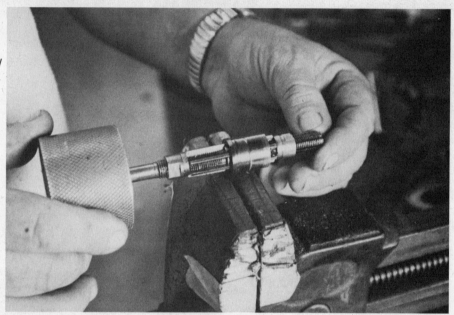

*Pistolsmith uses single-cut file to put clearance on the sides of the handgun's recoil spring guide.*

side of the ejection port. The lower side lets the oil ease down onto the slide stop. When shooting in a match, he oils several times during the shoot.

In cutting the lugs on the bottom of the barrel where the slide stop pin aligns, Day used a tool designed by one of Lackland's gunsmiths, Bobby Trapp. Day says it is the finest tool ever made to assist in accurizing the .45. This system is instantly adjustable to cut the precise amount of metal the smith wants removed. This, too, can be done by hand, but the tool makes it much faster.

Asked about the life of a barrel Day feels one should last through 10,000 rounds of hardball and 12,000 rounds or more with wadcutter or good handloads. He says the outside of the barrel wears out before the inside.

In fitting the link, he uses oversize pins, the size depending upon each individual barrel. Ordinarily starting with .013-inch, he sometimes goes to .017 or .021-inch. To check the proper fit, he lays the barrel on the receiver, then presses down on it and tries to put the slide stop pin through the hole. It should drop through with no interference. Otherwise there would not be sufficient clearance for the barrel to come out of battery.

Some smiths, not really understanding the workings of the .45, try to correct this by wallowing out the hole to make it larger. This will work to a degree, but on the feeding cycle the slide stop pin will hit against the lugs on the front of the barrel, really battering the devil out of it. Day has learned from experience that this detracts from the accuracy of the gun.

As to how his accurized guns shoot, Bob Day pointed out it depended entirely on the ammunition, but the average groups will be within a quarter-inch of the capabilities of the barrel-ammo combo. This has been proven over and over again by putting the barrel in a test device and shooting with a specific lot of ammo. If the

Day holds trigger yoke from which vertical clearance has been removed by means of technique called staking

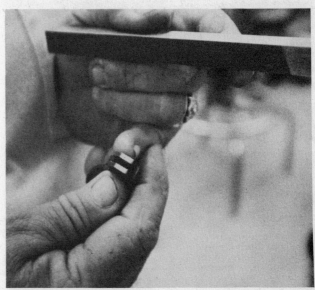

Pistolsmith inspects hammer of the autoloader, while holding the square file used on it and the gun's sear.

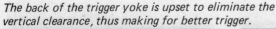

The back of the trigger yoke is upset to eliminate the vertical clearance, thus making for better trigger.

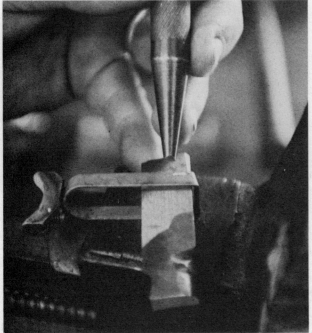

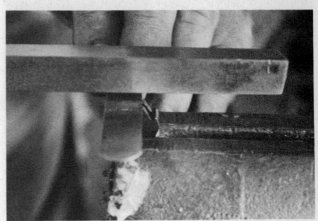

Using square file, hammer hooks are cut to proper height.

At left is the Mark IV hammer after alteration compared to a hammer for the same model which has not been touched.

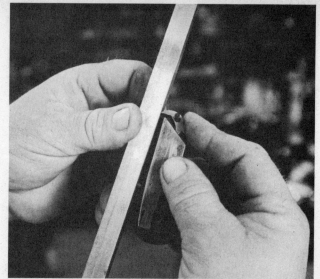

Using his file with care, the pistolsmith puts the face — or primary angle — on the sear for the modification.

Crude though it may appear, this is Bob Day's original sear jig, which he has used from start of his career.

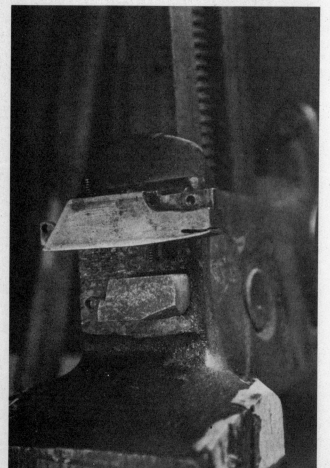

group was 1¾ inches at fifty yards his finished accurized gun would hold to no more than two inches. After all this, Day said he would still probably go to a .001-inch smaller slide stop pin when the fitted barrel bushing was installed.

Up to this point all of the fitting of the barrel, head space, et cetera, had been done with that old GI work bushing. Day now started with a special bushing that is oversize on the outside and undersize inside. In this instance, he picked one that fit the slide almost perfectly. A real snug fit, it could be pressed into place and pried back out. And with a bushing wrench, it could be turned without any undue effort.

New Series MK IV barrels are slightly larger at the muzzle than the overall barrel, about .012-inch smaller back of this larger muzzle area, so the barrel can have complete freedom of movement when it is in any position other than

The sear is inspected carefully after cut has been made.

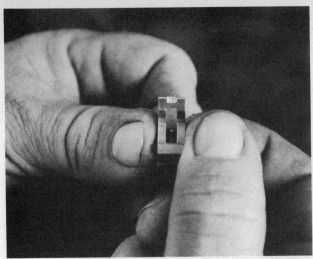

Cut through the sear is made so hammer half-cock clears.

battery. The collet-type bushing in these MK IVs tightens only as the barrel is in battery, thus, supposedly, positioning the barrel exactly the same for each shot.

"It has been my experience over the years, particularly watching guns being shot from a machine rest, that any time a spring of any kind holds the barrel down out of battery, and the lug and/or lugs on the bottom of the barrel are trying to lift it up into battery — thus under any spring tension at all — the gun will have a tendency to string the shots vertically on the target. This is the primary reason I don't like the collet-type bushing."

Concerning an expandable adjustable reamer he used, Day said, "It works real fine for holes that have to be fitted quite closely to an odd size like .579-inch, which this barrel measures."

With the bushing nearly a dead-perfect fit to the barrel, Day announced such a fit meant it was too snug; the gun couldn't function because the barrel and bushing were in alignment with the barrel out of battery in the unlocked position. The bushing had to be relieved enough for the barrel to move up into battery. Had this relief not been given, the barrel would have a tendency to "spring back"

Surrounded by his equipment, Bob Day tests the trigger. Assembly, disassembly are continual as he checks progress.

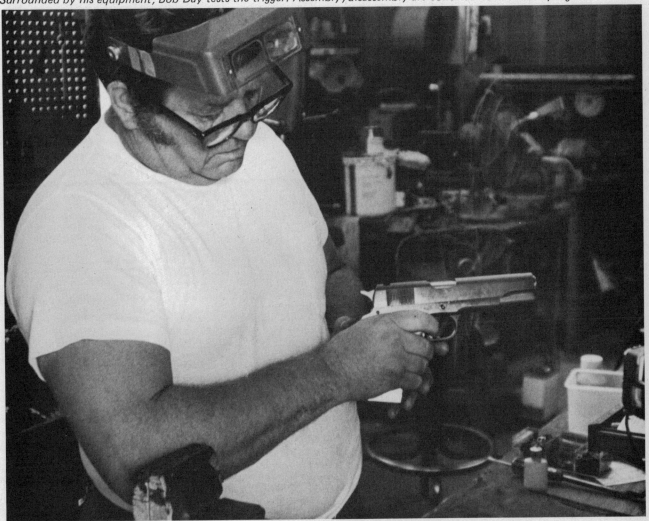

*The original rear sight has been cut in half by Bob Day, then reinstalled.*

meaning it wanted to pop out of battery. This condition is highly detrimental to accuracy.

To gain this necessary relief, Day used the same reamer; but by hand. The idea was to remove only a little metal from the bottom front of the bushing and an equally small amount from the upper rear. Thus, the barrel will fit closely to the overall diameter, yet have the freedom to move up and down, or tip, as referred to by gunsmiths.

Day said this same principle was applied to the S&W Model 52 by use of an oversize portion on the muzzle with a spherical radius. "A great theory," he added.

The fitted barrel and bushing went back together with the barrel readily moving to full engagement with virtually no tendency to spring back. Day said he considers one-sixty-fourth-inch spring back perfect, "because, with a little use, it will wear to complete elimination."

"If it's loose to start, it can't do anything but get worse," he added. "The combination of the slide to barrel fit and the fit of the lugs and link area are about ninety percent of an accuracy job.

"I can make a gun shoot great off a machine rest or out of a hand without ever touching the slide — just fit the lugs tight — but it won't be near as durable as if everything fits perfectly," Day contends.

At this point he decided to take .001-inch off the head-space extension, then pronounced the fit as perfect.

*The excess welded material filling rear sight slot must be ground off.*

*A hole is drilled into the top of the slide for the 1/16-inch pin that will hold the slot filler material in place.*

He said all the tension would be out in a hundred rounds or less.

In describing the way he fits bushings he said, "If you look at the wear pattern on the barrel after five hundred or a thousand rounds, there will be a wide bearing point on the bottom of the front and the rear of the top, maybe even to seeing a fine line on the side showing it to be a perfect fit."

Without the recoil spring, the slide closed readily when the gun was put back together. Bob said here that the last three-thirty-seconds-inch is the point at which the slide stop pin bears quite hard on the lugs that were built-up on the bottom of the barrel and recut. It is here the precision work shows up. If properly fitted, all vertical clearances between the slide stop pin, receiver, barrel, and slide are gone.

This particular gun is going to be loosened up a bit, because it belongs to a field shooter who won't want to go through a break-in period.

Day pointed to a little burnished mark on the lugs, the area where the three-thirty-seconds-inch resistance came

*Using a ballpeen hammer, the pistolsmith installs the pins that will hold the slot-filling material in place.*

*After being cleaned up, the filler material in the slide is nearly invisible and the rear sight is repositioned.*

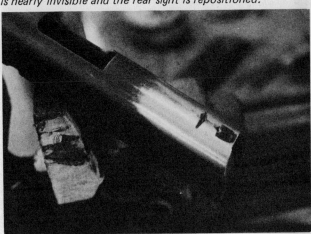

into being. This is done as the barrel and slide are moving along parallel to the receiver when the .45 is fired, because the barrel and slide are in motion before the bullet leaves the barrel. By doing this with the slide, it assures the barrel and slide stay aligned with the receiver until the bullet leaves the barrel.

Still not quite satisfied, Day stripped the .45 down again and relieved either side of the recoil spring guide to make certain it wouldn't bind.

Reassembled, there actually was a ringing sound as it went into battery. This, according to Day, means the handgun has become a solid piece of metal so far as the fitting is concerned. "And the beauty of it is that, when properly accurized, this old slab-sided rascal will shoot as if it were a solid piece of steel, because it will absolutely return the barrel and slide to exactly the same position from shot to shot," Day added.

Day pronounced this gun as being capable of going 6000 to 7000 rounds, then perhaps needing a tune-up, then another 6000 or 7000 rounds before finally wearing out the barrel. This would be with factory wadcutters, he explained. "Until the bore goes, it will give gilt-edge accuracy. The average shooter can't wear out a gun."

Day has had guns out of his shop fire over 20,000 rounds with nothing done except snug up the slide a bit. This has been with service match guns where daily records were kept so they knew exactly how many rounds had been

Bob Day keeps profuse notes on past work and can refer to them for proper machining dimensions for most guns.

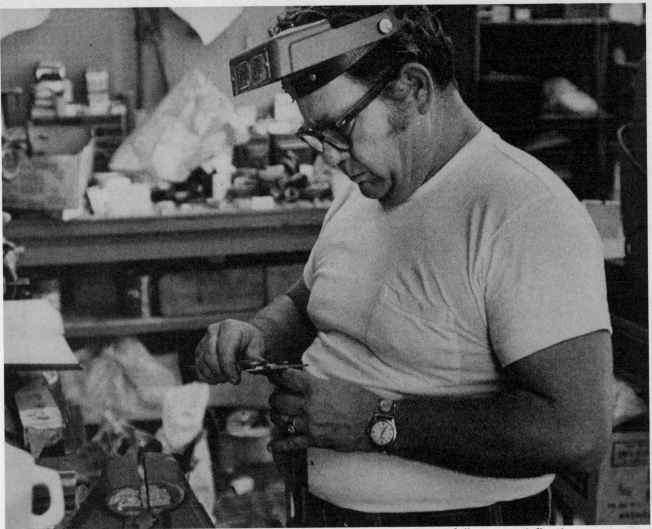
*For the ultimate target accuracy that is sought, even the most minute part must be carefully measured, fitted.*

fired. He mentioned several he had worked on personally that, after 20,000 rounds, still were turning out 2650s for the shooters.

Now it was trigger-fitting time. This one had to be drilled and tapped for a stop. Day takes out all vertical and horizontal movement.

"Sometimes the trigger yoke gives problems by moving up and down maybe only .003, .004 or .005-inch, but it's enough to cause a top shooter to throw a shot plumb over the fence." Day raised a little welt of metal to take out this play. It was so small one could hardly see it, but Day said it was sufficient to do the job. He worked with the trigger until satisfied it was perfect.

On the hammer, Day never cuts more off than absolutely necessary. The height of the hammer hooks can be regulated simply by using a hardened piece of steel of predetermined thickness and filing against the surface to get both hooks down to the height wanted. It is important that they be the same height.

The hammer hooks on this gun were cut to .018-inch. Ordinarily Day takes them a little lower on competition guns, but since this was to be a holster gun he was giving it

a little more hook. Setting it with a little more sear engagement with a little less angle makes it safer as a field gun. A strictly competition trigger could be hard to handle in the field unless the shooter really knows what he is doing.

Though the NRA minimum is 3½ pounds for trigger pull, Day planned to set this one at four pounds as a field gun. "But the shooter will think it is two, it will break so cleanly," he added.

He cut away part of the half-cock with a matching cut on the sear so the hammer could fall through without any interference or binding, the trigger stop set at its closest possible position, yet it will still catch on the half-cock if accidentally dropped.

"The gun will still be safe but it is more refined insofar as competitive shooting is concerned."

Day checked the holes through the receiver and hammer to make sure they were straight and to make certain the hammer didn't have a tendency to crowd one side or the other. If the hammer crowds either side, it indicates the holes are too far out of line to make a good gun.

In working the sear, Day uses a little gadget of his own

*The slide is held in padded jaws for second milling cut for installation of the Smith & Wesson K sight. The technique is discussed in the text.*

*With the amount of metal the milling machine eats, care must be exercised to assure that cut is not too deep.*

*The milling machine also is utilized by Day to cut relief for the bevel. The machine can save countless hours.*

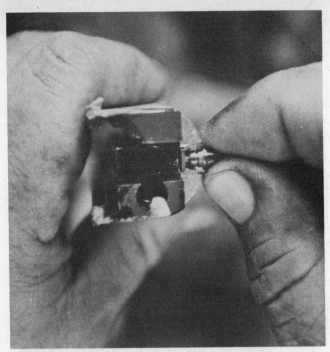

Pistolsmith checks the fit of T-slot cut in the slide.

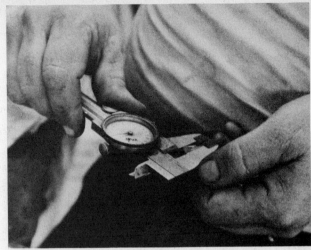

Day measures height of the front sight, using calipers.

Milling machine is used to cut slot for new front sight.

After sight slot is milled, file is used to clean up area.'

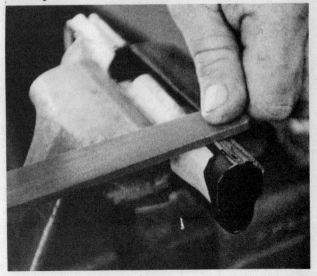

design. This particular tool, made eighteen years ago, is designed so the sear can be inserted, with its pin, then a stone or file used to cut the primary face or angle. The angle Day wants is very close to the original Government Model sear.

To set up such a tool, an untouched Parkerized sear is needed. Adjustments are made so the stone or file only cleans up the pristine sear. This will be the right angle. From here on, it becomes a matter of experience to alter the trigger pull by changing the angle. Bob Day emphasized, "This is for serious gunsmiths only."

This sear is to be set up with about .008 engagement on the hammer hooks with equal pressure on both hooks on a sear spring that is almost, but not quite, flat. Ordinarily this will give about a four-pound trigger, but it can't really be depended on, because springs vary.

"A trigger job is an individual thing on each individual gun. No two will be the same," Day said as he set the jig to cut the secondary angle on the sear.

This done Day assembled the gun, dry-fired it several times and pronounced it good but not good enough. Again it was stripped down for a bit of touch up here and there, then reassembled. This time he decided it was right.

Bob Day has been working on pistols for a little over twenty years and is a master of the "by feel" technique. If the slide doesn't feel right he corrects it. The same is true of the trigger, safety, and all functioning parts. It is this inner ability, coming from long years of experience, that sets apart the real gunsmith.

"There is only one way to handle an accurized gun," Day said, "When the slide is all the way to the rear, locked open, and a fresh magazine inserted, either the hammer must be held back against the grip safety when the slide is released or else the trigger has to be squeezed hard against the stop. This will prevent the hammer from following the

A new front sight — in this instance a Dan Wesson sight — is silver soldered into position in the new sight slot.

After the sight is soldered in place, the slide is polished to do away with burrs from cutting, any excess metal.

Larry Noel, who works with Bob Day, sandblasts the slide, observing his work through protective glass. (Lower right) Apprentice gunsmith Eddie Garcia checks the slide for conformity after it has been sandblasted.

slide or going to half-cock and damaging the sear and hammer." Day recommends holding the hammer, because that has to be done consciously. He emphasized that you don't do both as they could get a little out of sequence and, to use Day's words, "The gun will go bang."

Day also explained the possibility of the hammer following the slide. "The trigger in a .45 is a free-floating affair. It's not tied, hooked or hinged to any part of the gun. It's in there free as a bird. When the slide slams forward the gun is jerked in that direction, along with the arm and hand, but there is a tendency for the trigger to remain stationary. When this happens the rear of the trigger yoke can tap against the disconnector, which thumps the bottom leg of the sear just enough to knock the sear out from under the hammer, and the hammer will fall." He added, "With the trigger pulled all the way to the rear, the disconnector is disconnected from the bottom leg of the sear."

He reemphasized that .005 to .008-inch engagement is adequate insofar as the gun's safety is concerned, but it does require this precaution "just in case."

Colt overcomes this condition in their Gold Cup with a specially designed hammer and sear allowing an almost over-cocked position which serves to discourage following of the slide at the loading stage.

The San Antonio pistolsmith polishes receiver on buffer.

As with each handgun he accurizes, Bob Day treks to the range to test fire the Mark IV. If one fails to live up to his expectations for accuracy, it's back to the shop.

Day's bluing tanks are located out-of-doors, doing away with the need for an expensive ventilating system in shop. (Below) Polished slide, sandblasted receiver have been stabilized in the basket ready for the bluing solution.

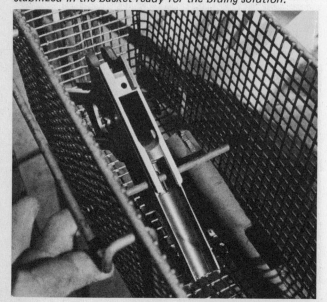

"This gun will be as safe as ever carried in the cocked and locked condition so common with most .45 users, those who have used them a lot and grown to love and depend on the gun." Day recommends, however, that the grip safety and safety be checked regularly to be sure they are functioning correctly. Depending on how much the gun is used, this should be done every three or four months.

"As long as the grip safety is working properly there is no way the gun is going to go off," he concluded.

As for the possibility of the hammer following the slide, gunsmiths recognize the problem, but none have come up with a foolproof solution. National Match guns used an aluminum trigger at one time to try and correct the condition. At another time, Colt inserted an additional spring and lever in their Gold Cup to help prevent the hammer falling. Day obviously doesn't care much for that solution and says most gunsmiths "lose" those two additional parts when working on the guns.

His own possible solution is to increase the amount of take-up on the trigger; all .45s have a certain amount before bearing metal to metal. Most of this take-up could be spring

While in the Air Force, Day was championship material and, it is said, could be a top contender even today.

*The first 10-shot test target fired was with Federal's 185-gr. wadcutter.*

*When second 10-shot group was fired with Remington's 185-gr. hollow point, the group remained just as tight, but moved to the right. This illustrates the differences in brands of ammo.*

loaded by the sear spring which would reduce the tendency for the hammer to fall. Some shooters object to this additional take-up, but seldom does a top-flight shooter. In fact, most like it, as it allows them to feel the trigger better thus enabling them to get everything perfect before letting the shot go.

"A finely tuned gun should never be loaned or given to someone else to shoot. It's for the owner only if it is to serve as it should," Bob Day contends.

Still another tidbit came out of his mouth. "A creditable trigger job can be done with nothing but a file, if the workman knows what he is doing."

With the inner workings of the gun finished, it was sight time. Day's first act was to take an issue rear sight and cut

it in half. Each half then was driven into the rear sight slot from opposite sides with no effort to make sure the center was filled. A one-sixteenth-inch hole was drilled through each half, from the top, into the slide. A piece of steel welding rod then was driven into each hole to ensure the pieces of metal never slipped. Once firmly in place, those cut-in-half rear sight segments were ground to a near fit, then peened until there was no indication they weren't part of the original slide.

"It isn't necessary," Day pointed out, "to fill the center because that will be milled out anyway."

None of this has anything to do with the accuracy of the gun. Good sights simply help to extract whatever accuracy is built into that gun. Day normally uses S&W K-frame

The fully accurized Colt Mark IV .45 in the hand of Bob Day, who did the work. Note the Dan Wesson front sight, the Smith & Wesson K rear sight and King Combat Speed Safety; these installations are only a small part of work.

Air Force gunsmith Bob Roripaugh (left) tells student, Bob Day, how a job should be done. This was in latter's early days in the gun shop at Lackland Air Force Base.

sights, but will install whatever good target sight the customer wants. Fitting the "K" sight requires five separate cutting acts, then one more for the front sight. Bob Day makes his own target front sights from a blank after it is silver soldered to the slide. In this case, because it is a field gun, a Dan Wesson front sight was installed, as this shooter wanted a colored insert.

Day does his own polishing and bluing and it's at least as good as a factory job. Once that chore was finished, the gun was put together. A white-outlined rear sight blade was installed along with the Dan Wesson yellow insert.

But the gun still was not finished. Magazines also are fitted to each gun.

Day started with a new Colt factory magazine. Using a steel form slipped into the magazine, the lips were peened against the form for better shape and fit. Day then made sure the magazine fit the gun securely. Thumbing two cartridges into the magazine, he fired them into his bullet trap for functioning. Two more magazines were fitted in the same manner. Then moving over to the vise, he took a

*In 1960, when Bob Day was initially assigned to the USAF Marksmanship Gunsmith Section, he worked competition guns.*

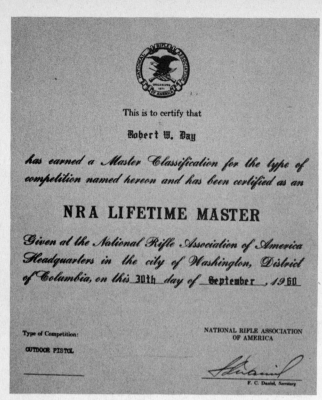

This is to certify that

**Robert W. Day**

has earned a Master Classification for the type of competition named hereon and has been certified as an

## NRA LIFETIME MASTER

Given at the National Rifle Association of America Headquarters in the city of Washington, District of Columbia, on this 30th day of September, 1960.

Type of Competition:

OUTDOOR PISTOL

NATIONAL RIFLE ASSOCIATION OF AMERICA

F. C. Daniel, Secretary

*As a pistol competitor, Day received his NRA Lifetime Master certificate in 1960, competing when he wasn't rebuilding handguns. (Below) A special order from the Dept. of the Air Force awarded Day USAF Badge 34 as a distinguished pistol shot during the same time frame.*

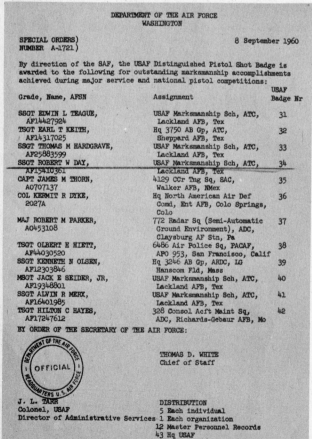

DEPARTMENT OF THE AIR FORCE
WASHINGTON

SPECIAL ORDERS)                          8 September 1960
NUMBER A-1721)

By direction of the SAF, the USAF Distinguished Pistol Shot Badge is awarded to the following for outstanding marksmanship accomplishments achieved during major service and national pistol competitions:

| Grade, Name, AFSN | Assignment | USAF Badge Nr |
|---|---|---|
| SSGT EDWIN L TEAGUE, AF14427924 | USAF Marksmanship Sch, ATC, Lackland AFB, Tex | 31 |
| TSGT EARL T KEITH, AF14317025 | Hq 3750 AB Gp, ATC, Sheppard AFB, Tex | 32 |
| SSGT THOMAS M HARDGRAVE, AF25883599 | USAF Marksmanship Sch, ATC, Lackland AFB, Tex | 33 |
| SSGT ROBERT W DAY, AF15410361 | USAF Marksmanship Sch, ATC, Lackland AFB, Tex | 34 |
| CAPT JAMES M THORN, A0707137 | 4129 CCr Tng Sq, SAC, Walker AFB, NMex | 35 |
| COL KERMIT R DYKE, 2027A | Hq North American Air Def Comd, Ent AFB, Colo Springs, Colo | 36 |
| MAJ ROBERT M PARKER, A0453108 | 772 Radar Sq (Semi-Automatic Ground Environment), ADC, Claysburg AF Stn, Pa | 37 |
| TSGT OLBERT H HIETT, AF44030520 | 6486 Air Police Sq, PACAF, APO 953, San Francisco, Calif | 38 |
| SSGT KENNETH N OLSEN, AF12303846 | Hq 3246 AB Gp, ARDC, LG Hanscom Fld, Mass | 39 |
| MSGT JACK E SEIDER, JR, AF19348801 | USAF Marksmanship Sch, ATC, Lackland AFB, Tex | 40 |
| SSGT ALVIN R MERX, AF16401985 | USAF Marksmanship Sch, ATC, Lackland AFB, Tex | 41 |
| TSGT HILTON C HAYES, AF17247612 | 328 Consol Acft Maint Sq, ADC, Richards-Gebaur AFB, Mo | 42 |

BY ORDER OF THE SECRETARY OF THE AIR FORCE:

THOMAS D. WHITE
Chief of Staff

J. L. TARR
Colonel, USAF
Director of Administrative Services

DISTRIBUTION
5 Each individual
1 Each organization
12 Master Personnel Records
43 Hq USAF

A-1721

2600

ROBERT W. DAY

*The penholder which graces the desk in Bob Day's office today was for his 2600 score in three-caliber shooting.*

little electric engraving tool and inscribed the last four digits of the gun's serial number into the bottom, along with numbering each: 1, 2, and 3.

Then came the acid test: Would it shoot?

Those 2600 ratings don't come in Cracker Jack boxes, and with the wind blowing, Day did mention it made close grouping harder. The first ten-shot group was fired with match wadcutter ammo. The gun printed six tens, three nines and a called eight (3Xs) straight from the bench, sights set the way he felt they should be, but with no shots fired to see if he was right.

*On this field gun, the pistolsmith installed a Dan Wesson sight with a yellow insert, but the autoloader also received full treatment as though it was a target gun.*

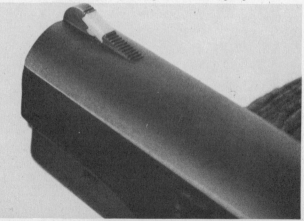

A white-outlined blade was used with the S&W K sight. Photo also shows how King Combat Speed Safety is easily reached. (Right) Both the main spring housing and the front of autoloader's grip have been heavily stippled.

Day put ten Federal 185-grain Match wadcutters into the twenty-five-yard pistol target. It printed seven tens and three nines (6Xs).

Trying another load, Day fired ten Federal 185-grain hollow point Match cartridges for another seven tens and three nines with five Xs.

Going to still another load, the Remington 185-grain hollow points were fired, as this particular gun was for a field shooter who used this ammo. Those Remingtons printed seven tens and three nines but with only two Xs. The reason for this was the group moved enough to the right that six of the shots would have been X-ring had the gun been sighted in for this load. Changing from Federal to Remington moved the group center a full inch to the right.

This job required parts of eight days stretched out over nearly three weeks. A minimum of twenty-five hours went into the gun and probably closer to thirty. Day had stated about eighteen hours normally was enough for accurizing a pistol. The additional time is where that "labor of love" comes in.

The price is $150 plus sights. Figure out his hourly wage and we are fast back to that "labor of love."

Bob Day isn't soliciting work because he's already behind and has been for a long time, but his work is well worth waiting for if accuracy is your game. The trick is to get your name on the list.

Fully accurized Colt Mark IV .45 shows the work that went into the exterior at the hands of Bob Day.

# Chapter 15

# Building And Rebuilding The .45 AUTO

**T**HE ONLY PEOPLE who remain neutral about the Government Model Colt .45 ACP autoloader are the ones who've yet to encounter it. The old, slab-sided thumb-buster has a strong tendency to polarize all the rest into either devout fans or bitter enemies. Introduced and adopted in 1911, the venerable self-stuffer has lent its stout voice to the resolution of every conflict in which this country has gotten embroiled from that year to the present, often rather decisively, and it shows no clear indication of being replaced, even some seventy years after the design came from the singularly gifted drafting pen of John Moses Browning.

When a hunk of hardware endures for seven decades without anything demonstrably better coming along, that has to stand as some sort of reasonably impressive accomplishment. Along the way, the Model 1911 Colt and its successor, the Model 1911A1, have built up their distinctive mystique, partially founded upon solid fact, partially teetering upon the feathery foundation of pure myth. If you conduct a poll, you will encounter people who remain firmly convinced that a hit from the M1911 on the tip of a victim's little finger will spin him around and around and drop him dead at your feet. Facts do not support this dewy-eyed hypothesis. It is in the same league with the calm conviction that the .357 magnum bullet will shatter an engine block.

Others hold and will fight to defend the belief that nobody can hit a man-sized target with the .45 auto farther away than the opposite side of a small card table. Again, the theory is demonstrably false to fact. Even the most goose-loose of all .45 autos, properly handled, can and will terrorize the daylights out of any target the size of a dinner plate, to a distance of seventy-five feet or a bit more. In reasonably skilled hands, the same gun and load will cause grave concern to a target the size of the human torso, at three hundred yards. At that distance, the drop is right around fourteen feet and yes, it takes a bit of doing.

A good .45 auto, with good ammo, in the hands of one of its better manipulators, will clip a half-dollar, practically every time, from seventy-five feet. A really great .45, with top-notch loads in hands singularly gifted, will do the same to a dime, from the same distance.

There are handguns that practically any neophyte can grab at first encounter and fire like an expert from the first round on. The Government Model Colt is not one of these. It is a gun that demands a great deal of fanatical devotion to master, and a bit more, after that. It is incredibly noisy, and it kicks like a goosed mule. It causes even the most steely-hearted shooter to flinch, and badly. That is the first, and highest hurdle toward its mastery.

Let us assume that those who remain disenchanted with the GI .45 auto have shrugged and skipped along to

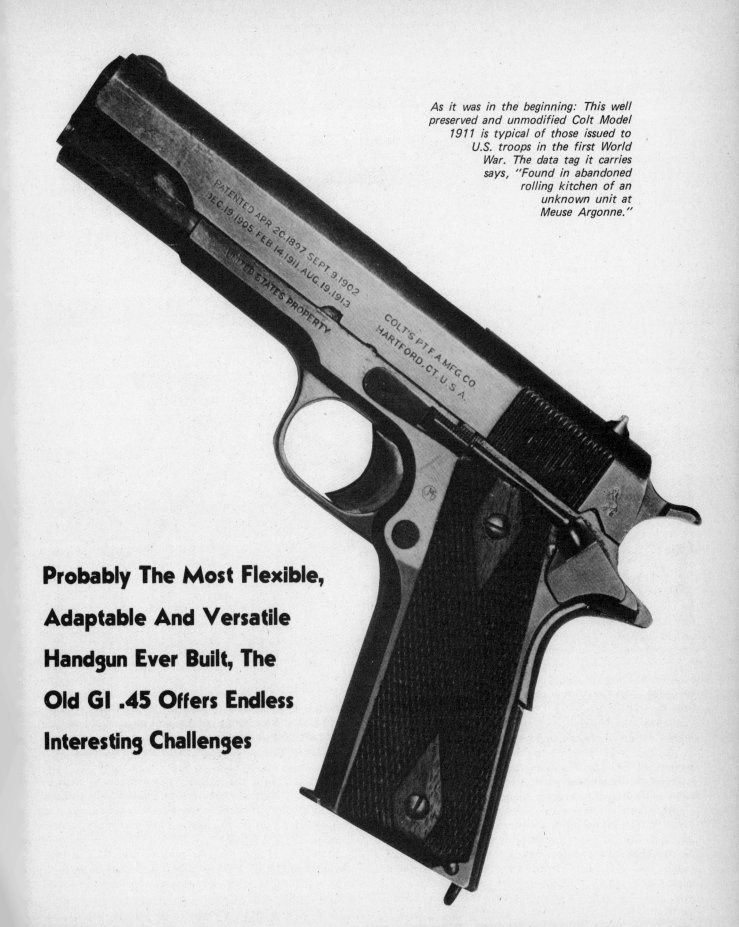

As it was in the beginning: This well preserved and unmodified Colt Model 1911 is typical of those issued to U.S. troops in the first World War. The data tag it carries says, "Found in abandoned rolling kitchen of an unknown unit at Meuse Argonne."

# Probably The Most Flexible, Adaptable And Versatile Handgun Ever Built, The Old GI .45 Offers Endless Interesting Challenges

*Stainless slide and receiver by Vega, from Pacific International, can be used in making up a complete gun such as the one here. Note forward-raked cocking grooves at rear of slide.*

*Unfinished plain steel receiver from Essex Arms has its plunger tube installed and stock screw bushings in place. Details on attaching plunger tube are illustrated in photos on opposite page.*

following chapters at about this point. The discussion that follows is predicated upon nobody being left but admirers of the burly old boomer.

If you don't have one, and want one, you've a choice of buying one or building one. In the days at immediate hand, buying one usually soaks up around $300. There have been times when the tab was one-twelfth that amount, but you can't go there from here. Sorry about that.

Spare small parts for the .45 auto remain reasonably available from a number of sources. There is, however, one lone part that isn't overly accessible and it's the receiver, or frame. That's the part that carries the serial number and maker's name. It can be viewed as sort of the heart and soul of the basic gun. If you have a receiver, you can build a gun around it. If you don't, all you have is a collection of small parts.

For purposes of the present discussion, let's assume that a receiver is at hand, with most if not all of the requisite minor pieces. Even with all of the parts on hand, the Model 1911 pistol and its descendants are no snap to put together. We will now turn our attention to the several intricacies.

Reference will be made to the nomenclature and part numbers as given in the exploded view reproduced on page 232. The one fairly iffy item is part number 32, the plunger tube. If it comes attached to the receiver, you're happily in business. If it doesn't, you have a small problem of buying it and staking it into place.

In theory, if not in actual practice, the GI Colt was produced so that all parts would be interchangeable with all guns. It didn't quite work out that way, but it was a noble goal, if nothing else.

When Colt went ot the Model 1911A1 format, in the

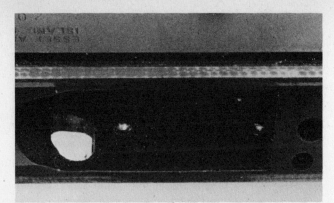

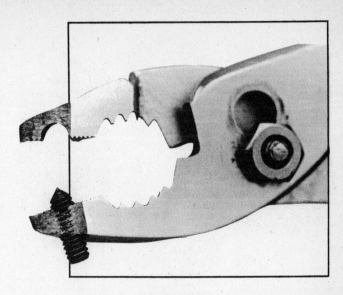

Above, a view inside magazine well of the Essex receiver shows how the pins holding the plunger tube in place are staked for a secure hold. Right, a pair of pliers has been modified to serve as a tool for staking.

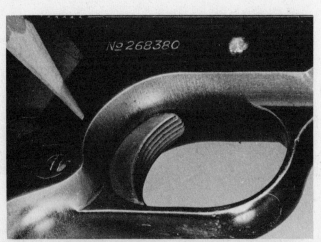

Pencil points to the area on Model 1911 (above) and on a Model 1911A1 (below) where a crescent cut was made to increase clearance on the A1 version. You'll note that the Model M1911 has been retrofitted with an A1-type trigger.

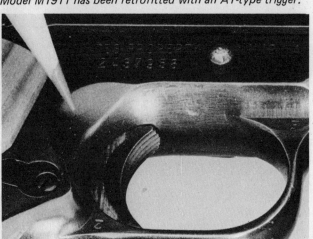

Here the modified pliers at the top of the page are in use to stake the front holding pin of the plunger tube in place.

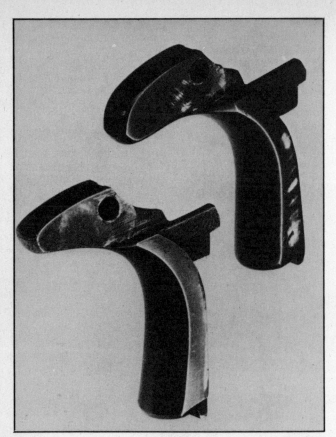

*Upper grip safety has the longer tang of the Model 1911A1 version, while the lower one is of original 1911 pattern.*

one can hear parts clattering merrily against each other. That may not be a serious matter if one proposes to use the gun for large targets at close distances, and such guns tend to be notably reliable as to feeding and functioning. They are not, however, capable of achieving the impressive accuracy of the Model 1911/A1 and the .45 Automatic Colt Pistol (ACP) cartridge, when everything is tuned and fitted to the highest degree.

So let's assume that we have a receiver and all of the other necessary parts and pieces on hand and take up the procedures for assembling them. If at all possible, try to obtain the receiver with the plunger tube (32) already installed, because that is the one installation most apt to pose problems for the inexperienced builder. The tube is staked into place by judicious riveting of two tiny tangs that extend through holes in the receiver into the inner surface of the magazine well and it is somewhat challenging to get at the working area to achieve a workmanlike installation. If you have no choice other than to install the

*Loctite Stud N' Bearing Mount is one of the strongest grades of that line of sealants and, as discussed in the text, it can serve usefully to keep parts from loosening.*

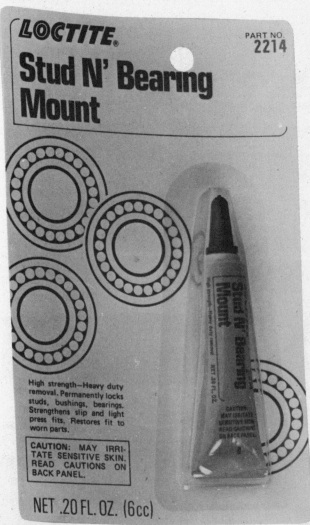

early Twenties, they made certain changes. They cut a crescent clearance behind the trigger, the only basic change in the receiver, itself. They lengthened the tang of the grip safety. They trimmed back the trigger and modified the spur of the hammer to keep from colliding with the longer grip safety tang. The mainspring housing was rounded from its original straight contour and both the front and rear sights were broadened in blade and notch width. The changed checkering of the stocks constituted the final phase of the modification.

In theory, at least, the military .45 pistol was produced on an all-parts-interchangeable basis, regardless of the maker or subcontractor. Actually, there are a few minor exceptions, principally the matter of the M1911 hammer spurs interfering with the longer grip safety tangs of the M1911A1, as noted. In fact, the M1911 grip safeties may not function in M1911A1 receivers, since a small bevel was incorporated on the two lower side corners at the same time the tang was lengthened. Old grip safeties may require grinding at these points for proper clearance, if installed in the newer receivers.

The all-parts-interchangeable approach has certain advantages and with them a few disadvantages. The slightly charitable tolerances that make all parts fit with all other parts tends to result in a final assembly with many of the component parts in rather casual relationship to each other. The colloquial term among .45 fans for such a gun is goose-loose. Grasping such a gun by the grip and shaking it,

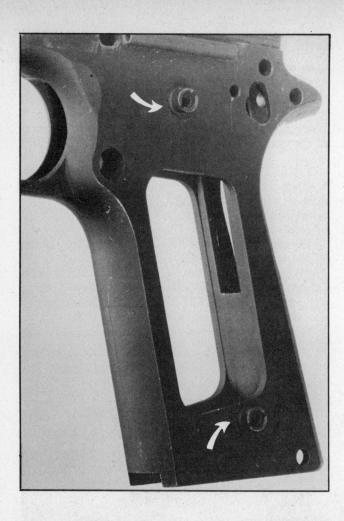

*The two stock screw bushings (arrows) shown here are somewhat prone to work loose in normal use and are an example of an application that can benefit from Loctite.*

tube yourself, apply some Loctite to the various mating surfaces.

Loctite is an adhesive/sealant made by the Loctite Corporation, Newington, Connecticut, and it is available in various grades. The one termed Stud N' Bearing Mount sets up to the strongest, toughest adherance of the grades readily available and it is the best choice for purposes such as those under discussion.

Loctite contains a metacrylic ester and it's a sort of chemical cousin to the cyanoacrylate wonder glues such as Krazy Glue and the like. Loctite, however, does not set up in seconds, requiring from fifteen minutes to three hours, depending upon the type of metal and nature of application. If haste is of the essence, it can be heated to 200F to accelerate the curing. Once a joint or assembly has been sealed with properly cured Loctite, it becomes damnably difficult to take apart again and that fact should be kept firmly in mind; Locktited in mind, perhaps. Don't use the stuff unless you're totally certain that you want the parts in that particular relationship for an interval amounting to forever, plus six months! Loctite is available from most gunsmith supply houses, and it's usually stocked by suppliers of automotive parts.

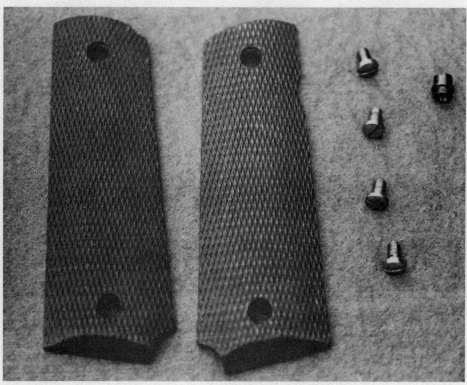

*Left and right-hand stocks, in a checkered pattern, with the four stock screws and one stock screw bushing.*

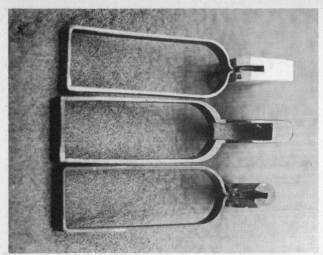

*Trigger designs can show considerable variation from one source to another. The one with a light-colored alloy trigger has an adjustable trigger stop that bears on the magazine catch to arrest rearward motion after firing.*

For clarity and simplicity, the first reference to each part will be accompanied by parenthetical listing of the part number in the accompanying illustration.

With the plunger tube installed, proceed to install the four stock screw bushings (48). This is another place where Loctite is indicated, since the bushings tend to come loose when you unscrew the stock screws (47), as in replacement of the right or left stocks (46 or 45, respectively). If your receiver (34) is one of the lightweight types, made of aluminum alloy, frequent retightening of the stock screw bushings can strip the mating threads in the receiver. If the receiver is of steel, it is the bushing's threads that are vulnerable to stripping. Either way, LocTite solves the problem nicely.

The trigger assembly (49) can now be installed, with its sloping rear surface parallel to the adjacent flat surface at the rear of the receiver. The trigger should move easily back and forth in its slots, by gravity as the receiver is tilted up and down. If it seems to bind to some extent, stone the sides of the trigger loop to relieve the interference.

The trigger is held in place by the magazine catch

*This is the first step of sliding the trigger into its grooves within the receiver. Note that the magazine catch is not in place at this point.*

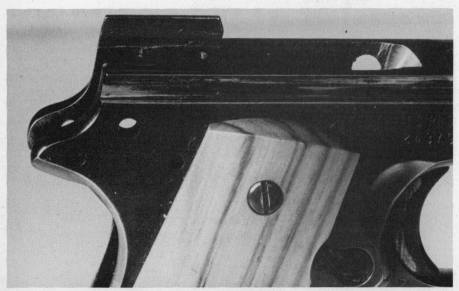

*Here the trigger is fully forward and we're ready to install the magazine catch that will hold it in place. Details are on next page.*

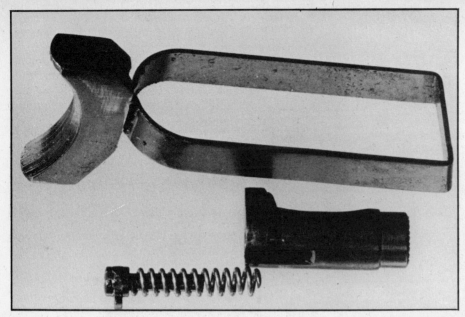

*At left, the trigger with the magazine catch, magazine catch lock and magazine catch lock spring ready for assembly. Below, the lock and spring have been inserted and partially turned into assembly position.*

assembly, consisting of the magazine catch (19), magazine catch lock (20) and magazine catch lock spring (21). Assembly of the three parts is relatively simple: Slip the shank of the magazine catch lock into the magazine catch lock spring, then slide both into the magazine catch, using a small screwdriver to compress the spring until the little ear on the slotted head of the magazine lock catch can be given one-quarter turn, counterclockwise, to engage the cut in the magazine lock. When thus assembled, slip the entire assembly into the receiver from the right-hand side, maintaining a light, clockwise torque on the screwdriver against the magazine catch lock until the ear of the magazine catch lock is felt to engage the slot milled in the receiver. A one-quarter clockwise turn of the magazine

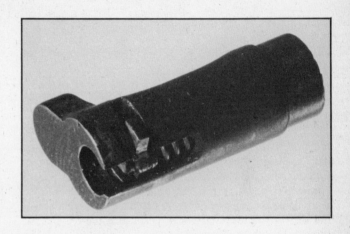

*With the magazine catch assembly in place, the slot on the catch lock can be given a quarter-turn to engage a milled slot in the receiver to lock in place for normal use.*

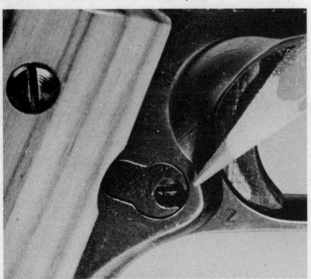

*Here the catch lock has been turned in place as described at left. As a rule, it will be necessary to move the catch assembly in and out, with torque, to feel for the groove.*

*As discussed in the text, the sear spring makes a handy improvised screwdriver for removing or installing the magazine catch assembly and similar low-stress applications with the M1911s.*

catch lock at that point causes the entire assembly to snap into place and removal, if desired, is a simple matter of pressing the knurled area inward from the left, with a screwdriver engaging the slot of the magazine catch lock, with light counterclockwise torque until the ear matches the slot in the magazine catch, permitting the one-quarter turn for release and removal.

Lacking a screwdriver, the right-hand tip of the sear spring (41), as normally viewed with the gun in firing position, can be used to remove or install the magazine catch assembly. It is an impressive feature of the .45 auto

that the complete gun, in being field stripped, produces parts that can be used as tools for further disassembly.

If the receiver did not come with the ejector (6) in place, that can be installed at this time. The two projections on the ejector's lower surface go into two matching holes in the top of the receiver, with the longer of the two to the front. Directions, for the purpose of this discussion, assume that the gun is viewed in normal firing position, thus "front" means toward the muzzle end of the assembled gun, and so on.

Note that there is a small, semicircular clearance cut,

*The ejector, laid out in its proper relationship to the receiver. Note the small, semicircular cut on the front surface of the front post to accept the ejector pin.*

*The ejector has been partially inserted into the mating holes on the top of the receiver. When pressed fully into place, the ejector pin can be driven to hold it in position.*

*Left, the plunger assembly, ready for insertion into the plunger tube. Plunger with small end goes to the front. The slight kink in the spring serves to hold the assembly in its place and should not be straightened. Below, rear sight, as seen from the front, carries a center witness line.*

about halfway down the front of the longer leg of the ejector to accommodate the ejector pin (7). With the ejector fully seated in place, check by looking through the hole in the receiver to verify that the clearance cut lines up before driving the ejector pin into place. Make sure that neither end of the ejector pin projects beyond the surface of the slot in the receiver, because that would interfere with free movement of the slide (42), later.

The legs of the ejector usually are a rather tight fit in the mating holes of the receiver. Check the fit visually — a jeweler's loupe or magnifying glass is handy for this — to see whether it may be necessary to relieve a little metal from the front or rear of the rear leg before making the all-out effort to seat the ejector home. Once in place the ejector is difficult to remove if everything isn't just right. It is better to avoid the LocTite for this application.

*Components of the slide assembly, including one of the Vega stainless steel slides with fixed sights, the ejector in its correct relationship to the slide, the firing pin, firing pin spring and firing pin stop, ready to be put together.*

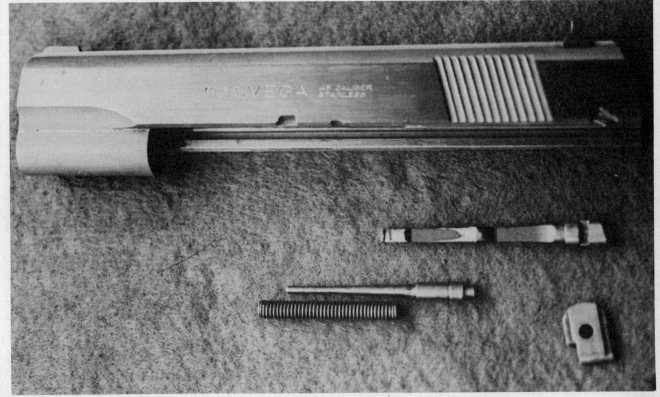

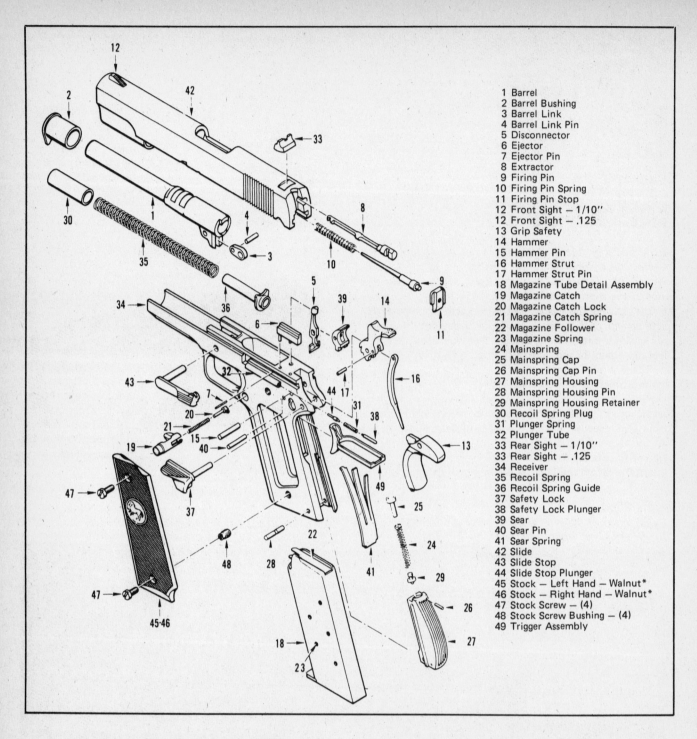

1 Barrel
2 Barrel Bushing
3 Barrel Link
4 Barrel Link Pin
5 Disconnector
6 Ejector
7 Ejector Pin
8 Extractor
9 Firing Pin
10 Firing Pin Spring
11 Firing Pin Stop
12 Front Sight — 1/10″
12 Front Sight — .125
13 Grip Safety
14 Hammer
15 Hammer Pin
16 Hammer Strut
17 Hammer Strut Pin
18 Magazine Tube Detail Assembly
19 Magazine Catch
20 Magazine Catch Lock
21 Magazine Catch Spring
22 Magazine Follower
23 Magazine Spring
24 Mainspring
25 Mainspring Cap
26 Mainspring Cap Pin
27 Mainspring Housing
28 Mainspring Housing Pin
29 Mainspring Housing Retainer
30 Recoil Spring Plug
31 Plunger Spring
32 Plunger Tube
33 Rear Sight — 1/10″
33 Rear Sight — .125
34 Receiver
35 Recoil Spring
36 Recoil Spring Guide
37 Safety Lock
38 Safety Lock Plunger
39 Sear
40 Sear Pin
41 Sear Spring
42 Slide
43 Slide Stop
44 Slide Stop Plunger
45 Stock — Left Hand — Walnut*
46 Stock — Right Hand — Walnut*
47 Stock Screw — (4)
48 Stock Screw Bushing — (4)
49 Trigger Assembly

The slide stop plunger (44) can now be installed on one end of the plunger spring (31) and the safety lock plunger on the other end. The resulting assembly, with slide stop plunger to the fore, is inserted into the plunger tube, where it is held in place by a light friction fit. Note, in the exploded view, that the longer end of the slide stop plunger goes to the front.

If the component parts of the slide assembly remain unassembled, they can be put together at this point. Decide which face of the front sight (12) you want to the front or rear, fit the tang into place in the opening at the front upper end of the slide. Hold the parts in proper relationship to each other by securing them in a vise, preferably a vise with its jaws covered by brass or aluminum plates to prevent marring the gun parts. Use a small punch to stake the lower end of the front sight tang securely into place. This is an application where a drop of Loctite can be helpful.

The rear sight (33) is driven into its mating dovetail from right to left, with the slide held in the padded vise, using a brass drift punch to avoid marring the sight or slide. The small witness line on the rear sight goes to the front and the sight is tapped in until the line on the sight aligns with the corresponding line on the top of the slide, just ahead of the dovetail. Avoid using Loctite here. You may wish to tap the rear sight to one side or the other at some future time, in order to correct the left/right bullet placement, or windage.

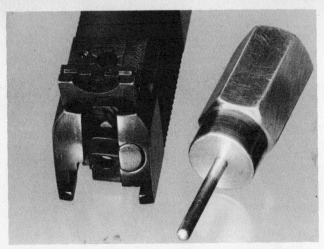

*The firing pin spring has been slipped over the firing pin and compressed into its recess to slide the firing pin stop into position, using the homemade .45 tool with brass pin.*

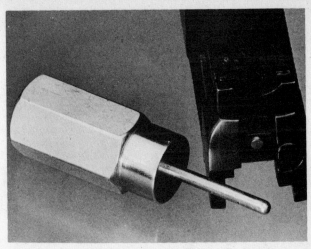

*The firing pin stop has now been pushed fully into its correct position and the rear tip of the pin pops through the central hole to hold everything together correctly.*

The extractor (8) is installed in the hole at the right rear of the slide, with its slot to the inside. The firing pin (9) is slipped into one end of the firing pin spring (10) and rotated against the coiling of the spring to get it fully into place with a light friction fit. Usually one end of the firing pin spring is a slightly snugger fit than the other. Install the firing pin in the tighter of the two ends, if there is a difference.

Install the assembled firing pin and firing pin spring in the central hole at the rear of the slide, spring foremost, and use a small screwdriver or similar tool to depress the rear of the firing pin far enough, under spring tension, to permit the firing pin stop (11) to be slid up from below. Once the front face of the firing pin stop slides over the rear of the firing pin, it is pushed on upward until the rear of the firing pin pops back to hold it in place. Disassemble by pushing inward on the firing pin and downward on the firing pin stop until it releases.

*The barrel, barrel bushing, barrel link, barrel link pin and slide stop, all arranged in approximately their proper relationship. The smaller of the two holes in the barrel link is the one through which the link pin is driven to assemble.*

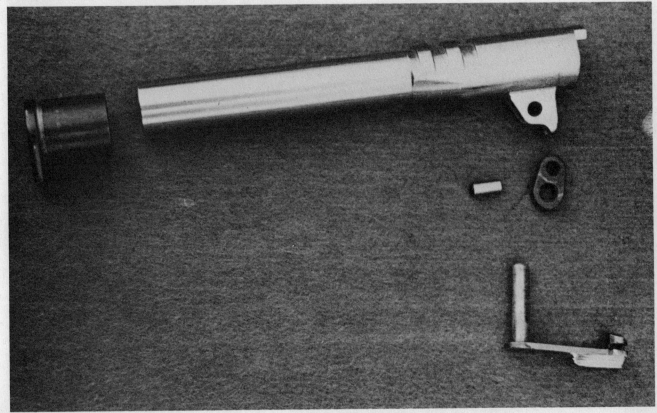

*Here is a mainspring housing group, assembled, with the mainspring cap, mainspring and mainspring housing retainer. Visible in the assembly, but not shown fully is the mainspring cap pin. Housing is of 1911A1 type.*

*From left, an early 1911 housing, with lanyard loop; a straight housing as used on Colt Gold Cup; and an arched housing, per Model 1911A1.*

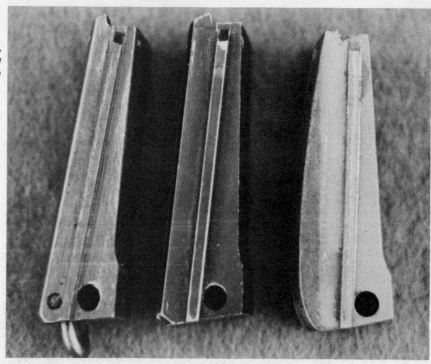

If the barrel link pin (4) and barrel link (3) are not installed on the barrel (1) at this point, put them together. The barrel link pin goes in from the right-hand side of the barrel, through the smaller of the two holes in the barrel link. This is a fairly tight friction fit and you should use a brass drift punch to get both ends of the pin flush with the side surfaces of the barrel lug. There is no need to use Loctite here. The barrel link should move freely, once installed. If it shows frictional resistance, remove it and stone the two sides lightly, repeating as necessary until it moves easily.

If your mainspring assembly is still in its component parts at this point, put the mainspring housing (27) in the padded vise, top-end-up, put the mainspring housing pin retainer (29) into one end of the mainspring (24) and the mainspring cap (25) into the other and drop the assembly into the hole in the mainspring housing, with the mainspring cap uppermost, as shown in the exploded view. Use a brass drift punch to compress the mainspring by pressing against the cupper upper surface of the mainspring cap so that the mainspring cap pin can be inserted from the rear of the mainspring housing and seated with a pin punch of the appropriate diameter.

If the magazine assembly has not been put together, put the magazine spring (23 – not visible in the exploded view) into the outer part of the magazine (called out in the exploded view as 18 magazine tube detail assembly) with the small loop uppermost and facing toward the rear of the magazine, as shown in the accompanying photo. Use a flat stick or similar tool to compress the magazine spring a bit over one inch below the top of the magazine, then insert a pin punch through the upper part of view holes in the magazine to hold it in place as you install the magazine follower, sliding its flat end between the coils of the compressed magazine spring and the rear face of the magazine. Reapply pressure to the magazine follower as you remove the pin punch to free the coils of the magazine spring and ease the follower back to the top of its travel. Don't just yank the punch out and let the follower snap up, because that could damage the follower and/or the feed lips of the magazine and it is vital that both remain in good condition to assure reliability of feeding and functioning.

If the hammer assembly requires putting together, do so by laying the hammer (14) on its left side, aligning the hole in the top of the hammer strut (16) with the smaller of the two holes drilled through the hammer and use a brass drift punch to drive the hammer strut pin (17) into place, with neither end projecting above the side surfaces of the hammer. This is a moderately tight press fit and there is no need to use Loctite. The strut and hammer should move freely. If there are indications of frictional binding, disassemble and stone the sides of the upper end of the

Here's a close look at the frontal area of a healthy hammer, showing the ledges to engage the tip of the sear and the half-cock notch as it should appear.

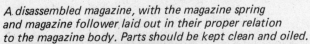

A disassembled magazine, with the magazine spring and magazine follower laid out in their proper relation to the magazine body. Parts should be kept clean and oiled.

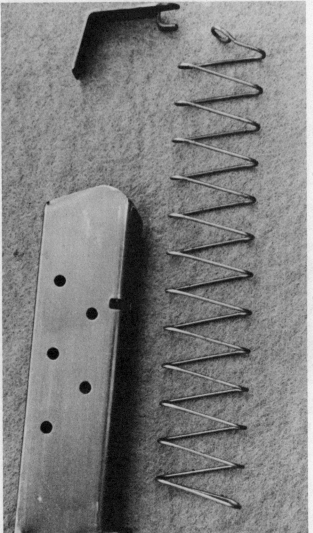

This is the hammer assembly, with the hammer strut held in place by the hammer strut pin. A hammer with a narrow tang, such as this one, is the type usually used with 1911A1.

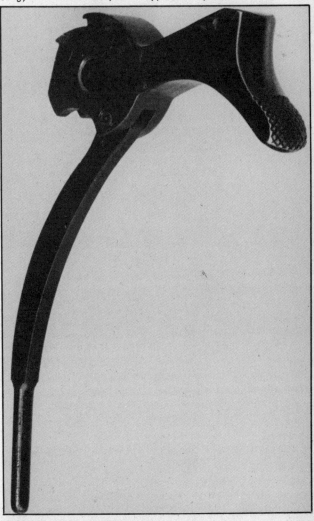

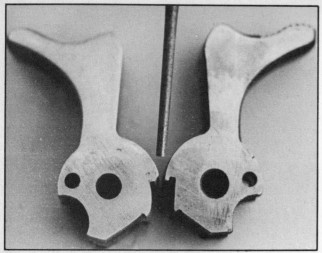

Hammer at left has a broken half-cock notch, as seen at tip of punch, and it should not be used. Hammer at right has its engaging surfaces in acceptable condition for use.

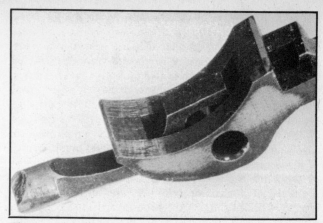

The sear and disconnector have been put together before inserting in the receiver. Sear lugs must touch ledge at the lower end of the disconnector for proper installation.

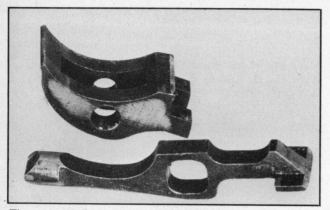

The sear and disconnector, arranged in their correct relationship to each other, before positioning to install.

The assembled sear and disconnector are placed into the receiver in this manner, with disconnector tip on trigger.

hammer strut lightly. Reassemble and recheck, repeating as necessary. The strut assembles to the hammer in the relationship shown in the exploded view.

With such assemblies as the slide, barrel, magazine, mainspring unit and hammer all put together, proceed with the final assembly of the gun.

Attach the stocks (45 and 46) by means of the four stock screws (47), tightening them with judicious pressure. You don't want them coming loose, but don't tighten them so savagely as to damage the stock material.

With the trigger and magazine catch assembly in place, as discussed earlier, place the sear (39) astraddle of the disconnector (5) in the relationship shown in the exploded view and accompanying photo. With the receiver held in one hand, muzzle down, grasp the disconnector by the lower end, slanted side to the rear, with the sear in place on it, and insert the upper end of the disconnector through its opening on the upper surface of the receiver. Insert the sear pin (40) from the left side of the receiver, into the small hole just ahead of the irregular opening. Note that the sear pin has a shallow flange on its outer end.

To get the sear pin inserted fully, you may find it

helpful to insert the rounded tip of the hammer strut from the right-hand side to prealign the holes, pushing it out as you insert the sear pin from the left.

With the disconnector and sear in place, push forward on the upper end of the sear, so the disconnector can be moved upward fully to the limit of its vertical travel. The two small lugs on the lower end of the sear must be resting against the rear face of the lower end of the disconnector before assembly can be carried forward.

With the parts in the positions described, lay the sear spring (41) into place, with its shallow lower tongue inserted in the crosswise slot near the lower end of the back face of the receiver. Hold the sear spring in place by sliding the mainspring assembly about one inch or so into its milled slots.

Now put the hammer assembly in place and line its hole

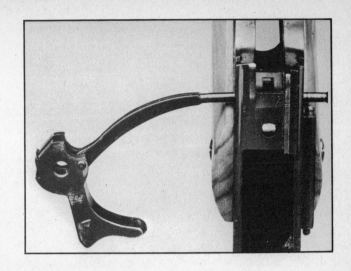

*Above, rounded tip of the hammer strut makes a handy tool to align holes of the sear and disconnector so that the sear pin can be placed from opposite side for assembly. Left, arrow indicates proper protrusion of disconnector tip. It mates with a semicircular recess in the bottom of the slide to keep gun from firing without full closure.*

*The sear spring, here with its front surface uppermost, performs several vital functions in operation.*

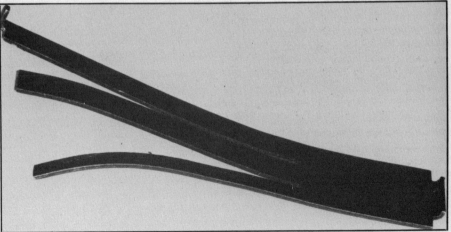

*Sear spring fits into place as at left, with its shallow lower lip inserted into receiver slot.*

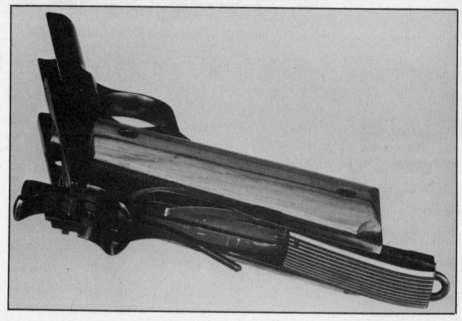

*After installing sear spring, as above, mainspring housing is slid partially into place to hold spring for next steps.*

with the upper hole in the left side of the receiver, inserting the hammer pin (15) from the left side, flanged and outermost. Pull the trigger to get the hammer fully forward in order to proceed with the assembly.

Insert the grip safety (13) and align its hole with the rearmost hole in the left side of the receiver, inserting the pin of the safety lock (37) through the hole in the receiver from the left to hold the grip safety in place. The safety lock will not go in fully at this time.

Holding the butt of the gun about vertical, hammer side up and hammer fully forward, slide the mainspring assembly upward, guiding the tip of the hammer strut into the center of the cup at the top of the mainspring cap (25), squeezing inward slightly on the lower end of the grip safety until the hole at the lower end of the mainspring assembly is seen to be aligned with the mating holes through the lower rear corner of the receiver. Insert the mainspring housing pin (28) from the left, rounded end

first and tap it carefully into place, using a brass drift with a rounded end until the lower tip of the mainspring housing pin retainer (29) aligns with the groove around the midpoint of the mainspring housing pin, holding it in place.

All that remains in completing the receiver assembly is to maneuver the safety lock (37) back into its proper position. Cock the hammer and grasp the safety lock by its knurled ear and move it about slightly, meanwhile using a small punch or screwdriver to push the exposed tip of the safety lock plunger (38) forward slightly. The safety lock should click into place with little or no difficulty.

A word of caution: Never pull the trigger to drop the hammer when the .45 is disassembled! If you are so injudicious as to do so, there is a strong possibility that the hammer will break; even if it doesn't, it will burr the contacting surfaces in a most unsightly manner. This falls into about the same category as closing the swing-out revolver cylinders with a snap of the wrist, as those idiots

Hammer is held in place by hammer pin, which is inserted into receiver from the left, as illustrated here.

With hammer forward, mainspring housing is pushed up and secured with mainspring housing pin. Then the grip safety is positioned and partially secured by safety lock.

A close look at the inner surfaces of the safety lock.

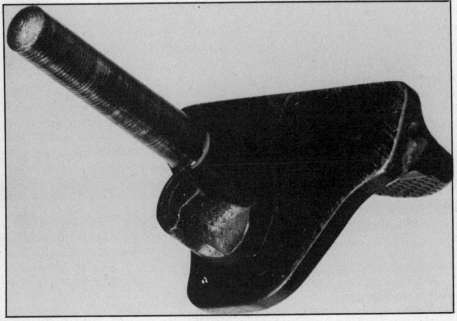

With the hammer cocked, plus perhaps a bit of wiggling, the safety lock can be slid into the receiver until (arrow) it contacts the safety lock plunger, which is pushed ahead.

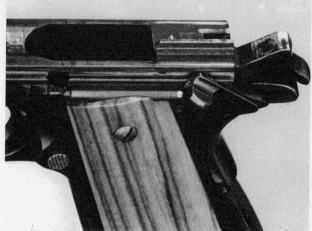

With safety lock plunger held forward, the safety lock can be pushed into place for the remaining distance. It is a good idea, per text, to put the safety up to the lock the action if the receiver assembly is set aside until final assembly.

are so fond of doing on the boob tube.

With the hammer cocked and safety lock in its down or off position, set the receiver aside and perform the preliminary assembly of the barrel and slide components by inserting the rear of the barrel into the front of the slide, pushing it fully to the rear.

The recoil spring (35) usually will have one end with the coils a trifle tighter than the other. Insert the round end of the recoil spring guide (36) into the tighter end of the recoil spring, twisting slightly to insert it fully. Slide the front of the recoil spring, from the rear, through the opening at the lower front of the slide, resting the concave portion of the flange at the rear of the recoil spring guide against the barrel, just ahead of the lug.

Install the barrel bushing (2) over the muzzle, noting the position of the small lug on its lower surface and rotating it so that the lug passes through the opening in the front of the slide. When the barrel bushing is seated fully, leave it in

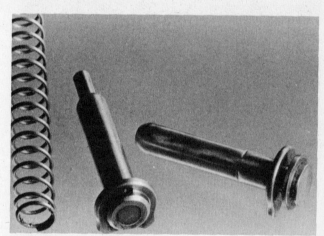

Here's the tighter end of the recoil spring into which the recoil spring guide shaft is inserted. Guides shown are recoil-buffing type by Bar-Sto (left) and Dinan (right).

Below, barrel has been placed in the slide and the latter has been inverted for further steps of the assembly procedure.

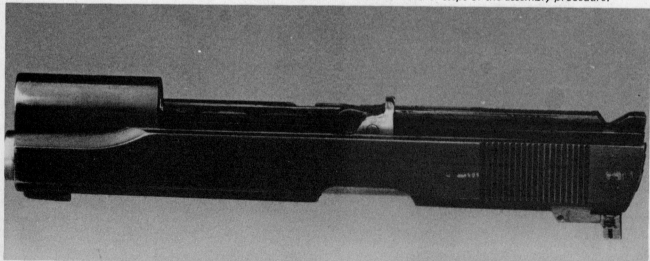

THE GUN DIGEST BOOK OF PISTOLSMITHING

Barrel bushing is slipped over barrel muzzle and rotated as shown above, permitting lug clearance for full seating.

*Above, bushing has been pushed fully rearward to ready it for the next step. Below, bushing is rotated as shown.*

Following the steps above, recoil spring and guide are inserted, with front of spring extending up through end of slide.

*Still uncompressed at this point, the front of the recoil spring projects from its opening in the front of slide.*

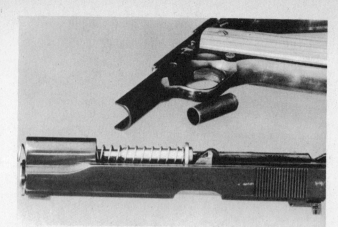

*Slide assembly is ready for attachment of receiver and recoil spring plug. If safety was put up, push it back down.*

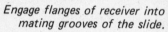

*Engage flanges of receiver into mating grooves of the slide.*

*Push receiver forward until the square notch (arrow) in receiver lines up with curved slide notch.*

As described in text, slide stop is positioned carefully and pushed straight down until it encounters the projecting tip of the slide stop plunger, which is pushed rearward to let the slide stop continue into its proper position against receiver.

properly, and much better so.

With the slide stop installed, push the slide forward fully and put the safety lock (37) into its upper (safe) position, to lock the slide in place for the final steps of assembly. Slip the recoil spring plug (30) over the end of the recoil spring and, using a bit of care and caution, swing the barrel bushing clockwise to the limit of its travel and compress the recoil spring by pushing downward on the recoil spring plug, guiding it into the opening at the front of the slide until its knurled outer surface is flush with the front of the slide. Then, holding the recoil spring plug in place, rotate the barrel bushing counterclockwise until its lower end, with the concave arc, aligns with the knurled tip of the recoil spring plug.

Push down on the safety lock, take a firm hold on the hammer spur, and pull the trigger to lower the hammer. Insert the magazine and the assembly of the pistol is

The safety lock is put back up to hold the slide in its proper position (fully forward) for final assembly.

that position for the immediate present.

Holding the slide and its parts upside down, engage the flanges at the top of the inverted receiver with the mating grooves along the lower edge of the slide and push the receiver forward, meanwhile rotating it back to right-side up position. Push the slide on to the rear until the small, rounded notch on the lower left edge of the slide lines up with the square opening in the receiver just ahead of the slide stop plunger (44). Insert the rounded end of the slide stop (43) pin into the round hole above and slightly ahead of the trigger and gently guide it through the hole at the lower end of the barrel link (3). There is a right way to install the slide stop. Hold the lever portion firmly between the thumbs and forefingers of both hands and guide it into place so that the rounded rear portion of the lever pushes the slide stop plunger rearward as it goes into place. The wrong way of doing it is to drop in the slide stop, willy-nilly, skating it up across the receiver to wear an unsightly arc of bright metal against the blued finish, thereby branding the gun as having been abused by a bungler. This is one of those things that is just as easy to do

The recoil plug is slipped over the end of the recoil spring in preparation for further assembly. Some plugs have a small inner protuberance to engage the end of the spring. Compress the recoil spring carefully, guiding its coils back into the slide until the barrel bushing can be swung over to hold against the flange of the recoil plug, as here.

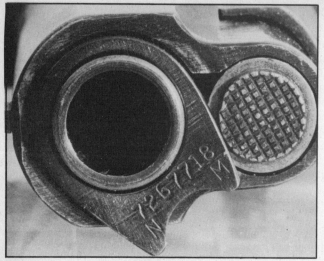

Compress the recoil spring carefully, guiding its coils back into the slide until the barrel bushing can be swung over to hold against the flange of the recoil plug, as here.

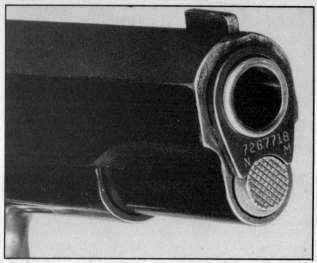

Then press the recoil plug down to permit the barrel bushing to be turned to its normal position, as above. If the bushing is a tight fit, you may need a bushing wrench.

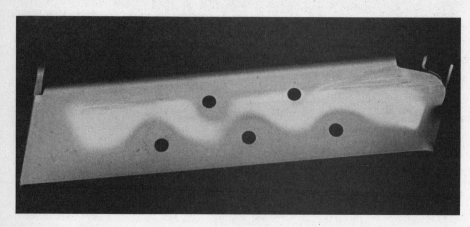

Irregular lighter areas on this stainless magazine show where metal was removed by 400-grit paper for an easy release. Paper was fastened to a flat surface and used on both sides.

This late model receiver has been fitted to a Kart conversion, firing the .22 LR cartridge with exceptionally good accuracy.

*The Kart conversion on facing page appears above with its action locked open. With it is the Service Model Ace, also firing the .22 LR cartridge. Latter was reintroduced by Colt in 1978. Custom Ace stocks are by Sid Bell, Tully, NY.*

completed. The magazine should be an easy slip-fit in the magazine well, so that the magazine will drop free by gravity if the magazine catch is depressed with the butt vertical. If the magazine shows frictional resistance, the easiest approach to remove a small amount of metal from one or both sides of the magazine, checking as you go along and stopping when the condition has been corrected.

It is easy, inexpensive and simple to construct one or more improvised hones for work on the .45 auto in applications such as slimming-down the magazines. Take a piece of board — particle board is fine for the purpose — and glue a sheet of Tri-M-Ite WetOrDry waterproof silicon carbide paper (rough-side out!) to one side and a small block of wood to the other. In use, the block is secured in the bench vise and a small amount of honing oil is applied to the working surface of the paper. The honing oil serves to keep the grit from blocking up with metal particles as the work progresses; it has no lubricating effect. You can make up a series of such hones, with paper of the different grits, perhaps starting with the 220 grit to remove the major amount of metal, then progressing down through 320, 400 and 600 to leave an attractive finish.

If your receiver and/or other components came "in the white," you probably will want to apply a matching finish, throughout, unless the parts are of stainless steel. The conventional blued — actually, more accurately, black oxide — finish is a good choice, being attractive and traditional. Unless your shop facilities are at a lofty level of sophistication, bluing is not a do-it-yourself operation because the equipment is costly and the procedures quite exacting.

The so-called "cold-bluing" preparations sold under a variety of trade names should not be regarded as suitable for a permanent finish on the entire gun unless your standards are charitable, indeed. Such cold blue formulas operate by depositing a thin wash of copper atop the surface of the steel, simultaneously discoloring it to a hue that more or less resembles black oxide. The wearing properties of the colored copper are severely limited, as you might imagine, and the resulting appearance is pretty dreadful.

It is a considerably wiser course to put the gun in the hands of the best gunsmith you can manage to track down and let him attend to the finishing, which will usually add more to the value of the gun than his charge for the service, and you'll be able to look at it without wincing painfully. If you're in doubt as to the gunsmith's credentials, ask to see some guns that he has blued. Check for signs of over-buffing, such as rounded corners that should be square and stamped letters blurred nearly beyond legibility. If you

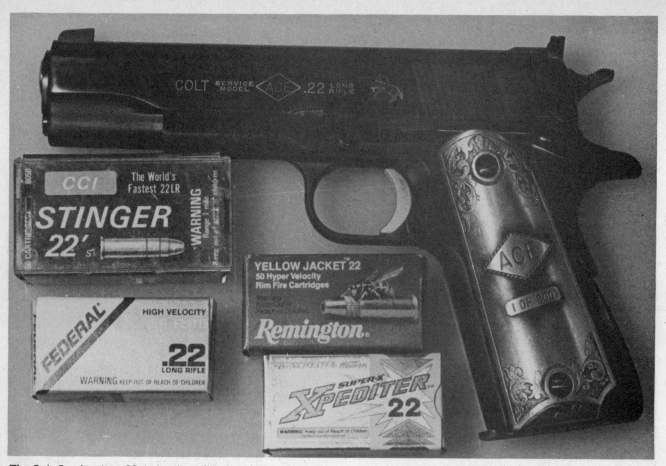

The Colt Service Ace .22 embodies a floating chamber to augment the modest recoil of the smaller cartridge for reliable functioning of the heavier action. Modern high-energy .22 LR loads such as these perform well in the Ace.

An unusual variant, this .45 has been fitted with a scoped slide carrying the Redfield 1½X on Redfield mounts, plus an extended magazine to provide about 21-round firing capability.

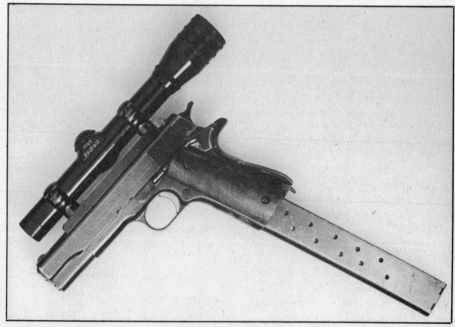

*Another odd item, this one was built up from spare parts on a lightweight alloy receiver from A.R. Sales Company. It has the Caraville Double Ace cocking system (in carrying mode at right), Springfield Armory slide with S&W rear sight and two Sid Bell stock designs.*

*A.R. Sales will provide custom serial number at slight extra charge, if not used earlier. This one consists of the builder's initials plus his WWII MOS number.*

note such things, hand the sample gun back, wish him a happy day and continue your quest for a good gunsmith you can entrust with the project.

There are other finishes, the more desirable of which are industrial hard chrome and nickel, in about that order.

Once you have completed the building of your .45 auto, there are countless tinkery and delightful projects you can tackle by way of modifying and perhaps improving its appearance or performance, or both. There are conversion units that will enable it to handle the inexpensive .22 long rifle cartridge for a saving on cost of practice ammunition and a reduction of the lusty kick and bellow of the .45 ACP cartridge. There are extended magazines, which can increase the gun's firepower beyond the usual seven in the magazine plus one in the chamber. There are accessories such as the Caraville Double Ace device that enable the gun to be carried in safe mode, with a round in the chamber, ready to go into action by a quick squeeze of the lever that replaces the grip safety. There are any number of stocks available to beautify the gun, improve its holding qualities, or both.

You can add target sights, or the adjustable rear sight from Miniature Machine Company. The latter has the advantage of being easy to install and it's designed to work with the conventional front sight of the non-adjustable sight set. If you go for the taller, target-type front sight, you may wish to add a colored insert on the rear surface of it, using a kit such as the one offered by Bullshooter's Supply.

*These target sights were installed by Armand Swenson of Fallbrook, California. He milled the rear of the slide to position the Micro rear sight down as far as possible for low profile.*

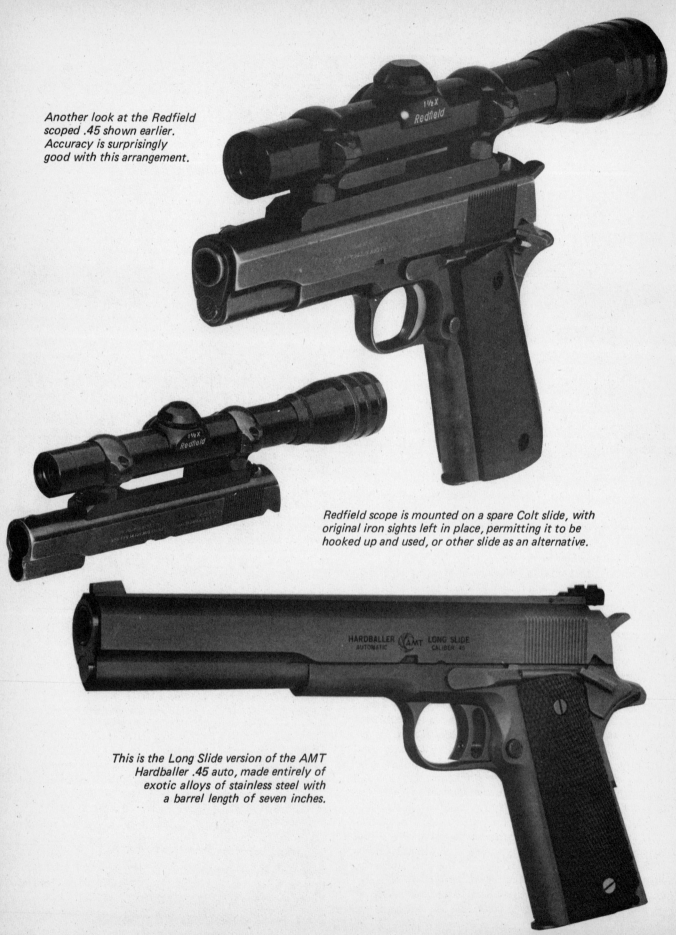

*Another look at the Redfield scoped .45 shown earlier. Accuracy is surprisingly good with this arrangement.*

*Redfield scope is mounted on a spare Colt slide, with original iron sights left in place, permitting it to be hooked up and used, or other slide as an alternative.*

*This is the Long Slide version of the AMT Hardballer .45 auto, made entirely of exotic alloys of stainless steel with a barrel length of seven inches.*

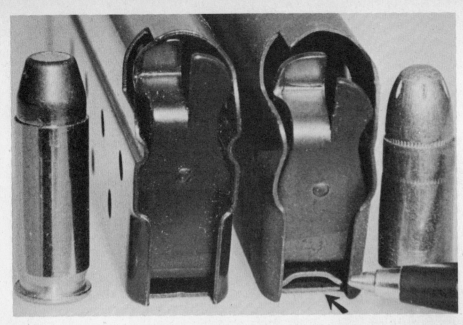

*Left and below, magazines for the .38 Colt Super and 9mm Luger should be used with their respective cartridges for best results. Note the thin spacer strip at rear of 9mm version.*

A further variant is to install the base and mounting rings from Redfield, with one of their telescopic sights. This approach is surprisingly effective as to accuracy and the weight it adds to the slide does not seem to hamper the reliability of the functioning with standard, "hardball" loads. Nor does the 1.5X Redfield scope seem bothered by the violent jouncing back and forth atop the slide. It does, however, have the handicap of making the .45 auto considerably bulkier and heavier and, due to that fact, it is better to mount the scope on a spare slide, retaining another of more conventional configuration to substitute for those times when compactness is more to be desired than ultimate accuracy.

A barrel chambered for the wildcat caliber .38-45 Clerke cartridge can be substituted for the standard .45 ACP barrel. The .38-45 Clerke is made by necking down the regular .45 ACP case to accept bullets of .355-inch (9mm) diameter, using special case forming dies that are available from RCBS, together with the reloading die sets. Exceptionally good .38-45 Clerke barrels are available from Bar-Sto Precision, as are barrels in .45 ACP, .38 Super and 9mm Luger chambering. Lengths are offered for both the Government Model and Commander, all with the collet-type barrel bushing similar to the one introduced by Colt in 1970 for their Mark IV series of the Model 1911A1. The Bar-Sto barrels are unusually precise and accurate, usually requiring little or no hand fitting when installed in most guns. The standard .45 ACP magazine is used with the .38-45 Clerke cartridge.

Various sources have offered extra-length barrels for the .45 auto and in the other two calibers — .38 Colt Super and 9mm Luger — but the resulting gain in velocity with a

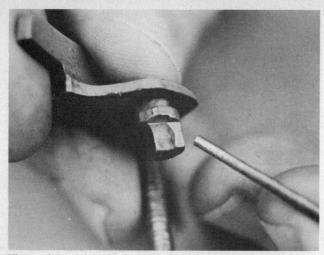

The surface pointed out here on safety lock engages the left lower lug of the sear, when up, to prevent release of the sear/hammer engagement. Text details checking steps.

longer barrel is not usually as much as one might expect. This seems particularly true of the .45 ACP cartridge, which shows no more than modest velocity gains, even when fired from the ten-inch barrel that Thompson/Center Arms used to offer for their single-shot Contender pistol.

It was noted earlier that all parts for all Model 1911 and 1911A1 pistols are theoretically more or less interchangeable but there are several exceptions, apart from the hammer spurs and tang lengths of the grip safeties, as discussed. Some of the parts for the shorter-barreled Commanders do not interchange with those of the

Government Model. The design and location of the ejectors on the 9mm and .38 Super autoloaders is different from that of the .45 ACP guns, preventing an easy and simple interchange between the two smaller cartridges and the .45 ACP. It is possible to convert the .38 Super to handle the 9mm Luger, by changing barrels. The 9mm may feed from the .38 Super magazine, although feeding usually is better if a 9mm magazine is obtained and used. The lower power of the 9mm cartridge usually requires the substitution of a somewhat weaker recoil spring for reliable functioning.

When building up an autoloading pistol of the general Model 1911 pattern, including the several subvariants of it, the builder is well advised to obtain new parts of high quality, rather than relying upon parts accumulated casually. The reason is that the surplus parts may and quite probably have seen extensive previous wear and use. The assembler should be aware that such wear can change certain critical dimensions in ways that affect accuracy, reliability and — even more urgently important — safety.

As an example, a safety lock with its inner surfaces worn or modified to contours and dimensions other than standard can function in such a way that, if the trigger is pulled when the safety is up — in safe position — the gun may fire when the safety lock is pushed back down. Even if it does not fire under such conditions, the trigger pull may be reduced to a marked degree.

One way to check for the existence of such a condition is to make certain the chamber is empty, cock the hammer, put up the safety lock and — keeping the muzzle pointed in a safe direction — pull the trigger. Maintaining the muzzle position, push the safety lock back down. Now pull back on the hammer spur, as you would in cocking the hammer, listening carefully. If a slight click is heard, that indicates

The receiver has been assembled temporarily — note protruding housing pin — without the grip safety in order to make a visual check of the operation of the safety catch. For further details, see photos at top of facing page.

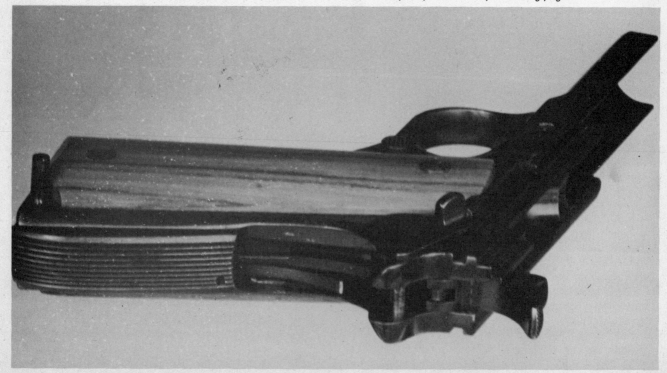

With hammer cocked and safety locked down (off), the lug of the safety lock (arrow) is seen to be well clear of the sear.

With safety lock up (on), its lug makes contact with the left lug of the sear (arrow) and must bar hammer release when in this configuration. If not, corrective action is needed.

Here the barrel and receiver have been placed in their relationship when the slide is back, as in feeding. The ramps must be free of snags as discussed in the text.

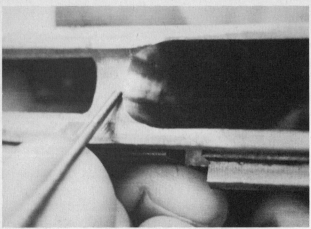

*Front edge of receiver feed ramp must not be ground so as to move it forward or bullets will hang up on barrel.*

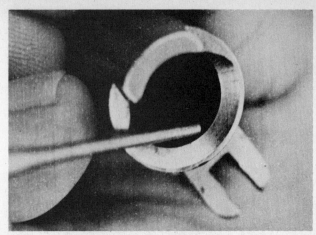

*Edge of barrel ramp must not be moved or it will reduce support of case head and may cause dangerous case rupture.*

that some amount of sear engagement was lost as the trigger was pulled with the safety lock in safe position. A condition such as the one described requires correction by the assembler or by a competent, professional gunsmith.

In the same manner, the functional integrity of the other safety provisions of the general Model 1911 design should be checked and verified, with corrective action taken if they do not perform as they should.

The three most critically important parts, in terms of functional reliability and safety are the hammer, sear and

safety lock, with the disconnector as a close runner-up. One of the main problems arising from incorporation of used parts, in addition to normal wear, is the fact that someone may have worked over the engaging surfaces at some previous time, leaving them no longer in correct relationship to each other.

One way of checking the operation of the safety lock, sear and disconnector is to assemble the gun without the grip safety in place. This permits the interaction of the remaining mentioned parts to be observed and checked.

The engagement between the contacting surfaces of the hammer and sear can be checked by applying a little color to the upper edge of the sear, perhaps with a felt-tipped marker, or a thin wipe of prussian blue oil pigment, then reassemble the gun, verify that it is empty, and cock and snap the hammer a few times. Disassemble and examine the colored area on the sear to see where the pigment has been rubbed off. This is a good way to detect uneven engagement and check the corrective measures taken or the need for replacement with a new part or parts.

When the gun is disassembled, the barrel can be held to the receiver so that the feed ramps of both the receiver at the upper front edge of the magazine well and around the lower edge of the chamber are in the same relation as when the gun is assembled. If the barrel ramp projects slightly behind the edge of the magazine well ramp, it creates a snag that will catch the nose of the bullet on the way to being chambered. It is a condition that causes unreliable feeding. The problem usually is an indication that someone has made ill advised attempts to modify the magazine well ramp in an effort to improve the feeding with semi-wadcutter cast bullets.

There are two lines on the magazine well ramp and the barrel feed ramp that should not be changed or modified, as

*This view of a chambered round shows normal headspacing flush with rear surface of barrel shroud, also the area of the cartridge head that is unsupported during firing cycle.*

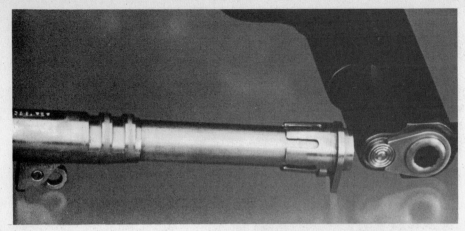

*A 9mm barrel from Bar-Sto Precision, installed in .38 Super.*

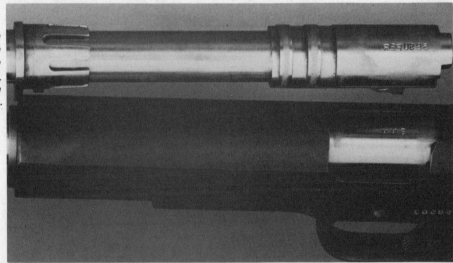

*Another view of the installed 9mm barrel and .38 Super version, both by Bar-Sto. These are the five-inch length for the Government Model, but 4¼-inch Commander length barrels are available from same source.*

*A better look at the collet-type barrel bushing supplied with the Bar-Sto stainless steel barrels, likewise available in .45 ACP and .38-45 Clerke. Same source offers stainless recoil spring plugs (top photo), spring sets, other items.*

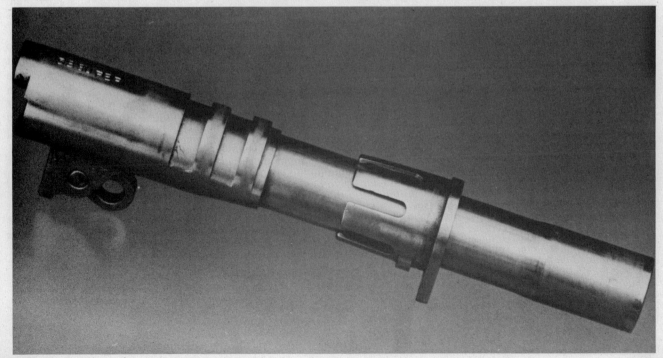

*One of the barrel bushing wrenches, discussed earlier, is in use here. It has an opening to match the shape of the bushing flange and a central tongue to depress tip of recoil spring plug for convenience. These are handy with tight bushings, but the lower edge of a magazine can be used with care for the same task, if needed.*

*This Government Model Colt Super .38 Automatic has been fitted with target sights and an accessory grip adapter of Nylon that's no longer made.*

shown in the accompanying photos. Pushing the front edge of the magazine well ramp forward creates the snagging problem just discussed. Moving the upper edge of the barrel feed ramp forward takes away the vital support for the cartridge case head at that point, creating a highly hazardous condition. Loss of support from the chamber can cause the case head to rupture, releasing high-pressure gases into the top of the magazine well. If loaded rounds remain in the magazine, it can set them off in a chain reaction.

It is permissible to polish the two sections of feed ramp, by way of reducing frictional resistance, so long as the locations of the two critical edges are not changed.

The Model 1911 pattern pistol has been produced in various forms by many makers during its career and those

*Military .45s bear numerous cryptic markings. FJA stands for Lt. Col. F.J. Atwood, who inspected the WWII output of Ithaca, Union Switch & Signal, and Remington-Rand, maker of gun pictured here.*

*This stainless Vega Combat Match .45 is of modern manufacture, but you'll note that it has the long trigger and straight mainspring housing of the early 1911 appearing at the start of this chapter. Many shooters prefer the longer trigger and straight housing.*

produced by certain firms tend to have a somewhat higher value, particularly among collectors. Two examples are the Springfield Armory pistols and those made by Union Switch and Signal of Swissvale, Pennsylvania. Relatively few of the Springfield Armory pistols were built, and only in the years 1914 and 1915. Remington built about 21,000 of the Model 1911, late in WWI, using their own set of serial numbers that ranged from 1 to 21676. All other military .45 autos carry serial numbers from assigned sequences between 1 in 1912 to 2693613; the last produced by Ithaca in 1945.

The fact that it is comparatively easy to swap parts between pistols is good and sufficient reason for the buyer to be wary when offered one of the more highly prized

*Here are right and left views of the Model 1911A1 from Remington-Rand, all put together, with no pieces left over. Those handsome stocks are of tulipwood, with vivid orange streaks on bright canary yellow. Steve Herrett, head of Herrett Stocks in Twin Falls, Idaho, made them about 1970, but says he's no longer able to obtain supplies of that particular scarce and exotic wood.*

examples of the .45 Government Model breed. The reason that the Union Switch & Signal .45s are so warmly regarded is that they were made and put together with truly exceptional precision and uniformity. The mere fact that the slide bears the US&S trademark is by no means solid assurance that the entire gun is made up of parts that came out of Swissvale.

It is generally believed that US&S made a lot more slides than complete pistols, furnishing their excellent slides to other makers. During most of its career to the present, the military .45 bore its maker's name on the slide and only the serial number and inspector's stamp on the receiver. According to E.J. Hoffschmidt's excellent and scholarly book, *Know Your .45 Auto Pistols*, the serial number range assigned to US&S spanned from 958101 through 1088725. Accordingly, unless the receiver bears a serial number between those two limits, it's not a US&S receiver, no matter what it says on the left side of the slide.

The basic Model 1911 design incorporates several safety features, including the thumb operated safety lock, the grip

A broad trigger shoe, such as this one from Pacific Tool Company of Grand Island, Nebraska, increases trigger surface and gives the impression of a lighter trigger pull.

Specifications say that the 9mmP case is .754-inch in length, but you won't find many that long. Usually, as in this one, they seat beyond the barrel shroud, per arrow. As a result, it's a challenge to get tight 9mm Luger groups.

The pertinent consideration with the Model 1911 is that a sharp amount of force against its muzzle can cause the gun to move back so abruptly that the firing pin moves forward under inertia against the firing pin spring and it can fire a chambered round in this manner, even if the hammer is back and the safety up, or if the hammer is fully forward. For that reason, it is the policy of most military organizations using the Model 1911/A1 to carry it with a fully charged magazine and empty chamber. It is a quick and positive operation to haul the slide back and let it go forward to place the gun in readiness for instant firing and it avoids completely the hazard of the chambered cartridge.

Curiously enough, some of the National Match grade Model 1911A1s, made for commercial sale shortly before WWII, incorporated a modification so that the forward travel of the firing pin was blocked when the hammer was cocked and the safety lock in its upper (safe) position. It is a bit mystifying that this practical modification has not been made more readily available in the years since.

safety and an inertia-type firing pin. The idea behind the inertia firing pin is that, if the hammer is down, a blow against the spur of the hammer will not fire a chambered round. Many revolvers, including most of the single-action design, will fire the chambered round under sharp stress against the spur of the lowered hammer. An exception is the New Model Ruger single-action, with its transfer bar, of course.

Using the homemade .45 tool to push out the mainspring housing pin, which has a shallow groove in its center.

Commercial Colt magazines carry stamp as below. The magazine's condition has important bearing on reliability.

*These two pictures show details of the pre-WWII National Match Colt incorporating a locked-up firing pin when safety lock is up (safe). At left you can see the tiny nub projecting below tip of disconnector to engage stud visible above the disconnector cut at the rear of the slide.*

*Below, a closer look at the area around the stud at the rear of the slide. When the National Match is in firing readiness, the nub in the receiver pushes the stud upward to disengage the locking block around the firing pin.*

Right, looking up into rear of the slide, with the firing pin and firing pin stop removed, you can see the spring-loaded locking plate that comes down to arrest forward movement of the firing pin. Below, the National Match firing pin, distinguished by its groove at the rear, is shown above a standard firing pin.

Here's one final close-in look at the National Match modification. There are not many of these guns around. They were factory honed, tuned and polished to incredible smoothness.

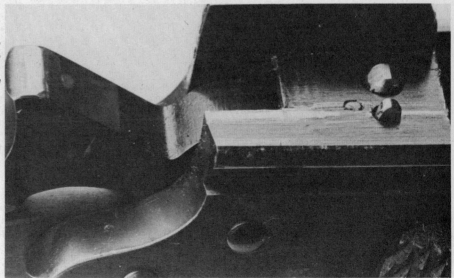

# Chapter 16

# THE OLD SHELL GAME

## Mother-Of-Pearl Has Been Used Decoratively For Centuries; Now It's Within Your Grasp!

**I** STOOD BEFORE the Art Jewel Enterprises display booth. We were at the National Sporting Goods Association show; outside it was depressing, cold even for Chicago, roads and highways clogged with snow. Inside the convention center, row after row of manufacturers and distributors showcased the coming year's new products for the trade. But I'd been drawn to the Art Jewel booth by the eye-catching ivory and rosewood pistol grips on display.

I'd worked with ivory myself a year earlier and was interested in talking to anyone who knew anything at all about working with it. Only after my initial ivory project had I learned one should work in a well ventilated room and wear a mask; should the powder-like ivory grindings get into the lungs, this can cause serious health problems.

Looking over the beautifully carved, highly polished ivory grips I figured if anyone knew anything about working ivory, it would be these folks. I was impressed also with the polished, carved rosewood grips, but in a corner were mother-of-pearl grips for the Colt Single Action. "Really nice looking pistol grips, but not my style," I thought, my attention still held by the exotic solid ivory.

Jack Lewis, next to me, was entranced by this company's products. Talking to Mike Lavarra, sales manager, we were surprised by the reasonable retail prices of their entire line in view of the growing scarcity of both ivory and mother-of-pearl.

The company features their Eagle line of solid rosewood grips which are available with high relief carvings. There are four individual styles for revolvers: oversize, finger position, target, and regular. They also make grips for autoloading handguns.

Lewis decided to buy a matching set of grips for each of the two Colt Single Action pistols he prizes. With one of

*This pair of Colt Single-Action Army revolvers has been custom-fitted with mother-of-pearl grips from Art Jewel firm. The growing scarcity of such grip materials will do much in coming years to increase collector values.*

*Shells for custom mother-of-pearl grips must be at least 10 inches in diameter.*

the executives of Art Jewel Enterprises, Harbans Singh, we looked over the many choices available for this particular handgun model.

Finally, Lewis ordered two sets of mother-of-pearl grips for his beloved Colts. I'd been sure he would have picked ivory, or that the high relief carved solid rosewood would be his second choice. Singh made shipping arrangements for the grips.

The more I thought about it, the more I realized that mother-of-pearl would not be my own first choice for pistol grips. That led to questioning why I didn't seem to like this particular material. Granted, it certainly isn't very durable and never would win first choice as the least obvious grips for an undercover gun. But those practical considerations aside, I realized I was prejudiced. Since I'd never worked

with it, I knew I didn't dislike the shell material due to past experience.

It finally dawned on me. I didn't like mother-of-pearl because of General George Patton. I remembered reading an interview wherein a reporter made reference to Patton's mother-of-pearl-gripped pistols he allegedly wore in the field. The general corrected the reporter with the fact that his guns carried ivory grips. The outspoken general added something to the effect that only pimps would have mother-of-pearl on their guns.

There it was: I was prejudiced against one of the most beautiful of nature's treasures because of a quote that had stuck in my mind all these years. Over the next few months, I asked several gunsmithing friends, as well as other acquaintances, if they'd ever heard the general's quote

*Shell's exterior doesn't reflect the inner beauty of material. Shells are five years old.*

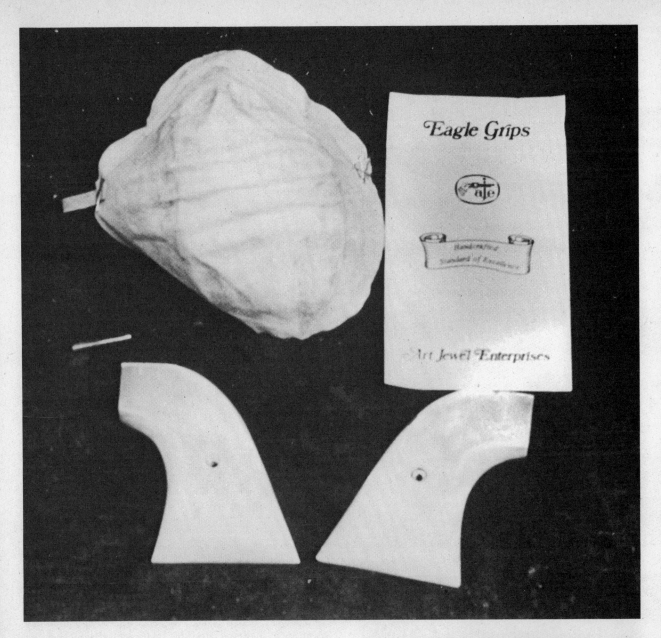

*Each pair of Art Jewel grips is cut slightly oversize and require custom fitting to the individual handgun. (Right) Filipino workers wear protective masks as they rough-shape the shells on grinding wheels. Approximately 30 percent of the shells are rejected due to imperfections.*

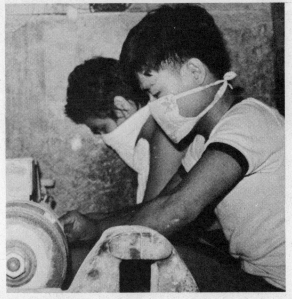

pertaining to mother-of-pearl. I was surprised at how well remembered that quote still is today.

Other than the fact that the general didn't seem to think much of mother-of-pearl, that this material is too brittle to stand up under heavy and continuous use, it is valued universally because of its iridescent qualities. Anyone who has ever seen real mother-of-pearl in bright sunlight and viewed its shifting changes in color from different angles will recognize its beauty.

When the mother-of-pearl grips arrived at our offices, I took them and the two Colt Single Actions to my shop. While awaiting delivery, I'd done some homework on mother-of-pearl and had changed my earlier opinion considerably.

*Mother-of-pearl grips are final shaped by sanding with various grades of aluminum oxide paper to match contour of the Colt Single-Action Army frame. Author found that approximately 3½ hours was required for the operation.*

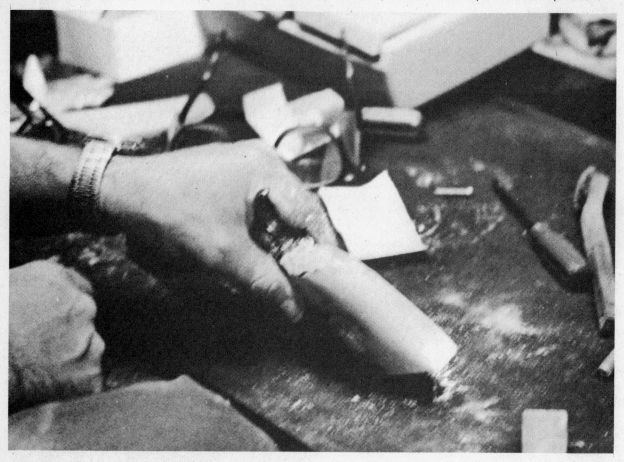

*Care, patience are keys to fitting slightly oversize grips. Mother-of-pearl is much more difficult to work than most other grip materials, as it tends to be hard, brittle.*

Attempting to learn a few basic working fundamentals for shaping and polishing mother-of-pearl, I called a custom knifemaker friend I thought might be able to enlighten me. After some working tips, he cautioned that it was an extremely dangerous material with which to work. I should definitely wear a mask at all times while sanding or polishing the shell. In the next few days, I called several other people in the custom firearms and knifemaking business. Each who had worked with it echoed the fact that mother-of-pearl could be hazardous to your health if you breathe the dust while grinding or polishing the material.

I knew that working with ivory was dangerous due to the possibility of inhaling its needle-like particles. With mother-of-pearl, I wanted to learn whether it is considered harmful because it is toxic, or because the powder physically damages the lungs. I quickly learned that few people know much about mother-of-pearl.

After additional warnings, I began researching various scientific journals looking for origins and characteristics. I finally contacted John Sampson White, the associate curator of Minerals and Gems, Department of Mineral Sciences, for the U.S. National Museum of Natural History in Washington, D.C.

After outlining my frustrations in learning whether

*Sanding requires both square and round blocks as backing to paper. Good wire brush should be used to remove powder residue from the sandpaper during operation. (Below) The variable speed Dremel Moto-Tool, with felt polishing wheel, jeweler's rouge, was used by Mitchell for final polishing work.*

mother-of-pearl is a dangerous toxic substance, White replied, "That is total poppycock. There is nothing about the chemistry of mother-of-pearl that I know of to be harmful. It is composed of calcium carbonate which means it could either be calcite or aragonite, or a combination of the two. Both are crystals found in nature that are not harmful to humans from a chemical standpoint. If there is a problem, it might stem from the inhalation of the powder into the lungs and that possibly might cause a problem."

Since every person I have talked with about working with mother-of-pearl recommended the work area to be well ventilated and masks worn, I'd suggest adherance to those few safety rules.

My research revealed that mother-of-pearl is becoming increasingly difficult to obtain, especially in sizes large enough for pistol grips. Like everything else in this world, as the supply diminishes, the value increases dramatically.

Mother-of-pearl might well be one of the best investments in today's firearms collecting field.

Genuine mother-of-pearl comes from shells in the mollusk family. Clams, mussels, oysters, snails, and abalone come under this heading. Although many different types of shells labeled mother-of-pearl are used for ornamentation, the particular type sold through Art Jewel Enterprises and used throughout the industry for pistol grips is becoming increasingly difficult to obtain, as stated earlier.

To make one grip for one side of the handgun requires a shell properly aged, and free of defects. That doesn't sound like such a tall order until you understand that it takes an abalone shell of ten to twelve inches in diameter to furnish material for one grip. A shell this size weighs approximately five pounds and is about five years old. And only seventy percent of all shells large enough are worm- and defect-free after being ground to size.

The Philippines, Australia, Thailand, and a few other Pacific Islands are the only places in the world where shells of adequate size still are found. Even in such exotic locales there are damn few large shells left and the supply is diminishing rapidly.

Most of the abalone shells of pistol grip size must be taken at a depth of around 120 feet. Diving at that depth, a diver can stay down a very limited time for each dive. In each ton of shell gathered commercially only two or three individual shells will be large enough and sufficiently free of defects to be used for pistol grips. Each half of the pistol grip is mated to the other only after many are rough cut at the Jewel Enterprises factory in the Philippines. Obviously, a sameness of design and color are important factors in the mating process. And since Mother Nature never makes any two things exactly alike one can begin to understand

reasons for the value of the mother-of-pearl grips.

Scientifically speaking, the actual mother-of-pearl shell consists of extremely fine layers of aragonite and/or calcite deposited parallel to the surface of the shell. These layers can number anywhere from 450 to 5000 layers per each 1/25-inch of thickness. It is these layers of crystals lying horizontally that catch and interact with light waves to give mother-of-pearl its iridescent quality.

Water temperature has a great deal to do with the broad spectrum of beautiful colors found in abalone shells. According to a marine biologist whom I questioned, the colder the water, the greater the density and profusion of the color patterns in the shell. For example, shells of the abalone family gathered in Northern California or Oregon usually are much darker with greater variations of color patterns than in those found in Southern California waters.

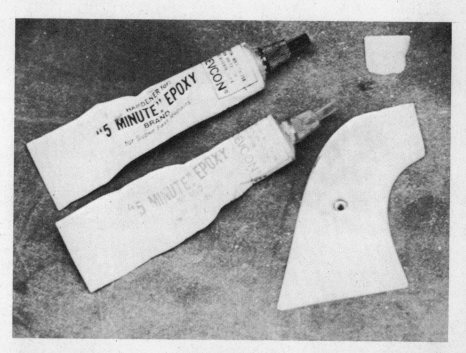

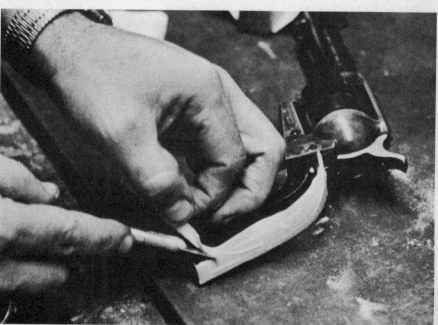

*Broken chip from the material was epoxied in place carefully. The epoxy was allowed to cure, then grips were sanded to completely hide the small repaired area. (Lower right) As grips must be attached to pistol in shaping, exposed metal surface should be protected with fiberglass reinforced shipping tape.*

The water temperature between these two areas seldom varies more than twenty degrees, yet the density of color is so different one can understand why mother-of-pearl gathered from the warmer waters off the Philippines or Thailand with their overwhelmingly white shell color is so valuable for grips.

Abalone and other shells have been used by man since the beginning of recorded time. It should not be surprising that some of the finest guns ever built have used abalone shell and mother-of-pearl as part of their ornamentation. Looking for a good example of mother-of-pearl used historically required further investigations. I contacted the Smithsonian Institute to talk with Craddock Goings, curator of Firearms and Edged Weapons. He informed me that, although they did indeed have firearms at the Smithsonian with mother-of-pearl inlays, there were some tremendous art examples at the Metropolitan Museum of Art in New York City.

At the Metropolitan, I spoke with Dr. Helmut Nickel, in charge of arms and armament at the museum. Dr. Nickel informed me that mother-of-pearl was used decoratively for certain firearms beginning in the mid-Sixteenth Century. These were mostly wheelocks made in Germany and France. The shell has been gathered from the North Sea and Mediterranean, although local mussels were used occasionally.

The Metropolitan Museum has on display an early

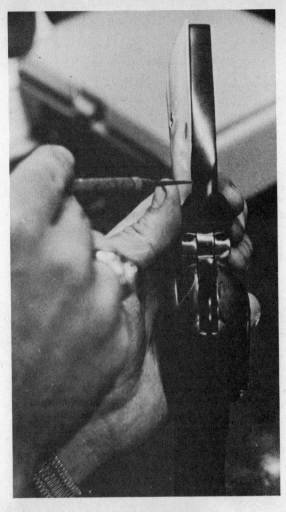

*Right: The low spot visible on the grip is the work of Mother Nature, not a mistake by the gunsmith. (Below) Stock pin holes in the Art Jewel grips were slightly undersize. Careful drilling resulted in a perfect fit.*

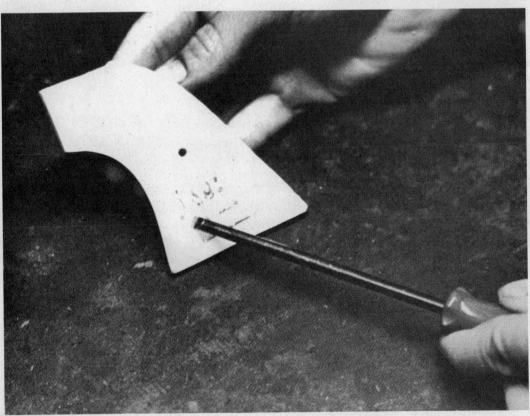

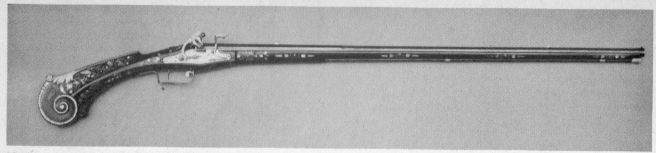

*Mother-of-pearl inlays were used to artistic advantage in this early flintlock rifle made especially for King Louis XIII of France in about 1615 by the LeBourgeoy brothers. It's displayed at the Metropolitan Museum.*

flintlock made in 1615 especially for Louis XIII, King of France. The gun was built by three gunmaking brothers named LeBourgeoy, who were living in the small French village of Lisieux.

After staring at photos of the Louis XIII flintlock, I began to feel General Patton just might have been wrong in his assessment of mother-of-pearl. As an old non-commissioned officer, I knew it wasn't unheard of for an enlisted soldier to disagree with the general once in a while — quietly of course.

Really getting into mother-of-pearl, I contacted John Bianchi of Bianchi Leather in Temecula, California. Bianchi has several famous guns of the Old West with mother-of-pearl grips in the museum facility located at his factory.

Bianchi's collection of Old West firearms is impressive. Surprisingly, in the entire collection, I found no pearl-handled guns that had belonged to pimps. Actually,

all of the handguns once belonged to lawmen.

Some of the most famous characters out of our Western frontier carried pearl-handled revolvers. Wyatt Earp occasionally carried such a Colt Single Action .44-40 with a 7½-inch barrel. Since the gun was profusely engraved and inlayed with gold and silver, Earp did not carry it on a daily basis.

Tom Threepersons carried a nickel-plated Colt SAA in .44 Special that had mother-of-pearl grips with a Texas steer head carved into each of them. He had been a Northwest Mounted Policeman, a renowned rodeo rider, a lawman in El Paso and a scout against Pancho Villa for General "Blackjack" Pershing.

Bianchi has in his collection pearl-handled Colts that once belonged to Bob Dalton of outlaw fame and another that once was the property of Jeff Milton, a one-time Texas Ranger and chief of police in El Paso.

It was becoming obvious that mother-of-pearl grips were

*Colt SAA with mother-of-pearl grips belonged to outlaw Bob Dalton, now is a part of collection of John Bianchi.*

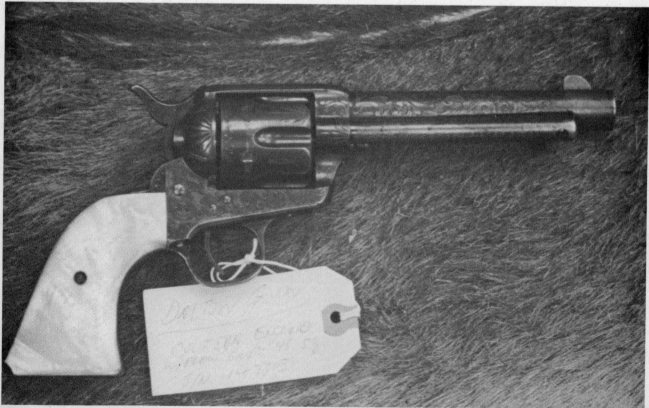

Cherokee Indian lawman Tom Threepersons favored mother-of-pearl grips with a Texas longhorn carved into shell.

favorites for many famous characters of the Old West. Since guns were working tools for lawmen and cowboys, they often were subjected to hard use. Inspection of the pieces in the Bianchi Collection indicate that the pearl grips stood up quite well.

I was beginning to wonder if the general had ever really known a pimp, particularly one with a pearl-handled shootin' iron!

With all the research that threatened to become a career, I hadn't done much to fit the pearl grips to Jack Lewis' Colt Single Action .45s. The easiest, fastest, and safest way to work with mother-of-pearl, I had learned, is to use

El Paso lawman Jeff Milton also preferred mother-of-pearl. Grips appear to be factory option.

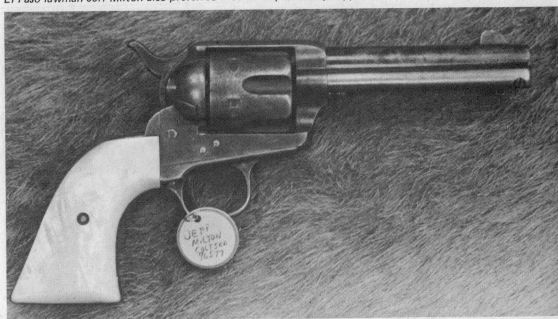

Replicas of guns Gen. George S. Patton carried in World War II boasts ivory grips, not mother-of-pearl.

lapidary equipment, including gem-cutting diamond wheel cutters, special lapidary grinding wheels, and exceedingly fine polishing abrasives.

The final high polishing of stones and/or mother-of-pearl is accomplished with what is called a vibrating lap. This is a flat pan that floats on rubber balls and is vibrated rapidly by a motor. The pieces of shell are placed in the pan, separated by small plastic rings to keep the parts from

bumping into each other and breaking. The proper polishing grit is selected and added to water, the switch is turned on — and several hours later the pieces are finish polished.

However, I didn't have access to this equipment, so a call for help to gunsmith and knifesmith friends resulted in the simple advice that led to the tedious task of hand sanding the grip material to fit, then polishing with a Dremel

When appreciative citizens ordered special SAA for Wyatt Earp, they made certain of pearl grips. The gun, now in the Bianchi collection also is heavily engraved, inlaid with gold and silver, matching the lawman's flamboyance.

Moto-Tool and jeweler's rouge.

Beginning by opening all the doors and windows to my small garage shop and adjusting a mask over my nose and mouth, I fit the grips to the individual guns. The holes pre-drilled on the inside of the Art Jewel grips to mate with the Colt stock pins or detents were a bit undersized for these particular models and I had to drill them out to a custom fit. Drilling had to be slow and careful not to chip or crack the brittle mother-of-pearl.

Before I'd even started fitting the grips I'd noticed that one of the grips had been chipped during shipment. Using a good epoxy to affix the broken chip into place was all that was required to resolve that problem.

Protection of the bluing on the Colts while sanding down the grips to fit was a bit of concern to me. One little slip and the 60-grit fastcut paper I'd selected to rough shape the grips would scratch the metal and require a new blue job. To protect the metal, I used fiberglass-reinforced tape. It is the best stuff I've found for protecting metal surfaces when using sandpaper or files. I managed to slip a few times, but the tape prevented the rough paper from touching the metal.

Progressing from the 60-grit paper to finish shaping and smoothing down the work with 280-grit fine paper, I was ready to final polish the grips. Having no regular lapidary polishes, I opted for jeweler's rouge and my Dremel tool with the felt polishing wheel turned up to fast speed. The grip polished up to incredible brilliance and iridescence.

In all honesty, I did the best job possible to fit the grips, but there were two small places where Mother Nature had seen fit to leave a low spot or two in her shells. However, even with a slightly less than perfect fit, they looked sensational on the two Colts.

Fitting the grips to one gun, getting the stock pin holes to line up properly by slightly altering the escutcheon screw fit, and final polishing had taken me approximately 3½ hours. Total working hours for both sets of grips required just under seven hours. However, I had done it the slow way, using only sandpaper and polishing rouge.

A pair of mother-of-pearl grips for a Colt Single Action from Art Jewel Enterprises currently runs around $135. I called a few more gunsmith buddies to find out if they had any idea of gunsmith charges for such work. Most seemed to feel that a median price would be about $50 per set. So, for approximately $185 it is possible to buy and have custom-fitted a set of mother-of-pearl grips on that favorite presentation handgun.

From a gunsmithing standpoint, I still prefer ivory because it works so easily, is almost as distinctive as mother-of-pearl, and certainly more durable. And although ivory is becoming increasingly more difficult to obtain, it still is more prevalent than mother-of-pearl.

From a pure investment standpoint, mother-of-pearl has to be the choice. And with the traditional gathering grounds offshore from the Philippines almost depleted, within a few years, the material probably will not be available. As suggested, this just might be the best investment in the firearms collecting field.

For more information and a catalog of exotic mother-of-pearl, ivory, and rosewood custom grips from Art Jewel Enterprises, send $1 to P.O. Box 819, Berkeley, Illinois 60163.

So cry, General Patton — wherever you are!

*These are the matching sixguns with new custom-fitted mother-of-pearl grips on which Jack Mitchell worked. Raw materials were from Illinois' Art Jewel Enterprises.*

# Chapter 17

# IMPROVING THE BREED

*This Loveless-customized Colt Commander in .45 ACP caliber has been worked over extensively to eliminate sharp corners and rough edges, as well as internal refinements to improve accuracy.*

**T**HE FIRST TIME Bob Loveless ever heard the Colt Model 1911 bad-mouthed, was by an Air Force sergeant on the pistol range at Keesler Field, Mississippi, in 1946. "We were a bunch of raw youngsters," Loveless relates, "and by the time the sergeant was done talking, we were already half scared of the brute. Luckily, we fired only for familiarization; we didn't have to qualify with the gun."

Loveless, who operates out of Riverside, California, these days, is considered one of the nation's top custom knifemakers. However, he also has gained more than a passing reputation as a gunsmith, limiting his work largely to his own handguns and those of his immediate friends.

When his enlistment was over, Loveless went back to civilian life, and within a year or two, bought his first handgun. It was a Colt Commander, in .45 ACP, with the first aluminum frame ever used on a big bore pistol.

"I thought it was a most efficient performer, and I've kept it all these years. But somehow I never shot it much, perhaps a few magazines on the odd Sunday afternoon. I never did settle down to really master the pistol and what could be done with it. Still, I felt it was a damned good gun to have around: lots of power, with the least possible weight for the caliber," Loveless says.

"In the years since, I've run into fellows who claim the Colt .45 auto is a bad one, that it kicks like a mule, and

# A Few Simple Custom Modifications Can Do Much To Improve Any Autoloader's Performance

isn't accurate. Not too many years ago, a friend bought a Government Model and went to work with it. Three months later, after shooting up most of a case of surplus ammo, he sold the gun and to this day bears a small scar on the web of his shooting hand. He claims that he'll never again mess with big bore automatics and presently shoots rimfire revolvers.

"During these years, I've messed with all kinds of handguns. But somehow I've never gotten really confident with the Colt .45 auto. It has always hurt me and I never felt it was a fun gun to shoot. But a few months ago I had a chance to go over to Jeff Cooper's Gunsite Ranch, in Arizona, to take the Basic Pistol Course. A week before heading for Gunsite, I hauled out a pair of Commanders, one in alloy and one steel-framed, and went to the range to work with them."

In the course of shooting some 225 rounds, in about three hours, Loveless found his hand beaten up something fierce; the web between thumb and forefinger was open and bleeding. He went back to his shop and quickly made up two beavertail-tanged safeties. Figuring this would cure the problem, he was able to shoot the guns without further damage to his hand and, a week later, took off for Gunsite full of fresh beans and vinegar, as they say.

"The Basic Pistol Course at Cooper's place starts off easy; I fired only a few shots that Monday afternoon. But by Thursday I was shooting almost one hundred rounds a day. Late that afternoon, on a time problem, I made a grab for the gun, got into it a little high, squeezed off the shot, and right away knew I'd done something wrong. I looked at my hand and saw fresh blood on the web. From that shot, everything went downhill, and I was lucky to graduate the

*Above, Loveless checks the sights on one of the .22 LR Field Guns he builds from the S&W Model 41 auto. Far left, a Model 1911A1, with one of Loveless' customized Commanders.*

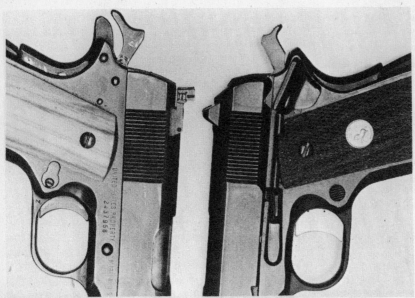

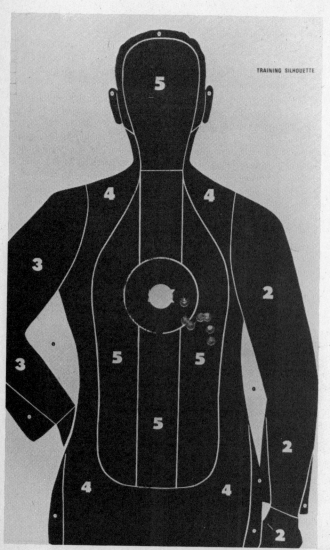

*Right, Loveless observes the functioning of one of his guns as Ray Randall fires seven rounds from twenty-five yards at the silhouette target, below.*

TRAINING SILHOUETTE

course with a rating as Marksman."

Early Saturday afternoon, while several of Cooper's students were sitting around a table, they began comparing notes. Loveless noticed that more than half had moderate to severe hand damage from the constant shooting. Then he realized this was the first time in his shooting career that he'd been required to shoot the gun every day, with no days off to recuperate.

"At other times in my life, I had done a lot of shooting, but never day in and day out, a hundred rounds or so a day, working against time limits. Finally, after years of owning a big-bore pistol, I was actually learning something about shooting it. Gunsite was a great experience. I learned to shoot quickly and accurately and only now can I appreciate what is possible for the well-trained pistolero using the proper gun."

The Colt Model 1911, in any of its variations, is the preferred choice of the International Practical Shooting Confederation and similar events, because of its major caliber classification and because such men as Jeff Cooper, Roy Chapman and other leading shooters use it.

Yet it is notoriously hard on the shooter. It doesn't hurt every man who uses it and some can handle it with no strain or pain. But it's safe to say that most of us have trouble with it and some end up quite goosey about the subject, even as they head out on a weekend for another league match.

Upon returning from Gunsite, Loveless settled in for a serious look at the M1911. Although he had been raised with the idea that sharp edges are the mark of fine gunsmithing, it was soon obvious that the sharp edges on this gun caused damage where they made contact with the web of the shooter's hand. The tang of the grip safety is the main culprit, as the guns come from the factory. Yet even his beavertail tangs hadn't solved the problem during fast shooting.

"Among my current handguns is a cut-down version of

Loveless has produced his custom guns in both blued or black oxide finish and in industrial hard chrome. Details of the chromed version are depicted in photo at right.

the Smith & Wesson Model 39. The maker shortened the barrel and slide, cut off part of the grip and completely removed the rear frame tang. I got this gun out, loaded it up and cut loose with a magazine full.

"Sure enough, there was no pain to my hand. I began to wonder if maybe we hadn't been going at this problem all wrong. I took the alloy Commander to the belt grinder and quickly removed the tang of the grip safety. A bit of careful work smoothed up all the edges at the rear of the gun and made it feel a whole lot better in my hand," Loveless recalls.

"A bullet trap out of three-eighths-inch steel plate sits just behind my line of knife grinders — too damned heavy to move around — and is one of my life's treasures. So after cleaning up the rear of the gun, I loaded a magazine full of military ball loads and tried it out. Wonder of wonders, even with my hand beat up from Gunsite a week before, there was no pain; it didn't hurt, not even a little. Could it be that this was the simple answer all along: Take away the part that hurts, so that the tang just isn't there anymore to bite you?

"Three magazines later, it seemed to be an answer. I now had a messed up gun and did a little more thinking, remembering how, every once in a while when shoving the gun down inside my waist for a right kidney hold, the muzzle would catch on my clothing, from the squared edges around the muzzle.

"A few more strokes on the belt grinder and that problem was solved. Now the gun was smooth at both ends, although it did look somewhat like it had the measles.

"One other thing that had been bothering me for years was the poor visibility of most pistol sights. I remembered reading in Bob Nichol's book about double-action shooting

*Above, size of indoor test group can be gauged by comparing it to the 1¼" red aiming paster. Right, a close look at the novel stippling on the front grip area of the Loveless-reworked Colt.*

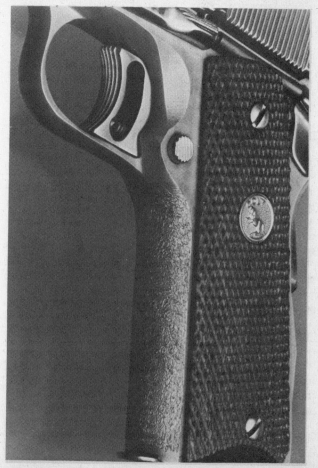

of the need for better sights. The main complaint is that existing sights are too fine, too hard to see. Well, it took a couple hours of work on the little Clausing vertical mill and I had a fine new set of fixed sights. The new red-ramped front sight was .173-inch in width and dropped into the darkened U of the new and larger rear sight, giving me a big, bright sight picture. It also gave me much faster target acquisition, which is an important part of this new — to me — kind of shooting. I've been using red-ramped sights for years and I still like them, although some shooters claim such sights distract them or that the red front shoots to the light. But for me, the big red ramp works in any light, against any target and that is exactly what I feel is needed on a law enforcement duty handgun."

At this point Loveless had a smoothed-up gun that didn't hurt any more, new sights that he could see much better and faster; what else was left?

"One of the things I've always liked about the S&W M39 was the profile of the lower rear grip frame. It has always seemed to fit my hand quite nicely, filling the hollow in the middle of the palm."

Loveless took a hard look at the arched housing on the Colt, went back to the grinder and quickly made a housing he liked a lot better. There was no longer a lump on the bottom, punching its way into the heel of his hand. Now it fit the way it should.

The usual loop-type hammer tang of the worked-over Colt Commander has been ground by Loveless to eliminate the gun's objectionable tendency to nip the hand's web.

Loveless' usual tendency has been to stay with the factory checkered stocks, in handsome walnut, with gold-colored medallions. His modification of the mainspring housing is remarkably steady in sighting and secure from recoil shift.

"Once again I loaded a magazine, lined up on my bullet trap at eleven yards and cut loose, this time with a two-handed hold from rest. I got something that looked like about three inches and did some more thinking.

"My first friend, when I arrived in Modesto, California, in early 1959, was Cassius P. 'Cash' Gustin, then serving on the Highway Patrol. Cash had been on the CHP Perry team 'way back and, in 1968, developed and patented the slickest and quickest way of making a short-recoil pistol shoot tight groups that I'd ever seen."

The Gustin accuracy job consists of two set screws, set into the slide at the right place, that act to limit lock-up action which provides consistent battery position. This is exactly what most accuracy jobs attempt to do, of course.

"Most of us, in the past, have squeezed the slide slightly closed to limit slide-to-frame movement, then fitted tight front barrel bushings, and sometimes long links, ending up with finicky guns that do not tolerate any dirt at all. You may have seen such a gun, if you've gone to one of the pistol league matches, hang up right in the middle of a string. Some authorities suggest that new shooters should not even bother with an accuracy job but shoot the gun right out of the box. Guns that are fitted up too tight directly contradict the very quality of the Model 1911 so prized by the military — its ability to eat dirt and come up

shooting."

The Gustin accuracy job does not reduce the reliability of the gun in any way. It just makes the pistol put all its shots into a smaller area, which is exactly what it should do. Gustin's patent, first issued in 1968, covers such guns as the Colt, the Browning P-35, the S&W M39, the Tokarev, and even the SIG P-210.

After setting up a V-block in the mill and drilling and tapping the holes, Loveless set the screws in place, adjusted the return stroke of the slide and went back to the shooting rest. This time, with a two-handed hold, the gun shot into one ragged hole, giving a group of seven shots that measured about one-quarter-inch center to center.

"After finishing work on the alloy gun, I worked up the Combat Commander and began thinking about the refinishing work. Considering that the lightweight model would be my No. 1 gun, the choice was easy; it would have to be hard-chromed.

"Having done a bit of business with this gent previously, I contacted John B. Williams, in Fullerton. He agreed to handle the job, so I shagged the lightweight over to him, and in the next few days, he performed his usual magic with conversion coatings and other arcane techniques. I took the Combat Commander to Terry Jirsa, of Accurate Gun Works in San Bernardino, who did a fine job of

At far left, an S&W Model 41, in factory condition, with the left stock removed, compared to Loveless' version.

rebluing it," Loveless reports.

"Bruce Nelson, one of IPSC's leading shooters and a staff instructor at Gunsite, happened by a few days after I had done all this messing around. Now this dude, when it comes to Colts, is about as smart as an outhouse rat. He's handled a lot of Colts, uses an alloy Commander on daily duty and can be considered generally qualified to pass judgment on the job. His verdict, after test shooting both guns, was enthusiastic; said he wanted to shoot one of the guns at an IPSC event, even.

"For me, at this point, I have something I never expected to have; a pair of Commanders that don't hurt me — and thus don't scare me into reflexive flinching — a sighting system that helps these tired old eyes see better and quicker and guns that shoot like short rifles, with no reliability problems.

"What are the disdavantages? Well, frankly, I don't know. We'll have to shoot several thousand rounds and keep track of the problems, correcting them as they come up, before we'll know for sure if this has all been worth doing. So far everything works but only time and lots of use will tell the tale. Even now I find myself grabbing one of the guns, at odd moments during the day, loading up, and busting loose at a target on the bullet trap."

Bob Loveless holds a deep-seated conviction that few human activities are much more enjoyable than shooting.

As Dean Grennell observes via binoculars, Loveless fires a test group from Ransom rest. Note the ejected empty case.

"I wanted a .22 auto that would be compact and pleasant to carry, with no sacrifice in accuracy, reliability or capability," Loveless says of his Field Gun modified from S&W M41.

Of all the many aspects of the shooting sports, the one he finds most enthralling is plinking at tin cans, or perhaps at jackrabbits, ground squirrels and the like with a handgun. Focusing to a still smaller area, his tastes run strongly to an autoloading pistol chambered for the familiar .22 long rifle cartridge. Also Loveless is one of those constructively malcontent souls who cannot seem to find total satisfaction with gadgetry the way it was built by its maker.

"I guess at one time or another, I've owned just about every make of .22 auto pistol," he recalls, "but I couldn't seem to find one exactly suited to my personal taste. The ones capable of the accuracy I expected and demanded were all too big, bulky, clumsy and unwieldy. If they were small, light and handy, they just wouldn't deliver the slugs to the place I had in mind."

When Smith & Wesson introduced their Model 41 target auto, in the latter years of the Fifties, Loveless bought one and found it offered many things to his liking, with a few features to which he objected. The good news was its capability for excellent accuracy, combined with trouble-free functioning. The bad news was that it weighed about forty-three ounces and, with the detachable muzzle brake in place on the 7-3/8-inch barrel, it stretched to about one full foot in overall length.

Most of the modern .22 auto pistols can trace some portion of their design concept back to John M. Browning, drafter of the blueprints for the Colt Woodsman, which several other makes and models resemble to greater or less degrees. The common traits include a relatively long breechblock that carries the recoil spring, recoil spring

guide and, in most instances, conceals the hammer. This adds a substantial length of slide assembly to the barrel, with little or no way to reduce the slide length. Thus, any modification must concern itself with bobbing metal off the barrel, with a resulting loss of velocity and length of

*Blued and hard-chromed versions of the Loveless Field Gun, from right and left sides, with slide open and closed.*

sight radius.

Unlike most of its contemporaries among American-made .22 autos, the S&W Model 41 design has more of a European flavor, harking back to the Paul Walther approach of putting the recoil spring and its guide rod up front, beneath the barrel. With those components taken from the slide, its length is shortened slightly, though it continues to conceal the hammer in the unmodified Model 41, with a small pin that protrudes to the rear of the receiver to serve as a cocking indicator. (Newer versions of the Model 41, incidentally, are sans this indicator and have no muzzlebrake.)

Among Loveless' many strong convictions is a preference for a visible hammer as a safety feature and, in taking a long, thoughtful look at the Model 41, he felt it would be an advantage to trim nearly an inch of metal off the back of the slide, thereby exposing the hammer and reducing the overall length without taking it from the barrel. Since the Model 41 does not have a floating firing pin, when its hammer is down and a live round is in the chamber, it could be fired by a sharp impact against the hammer spur. Loveless chose to overcome this problem by utilizing the half-cock notch for the hammer. The sear mechanism of the Model 41 is not engaged until the hammer is drawn to full-cock. Thus there is no serious risk that the hammer could be dropped from half-cock by a pull of the trigger,

this being a hazard with certain other auto pistol designs.

The barrel of the Model 41 is locked securely to the receiver, with the pivoting trigger guard serving as the lever for taking down or locking up on reassembly. The barrel assembly includes an upper extension, projecting rearward from the breech for about three inches to carry the rear sight. This has the desirable property of maintaining both sights in rigid relationship to the bore.

In the original Model 41 design, the front of the recoil spring and guide rod are about flush with the front of the slide extension, although the muzzle and muzzle brake of

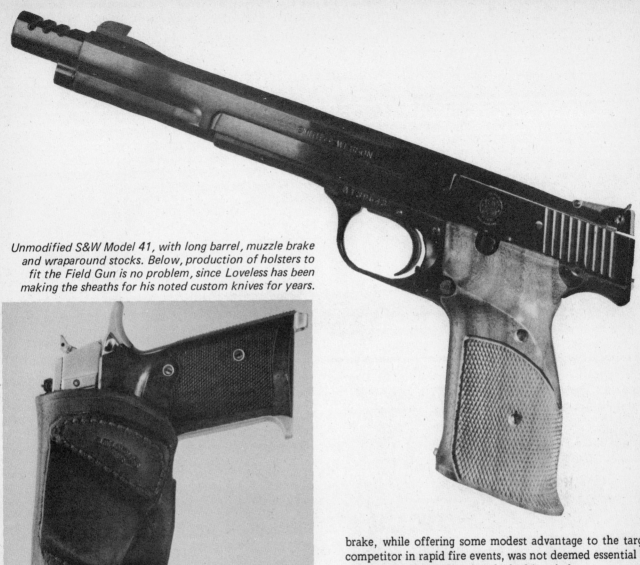

*Unmodified S&W Model 41, with long barrel, muzzle brake and wraparound stocks. Below, production of holsters to fit the Field Gun is no problem, since Loveless has been making the sheaths for his noted custom knives for years.*

the 7-3/8-inch barrel continue forward for a good four inches beyond that point. Experience with several other guns indicated that the .22 long rifle cartridge could develop an adequate level of punch within a barrel length of about four inches.

Cutting off the barrel flush with the front of the slide leaves a dimension of about 4.350 inches from the muzzle to the face of the breechblock. At the same time, it gives lengths of 7¼ inches from the muzzle to the rear of the hammer spur and 7½ inches to the rear of the grip tang. This effects a net reduction of nearly five inches off the original length, meanwhile sacrificing a hair less than 2¾ inches of actual swept length within the bore. The muzzle

brake, while offering some modest advantage to the target competitor in rapid fire events, was not deemed essential by Loveless for the applications he had in mind.

Another feature of the Model 41, regarded by Loveless as great for paper-punchers, but less than ideal for plinking purposes, was the shape and contour of the factory grips. These are fairly bulky, nearly symmetrical as to right and left, for use in either hand and the wood goes around the rear of the grip fully. This encloses the coil-type hammer spring and its guide rod that extends upward to serve as the hammer strut. These components are exposed when the grips are removed.

Loveless chose to make up a mainspring housing from scratch to cover the area. He chose a high-tensile aluminum alloy, contouring it in a straight line, parallel to the front of the grip and fairing it smoothly into the sweep of the tang at the upper rear of the grip. An area along the center of the lower two-thirds was left as raised checkering and he incorporated an integral lanyard loop at the lower rear corner. After polishing, the aluminum housing is anodized in a gold color.

The thumb/finger ridges, jutting from each side of the Model 41 factory grips, give the gun a maximum thickness of some 1.675 inches at that point. Loveless found that he could trim this dimension down to 1.275 inches, without notable loss of feel to the hand or security in holding. In

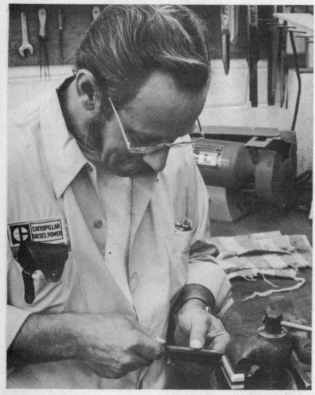

hip if carried in pocket or holster but, at the same time, one that welds itself unobtrusively but solidly into the shooting hand in a most impressive manner.

In removing metal from the rear of the slide, the original finger grooves are taken off and the surface is milled down flat where the three front ridges were located. A new series of finger grooves are cut into the slide, at a spacing of twenty lines to the inch. A portion of the rear barrel extension is retained, being inletted for installation of an adjustable rear sight originally supplied for S&W's kit guns. A rounded blade front sight, 0.180-inch in width, is fitted with a bright red plastic insert on its rear face and the rear sight notch is outlined in white. This particular color combination is favored for quick aim on moving targets, although it is less suitable for formal firing at conventional paper targets.

A small amount of metal is removed from the tang projecting from the front lower corner of the magazine, so as to fit the recess in the reworked butt. Model 41 magazines are custom-fitted to the individual gun and are stamped with the final four digits of its serial number by way of identification.

The standard safety catch of the unmodified Model 41 is quite incredible as to difficulty of function. By bracing the gun on a scale platform and watching the dial, it appears that the safety engages under about ten pounds of static force, with something like thirteen pounds being required to disengage it.

Loveless' philosophy in regard to the refractory factory safety is to trim it down a bit and try to forget about it. He

the process, he trimmed about .130-inch off the projecting end of the magazine release button, leaving the exposed end grooved, rather than checkered.

A further area of grip modification consisted of building up metal around the lower front corner of the grip, reshaping it into a graceful tang to project ahead of the little finger of the shooting hand. The result is a grip that is considerably smaller, much less prone to gouge the user's

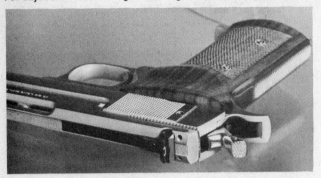

*An adjustable S&W kit gun rear sight replaces original one.*

feels that carrying the hammer on half-cock serves the same function, at least as well and with vastly greater convenience. At the same time, he has designed the holsters that he makes and supplies with the cut-down guns in such a way that the muzzle is canted well to the rear. In this way, if the gun should discharge in the holster — which is highly unlikely — the muzzle is pointed in the direction least apt to cause injury. It is a convenient angle for carrying the gun under routine conditions.

The original Model 41 design incorporates a magazine disconnect, so that a round in the chamber cannot be fired with the magazine removed or not seated fully. Loveless considers that a useful safety feature and has retained it in his field gun modification.

Many handgunners feel that a magazine disconnect is of dubious value in a gun that might have to be used against armed human adversaries. This envisions the possibility of having to keep someone covered while replacing a depleted magazine, without sacrifice of firing capability. Since neither the target nor the plinking/hunting applications are apt to pose the need of uninterrupted shootability, the

magazine disconnect makes good sense in the example at hand.

Smith & Wesson offers three additional versions of their .22 target auto: two Model 41s with 5½-inch heavy barrels, one having an extendible front sight; plus a long-discontinued Model 46 having a satin blue finish in place of the bright blue, and moulded nylon stocks rather than checkered walnut. The Model 46 can be had in standard-weight barrels of five or seven inches, as well as a 5½-inch heavy barrel pattern.

Loveless has produced a few experimental modifications of the heavy barrel versions, but feels the standard-weight barrel is much to be preferred. One further operation consists of milling a quarter-circular groove down each upper corner of the barrel and milling slots into the resulting rib for ventilation. He admits that this step is purely cosmetic, beyond reducing the weight through removal of the steel involved.

An example of Loveless' Model 41 field gun — to use the term he prefers — tips the scale at 30¼ ounces, nearly a pound less than the long-barreled factory version.

If S&W has a particular forte for which they're noteworthy, their trigger pulls would have to be listed as a strong contender. Even out of the factory box, the pull on the Model 41 leaves little if any just cause for complaint. By the time Loveless calls it a day, the pull is considerably better than factory-issue; just firm enough to be safe and almost sinfully light, crisp and delicious. Of all the many factors that can contribute toward handgun accuracy, excellence of trigger pull is one of the most significant, if not the single strongest consideration.

Quizzed as to the approximate number of shop hours required for each conversion, Loveless has not run an accurate accounting, but he estimates that somewhere between seventy-five and one hundred man-hours went into each gun.

A source of the delay in completion is connected with ordering new parts and waiting for them to turn up. Several of the component parts are purchased new and reworked for installation.

*Loveless examines the milling on the ventilated rib of one of the Model 41s being modified to Field Gun mode.*

# Gunsmith Directory

## PISTOLSMITHS

Accuracy Unlimited (Frank Glenn), 5425 W. Thomas Road, Phoenix, AZ 85031

Actionworks (Charles Lowden), P.O. Box 23028, Richfield, MN 55423

Allen Assoc., 7502 Limekiln Pike, Philadelphia, PA 19150 (speedcock lever for .45 ACP)

Bain and Davis Sptg. Gds., 559 W. Las Tunas Dr., San Gabriel, CA 91776

Bar-Sto Precision Machine, 633 So. Victory Blvd., Burbank, CA 91502 (S.S. bbls. f. .45 ACP)

Behlert Custom Guns Inc., 725 Lehigh Ave., Union, NJ 07083 (short actions)

Bullseye Gun Shop, 5091-F Buford Hwy., Doraville, GA 30340

Andy Cannon, Box 632, Center Harbor, NH 03226

Centaur Systems, 1653 S. Magnolia Ave., Monrovia, CA 91016

Cheshire & Perez Distributors, 136 E. Walnut Ave., Monrovia, CA 91016

F. Bob Chow, Gun Shop, 3185 Mission, San Francisco, CA 94110

J.E. Clark, Rte. 2, Box 22A, Keithville, LA 71047

Cleveland Blueing Company, 1024 East 185th St., Cleveland, OH 44119

Colt Custom Gun Shop, 150 Huyshope Avenue, Hartford, CT 06102

Crawford's Gunsmithing, Swain Drive, Pleasant Valley, NY 12569

Custom Gun Shop, 725 Lehigh Ave., Union, NJ 07083

Cylinder & Slide Shop, Bill Laughridge, 523 No. Main St., Fremont, NE 68025

Darlington Gun Works (Jim Kelly), Box 698, 516 S. 52 By-Pass, Darlington, SC 29532

Cake Davis Co., 1200 Fifth St., Berkeley, CA 94710; 415-526-9124

Day Arms Corp., 2412 S.W. Loop 410, San Antonio, TX 78227

Devel Corp. (Charles Kelsey, Jr.), 3441 W. Brainard Place, Cleveland, OH 44122

Dominic DiStefano, 4303 Friar Lane, Colorado Springs, CO 80907 (accurizing)

Dan Dwyer, 915 W. Washington, San Diego, CA 92103

Ehresman Tool Co., Inc., 5425 Planeview Dr., Ft. Wayne, IN 46805 (custom)

Ken Eversull Gunsmith Inc., P.O. Box 1766, Alexandria, VA 71301

Fisher Custom Firearms (Don Fisher), 2199 S. Kittredge Way, Aurora, CO 80013

Fred's Gun Shop, 5904 Signal Hill Road, Mechanicsville, VA 23111

Gateway Shooters Supply, 10145 103rd St., Jacksonville, FL 32210

Giles' .45 Shop, Rt. 2, Box 847, Odessa, FL 33556

The Gunshop (R.D. Wallace), 320 Overland Rd., Prescott, AZ 86301

Jack Gutridge, 5332 14th St., Dyer, IN 46311

Keith Hamilton, P.O. Box 871, Gridley, CA 95948

Gil Hebard Guns, Box 1, Knoxville, IL 61448

Richard Heinie, 821 E. Adams, Havana, IL 62644

James Hoag, 8523 Canoga Avenue, Suite C, Canoga Park, CA 91304

Duane Hobbie, 2412 Pattie, Wichita, KS 67216

Laddie V. Houck, P.O. Box 1071, Monticello, UT 84535

Innovation Inc., P.O. Box 43, Angola, IN 46703

Jack's Guns & Reloading (Jack Abene), 1607 W. Kennedy Blvd., Tampa, FL 33606

JJL Customs, 1333 Highland Pkwy., St. Paul, MN 55116

Reeves Jungkind, Box 4087, Austin, TX 78773

Lee E. Jurras & Assoc., Inc., P.O. Drawer F, Hagerman, NM 88232

Joe K's Inc. (Joe Kassay & Jim Arbes), 500 High St., Perth Amboy, NJ 08861

Kart Sptg. Arms Corp., RD 2, Box 929-Broad Ave., Riverhead, NY 11901 (handgun conversions)

King's Gun Works, 1837 W. Glenoaks Blvd., Glendale, CA 91201 (makes "King-Tappan" combat .45 pistol sights)

Reed Knight, 1306 29th, Vero Beach, FL 32960

John Lawson, 1802 E. Columbia Avenue, Tacoma, WA 98404

Lenz Firearms Co., 1480 Elkay Dr., Eugene, OR 97404

Kent Lomont, 4421 South Wayne, Ft. Wayne, IN 46807

Mag-na-port Arms (Larry Kelly), 30016 S. River Road, Mt. Clemens, MI 48045

Rudolf Marent, 9711 Tiltree, Houston, TX 77075 (Hammerli)

Alan Marvel, 3922 Madonna Road, Jarrettsville, MD 21084

Maryland Gun Works (Lou Ciamillo), 26200 Frederick Road, Hyattstown, MD 20734

Fred R. Miller, 2620 E. 32nd St., Davenport, IA 52807

John Miller, c/o Photo Center, 132 Putnam St., Marietta, OH 45750

Moran Custom Guns, 2275 E. Farrand Road, Clio, MI 48420

North Valley Gun Shop (Charles Clemens), 179 East Avenue, Chico, CA 95926

Nu-line Guns, 3727 Jennings Rd., St. Louis, MO 63121

Pachmayr Gun Works, 1220 S. Grand Ave., Los Angeles, CA 90015

Patton's Custom Guns (Charles Clemens), 612 Chenevert, Houston, TX 77003

Power Custom, Inc. (Ron Powers), Box 1604, Independence, MO 64055

Robert A. Richter, 5792 Vista De Oro, Riverside, CA 92509

Chuck Ries, P.O. Box 205, Culver City, CA 90230

Fred Sadowski, Sr. Gun Service, 4655 Washington St., Denver, CO 80216

Schneider Gunsmithing, 404 W. Garbry Road, Piqua, OH 45356

Schone Tool & Model Co. (Don Schone), 309 13th Ave. West, West Fargo, ND 58078

L.W. Seecamp Co., Inc., Box 255, New Haven, CT 06502 (DA Colt auto conversions)

Walt Sherman Custom Guns, 9621 Rose Road, Tallahassee, FL 32301

Harold Shockley, Box 116, Hanna City, IL 61536

Silver Dollar Guns, P.O. Box 475, 10 Frances St., Franklin, NH 03235 (.45 ACP)

Bob Snapp Gun Shop, 6911 E. Washington Road, Clare, MI 48617

Spokhandguns, Inc., E. 1911 Sprague Avenue, Spokane, WA 99202

Sportsmens Equipmt. Co., 915 W. Washington, San Diego, CA 92103

Ikey Starks Sports West, 2200 W. Alameda Ave., Denver, CO 80223

Irving O. Stone, Jr., 633 S. Victory Blvd., Burbank, CA 91502

Travis R. Strahan, Route 7, Ringgold, GA 30736

Victor W. Strawbridge, 6 Pineview Dr., Dover Pt., Dover, NH 03820

Earl Stroup, 30506 Flossmoor Way, Hayward, CA 94544

A.D. Swenson's .45 Shop, P.O. Box 606, Fallbrook, CA 92028

Trapper Gun, Inc., 28019 Harper, St. Clair Shores, MI 48081

Dennis A. "Doc" Ulrich, 2511 S. 57th Ave., Cicero, IL 60650

Steve Vaniadis, 4657 E. 57th Place, Tulsa, OK 74135

Vic's Gun Refinishing, 6 Pineview Dr., Dover, NH 03820

Walker Arms Company (Ralph Walker), Rte. 2, Box 73, Selma, AL 36701

Walters Industries, 6226 Park Lane, Dallas, TX 75225

Royce Weddle, 411 24th Avenue N.W., Norman, OK 73069

Bill Wilson's Gun Shop, 101-103 Public Sq., Berryville, AR 72616

W.C. Wolf Company, Box 232, Ardmore, PA 19003 (makes 18½-lb. compression springs for combat .45s; also firing pin springs)

Dave Woodruff, Box 5, Bear, DE 19701

## BOOKS (ARMS), Publishers and Dealers

Beinfeld Publishing, Inc., 12767 Saticoy St., No. Hollywood, CA 91605/213-982-3700
Blacktail Mountain Books, P.O. Box 1699, Kalispell, MT 59901
DBI Books, Inc., One Northfield Plaza, Northfield, IL 60093/312-441-7010
EPCO Publ. Co., 75-24 64 St., Glendale, NY 11227
Empire Press, P.O. Box 2902, Santa Fe, NM 87501
Fairfield Book Co., Inc., P.O. Box 289, Brookfield Center, CT 06805
Fortress Publications Inc., P.O. Box 241, Stoney Creek, Ont. L8G 3X9, Canada
Handgun Press, 5832 S. Green, Chicago, IL 60621
Jackson Arms, 6209 Hillcrest Ave., Dallas, TX 75205
Ridge Guncraft Inc., M. C. Wiest, 234 N. Tulane Ave., Oak Ridge, TN 37830
Ray Riling Arms Books Co., 6844 Gorsten St., Philadelphia, PA 19119
Rutgers Book Center, Mark Aziz, 127 Raritan Ave., Highland Park, NJ 08904
James C. Tillinghast, Box 568, Marlow, NH 03456
Ken Trotman, 2-6 Hampstead High St., London, NW3 1PR, England

## CHRONOGRAPHS AND PRESSURE TOOLS

B-Square Co., Box 11281, Ft. Worth, Tex. 76110
Chronograph Specialists, P.O. Box 5005, Santa Ana, Calif. 92704
Custom Chronograph Co., Rt. 1, Box 193A, Tonasket, WA 98855/508-486-4379
Herter's, Waseca, Minn. 56093
Diverter Arms, Inc., P.O. Box 22084, Houston, TX 77027 (press. tool)
Robert P. Medaris, 15412 Webster, Westminster, CA 92683
Oehler Research, P.O. Box 9135, Austin, Tex. 78756
The Precisionics Co., P.O. Box 502, Moss Point, MS 39563 (Tepeco Speed-Meter)
Schmidt-Weston Co., Box 9, West Islip, NY 11795
Sundtek Co., P.O. Box 744, Springfield, Ore. 97477
Telepacific Electronics Co., Inc., P.O. Box 2210, Escondido, CA 92025
Vibra-Tek, 2807 N. Prospect St., Colorado Springs, CO 80907 (Kronoscope)
M. York, 19381 Keymar Way, Gaithersburg, MD 20760 (press. tool)

## CLEANING & REFINISHING SUPPLIES

A 'n A Co., Box 571, King of Prussia, PA 19406 (Valet shotgun cleaner)
Armite Labs., 1845 Randolph St., Los Angeles, CA 90001 (pen oiler)
Armoloy Co. of Ft. Worth, 204 E. Daggett St., Ft. Worth, TX 76104
Birchwood-Casey, 7900 Fuller Rd., Eden Prairie, MN 55344/612-927-1733
Bisonite Co., Inc., P.O. Box 84, Kenmore Station, Buffalo, NY 14217
Blue and Gray Prods., Inc., 817 E. Main St., Bradford, Pa. 16701
Jim Brobst, 299 Poplar St., Hamburg, Pa. 19526 (J-B Compound)
GB Prods. Dept., H & R, Inc., Industrial Rowe, Gardner, MA 01440
Browning Arms, Rt. 4, Box 24-B, Arnold, Mo. 63010
J. M. Bucheimer Co., P.O. Box 280, Airport Rd., Frederick, MD 21701/301-662-5101
Burnishine Prod. Co., 8140 N. Ridgeway, Skokie, Ill. 60076 (Stock Glaze)
Caddie Products Corp., Div. of Jet-Aer, Paterson, NJ 07524 (the Cloth)
Chem-Pak Inc., Winchester, VA 22601 (Gun-Savr. protect. & lubricant)
Chopie Mfg. Inc., 531 Copeland, La Crosse, Wis. 54601 (Black-Solve)
Clenzoil Co., Box 1226, Sta. C, Canton, O. 44708
Clover Mfg. Co., 139 Woodward Ave., Norwalk, CT 06856 (Clover compound)
Dri-Slide, Inc., Industrial Park, 1210 Locust St., Fremont, MI 49412
Durango U.S.A., P.O. Box 1029, Durango, CO 81301 (cleaning rods)
Forty-Five Ranch Enterpr., 119 S. Main St., Miami, Okla. 74354
Gun-All Products, Box 244, Dowagiac, Mich. 49047
Frank C. Hoppe Div., Penguin Ind., Inc., Airport Industrial Mall, Coatesville, PA 19320/215-384-6000
J & G Rifle Ranch, Box S 80, Turner, MT 59542
Jet-Aer Corp., 100 Sixth Ave., Paterson, N.J. 07524 (blues & oils)
Kellog's Professional Prods., Inc., P.O. Box 1201, Sandusky, OH 44870
K.W. Kleinendorst, 48 Taylortown Rd., Montville, N.J. 07045 (rifle clg. cables)
LPS Res. Labs. Inc., 2050 Cotner Ave., Los Angeles, Calif. 90025
LEM Gun Spec., Box 31, College Park, Ga 30337 (Lewis Lead Remover)
Liquid Wrench, Box 10628, Charlotte, N.C. 28201 (pen. oil)
Loner Products, Inc., P.O. Box 219, Yorktown Heights, NY 10598
Lynx Line Gun Prods. Div., Protective Coatings, Inc., 20626 Fenkell Ave., Detroit, MI 48223
Marble Arms Co., 420 Industrial Pk., Gladstone, Mich. 49837
Micro Sight Co., 242 Harbor Blvd., Belmont, Ca. 94002 (bedding)
Mirror-Lube, P.O. Box 693, San Juan Capistrano, CA 92675
New Method Mfg. Co., Box 175, Bradford, Pa. 16701 (gun blue)
Northern Instruments, Inc., 6680 North Highway 49, Lino Lake, MN 55014 (Stor-Safe rust preventer)

Numrich Arms Co., West Hurley, N.Y. 12491 (44-40 gun blue)
Old World Oil Products, 3827 Queen Ave. No., Minneapolis, MN 55412
Original Mink Oil, Inc., P.O. Box 20191, 10652 N.E. Holman, Portland, OR 97220/503-255-2814
Outers Laboratories, Route 2, Onalaska, WI 54650/608-783-1515 (Gunslick kits)
Radiator Spec. Co., 1400 Independence Blvd., Charlotte, N.C. 28201 (liquid wrench)
Reardon Prod., 103 W. Market St., Morrison, IL 61270 (Dry-Lube)
Rice Gun Coatings, 1521-43rd St., West Palm Beach, FL 33407
Rig Products Co., Div. of Mitann, Inc., 21320 Deering Ct., Canoga Park, CA 91304/213-883-4700
Rusteprufe Labs., Sparta, WI 54656
San/Bar Corp., Chemicals Div., P.O. Box 11787, 17422 Pullman St., Santa Ana, CA 92711 (Break-Free)
Saunders Sptg. Gds., 338 Somerset, No. Plainfield, NJ 07060 (Sav-Bore)
Schultea's Gun String, 67 Burress, Houston, TX 77022 (pocket-size rifle cleaning kit)
Service Armament, 689 Bergen Blvd., Ridgefield, N. J. 07657 (Parker-Hale)
Silicote Corp., Box 359, Oshkosh, Wis. 54901 (Silicone cloths)
Silver Dollar Guns, P.O. Box 475, 10 Frances St., Franklin, NH 03235 (Silicone oil)
Sportsmen's Labs., Inc., Box 732, Anoka, Minn. 55303 (Gun Life lube)
Taylor & Robbins, Box 164, Rixford, Pa. 16745 (Throat Saver)
Testing Systems, Inc., 220 Pegasus Ave., Northvale, NJ 07647/201-767-7300 (gun lube)
Texas Platers Supply Co., 2453 W. Five Mile Parkway, Dallas, TX 75233 (plating kit)
Totally Dependable Prods., Inc., P.O. Box 277, Zieglerville, PA 19492
C. S. Van Gorden, 120 Tenth Ave., Eau Claire, Wis. 54701 (Instant Blue)
WD-40 Co., 1061 Cudahy Pl., San Diego, CA 92110
West Coast Secoa, 3915 U S Hwy. 98S, Lakeland, FL 33801 (Teflon coatings)
Williams Gun Sight, 7389 Lapeer Rd., Davison, Mich. 48423 (finish kit)
Winslow Arms Inc., P.O. Box 783, Camden, SC 29020 (refinishing kit)
Wisconsin Platers Supply Co., see: Texas Platers Supply Co.
Woodstream Corp., P.O. Box 327, Lititz, Pa. 17543 (Mask)
Zip Aerosol Prods., 21320 Deering Court, Canoga Park, CA 91304

## ENGRAVERS, ENGRAVING TOOLS

John J. Adams, 47 Brown Ave., Mansfield, MA 02048/617-339-4613
Aurum Etchings, P.O. Box 401059, Garland, TX 75040 (acid engraving)
Austrian Gunworks Reg'd., P.O. Box 136, Eastman, Que., Canada, J0E 1P0
Joseph C. Bayer, 439 Sunset Ave., Sunset Hill Griggstown, RD 1, Princeton, NJ 08540/201-359-7283
Sid Bell Originals, R.D. 2, Tully, NY 13159
Bergevin et Marechal, 69 rue du Bois-Saint-Martin, 77340 Pontault-Combault, France
Weldon Bledsoe, 6812 Park Place Dr., Fort Worth, Tex. 76118
Carl & Roger Bleile, Box 11285, Cincinnati, OH 45211
Erich Boessler, Am Vogeltal 3, 8732 Münnerstadt, W. Germany
Henry "Hank" Bonham, 218 Franklin Ave., Seaside Heights, NJ 08751
Bryan Bridges, 6350 E. Paseo San Andres, Tucson, AZ 85710
Burgess Vibrocrafters (BVI), Rt. 83, Grayslake, Ill. 60030
Winston Churchill, Twenty Mile Stream Rd., Rt.1, Box 29B, Proctorsville, VT 05153
Crocker Engraving, 1510 - 42nd St., Los Alamos, NM 87544
Art A. Darakis, RD #1 Leavitt Rd., Amherst, OH 44001
Tim Davis, 230 S. Main St., Eldorado, OH 45321
James R. DeMunck, 3012 English Rd., Rochester, NY 14616
Howard M. Dove, 402 Roanoke St., Blacksburg, VA 24060
Ernest Dumoulin-Deleye, 8 rue Florent Boclinville, 4410 Herstal (Vottem), Belgium
Bill Dyer, P.O. Box 75255, Oklahoma City, Okla. 73107
Wilton L. English, 12009-B Barksdale Dr., Omaha, NB 68123
Ken Eyster, Heritage Gunsmiths Inc., 6441 Bishop Rd., Centerburg, OH 43011/614-625-6131
John Fanzoi, P.O. Box 25, Ferlach, Austria 9170
Jacqueline Favre, 3212-B Wynn Rd., Suite 214, Las Vegas, NV 89102
Armi FERLIB, 46 Via Costa, 25063 Gardone V.T. (Brescia), Italy
Lynn Fliger, 5036 Hughes Ave. NE, Fridley, MN 55421
H. H. Frank, 210 Meadow Rd., Whitefish, MT 59937/406-862-2681
J. R. French, 2633 Quail Valley, Irving TX 75060
GRS Corp., P.O. Box 1153, Emporia, KS 66801/316-343-1084 (Gravermeister tool)
Ed F. Giles, 204 Tremont St., Rehoboth, MA 02769
Donald Glaser, 1520 West St., Emporia, Kans. 66801
Eric Gold, Box 1904, Flagstaff, AZ 86002
Daniel Goodwin, 2033 Broad St., East Petersburg, PA 17520/717-569-5654
Howard V. Grant, P.O. Box 396, Lac Du Flambeau, WI 54538
John Gray, 3923 Richard Dr. NE, Cedar Rapids, IA 52402

Griffin & Howe, 589 Broadway, N.Y., N.Y. 10012
F. R. Gurney Engraving Method Ltd., #2301, 9925 Jasper Ave., Edmonton, Alberta, Can. T5J 2X4/403-426-7474
Neil Hartliep, Box 733, Fairmont, Minn. 56031
Frank E. Hendricks, Inc., Rt. 2, Box 189J, San Antonio, TX 78229
Heide Hiptmayer, P.O. Box 136, Eastman, Que., Canada J0E 1P0
Steve Huff, P.O. Box 8663, Missoula, MT 59807/406-721-1740
Ken Hunt, c/o Trevallion, 3442 S. Post Rd., Indianapolis, IN 46239
Ralph W. Ingle, #4 Missing Link, Rossville, GA 30741
Paul Jaeger, 211 Leedom, Jenkintown, Pa. 19046
Bill Johns, 2217 No. 10th, McAllen, TX 78501
T. J. Kaye, 4745 Dellwood, Beaumont, TX 77706
Lance Kelly, 4226 Lamar St., Decatur, GA 30035
Jim Kelso, P.O. Box 518, Preston, WA 98050
Kleinguenther's, P.O. Box 1261, Seguin, TX 78155
E. J. Koevenig, Keystone, SD 57751
John Kudlas, 622-14th St. S.E., Rochester, MN 55901
Ben Lane, Jr., 2118 Lipscomb St., Amarillo, TX 79109
Beth Lane, 201 S. Main St., Pontiac, IL 61764
W. Neal Lewis, 6300 Mixon Rd., Palmetto, GA 30268
Frank Lindsay, 1326 Tenth Ave., Holdrege, NB 68949
London Guns, 1528-20th St., Santa Monica, CA 90404
Ed. J. Machu, Jr., Sportsman's Bailiwick, 5306 Broadway, San Antonio, TX 78209
Lynton S.M. McKenzie, 5589 Arapahoe, Unit 104, Boulder, CO 80301
Wm. H. Mains, 3212 B. Wynn Rd., Suite 214, Las Vegas, NV 89102
Robert E. Maki, 818 Revere, Glenview, IL 60025
Rudy Marek, Rt. 1, Box 1A, Banks, Ore. 97106
Franz Marktl, P.O. Box 716, Kalispell, MT 59901
Ray Mellen, Box 101, Winston, GA 30187
S. A. Miller, Miller Gun Works, P.O. Box 7326, Tamuning, Guam 96911
Frank Mittermeier, 3577 E. Tremont Ave., New York, N.Y. 10465
NgraveR Co., 879 Raymond Hill Rd., Oakdale, CT 06370 (engr. tool)
New Orleans Jewelers Supply, 206 Chartres St., New Orleans, LA 70130
Hans Obiltschnig, 12. November St. 7, 9170 Ferlach, Austria
Warren E. Offenberger, Star Route, Reno, OH 45773
Oker's Engraving, 280 Illinois St., Crystal Lake, IL 60014
Tom Overbey, 612 Azalea Ave., Richmond, VA 23227
Pachmayr Gun Works, Inc., 1220 S. Grand Ave., Los Angeles, CA 90015/213-748-7271
Marcello Pedini, 48 Barnes Ave., Worcester, MA 01605
Hans Pfeiffer, 286 Illinois St., Elmhurst, IL 60126
Barbara Pierce, 248 E. Ridgeway, Hermiston, OR 97838/503-567-1661
Arthur Pitetti, Hawk Hollow Rd., Denver, NY 12421
Jeremy W. Potts, Box 85, Pine Bluff, WY 82082
Wayne E. Potts, 912 Poplar St., Denver, CO 80220
E. C. Prudhomme, 513 Ricou-Brewster Bldg., Shreveport, LA 71101
John and Hans Rohner, Sunshine Canyon, Boulder, Colo. 80302
Joe Rundall, 6198 Frances Rd., Clio, MI 48420
Robert P. Runge, 94 Grove St., Ilion, N.Y. 13357
A. E. Scott, 609 E. Jackson, Pasadena, TX 77506
Shaw-Leibowitz, Rt. 1, Box 421, New Cumberland, W.Va. 26047 (etchers)
George Sherwood, Box 735, Winchester, OR 97495/503-672-3159
Ben Shostle, The Gun Room, 1201 Burlington Dr., Muncie, IN 47302
Ron Skaggs, 508 W. Central, Princeton, IL 61536
Russell J. Smith, 231 Springdale Rd., Westfield, Mass. 01085
George B. Spring, 9 Pratt St., Essex, CT 06424
Robt. Swartley, 2800 Pine St., Napa, Calif. 94559
George W. Thiewes, 1846 Allen Lane, St. Charles, IL 60174/312-584-1383
Anthony Tuscano, 1473 Felton Rd., South Euclid, OH 44121
Robert Valade, Rte. 1, Box 30-A, Cove, OR 97824
John Vest, 6715 Shasta Way, Klamath Falls, OR 97601
Ray Viramontez, 4348 Newberry Ct., Dayton, OH 45432
Louis Vrancken, 30-rue sur le bois, 4531 Argenteau (Liege), Belgium
Vernon G. Wagoner, 12271 N. Chama Dr., Fountain Hills, AZ 85268/602-837-1789
Terry Wallace, 385 San Marino, Vallejo, CA 94590
Floyd E. Warren, 1273 St. Rt. 305 N.E. #3, Cortland, OH 44410
John E. Warren, P.O. Box 72, Eastham, Mass. 02642
Rachel Wells, 110 N. Summit St., Prescott, AZ 86301
Sam Welch, Box 2152, Kodiak, AK 99615
Mel Wood, 3901 Crestmont Dr., Santa Maria, CA 93454
Dwain Wright, 67168 Central, Bend, OR 97701/503-389-5558 (ctlg. $3)

## GUN PARTS, U. S. AND FOREIGN

Badger Shooter's Supply, Box 397, Owen, WI 54460
Behlert Custom Guns, Inc., 725 Lehigh Ave., Union, NJ 07083 (handgun parts)
Philip R. Crouthamel, 513 E. Baltimore, E. Lansdowne, Pa. 19050
Charles E. Duffy, Williams Lane, West Hurley, N.Y. 12491
Federal Ordnance Inc., 9649 Alpaca St., So. El Monte, CA 91733/213-283-3880
Fenwick's Gun Annex, P.O. Box 38, Weisberg Rd., Whitehall, MD 21161
Jack First, The Gunshop, Inc., 44633 Sierra Highway, Lancaster, CA 93534

Greg's Winchester Parts, P.O. Box 8125, W. Palm Beach, FL 33407
Hunter's Haven, Zero Prince St., Alexandria, Va. 22314
Walter H. Lodewick, 2816 N.E. Halsey, Portland, OR 97232
Marsh Al's, Rte. #3, Box 729, Preston, ID 83263 (Contender rifle)
Numrich Arms Co., West Hurley, N.Y. 12491
Pacific Intl. Merch. Corp., 2215 "J" St., Sacramento, CA 95816 (Vega 45 Colt mag.)
Potomac Arms Corp. (see Hunter's Haven)
Martin B. Retting, Inc., 11029 Washington, Culver City, Cal. 90230
Sarco, Inc., 323 Union St., Stirling, NJ 07980
Sherwood Distr. Inc., 18714 Parthenia St., Northridge, CA 91324
Simms, 2801 J St., Sacramento, CA 95816
Clifford L. Smires, R.D., Box 39, Columbus, NJ 08022 (Mauser rifles)
N. F. Strebe Gunworks, 4926 Marlboro Pike, S.E., Washington, D.C. 20027
Triple-K Mfg. Co., 568-6th Ave., San Diego, CA 92101 (magazines, gun parts)

## GUNS, SURPLUS—PARTS AND AMMUNITION

Century Arms, Inc., 3-5 Federal St., St. Albans, Vt. 05478
Walter Craig, Inc., Box 927-A, Selma, AL 36701
Eastern Firearms Co., 790 S. Arroyo Pkwy., Pasadena, Calif. 91105
Garcia National Gun Traders, 225 S.W. 22nd, Miami, Fla. 33135
Hunter's Lodge, 200 S. Union, Alexandria, Va. 22313
Lever Arms Serv. Ltd., 771 Dunsmuir St., Vancouver, B.C., Canada V6C IM9
Mars Equipment Corp., 3318 W. Devon, Chicago, Ill. 60645
Pacific Intl. Merch. Corp., 2215 "J" St., Sacramento, CA 95816
Plainfield Ordnance Co., Box 447, Dunellen, N.J. 08812
Sarco, Inc., 323 Union St., Stirling, NJ 07980/201-647-3800
Service Armament Co., 689 Bergen Blvd., Ridgefield, N.J. 07657
Sherwood Distrib. Inc., 18714 Parthenia St., Northridge, CA 91324

## GUNSMITH SCHOOLS

Colorado School of Trades, 1545 Hoyt, Lakewood, CO 80215
Lassen Community College, P.O. Box 3000, Susanville, CA 96130
Modern Gun Repair School Inc., 4225 N. Brown Ave., Scottsdale, AZ 85252
Montgomery Technical Institute, P.O. Drawer 487, Troy, NC 27371
Murray State College, Tishomingo, OK 73460
North American School of Firearms, 4401 Birch St., Newport Beach, CA 92663 (correspondence)
Oregon Institute of Technology, Small Arms Dept., Klamath Falls, OR 97601
Penn. Gunsmith School, 812 Ohio River Blvd., Avalon, Pittsburgh, Pa. 15202
Trinidad State Junior College, Trinidad, Colo. 81082

## GUNSMITH SUPPLIES, TOOLS, SERVICES

Albright Prod. Co., P.O. Box 1144, Portola, CA 96122 (trap buttplates)
Alley Supply Co., Carson Valley Industrial Park, Gardnerville, NV 89410
Amatek, Hunter Spring Div., One Spring Ave., Hatfield, PA 19440 (trigger gauge)
Ames Precision Machine Works, 5270 Geddes Rd., Ann Arbor, MI 48105 (portable hardness tester)
Anderson Mfg. Co., P.O. Box 3120, Yakima WA 98903 (tang safe)
Armite Labs., 1845 Randolph St., Los Angeles, Cal. 90001 (pen oiler)
B-Square Co., Box 11281, Ft. Worth, Tex. 76110
Jim Baiar, 490 Halfmoon Rd., Columbia Falls, MT 59912 (hex screws)
Behlert Custom Guns, Inc., 725 Lehigh Ave., Union, NJ 07083
Al Biesen, W. 2039 Sinto Ave., Spokane, WA 99201 (grip caps, buttplates)
Bonanza Sports Mfg. Co., 412 Western Ave., Faribault, Minn. 55021
Brookstone Co., 125 Vose Farm Rd., Peterborough, NH 03458
Bob Brownell's, Main & Third, Montezuma, Ia. 50171
W. E. Brownell, 1852 Alessandro Trail, Vista, Calif. 92083 (checkering tools)
Maynard P. Buehler, Inc., 17 Orinda Hwy., Orinda, Calif. 94563 (Rocol lube)
Burgess Vibrocrafters, Inc. (BVI), Rte. 83, Grayslake, Ill. 60030
M. H. Canjar, 500 E. 45th, Denver, Colo. 80216 (triggers, etc.)
Chapman Mfg. Co., Rte. 17 at Saw Mill Rd., Durham, CT 06422
Chase Chemical Corp., 3527 Smallman St., Pittsburgh, PA 15201 (Chubb Multigauge)
Chubb (see Chase Chem. Co.)
Chicago Wheel & Mfg. Co., 1101 W. Monroe St., Chicago, Ill. 60607 (Handee grinders)
Christy Gun Works, 875-57th St., Sacramento, Calif. 95819
Clover Mfg. Co., 139 Woodward Ave., Norwalk, CT 06856 (Clover compound)

Clymer Mfg. Co., 14241 W. 11 Mile Rd., Oak Park, Mich. 48237 (reamers)
Colbert Industries, 10107 Adella, South Gate, Calif. 90280 (Panavise)
A. Constantine & Son, Inc., 2050 Eastchester Rd., Bronx, N.Y. 10461 (wood)
Dave Cook, 720 Hancock Ave., Hancock, MI 49930 (metalsmithing only)
Cougar & Hunter, G 6398 W. Pierson Rd., Flushing, Mich. 48433 (scope jigs)
Alvin L. Davidson Prods. f. Shooters, 1215 Branson, Las Cruces, NM 88001 (action sleeves)
Dayton-Traister Co., 9322 - 900th West, P.O. Box 593, Oak Harbor, WA 98277 (triggers)
Delia Arm Sporting Goods, Highway 82 West, Indianola, MS 38751/601-887-5566 (Lightwood/England)
Dem-Bart Checkering Tools, Inc., 6807 Hiway # 2, Snohomish, WA 98290/206-568-7536
Dremel Mfg. Co., 4915-21st St., Racine, WI 53406 (grinders)
Chas. E. Duffy, Williams Lane, West Hurley, N.Y. 12491
Peter Dyson Ltd., 29-31 Church St., Honley, Huddersfield, Yorksh. HD7 2AH, England (accessories f. antique gun coll.)
E-Z Tool Co., P.O. Box 3186, 25 N.W. 44th Ave., Des Moines, Ia. 50313 (lathe taper attachment)
Edmund Scientific Co., 101 E. Glouster Pike, Barrington, N.J. 08007
F. K. Elliott, Box 785, Ramona, Calif. 92065 (reamers)
Forster Products, Inc., 82 E. Lanark Ave., Lanark, Ill. 61046
Keith Francis Inc., Rte. 4, Box 146, Coos Bay, OR 97420/503-269-2021 (reamers)
G. R. S. Corp., P.O. Box 1153, Emporia, KS 66801/316-343-1084 (Gravermeister)
Gager Gage and Tool Co., 27509 Industrial Blvd., Hayward, CA 94545 (speedlock triggers f. Rem. 1100 & 870 pumps)
Gilmore Pattern Works, P.O. Box 50231, Tulsa, OK 74150
Gold Lode, Inc., 181 Gary Ave., Wheaton, IL 60187 (gold inlay kit)
Gopher Shooter's Supply, Box 278, Faribault, MN 55021 (screwdrivers, etc.)
Grace Metal Prod., 115 Ames St., Elk Rapids, MI 49629 (screw drivers, drifts)
Gunline Tools Inc., 719 No. East St., Anaheim, CA 92805
Half Moon Rifle Shop, 490 Halfmoon Rd., Columbia Falls, MT 59912 (hex screws)
Hartford Reamer Co., Box 134, Lathrup Village. Mich. 48075
Paul Jaeger Inc., 211 Leedom St., Jenkintown, PA. 19046
Jeffredo Gunsight Co., 1629 Via Monserate, Fallbrook, CA 92028 (trap buttplate)
Jerrow's Inletting Service, 452 5th Ave., E.N., Kalispell, MT 59901
K&D Grinding Co., Box 1766, Alexandria, LA 71301/318-442-0569
Kasenite Co., Inc., 3 King St., Mahwah, N.J. 07430 (surface hrdng. comp.)
J. Korzinek, RD #2, Box R, Canton, PA 17724 (stainl. steel bluing)
LanDav Custom Guns, 7213 Lee Highway, Falls Church, VA 22046
John G. Lawson, 1802 E. Columbia Ave., Tacoma, WA 98404
Lea Mfg. Co., 237 E. Aurora St., Waterbury, Conn. 06720
Lightwood (Fieldsport) Ltd., Britannia Rd., Banbury, Oxfordsh. OX16 8TD, England
Lock's Phila. Gun Exch., 6700 Rowland Ave., Philadelphia, Pa. 19149
John McClure, 4549 Alamo Dr., San Diego, CA 92115 (electric checkering tool)
Marker Machine Co., Box 426, Charleston, Ill. 61920

Michaels of Oregon Co., P.O. Box 13010, Portland, Ore. 97213
Viggo Miller, P.O. Box 4181, Omaha, Neb. 68104 (trigger attachment)
Miller Single Trigger Mfg. Co., R.D. on Rt. 209, Millersburg, PA 17061
Frank Mittermeier, 3577 E. Tremont, N.Y., N.Y. 10465
Moderntools Corp, Box 407, Dept. GD, Woodside, N.Y. 11377
N&J Sales, Lime Kiln Rd., Northford, Conn. 06472 (screwdrivers)
Karl A. Neise, Inc., 5602 Roosevelt Ave., Woodside, N.Y. 11377
Palmgren Prods., Chicago Tool & Eng. Co., 8383 South Chicago Ave., Chicago, IL 60167 (vises, etc.)
Panavise Prods., Inc., 2850-29th St., Long Beach, CA 90806/213-595-7621
C. R. Pedersen & Son, Ludington, Mich. 49431
Richland Arms Co., 321 W. Adrian St., Blissfield, Mich. 49228
Riley's Supply Co., 121 No. Main St., Avilla, Ind. 46710 (Niedner buttplates, caps)
Ruhr-American Corp., So. Hwy #5, Glenwood, Minn. 56334
A. G. Russell, 1705 Hiway 71N, Springdale, AR 72764 (Arkansas oilstones)
Schaffner Mfg. Co., Emsworth, Pittsburgh, Pa. 15202 (polishing kits)
SGW, Inc. (formerly Schuetzen Gun Works), 624 Old Pacific Hwy. S.E., Olympia, WA 98503/206-456-3471
Shaw's, Rt. 2, Box 407-L, Escondido, CA 92025/714-728-7070
Southern Blueing, 6027-B N.W. 31st Ave., Ft. Lauderdale, FL 33309 (gun blueing & repairs)
L. S. Starrett Co., Athol, Mass. 01331
Texas Platers Supply Co., 2453 W. Five Mile Parkway, Dallas, TX 75233 (plating kit)
Timney Mfg. Co., 2847 E. Siesta Lane, Phoenix, AZ 85024
Stan de Treville, Box 33021, San Diego, Calif. 92103 (checkering patterns)
Twin City Steel Treating Co., Inc., 1114 S. 3rd, Minneapolis, Minn. 55415 (heat treating)
Will-Burt Co., 169 So. Main, Orrville, OH 44667 (vises)
Williams Gun Sight Co., 7389 Lapeer Rd., Davison, Mich. 48423

Wilson Arms Co., 63 Leetes Island Rd., Branford, CT 06405
Wisconsin Platers Supply Co., see: Texas Platers
W. C. Wolff Co., Box 232, Ardmore, PA 19003 (springs)
Woodcraft Supply Corp., 313 Montvale, Woburn, MA 01801

## HANDGUN ACCESSORIES

A. R. Sales Co., P.O. Box 3192, South El Monte, CA 91733
Baramie Corp., 6250 E. 7 Mile Rd., Detroit, MI 48234 (Hip-Grip)
Bar-Sto Precision Machine, 633 S. Victory Blvd., Burbank, CA 91502
Behlert Custom Guns, Inc., 725 Lehigh Ave., Union, NJ 07083
Belt Slide, Inc., 1114 N. Lamar, P.O. Box 15303, Austin, TX 78761/512-836-8772
Bingham Ltd., 1775-C Wilwat Dr., Norcross, GA 30093 (magazines)
C'Arco, P.O. Box 308, Highland, CA 92346 (Ransom Rest)
Case Master, 4675 E. 10 Ave., Miami, Fla. 33013
Central Specialties Co., 6030 Northwest Hwy., Chicago, Ill. 60631
D&E Magazines Mgf., P.O. Box 4579, Downey, CA 90242 (clips)
Bill Dyer, 503 Midwest Bldg., Oklahoma City, Okla. (grip caps)
Essex Arms, Box 345, Phaerring St., Island Pond, VT 05846 (45 Auto frames)
R. S. Frielich, 396 Broome St., New York, N.Y. 10013 (cases)
Jafin Prods., Jacob & Tiffin Inc., P.O. Box 547, Clanton,, AL 35045 (Light Load)
Laka Tool Co., 62 Kinkel St., Westbury, L.I., NY 11590 (stainless steel 45 Auto parts)
Lee Custom Engineering, Inc., 46 E. Jackson St., Hartford, WI 53027
Lee's Red Ramps, 7252 E. Ave. U-3, Littlerock, CA 93543 (illuminated sights)
Lee Precision Inc., 4275 Hwy. U, Hartford, WI 53027 (pistol rest holders)
Los Gatos Grip & Specialty Co., P.O. Box 1850, Los Gatos, CA 95030 (custom-made)
Mellmark Mfg. Co., P.O. Box 139, Turlock, CA 95380 (pistol safe)
W. A. Miller Co., Inc., Mingo Loop, Oguossoc, ME 04964 (cases)
No-Sho Mfg. Co., 10727 Glenfield Ct., Houston, TX 77096
Pachmayr, 1220 S. Grand, Los Angeles, Calif. 90015 (cases)
Pacific Intl. Mchdsg. Corp., 2215 ''J'' St., Sacramento, CA 95818 (Vega 45 Colt comb. mag.)
Pistolsafe, Dr. L., N. Chili, NY 14514 (handgun safe)
Platt Luggage, Inc., 2301 S. Prairie, Chicago, Ill. 60616 (cases)
Sile Distributors, 7 Centre Market Pl., New York, NY 10013
Sportsmen's Equipment Co., 415 W. Washington, San Diego, Calif. 92103
M. Tyler, 1326 W. Britton, Oklahoma City, Okla. 73114 (grip adaptor)
Whitney Sales, Inc., P.O. Box 875, Reseda, CA 91335
Dave Woodruff, Box 5, Bear, DE 19701 (relining and conversions)

## HANDGUN GRIPS

Art Jewel Enterprises, Box 819, Berkeley, IL 60163
Bingham Ltd., 1775-C Wilwat Dr., Norcross, GA 30093
Crest Carving Co., 8091 Bolsa Ave., Midway City, CA 92655
Fitz, 653 N. Hagar St., San Fernando, CA 91340
Gateway Shooters' Supply, Inc., 10145-103rd St., Jacksonville, FL 32210 (Rogers grips)
The Gunshop, R. D. Wallace, 320 Overland Rd., Prescott, AZ 86301
Herrett's, Box 741, Twin Falls, Ida. 83301
Mershon Co., Inc., 1230 S. Grand Ave., Los Angeles, Calif. 90015
Mustang Custom Pistol Grips, 28715 Via Montezuma, Temecula, CA 92390
Robert H. Newell, 55 Coyote, Los Alamos, NM 87544 (custom)
Rogers Grips (see: Gateway Shooters' Supply)
Safety Grip Corp., Box 456, Riverside St., Miami, Fla. 33135
Jean St. Henri, 6525 Dume Dr., Malibu, CA 90265 (custom)
Schiermeier, Box 704, Twin Falls, ID 83301 (Thompson/Contender)
Sile Dist., 7 Centre Market Pl., New York, N.Y. 10013
Southern Gun Exchange, Inc., 4311 Northeast Expressway, Atlanta (Doraville), GA 30340 (Outrider brand)
Sports Inc., P.O. Box 683, Park Ridge, IL 60068 (Franzite)

## LOAD TESTING and PRODUCT TESTING, CHRONOGRAPHING, BALLISTIC STUDIES

Hutton Rifle Ranch, 1802 S. Oak Park Dr., Rolling Hills, Tucson, AZ 85710
Kent Lomont, 4421 S. Wayne Ave., Ft. Wayne, IN 46807 (handguns, handgun ammunition)
Plum City Ballistics Range, Rte. 1, Box 29A, Plum City, WI 54761
John M. Tovey, 4710 - 104th Lane NE, Circle Pines, MN 55014
H. P. White Laboratory, Inc., 3114 Scarboro Rd., Street, MD 21154/301-838-6550

## REBORING AND RERIFLING

P.O. Ackley (see: Max B. Graff, Inc.)
Atkinson Gun Co., P.O. Box 512, Prescott, AZ 86301
Bain & Davis Sptg. Gds., 559 W. Las Tunas Dr., San Gabriel, Calif. 91776
Fuller Gun Shop, Cooper Landing, Alaska 99572
Max B. Graff, Inc., Rt. 1, Box 24, American Fork, UT 84003
Bruce Jones, 389 Calla Ave., Imperial Beach, CA 92032
Les' Gun Shop, (Les Bauska), Box 511, Kalispell, MT 59901
Morgan's Cust. Reboring, 707 Union Ave., Grants Pass, OR 97526
Nu-Line Guns, 3727 Jennings Rd., St. Louis, MO 63121 (handguns)
Al Petersen, Box 8, Riverhurst, Saskatchewan, Canada S0H3P0
SGW, Inc. (formerly Schuetzen Gun Works), 624 Old Pacific Hwy. S E., Olympia, WA 98503/206-456-3471
Sharon Gun Specialties, 14587 Peaceful Valley Rd., Sonora, CA 95370
Siegrist Gun Shop, 2689 McLean Rd., Whittemore, MI 48770
Snapp's Gunshop, 6911 E. Washington Rd., Clare, Mich. 48617
R. Southgate, Rt. 2, Franklin, Tenn. 37064 (Muzzleloaders)
J. W. Van Patten, Box 145, Foster Hill, Milford, Pa. 18337
Robt. G. West, 27211 Huey Ave., Eugene, OR 97402

## RESTS—BENCH, PORTABLE, ETC.

Bill Anderson, 551 Fletcher, Wayne, PA 19087
Bausch & Lomb, 635 St. Paul St., Rochester, NY 14602 (rifle rest)
Jim Brobst, 299 Poplar St., Hamburg, PA 19526 (bench rest pedestal)
C'Arco, P.O. Box 2043, San Bernardino, CA 92401 (Ransom handgun rest)
Cole's Acku-Rite Prod., Box 364, Ellington, NY 14732
Cravener's Gun Shop, 1627 - 5th Ave., Ford City, PA 16226 (portable)
Decker Shooting Products, 1729 Laguna Ave., Schofield, WI 54476 (rifle rests)
The Gun Case, 11035 Maplefield, El Monte, Cal. 91733
Harris Engr., Inc., Barlow, KY 42024
Rob. W. Hart & Son, 401 Montgomery St., Nescopeck, Pa. 18635
Tony Hidalgo, 6 Capp St., Carteret, NJ 07008 (shooters stools)
North Star Devices, Inc., P.O. Box 2095, North St. Paul, MN 55109 (Gun Slinger)
Progressive Prods., Inc., P.O. Box 41, Holmen, WI 54636 (Sandbagger rifle rest)
Rec. Prods., Res., Inc., 158 Franklin Ave., Ridgewood, N.J. 07450 (Butts Pi-pod)
D. E. Stanley, P.O. Box 833, Ringold, OK 74754 (portable shooting rest)
Suter's, 332 Tejon, Colorado Springs, CO 80902
Tuller & Co., 29 Germania, Galeton, PA 16922 (Protector sandbags)
Wichita Eng. & Supply, Inc., P.O. Box 11371, Wichita, KS 67202

## SIGHTS, METALLIC

Accura-Site Co., Inc., Box 193, Neenah, WI 54956
B-Square Eng. Co., Box 11281, Ft. Worth, Tex. 76110
Behlert Custom Sights, Inc., 725 Lehigh Ave., Union, NJ 07083
Bo-Mar Tool & Mfg. Co., Box 168, Carthage, Tex. 75633
Maynard P. Buehler, Inc., 17 Orinda Highway, Orinda, Calif. 94563
Christy Gun Works, 875 57th St., Sacramento, Calif. 95819
Jim Day, 902 N. Bownen Lane, Florence, SD 29501 (Chaba)
E-Z Mount, Ruelle Bros., P.O. Box 114, Ferndale, MT 48220

Freeland's Scope Stands, Inc., 3734-14th Ave., Rock Island, Ill. 61201
Paul T. Haberly, 2364 N. Neva, Chicago, IL 60635
Paul Jaeger, Inc., 211 Leedom St., Jenkintown, PA 19046
Lee's Red Ramps, 7252 E. Ave. U-3, Littlerock, CA 93543/805-944-4487 (illuminated sights)
Jim Lofland, 2275 Larkin Rd., Boothwyn, PA 19061
Lyman Products Corp., Rte. 147, Middlefield, Conn. 06455
Marble Arms Corp., 420 Industrial Park, Gladstone, Mich. 49837
Merit Gunsight Co., P.O. Box 995, Sequim, Wash. 98382
Micro Sight Co., 242 Harbor Blvd., Belmont, Calif. 94002
Miniature Machine Co., 210 E. Poplar, Deming, NM 88030/505-546-2151
Modern Industries, Inc., 613 W-11, Erie, PA 16501
C. R. Pedersen & Son, Ludington, Mich. 49431
Poly Choke Co., Inc., P.O. Box 296, Hartford, CT 06101
Redfield Gun Sight Co., 5800 E. Jewell St., Denver, Colo. 80222
Schwarz's Gun Shop, 41 - 15th St., Wellsburg, W. Va. 26070
Simmons Gun Specialties, Inc., 700 Rodgers Rd., Olathe, Kans. 66061
Slug Site Co., Whitetail Wilds, Lake Hubert, MN 56469
Sport Service Center, 2364 N. Neva, Chicago, IL 60635
Tradewinds, Inc., Box 1191, Tacoma, WA 98401
Williams Gun Sight Co., 7389 Lapeer Rd., Davison, Mich. 48423

## TRIGGERS, RELATED EQUIP.

Amatek, Hunter Spring Div., One Spring Ave., Hatfield, PA 19440 (trigger gauge)
M. H. Canjar Co., 500 E. 45th Ave., Denver, CO 80216 (triggers)
Custom Products/Neil A. Jones, 686 Baldwin St., Meadville, PA 16335 (trigger guard)
Dayton-Traister Co., 9322-900th West, P.O. Box 593, Oak Harbor, WA 98277 (triggers)
Electronic Trigger Systems, (Franklin C. Green), 530 W. Oak Grove Rd., Montrose, CO 81401
Flaig's, Babcock Blvd. & Thompson Run Rd., Millvale, PA 15209 (trigger shoe)
Gager Gage & Tool Co., 27509 Industrial Blvd., Hayward, CA 94545 (speedlock triggers f. Rem. 1100 and 870 shotguns)
Franklin C. Green, See Electronic Trigg. System
Bill Holmes, 2405 Pump Sta. Rd., Springdale, AR 72764 (trigger release)
Paul Jaeger, Inc., 211 Leedom St., Jenkintown, PA 19046
Michaels of Oregon Co., P.O. Box 13010, Portland, OR 97213 (trigger guards)
Miller Single Trigger Mfg. Co., R.D. 1 on Rte. 209, Millersburg, PA 17061
Viggo Miller, P.O. Box 4181, Omaha, NB 68104 (trigger attachment)
Ohaus Corp., 29 Hanover Rd., Florham Park, NJ 07932 (trigger pull gauge)
Pachmayr Gun Works, 1220 S. Grand Ave., Los Angeles, CA 90015 (trigger shoe)
Pacific Tool Co., P.O. Drawer 2048, Ordnance Plant Rd., Grand Island, NB 68801 (trigger shoe)
Richland Arms Co., 321 W. Adrian St., Blissfield, MI 49228 (trigger pull gauge)
Sport Service Center, 2364 N. Neva, Chicago, IL 60635 (release triggers)
Timney Mfg. Co., 2847 E. Siesta Lane, Phoenix, AZ 85024 (triggers)
Melvin Tyler, 1326 W. Britton Ave., Oklahoma City, OK 73114 (trigger shoe)
Williams Gun Sight Co., 7389 Lapeer Rd., Davison, MI 48423 (trigger shoe)